Microsoft

Microsoft
SQL Server™ 7.0 Performance Tuning Technical Reference

To Dave McKay,
It's great working
with you. I hope you
enjoy the Book!
Best wishes
Edward Whalen

Steve Adrien DeLuca,
Marcilina Garcia,
Jamie A. Reding, and
Edward Whalen

PUBLISHED BY
Microsoft Press
A Division of Microsoft Corporation
One Microsoft Way
Redmond, Washington 98052-6399

Library of Congress Cataloging-in-Publication Data
Microsoft SQL Server 7.0 Performance Tuning Technical Reference / Steve Adrien DeLuca
...[et al.].
      p. cm.
   Includes index.
   ISBN 0-7356-0909-8
   1. Client/server computing. 2. SQL Server. I. DeLuca, Steve Adrien.

QA76.9.C55 M5337   1999
005.75'85--dc21   99-052145

Printed and bound in the United States of America.

1 2 3 4 5 6 7 8 9   WCWC   5 4 3 2 1 0

Distributed in Canada by Penguin Books Canada Limited.

A CIP catalogue record for this book is available from the British Library.

Microsoft Press books are available through booksellers and distributors worldwide. For further information about international editions, contact your local Microsoft Corporation office or contact Microsoft Press International directly at fax (425) 936-7329. Visit our Web site at mspress.microsoft.com.

Acquisitions Editor: David Clark
Project Editor: Thom Votteler
Technical Editor: Marzena Makuta

Contents

Tables

Acknowledgments

Edward Whalen

In writing a book you rely not only on the people who have directly helped during the process, but also on much of the wisdom and experience that others have shared with you over the years. So, it is often necessary to thank those who have helped you get to where you are today.

First I would like to thank those people who helped with this book. This book would not be what it is without the dedication and skills of the great team of editors at Microsoft Press and at Argosy Publishing. Thanks to Thom Votteler, Tracy Thomsic, Cecelia Musselman, Marzena Makuta, Cindy Kogut, Arthur Brian Smith, and David Clark. Without you this book could not have been done. Also, thanks to Damien Lindauer and Charles Levine for their help. In addition, I would like to thank Bill Gates for making Windows NT and SQL Server possible.

I would especially like to thank my friends who worked with me on this book: Steve DeLuca, Marcilina Garcia, and Jamie Reding. All of you really made this a great book.

Finally I would like to thank my wife, Felicia, for putting up with all the time spent writing this book. Without her support this effort would have been much more difficult.

Jamie Reding

The writing of a book is not a solo process. In addition to the coauthors, there are many people who contributed mightily to the project. I would first like to acknowledge the efforts of the great editing teams at Microsoft Press and at Argosy Publishing. I truly appreciate their talents and patience. Cindy Kogut's and Marzena Makuta's abilities to translate my writing into actual English are a gift. I would also like to extend my thanks to Damien Lindauer, Maurice Franklin, Badriddine Khessib, and Charles Levine. They have taught me a great deal about SQL Server and performance. In addition I would like to thank Bill Gates, Steve Ballmer, and Paul Flessner. Without their vision, SQL Server would not be the great product that it is.

I would also like to extend my thanks to my friends who worked on the book: Steve DeLuca, Marcilina Garcia, and Ed Whalen. You really made this an enjoyable experience.

Finally, I would like to thank my wife, Sharon; my sons, Alex; and Jackson. Their patience and support during the writing process was invaluable and deeply appreciated. Without their support, none of this would have been possible

Marcilina Garcia

There are several people whom I would like to thank for their help and support with this book. First, I would like to thank my good friend and coauthor Edward Whalen, who made this book opportunity possible. Thanks again, Ed! I would also like to thank coauthor Jamie Reding, who is always willing to share his knowledge about SQL Server 7. And I would like to thank coauthor Steve DeLuca for his indispensable contribution to this book. Next I would like to thank the editors at Microsoft Press and at Argosy Publishing. They made the editing process quick and easy, and they did a great job asking the right questions!

In addition, I would like to thank my cool husband, Luis Garcia, for his support while I was writing this book. Happy Y2K, Luis! Also, thanks to my precious stepdaughter, Marilyn Nicole Garcia, for her encouragement. I also would like to thank my parents, Ron and Twila Jean Frohock, for their continued prayers and support, which give me the foundation to be successful. And above all, thank you, God.

Steve Adrien DeLuca

As in any endeavor, there are persons who support the project and contribute in some way to its overall success. I would like to take this opportunity to thank these people.

First, I'd like to thank the people on the great management staff at Microsoft and the Enterprise Server Division, including Brian Valentine, Brian Ball (remembering our Tandem years), Kevin Miller, and David Bishop (my direct manager and coinventor on two patents). Special thanks to Steve Ballmer and Bill Gates. Without them, none of this would be taking place in this reality. Thanks to such talented engineers as Dr. Kevin Hodge, Juhan Lee, Paul Darcy (coinventor with me on two other patents), and Kevin Hsu for working with me on the capacity planning solutions for my division and for Microsoft.

What can one say about close friends such as Ed Whalen, Marci Garcia, and Jamie Reding, who I have worked with and known for many years? How can I thank friends who have supported me during this and other projects, such as Pat Beadles, Dr. Kathryn B. Hodge, Chef Guido, and Cheryl D'Ambrosio? And last, but first in my thoughts, thanks to my family, especially my wife, Jean; my daughter, Tina; my sister, Sue; and my brother, Nick; who have always been there to support and help me.

A special thanks to the editing and publishing teams at Microsoft Press and at Argosy Publishing for so often turning my writing into English and making my English understandable.

Introduction

Since its introduction in 1989, Microsoft SQL Server has steadily gained in popularity. It has steadily moved from the desktop to the workgroup and finally to the enterprise computer room. With SQL Server's growth in popularity comes a greater responsibility for the database administrator and application designer. Because these systems service hundreds or thousands of users in mission-critical functions, the systems need to be well tuned. In addition, although a workgroup can sometimes get away with a lack of capacity planning, the enterprise cannot. It is unacceptable for a mission-critical enterprise server to run out of capacity with little or no notice. This has led to a new demand for sizing and capacity planning.

SQL Server 7 is easy to configure and manage and for the most part is self-tuning. No matter how smart the database engine is, however, it cannot compensate for an application that is doing unecessary work or for malformed indexes. Therefore, in addition to showing you how to tune the SQL Server engine itself, this book teaches you how to properly configure your I/O subsystem and tune your applications.

Who Should Use This Book

We have written this book with the intent of appealing to both the seasoned SQL Server administrator and the novice. We hope that for the experienced database administrator the information contained within this book can be a valuable reference and a resource for new ideas. For the novice, we hope that this book can show you how to debug and tune a SQL Server system. Some assumptions were made about the knowledge of the reader, however. Thus, a novice should use this book in conjunction with a SQL Server book, such as the *Microsoft SQL Server 7.0 Administrator's Companion*.

Regardless of whether you are an experienced SQL Server user, database administrator, or consultant, we feel that this book has something to offer you. We hope that you enjoy this book and find the information valuable.

What Is in This Book

Part I, "Basic Concepts," begins with how to tune the SQL Server engine and the server system that it is running on. This section of the book includes the basics upon which the remainder of the book is built. These chapters are intended to give you an insight into how SQL Server works as well as the proper configuration and use of the underlying hardware and OS platform. This section also includes an in-depth tour of the tools available to the database administor for discovering performance problems and configuring the system.

Part II, "Sizing and Capacity Planning," is a collection of chapters that teach you about the interesting world of sizing and capacity planning. These chapters provide the basics as well as advanced sizing and capacity planning topics as they walk through several sizing and capacity planning scenarios.

Part III, "Configuring and Tuning the System," provides specific information on configuring and tuning the most common type of SQL Server systems. These include online transaction processing (OLTP) systems, data warehouses, replicated systems, and high-performance backup and recovery systems.

Part IV, "Tuning SQL Statements," focuses on creating and tuning applications. This section includes chapters on tuning SQL statements, effectively using indexes and stored procedures, and using hints to improve performance. This section concludes the main portion of the book.

Part V consists of two appendixes designed as quick places to look up useful SQL Server information. Appendix A covers the SQL Server tuning parameters. Appendix B consists of the SQL Server Performance Monitor counters. This section also includes a glossary of terms used throughout this book.

Some Conventions Used in This Book

The following icons provide you with signposts to certain types of information throughout the book:

Note   A note underscores the importance of a specific concept or highlights a special case.

More Info   This is a cross reference to another section of the book or other reference material.

Caution   This advises readers that failure to take or avoid a specified action could be bad news for their users, systems, data integrity, and so forth.

Tip   This element indicates time-saving strategic advice.

Enjoy This Book!

This book has involved a lot of effort by many people, including a great editorial staff. We have striven to make this the best possible book that we could based on the combined experience of SQL Server experts both at Microsoft and in the field. We truly hope that you enjoy this book and that it is useful in your daily workSteve Adrien DeLuca
Program Manager responsible for developing performance tools at Microsoft Corporation since 1998, Mr. DeLuca is currently developing performance and capacity planning solutions for Microsoft's Enterprise Server Division. Prior to working at Microsoft, Mr. DeLuca worked as an architect engineer at Oracle Corporation, where he coinvented and developed the Oracle System Sizer. In addition to his work at Microsoft and Oracle, Mr. DeLuca has performed the function of performance engineer specializing in sizing and capacity planning for such organizations as DEC, Tandem, Apple, and the U.S. Air Force. Mr. DeLuca has been participating in performance benchmarks, developing performance tools, and lecturing about them around the world since 1980.

Part I
Basic Concepts

Chapter 1
Performance Tuning, Capacity Planning, and Sizing Overview

Performance tuning, capacity planning, and sizing are exciting subjects, offering a great deal of variety and new learning experiences. The tasks are constantly changing, as are the software and hardware. As this book goes to press, a new version of Microsoft SQL Server is already being tested. In addition, new central processing unit (CPU) chips or new system designs frequently complicate the equation.

Performance tuning can be challenging, exciting, and frustrating. Sometimes there is an easy solution to a performance problem, and sometimes there is no solution at all. Another challenge always lies ahead, because your system load and applications are always changing. Sizing and capacity planning present their own challenges. Not only must you project system capacity needs based on sometimes incomplete and inaccurate data, but you must also project anticipated workloads based on estimates of user needs. Incorrectly sizing a system can cause performance problems that lead to a frustrated and unhappy user community.

This chapter introduces you to the concepts and rationale behind performance tuning, sizing, and capacity planning. First we define performance tuning and introduce the three components to consider when fully tuning a SQL Server system. Then we talk briefly about sizing and capacity planning. Finally we discuss an effective performance tuning methodology and offer some tuning tips and recommendations.

Performance Tuning and Optimization

Performance tuning is the act of altering the performance of a system by modifying system parameters (software tuning) or by altering a system's configuration (hardware tuning). Performance tuning involves a detailed analysis of the hardware configuration, the operating system (OS) and *relational database management system* (RDBMS) configuration, and the applications that access those components.

One of the main goals in tuning a system is to remove bottlenecks. A *bottleneck* is a performance-limiting component. This component can be hardware or software and can severely affect performance in an otherwise properly configured and tuned system. Reducing bottlenecks maximizes the performance of a system.

To effectively tune a system you must follow a specific set of steps, or a *methodology*. You must also look at all components of the system, including applications, hardware, and

SQL Server. First let's look at the various components involved in tuning a system. We focus on methodology later in this chapter.

Application Tuning

Application tuning is usually the first step in tuning a SQL Server-based system and is done for several reasons. The application is the most likely component to cause a performance problem. In addition, the application is usually fairly easy to monitor and is sometimes easy to modify to achieve greater efficiency. By tuning the application first, you can then tune the hardware and SQL Server and be confident that your application is not using excessive resources.

Application tuning involves analyzing *structured query language* (SQL) statements and determining if the corresponding queries are efficient. Inefficient queries usually use excessive system resources and take an excessive amount of time to run. By tuning these SQL statements and the way in which the application accesses the database, you can dramatically change how a system performs.

SQL Server Tuning

SQL Server tuning and hardware tuning are closely related. SQL Server tuning involves modifying the way SQL Server allocates resources and how it functions by modifying its *configuration parameters.* Some of the configuration parameters are related to the utilization of resources; others are not. Those that are related to resource utilization are closely tied to the hardware resources available within a system. These parameters must be modified based on the type and amount of hardware resources available within the system.

For example, a system with multiple *processors,* such as a *symmetric multiprocessing* (SMP) system, may perform better with more SQL Server threads (processes) than a single-processor system would. A system with a lot of *memory* available should have SQL Server tuned to take advantage of that additional memory. The input/output (I/O) parameters should be modified to take advantage of the type of I/O system present on the system. SQL Server tuning and hardware tuning involve providing sufficient resources for the desired workload.

Hardware Tuning

Hardware tuning, which is the act of providing sufficient hardware resources for the desired workload, lies midway between sizing and capacity planning. To tune system hardware, you must determine which resources can be allocated to SQL Server to provide better performance. This may involve the addition of memory, CPUs, I/O resources, or a combination of all of these. Much of the effort in tuning a SQL Server system involves determining which resources must be added and in what amounts.

Hardware tuning is very important because many typical performance problems are caused by insufficient or misconfigured hardware components. The I/O subsystem is a critical component of database performance tuning. By providing sufficient CPU, memory, and I/O resources, many performance problems can be avoided.

Sizing and Capacity Planning

Capacity planning involves planning for the capacity of a system6 in order to maintain the level of service expected by the user community. This task comprises two main branches: precapacity planning and postcapacity planning. *Precapacity planning* involves capacity planning on a system that has not yet been built, whereas *postcapacity planning* involves capacity planning on a system that is already in service.

Precapacity planning, or *sizing,* involves anticipating the needed resources for a system based on an anticipated workload. This workload may or may not be accurately represented, depending on the quality of the available data. In some cases you may be able to get very reliable data on the type of workload, for example, when there is an existing system running the same or similar workload. In other cases the data is roughly estimated on paper. The quality of the results that sizing provides depends largely on the quality of the input data.

Sizing is an important operation, since a new system will be expected to meet the terms of a *service level agreement* (SLA). The SLA is a contract between the service provider (the Information Systems department) and the customer (your users) for a minimum level of service. This contract usually specifies maximum acceptable *response times* as well as the number and types of users to be serviced. To meet the SLA, you must purchase and configure a sufficient amount of hardware and software to provide for the specified user load, and you must also provide additional capacity for *peak utilization periods.* An inability to meet the SLA may cost your company time and revenue.

Postcapacity planning, or *predictive analysis,* is a complex and ongoing performance study of hardware and software resource consumption on a system that is already set up and running. This study is used to project resource consumption to plan for system capacity increases as needed. By anticipating these needs and acting before the needs become critical, you save both time and money. As with sizing, predictive analysis is only as good as the data used to perform the study. The better the input data, the better the results of the capacity planning study.

Capacity planning and sizing are complex tasks that can be both frustrating and rewarding. This book will teach you what is involved in sizing a system from scratch, as well as how to perform capacity planning on existing systems. We hope that you find capacity planning and sizing as challenging and rewarding as we do.

Server Tuning Methodology

A performance tuning methodology is a series of steps that will maximize your efficiency for solving performance problems on your system. In this section we introduce a tuning methodology that we use. This process for tuning a system is based on individual preference. You may have your own structured way of tuning, and that is fine. Take these steps as guidelines and adapt them to fit your needs.

Tuning Steps

We typically follow these steps in order to improve system performance in an organized manner:

1.   Determine the problem.
2.   Formulate the solution.
3.   Implement the solution.
4.   Analyze the results.

Following these steps will enable you to identify and solve performance problems that you might encounter. We also present a few tips and guidelines after discussing this methodology.

Determine the Problem

Before starting to tune a system, you must determine if any performance problems exist on the system. It is a waste of time, as well as a bad idea, to tune a system that is running well. You can determine if a system has a performance problem in several ways. The easiest and possibly the best way is to listen to the user community, which is a barometer of system performance. Users can tell you if the system performance has slowed and can also provide feedback as to which specific applications or queries are performing poorly.

Note   When interviewing users, be sure to take notes. Even if the result of the interview is that the system is performing well, a record of this report can be valuable. Record the date and time, the applications that this user runs, and how the user feels about the performance of the system. Ask pointed questions, such as, Are response times good? Is the system performing well? Record this information in a logbook for future reference.

Another good method of determining if a system's performance is degrading is to use the Windows NT Performance Monitor (PerfMon). Data from the Performance Monitor can be captured and saved for future use. By regularly creating PerfMon logs, you can compare performance from one week to the next. Look for changes in key parameters such as CPU usage and I/O usage. An increase in CPU usage could indicate an increased load on the system, which could lead to performance problems.

Yet another method of determining if SQL Server performance is degrading is to run a series of test queries that you have compiled. Recording the response times of these test queries at regular intervals will allow you to make comparisons of a system's responsiveness. If the response times increase over time, your system may need tuning or capacity planning.

Once you have determined that you have a problem, you must identify what kind of problem it is. Performance problems can consist of one or more of the following:

- **Hardware problems**   Hardware components could be malfunctioning. Faulty components can cause severe performance problems.
- **Hardware capacity**   You may be exceeding the capacity of the system components. You may need to complete a capacity planning exercise or reconfigure existing hardware.

- **Software tuning problems**   The system may be mistuned. Tuning SQL Server or Windows NT may solve the problem.
- **Application problems**   SQL statements may be inefficient, causing excessive usage of system resources.

How to determine if you have one or more of these problems is the heart of this book.

Formulate the Solution

Once a performance problem is identified, it is time to formulate a hypothesis about how to solve the problem. At this stage you may have an idea how to solve the problem, or you may be creating tests to help you further determine what the problem is. It is not necessary to know exactly how to solve the problem; in fact, often at this point you will not yet know what the cause of the problem is.

A key element of formulating the solution is to have an idea of what the solution should accomplish, so you will be able to judge its success. Let's look at a few examples. Suppose you have analyzed your system and determined that the I/O subsystem is causing a bottleneck. By modifying the I/O subsystem, you should anticipate a change in system performance, which would verify that the problem is actually with the I/O subsystem. If modifying the I/O subsystem does not change the performance of the system, perhaps the problem lies elsewhere.

Similarly, if you determine that the problem lies with the application, you should be able to anticipate how changes will affect the system. It is important to anticipate the effect of a change and verify that it improves or degrades system performance. Not every change that you make will be for the best, and sometimes you will have to reverse your changes to return to the original system performance.

This process doesn't have to be a big deal. Just think about the problem, the proposed changes, and how these changes should affect the performance of your system. This will lead to easier analysis of the results and better tests.

Implement the Solution

Implementing the solution involves putting into action the proposed changes from the previous step and observing the results. It may be difficult to determine how the solution actually affects the system, but by gathering as much data as possible you may be able to infer the results.

Implementing the solution might instantly improve the system or might moderately change the performance characteristics. Documenting any noticeable changes will enable you to determine the long-term effects of the change. As explained later, we recommend making only one change at a time. If you make multiple changes to a system, improvements and degradations might cancel each other out, thus preventing you from learning anything from your tests.

Analyze the Results

The final step in this tuning methodology is to analyze the results of your changes, documenting the changes you made as well as what you expected from each change and how it actually affected the system. This analysis will provide information on whether your hypothesis is correct and whether the change improves performance.

Whether your original hypothesis is correct is important, but equally important is whether you learn anything. An incorrect hypothesis can provide valuable information about the problem. As long as the result of the test provides information, the test is worthwhile.

By following this type of methodology you will be able to effectively tune a system in an organized, structured way. Organization, logical changes, and documentation make the difference between effective and ineffective tuning.

Tuning Tips and Recommendations

In this section we present tips and recommendations for more effectively tuning your system. As we mentioned earlier, organization is the key to effective tuning.

Document Everything

Documentation is an important part of database performance tuning and capacity planning. Documentation should be clear and concise and should consist of the following components:

- **Hardware configuration** This information should be complete so that it is possible to reproduce the system if necessary (this is also necessary for disaster recovery). Include details such as hardware components, RAID (redundant array of inexpensive disks) configuration, and file system layout.
- **Software components** Keep a list of the software components that are installed on the system. This should include software component revisions as well as all service packs that have been installed.
- **Configuration changes** Whenever you make configuration changes to the hardware, Windows NT, or SQL Server, keep a record in your server's logbook. You might want to note why the change was made.
- **Performance notes** Log any significant changes to system performance. This may be valuable information, and from it patterns might begin to emerge.

Regularly documenting system changes and logging the system configuration are habits that can really pay off in the long run.

Change One Thing at a Time

It is always a good idea to change only one thing at a time, and it is vital to document your changes. Doing so enables you to determine which changes improve system performance and which changes degrade it. We realize, of course, that this suggestion is often very difficult to follow. If performance has degraded to a critical state, it is often necessary to use what we call a "shotgun approach," in which multiple components are upgraded simultaneously. By upgrading several components at a time you have a good chance of improving performance, but you may not learn anything about what caused the problem. A shotgun approach may also turn out to consist of two or more components that cancel each other out, thus providing no performance improvement at all.

Don't Panic

It is easy for performance problems to escalate into an emergency. By remaining calm, however, you can avoid costly mistakes. Sometimes it is better to walk away from the problem for a few hours and get some rest rather than to make a mistake that may add to the problem. Don't be afraid to solicit help if you need it. Taking on a problem that you are not prepared to handle may lead to more problems. Here are a few tips for getting through emergencies:

- Don't panic, even if others become overexcited.
- Verify the problem. Don't just jump in based on what others tell you.
- Be cautious. Rushing to solve the problem can result in mistakes that can be even worse than the original problem.
- Don't work on little or no sleep. This is a disaster waiting to happen. It is better to fix problems when you are alert and can think coherently.
- Document everything. Documentation may save you in the long run.

Don't Be Afraid to Get Help

Sometimes performance problems can get you into trouble that you cannot get out of by yourself. If that happens, don't be afraid to call in outside specialists. Performance problems can be difficult to solve and may require solutions that you may not be able to implement safely on your own. By leveraging the experience of performance experts, you will most likely be able not only to solve the problem easier, but also able to learn a great deal. Calling in extra help is not necessarily a sign of weakness, but is often a sign of wi dom.

Summary

This chapter introduced performance tuning, capacity planning, and sizing, giving you a brief glimpse of what this book is all about. Throughout the book we will show you how to accomplish the tuning tasks—application tuning, hardware tuning, and software tuning—that were introduced here.

Each area of tuning is extremely important to the big picture and should be approached using a logical methodology. Keep in mind that not all problems are immediately solvable. Don't forget to document your work and to remain calm. Organization, logical changes, and documentation make the difference between effective and ineffective tuning. Performance tuning in conjunction with capacity planning and sizing will allow you to design, implement, and maintain a smoothly operating, well-running system.

The next chapter provides information concerning the internal architecture of SQL Server 7 as a foundation for tuning your system.

Chapter 2
SQL Server 7.0 Architecture

To know your database server well, not only should you know how to use and administer SQL Server, but you should also understand its internal architecture. This chapter explains several important architectural topics, knowledge of which will help you to better configure, tune, and understand your system.

SQL Server 7 has undergone several major changes in architecture from previous versions. Specifically, memory management, data storage, locking, thread management, the transaction log, and the backup and restore architecture have all been improved. We discuss each of these topics in detail in this chapter. For information on specific performance enhancements of SQL Server 7, see Chapter 5.

Memory Management

SQL Server 7 has a new memory management strategy. Unlike previous versions of SQL Server, version 7 is configured to automatically and dynamically allocate and deallocate memory as needed for optimal performance. This is the default behavior for SQL Server, but you can override it if necessary. This section describes some basic concepts related to memory, how SQL Server uses memory, and how to configure memory for SQL Server according to your needs.

Physical and Virtual Memory

To understand how SQL Server manages its memory, let's first discuss some memory concepts that we will need to build on. Your Windows NT/2000 or Windows 95/98 system has physical memory in the machine, which is the *random access memory* (RAM) of the system. The operating system also supports *virtual memory,* which allows applications, such as SQL Server, to use logical representations of memory instead of exact physical memory addresses; the operating system maps these logical addresses to physical memory addresses. This allows the operating system to move code or data around in physical memory when necessary, without affecting the application. The idea of virtual memory is to keep the internal management of physical memory hidden from the application.

The virtual memory operating system also creates a page file (or swap file) located on a disk drive; this page file can be used as an extension to the physical memory. The size of physical memory plus the size of the page file equals the total virtual memory available to the system. For example, if you have 512 MB of RAM and a page file of 512 MB, then 1 GB of address space is available for use by your applications: half of it resides in physical memory, and half of it resides on disk. The applications do not need to know where their data is being stored, whether in physical memory or in the page file-the operating system handles that layer of intelligence.

Data is accessed in memory and on disk in units called *pages*. Eventually, available physical memory will become filled up with data pages. In that case, when a page of data has been sitting in memory for a period of time without being referenced by an application (the page is aged), and space is needed for a new data page to be read into physical memory, the old page will be written to the page file on disk (a write operation to disk occurs) to free up space in memory for the new page. The old page is swapped out of memory and stored on disk. If that old page is later referenced, it will be read back into memory from the page file (a read from disk occurs); that is, the page is swapped from disk into memory.

Moving data between the page file and physical memory is known as *swapping* or *paging* and is handled by the operating system. Since I/Os to disk (reads or writes) are more expensive than are accesses to memory, in the sense of time and processing overhead, swapping is not desirable. Therefore, we do not want SQL Server pages to be swapped. We will see how SQL Server avoids paging later in this section. But first, let's build our understanding by learning how SQL Server uses memory.

How SQL Server Uses Memory

SQL Server allocates space from physical memory for two main components: executable code and the memory pool. Executable code includes SQL Server code, Open Data Services code, and other dynamic-link libraries (DLLs) and executable files. The *memory pool* (Figure 2-1) is an area of memory from which the following objects are

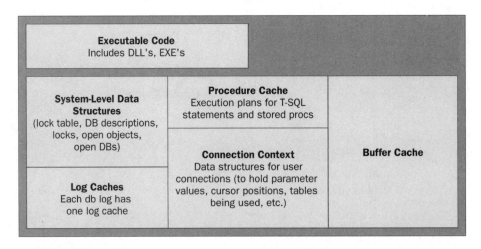

Figure 2-1 *Breakdown of SQL Server memory usage.*

allocated: system-level data structures, buffer cache, procedure cache, log cache, and connection context. System-level data structures hold data that is global to SQL Server, such as the lock table and database descriptors. The *buffer cache* is used to store data and index pages that have most recently been referenced. The *procedure cache* holds the execution plans for *Transact SQL* (T-SQL) statements and stored procedures. The *log cache* is used to read and write log pages. (There is one log cache for each database's log.) The *connection context* is a set of data structures that record the current state of a connection, such as the parameters used for a stored procedure or the tables being accessed.

With the default memory configuration, SQL Server automatically determines the size needed for each of these sections of the memory pool. For example, if more memory is needed to hold stored procedure execution plans, SQL Server will dynamically allocate more space from the available physical memory in the system. If no space is available, it will take memory from the buffer cache by freeing up pages there. SQL Server can change the size of the procedure cache, the log cache, and the buffer cache in this manner as needed to optimize performance. It will attempt to obtain more space from the available physical memory before taking it from the procedure, log, or buffer caches. Once physical memory has been used up, SQL Server adjusts the objects in the memory pool as needed. You do not have to specify a fixed amount of space for each of these objects, although you can specify minimum and maximum limits for the entire memory pool size.

Let's discuss in more detail the buffer cache area of the memory pool. The buffer cache (also known as the *data cache*) contains a singly linked list of pages that are free and therefore available for use. When SQL Server reads a page from disk, that page is stored in the first page of the buffer cache free list. If another process (or the same process) wants to read or modify the same page, it can read the page from or modify it in the buffer cache, instead of performing physical I/O operations to the disk.

Each buffer page contains header information about the page. This header holds a reference counter and an indicator of whether the page is dirty or not. A *dirty* page is one that has been modified in the buffer cache but whose changes have not yet been written to disk. Each time a page is referenced by a SQL statement, its reference counter is incremented by 1. Periodically, the buffer cache is scanned and the reference counter is divided by 4, with the remainder discarded. If the resulting number is 0, that means that the page has been referenced less than three times since the last scan, so the dirty page indicator is set for that page. This indicator causes the page to be added to the free list. If the page was modified, its modifications will first be written to disk; otherwise, the page will simply be freed without being written to disk. Basically, as more buffer pages are needed for new data pages to be read in, the least referenced pages will be freed.

When running SQL Server on Windows NT or Windows 2000, the work of scanning the buffer cache is performed by individual worker threads during the time interval between the scheduling of an asynchronous read and the completion of that read. The worker threads also take care of writing dirty pages to disk and adding pages to the free list. Writes are done asynchronously so they do not interfere with the thread's ability to complete its read.

A separate SQL Server thread called the *lazywriter* periodically checks to see that the free buffer list is not below a certain size (depending on the size of the buffer cache). If the free list has become too small, the lazywriter will scan through the cache, reclaim unused pages, and free up dirty pages that have a reference counter set to 0. For Windows NT and Windows 2000, most of the work is done by the individual threads mentioned above, so the lazywriter does not have much work to do. But in very I/O-intensive systems, the lazywriter becomes more useful because it is needed to help maintain the free list. Because Windows 95 and Windows 98 do not support asynchronous writes, the lazywriter performs all the work of freeing buffer pages and writing the dirty pages to disk. (The checkpoint thread also helps write out buffer pages but does not free pages; see the section "Checkpoints" later in this chapter.)

Caching describes the process of storing data in memory. One says that the data "gets cached" or it is "in cache." Data access is much faster when the data can be found in the buffer cache; therefore, you want SQL Server to have the most memory possible for its buffer cache. SQL Server attempts to use memory in such a way as to minimize costly disk I/O.

Dynamic and Manual Memory Configuration

As mentioned, SQL Server 7 can manage memory dynamically if you allow it to do so. This means that SQL Server will automatically allocate and deallocate memory for its memory pool as necessary. If SQL Server needs more memory for the memory pool, it will allocate it from the available physical memory in the system (if there is any available). If there are unused pages (pages that were previously allocated but are no longer in use) in the memory pool, SQL Server can deallocate them, thus freeing memory for other applications to use. However, if no other applications are requesting memory, SQL Server will maintain its memory pool at the current size, even if there are unused pages; it deallocates memory only if there is a need for it.

To avoid excessive paging (some paging by the operating system is normal), SQL Server automatically maintains its virtual memory space to be at least 5 MB less than available physical memory (plus or minus 200 KB). This allows SQL Server to have the largest memory pool possible while preventing SQL Server pages from swapping to the page file on disk. If the 5 MB of available memory begins to be consumed by some other application, SQL Server deallocates some more of its memory pool in order to keep 5 MB free physical memory on the system at all times. If the application then releases some memory, and SQL Server needs it, SQL Server will reallocate the memory (still leaving 5 MB free physical memory).

If other applications are running on your SQL Server system and require memory, SQL Server will free up memory from its memory pool to give to them. Other applications may attempt to steal SQL Server's total memory pool. To combat this, you can set a minimum size for the memory pool by configuring the *min server memory* parameter so that SQL Server will not release memory if doing so would cause the pool to fall below that size. For example, to ensure that SQL Server always has at least 256 MB of memory, set *min server memory* to 256. (This parameter is in megabytes.)

You may also want to put a maximum limit on the SQL Server memory pool so that other applications will be ensured a certain amount of memory for their own use that cannot be used by SQL Server. The parameter for this is *max server memory*. For example, to tell SQL Server not to use more than 512 MB of memory, set *max server memory* to 512. (This parameter is also in megabytes.)

When other applications are running on the same system as SQL Server, make sure you do not configure SQL Server memory settings in a manner that will cause excessive paging on the system. For example, if you set the *min server memory* parameter too high, it may cause other applications to have to page. Monitor the Windows NT Performance Monitor's Pages/sec counter (under the Memory object) to determine how much paging is occurring on the system. A low number is normal, but a continuous high number of pages per second indicates a paging problem that is slowing down the performance of your system. If you cannot avoid this paging, you need to put more physical memory in the machine.

We recommend that you allow SQL Server to dynamically configure its memory usage by leaving these two parameters at their defaults. Again, this is best when you have a dedicated machine for SQL Server and the memory size will not be changing much. When other applications demand memory on the server, you may need to adjust these parameters as mentioned. But even with a minimum or maximum memory size configured, SQL Server dynamically adjusts memory as needed without violating the upper or lower limits. To force SQL Server to allocate a fixed amount of memory, set the *min server memory* and *max server memory* parameters to the same value. SQL Server will allocate memory as needed up to the maximum configured value (or actually, up to the maximum memory available, because you could configure more physical memory than you actually have), and it will release that memory only if another application needs some, at which point SQL Server will page. Again, you do not want SQL Server to page, so do not set the fixed memory size too large for your system. Leave some memory free for other applications when necessary.

Min server memory and *max server memory* are both advanced options in SQL Server. To set them by using the stored procedure *sp_configure*, you must first enable the option *show advanced options* as follows:

```
sp_configure "show advanced options", 1

go

sp_configure "max server memory", 512

go

RECONFIGURE

go
```

> **Note** If you change a configuration value for an option that does not require SQL Server to be restarted, you must run RECONFIGURE in order for the new value to take effect as the run value (the value SQL Server will use while running).

Alternatively, you can configure the memory settings through SQL Server Enterprise Manager. To do this, open Enterprise Manager, expand the servers, right-click on the server you want, and select Properties from the context menu. Then go to the Memory tab. There you can set the minimum and maximum server memory values, or leave them at the defaults.

Again, we recommend that you allow SQL Server to dynamically configure memory by leaving the memory parameters set to their default values if you have a server dedicated to SQL Server. This memory management strategy is designed to improve SQL Server memory usage and to relieve the database administrator (DBA) of memory configuration worries.

Using Additional Memory

Microsoft Windows NT Server 4 supports 4 GB of memory, of which 2 GB is allocated for user processes and 2 GB is reserved for system use. This 2-GB limit represents the maximum amount of memory that can be allocated for SQL Server.

In Microsoft Windows NT 4 Enterprise Edition, the amount of virtual memory for a process is 50 percent larger—3 GB. A change in the allocation of virtual memory accounts for this increase: a user process can now be allotted up to 3 GB of virtual memory, and the system allocation has been reduced to 1 GB. This increase in virtual memory allotted to processes allows you to increase the size of the memory pool dramatically. To enable this support in Windows NT 4 Enterprise Edition, you must add the flag /3GB to the boot line in the boot.ini file. This can be done through the System icon that appears in the Control Panel.

Windows 2000 also supports additional physical memory—up to 64 GB with Windows 2000 Datacenter. To take advantage of this additional memory, you must be running Windows 2000 Advanced Server, or Windows 2000 Datacenter Server and Microsoft SQL Server 7 Enterprise Edition.

Note   At the time of publication, Microsoft was planning to add support for up to 8 GB of memory to Windows 2000 Advanced Server and 64 GB to Windows 2000 Datacenter Server.

Data Storage

The data storage architecture of SQL Server 7 has been redesigned. Files and filegroups have replaced the previously known devices and segments. Rows, pages, and extents of data have changed characteristics; tables and indexes have also evolved. All these changes are geared toward improving the efficiency and performance of SQL Server 7. The following sections describe the details of each of these data storage entities.

Data Files and Log Files

SQL Server 7 maps each database to a set of operating system files, which we will simply refer to as *files*. Files may reside on a Windows NT file system (NTFS) or file allocation table (FAT) file system (raw partitions are not recommended), but cannot reside on a compressed file system. A file is made up of smaller units of data called *pages*, which will be discussed in more detail in the next section. Each file is given a logical name and a physical name when created in SQL Server. The logical name is used to refer to the file in all T-SQL statements. The physical name is the path to the location of the physical file. SQL Server uses the following three categories of files for databases:

- **Primary data files**   A primary data file contains startup information for a database, points to the other files used by the database, stores system tables and objects, and can also store database data and objects. Each database has exactly one primary file. The recommended file extension for a primary data file is .mdf.

- **Secondary data files**   Secondary data files are optional for each database. They can be used to hold data and objects, such as tables and indexes, that are not in the primary file. A database might not have any secondary files, if all its data is placed in the primary file. On the other hand, a database might need one or more secondary files placed on separate disks in order to spread data across the disks. The recommended file extension is .ndf.

- **Log files**   A log file holds all the transaction log information for the database, and cannot be used to hold any other data. Every database has at least one log file, and can have multiple log files. The recommended file extension is .ldf.

A simple, small database might consist of only the primary data file and one log file. A larger, more complex database might consist of the primary data file, three secondary data files, and two log files. See Figures 2-2 and 2-3 for representations of the files that make up a simple and more complex version of a sample database called *Customers*.

Primary Data File - cust - pr (←Logical Name)
`C:\MSSOL7\Data\cust_pr.mdf` (←Physical Name)

Log File - log1
`D:\Data\log1.ldf`

Figure 2-2 *A simple* Customers *database.*

Primary Data File = cust-pr (←Logical Name)
`C:\MSSOL7\Data\cust_pr.mdf` (←Physical Name)

Secondary Data File 1 = cust-data1
`E:\Data\cust_data2.ndf`

Secondary Data File 2 = cust-data2
`F:\Data\cust_data2.ndf`

Secondary Data File 3 = cust-data3
`G:\Data\cust_data3.ndf`

Log File 1 = log1
`H:\Data\log1.ldf`

Log File 2 = log2
`I:\Data\log2.ldf`

Figure 2-3 *A more complex* Customers *database.*

> **Note** A SQL Server database can accommodate maximum file sizes of 32 terabytes (TB) for data files and 4 TB for log files. That will probably be enough space for your data storage needs!

Filegroups

If you create a database with one or more secondary data files, you can also create filegroups for those files. *Filegroups* provide a way to group secondary files together for data placement purposes, similar to the concept of grouping database devices with segments in previous versions of SQL Server. You indicate which secondary files are part of each filegroup when creating the database. You can later alter the database to add a filegroup and a new file, but you cannot move a file from one filegroup to another after the file has already been created.

When creating database objects, such as tables and indexes, you can specify in which filegroup to place those objects, in order to locate the data on specific disks or disk arrays (where the secondary files are located). You can have only one secondary file in a filegroup if you want. The purpose is the same as for assigning multiple files per filegroup—to place data on specific drives and to optimize disk performance. Figure 2-4 shows a representation of the *Customers* database using a filegroup named customers_fg to group the three secondary data files together.

Let's look at another example with filegroups. Let's say you have two disk arrays for data—one array of four disks and one array of two disks (see Chapter 3 for a discussion of RAID and disk arrays). You also have two tables to create, T1 and T2. T1 is highly accessed as read-only data. T2 is updated about once a minute, so it is not accessed as often as T1. You may want to place these tables on separate disks; for example, placing T1 on the four-disk array and T2 on the two-disk array. This allows more disks to per-

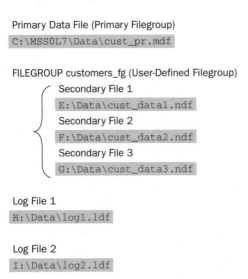

Figure 2-4 *Using a filegroup with the* Customers *database.*

form the high number of reads to T1, while keeping the writes to T2 from interrupting. This arrangement also allows two dedicated disks for the updates to T2.

To perform this kind of table placement, you must create a different filegroup with its own secondary files on each disk array. You can then create the tables on the appropriate filegroup, as shown in Figure 2-5. If the I/O rate is too high on some of the disks, you may need all six disk spindles to achieve better I/O performance for both tables. In this case you could create one filegroup to include both of the files so that the table data will be spread across both disk arrays, as shown in Figure 2-6.

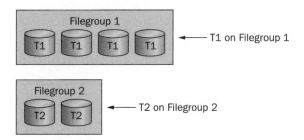

Figure 2-5 *Two different filegroups, each with its own secondary data files.*

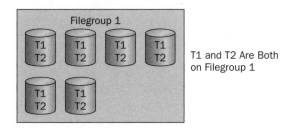

Figure 2-6 *One filegroup that includes both secondary data files.*

Generally, to optimize disk I/O performance on your system, you should distribute data across as many disks as possible in order to achieve more parallel data access (reads and writes). The use of filegroups can help you achieve more evenly distributed I/O. When data is loaded or inserted into a table that is placed on a filegroup, the data will be spread proportionately across all the files in the filegroup.

SQL Server uses a proportionate fill strategy per file in the filegroup. That is, SQL Server writes data to each file in an amount proportional to the free space in that file, rather than writing data to the first file until it is full, then filling up the second file, and so on. For example, if file F1 has 400 MB free and file F2 has 100 MB free, then 4 extents of pages are allocated from F1 and 1 extent from F2. (An *extent* is a unit of eight contiguous pages.) Both files will become full at about the same time, and data striping is optimized (here *data striping* refers to the distribution of data across files). This fill strategy is used whether you create your own filegroup or allow your files to be part of the default primary filegroup.

The three types of filegroups are as follows:

- **Primary filegroup** This filegroup contains the primary data file and all other files not put into another filegroup. The system tables are always allocated to the primary filegroup.

- **User-defined filegroups** These are any filegroups defined by the user during the process of creating the database. A table or index can be created in a specific user-defined filegroup.

- **Default filegroup** The default filegroup holds all pages for tables and indexes that do not have a specified filegroup when created. The default filegroup can be switched from one filegroup to another by members of the *db_owner* database role. Only one filegroup at a time can be the default. If no default filegroup is specified, the primary filegroup is the default. You can use the ALTER DATABASE command to change the default filegroup. See SQL Server Books Online for details on this command.

Note Log files are not part of any filegroup and may not be placed in any user-defined filegroup.

All files are by default part of the primary filegroup. The primary data file must be in the primary filegroup—this cannot be changed. Any secondary files created can be left in the default primary filegroup or created in a user-defined filegroup. If you create all files in the primary filegroup, then all your tables, indexes, and other objects will be spread across those files according to SQL Server's proportionate fill strategy. Keep in mind that for more specific placement of data, you may need to use user-defined filegroups.

One of the new features of SQL Server 7 to note is the ability to back up and restore sections of your database by file or filegroup. You can back up one file at a time or an entire filegroup as one operation. Knowing this may help you decide how many files you want to create and how to use filegroups to group them for your backup strategy. For example, if you want to have the ability to back up one table by itself, you will want to create a file and a filegroup and to create that table on the filegroup so that you can perform a filegroup backup to back up just that particular table. See Chapters 5 and 15 for more details on backup strategies.

Automatic File Growth

SQL Server 7 has another new feature: it allows files to grow automatically when needed. When a file is created, you can choose whether to allow SQL Server to automatically increase the size of the file. We recommend that you do choose automatic growth, because it saves the administrator the burden of manually monitoring and increasing file space.

A file is created with an initial size. When that initial space is filled up, SQL Server will increase the file size by a specified amount. This amount, called the *growth increment*, tells SQL Server how much more space to allocate to the file when the original space has been filled. When this new space fills, SQL Server will again allocate more space. The file will continue to grow at that rate as needed until the disk is full or until the maximum file size (if specified) is reached.

The *maximum file size* is just that—the maximum size to which a file is allowed to grow. This size is specified for each file individually at file creation or can be altered later. If there is no maximum size set for a file, SQL Server will continue to increase the size of the file as necessary until all available disk space is exhausted. To avoid completely running out of space on the disk, set a maximum size for each file. If you ever do reach the maximum size, you can add a new file or increase the maximum file size for more space.

We recommend that you use automatic file growth and maximum file sizes. When you create a database, allocate the largest size to which you think the files will ever grow. If you see that this initial space has been filled and automatic growth has taken place, you should reevaluate the space to determine whether more files or filegroups, or both, should be added. This evaluation helps you to avoid completely running out of space, either from reaching the maximum file size or by running out of disk space.

Pages, Extents, and Rows

The basic unit of data storage in SQL Server is a page, the term we have used already many times in this chapter. A SQL Server 7 page is 8 KB (as opposed to a 2-KB page size for previous versions of SQL Server). The SQL Server data files are made up of pages. (Log files, on the other hand, do not contain pages; they are made up of log records.) The beginning of each page contains a 96-byte header that stores information such as the type of page, the object ID of the object (table or index) that owns the page, the amount of free space on the page, and pointers to the previous and next pages for pages in a linked list. The six types of pages in SQL Server are as follows:

- **Data page**   Stores data rows with all types of data except data for text, ntext, and image data types
- **Index page**   Stores rows of index information
- **Text/image page**   Stores data for text, ntext, and image data types
- **Page Free Space page**   Stores information about free space available on pages
- **Global Allocation Map page**   Stores information about allocated extents
- **Index Allocation Map page**   Stores information about extents used by a table or index

An *extent* is a unit of eight contiguous pages, a total of 64 KB. Space is allocated to tables and indexes in extents.

A row on a data page can hold data for all data types except text, ntext, and image. For these data types, a pointer that points to the actual text, ntext, or image data in separate pages is stored in the data row. With this design, the maximum size of one row is 8060 bytes; therefore, a row will never span more than one page, a more efficient method than allowing a row to span pages. If a row spanned two pages, for example, retrieving that row would involve accessing two pages instead of only one, which could cause two disk I/Os instead of one.

Lock Management

The lock manager for SQL Server 7 has been optimized so that lock requests are completed faster, allowing for more concurrency for *online transaction processing* (OLTP) applications, especially when data rows are inserted often. Row-level locking has also been fully implemented for data and index pages. Let's take a look at what locking means and how SQL Server manages locks.

What Are Locks?

A *lock* is an object used by internal system software to indicate that a user has a dependency on some resource and therefore has an access right to it. That user is said to own a lock on the resource. Other users are not allowed to perform any operation on that same resource if doing so would cause a problem with the dependency of the user who owns the original lock. SQL Server uses locks to control concurrency for multiple users working with the same database at the same time. Locking ensures that multiple users can read and write to the same database without retrieving inconsistent data and without inadvertently overwriting each other's modifications.

Lock Granularity and Lock Modes

SQL Server has multigranular locking; that is, different types of locks can be locked by a user, from fine to coarse granularity. The finest granularity level is the row lock. A user may obtain a lock on a row of data when this will best fit the needs of the user. The coarsest level of lock granularity is the database lock, which locks an entire database. The types of resources that can be locked are as follows (from finest to coarsest level of granularity):

- **Row identifier (RID)**   A lock that locks a single row in a table
- **Key**   A row lock within an index
- **Page**   A lock on an 8-KB data or index page
- **Extent**   A lock on a contiguous group of eight data or index pages, or a 64-KB unit
- **Table**   A lock on an entire table and its indexes
- **Database**   A lock on an entire database

The finer the granularity of lock, the more concurrency is allowed but the more system overhead is incurred. On the other hand, the coarser the granularity, the less concurrency is allowed but the less system overhead is incurred. For example, many row-level locks allow greater concurrency for other transactions to access other rows in the table, but there is overhead incurred for each of the row-level locks. A table-level lock allows less concurrency for the table but does not require as much system overhead.

In addition to levels of granularity, SQL Server uses different modes for locks. These modes determine how the locked resource can be accessed by concurrent user transactions. The lock modes are as follows:

- **Shared**   Used for read-only operations, such as for a SELECT statement
- **Exclusive**   Used on resources for data modification statements, such as INSERT, UPDATE, and DELETE
- **Update**   Used on resources that may be updated
- **Intent**   Used to establish a locking hierarchy; includes intent shared, intent exclusive, and shared with intent exclusive
- **Schema**   Used for operations that perform a table *data definition language* (DDL) statement, such as adding a column or dropping a table
- **Bulk copy**   Used when bulk copying data into a table and also when the TABLOCK table hint is specified

SQL Server dynamically chooses the types of resources that should be locked for a transaction and the types of lock modes; you do not need to configure anything for this process to occur efficiently. SQL Server chooses the most cost-effective locks when the query is executed, based on the characteristics of the database schema and the query itself. This design provides ease of administration and improved performance because system overhead is reduced by automatically using the appropriate locking strategy for the task.

SQL Server also dynamically manages lock *escalation*—the conversion of many fine-grained locks into fewer, more coarse-grained locks. This conversion reduces the system overhead incurred when using a large number of fine-grained locks. For example, SQL Server will automatically convert row-level and page-level locks into table locks when the lock threshold is reached by a transaction. The lock escalation thresholds are determined dynamically by SQL Server and do not need to be configured, although they can be.

The *locks* Parameter

SQL Server allows administrators to manually configure the number of locks by using the *locks* parameter. You should not have to change this parameter in most cases, but we explain it here so you can understand the implications of changing it. Setting *locks* determines the maximum number of locks SQL Server is allowed to allocate. When left at its default of 0, SQL Server dynamically and very efficiently allocates and deallocates locks according to system needs. Each lock consumes 96 bytes of memory, and SQL Server will not allocate more than 40 percent of its memory to locks.

If you do set the *locks* parameter to a number other than 0, and you receive a message from SQL Server that you have run out of locks, increase the number. *Locks* is an advanced option in SQL Server, as are the memory options; you therefore must have the *show advanced options* parameter set to 1 to configure locks, and you must use the *sp_configure* stored procedure. You cannot configure locks through Enterprise Manager.

For details on how to specify in a query which type of lock you want SQL Server to use, see Chapter 19.

Thread Management

Complex applications may have several tasks or processes that need to be completed concurrently. A process has a thread of execution to perform the application's programming instructions. We refer to this thread of execution simply as a *thread*. SQL Server uses Windows NT operating system threads, and sometimes SQL Server fibers (see the discussion below), to execute concurrent tasks. (Fibers are not supported with Microsoft SQL Server Desktop Edition.) Threads are started by SQL Server, and then Windows NT distributes the threads evenly across the processors (CPUs) that are available for use by SQL Server. You can configure the processors that SQL Server is allowed to use either through Enterprise Manager or by setting the SQL Server configuration parameter *affinity mask*.

Most systems perform best by letting SQL Server use all the CPUs in the system. One thread can execute at a time on each CPU in the system. For example, a system with four CPUs can execute four threads concurrently. While one thread may be waiting for an I/O operation to complete, another thread can run on that same CPU, even in a single-CPU system. This increases the amount of work that can be performed.

Thread management is handled in the Windows NT kernel code. When one thread is moved off a CPU and another one is moved on, a *context switch* occurs. Context switching is a moderately costly operation because it requires a switch between the user mode of the application code and the kernel mode of the thread management code. Therefore, fewer context switches are better. To reduce context switching, SQL Server 7 has a new feature called *fibers*.

Fibers are subcomponents of threads. SQL Server does not use fibers by default, but can be configured to do so. Fibers are handled by code running in user mode; therefore, switching fibers is not as costly an operation as is switching threads because the mode does not have to change between kernel mode and user mode. The scheduling of fibers is handled by SQL Server, whereas thread scheduling is handled by Windows NT. Multiple fibers can run on one thread, and fibers can be switched on the thread, while the thread executes on the CPU without switching contexts. This greatly reduces the amount of context switching on the system. If your system is performing a lot of context switches, try running SQL Server in fiber mode. To do this, you must either select the option through Enterprise Manager or run *sp_configure* and set the parameter *lightweight pooling*, which is also an advanced option.

SQL Server maintains a pool of threads to execute SQL statements. If fiber mode is set, a pool of fibers is maintained instead of threads. The threads or fibers in this pool are known as *worker threads*. Worker thread pooling allows SQL Server to better allocate processing time on the CPUs when there are multiple SQL statements executing at the same time. You can configure the number of worker threads available to SQL Server with the configuration parameter *max worker threads*. The maximum value is 255. (This can be configured in Enterprise Manager or with the *sp_configure* stored procedure.)

When a SQL statement or batch of statements is sent to SQL Server for execution, SQL Server allocates a worker thread for the statement or batch if an existing thread is free in the pool. If no existing thread is free and the maximum number of worker threads has not yet been reached, SQL Server will start a new thread for the process. If the maximum is reached and no threads are free, the process must wait for another batch to complete its task and free a thread. This wait is normally not very long. If you see an error from SQL Server that you have reached the *max worker threads* limit, try increasing the parameter value. Remember, however, that allowing the creation of too many threads can cause more overhead and eventually degrade performance. The default value of 255 is sufficient for most systems. For systems that are not under a heavy load, you might experiment by setting this value lower and compare performance—in some cases the performance will improve because of the reduced overhead.

Note   Windows 95 and Windows 98 do not support thread pooling. Setting the *max worker thread* option will have no effect on those systems.

Transaction Log

The *transaction log* stores a sequential record of all *transactions* that make modifications to the database. This record makes database recovery possible. This section covers the transaction log for SQL Server 7, how it works, and how it is involved in database recovery.

Transaction Log Enhancements in SQL Server 7.0

The following enhancements have been made to the transaction log in SQL Server 7.

- The transaction log is no longer treated as a table; it is now treated as a completely separate set of files in the database   Thus, I/Os to the transaction log are not written in increments of the SQL Server page size. With SQL Server versions 6.5 and earlier, the log was treated as a database table and all I/Os were done using the SQL Server page size (2 KB in SQL Server 6.5). Now the log writer thread can write to the transaction log using whatever size it needs. The transaction log pages no longer follow the format of data pages. Thus, if the log writer thread needs to write only a small amount, it is not necessary to write an entire 8 KB of data (the size of a data page). If the system is performing heavy updates, the log write thread can write using a larger block size (for example, 16 KB or 32 KB).

- **The transaction log can be configured to automatically grow as needed**   This option allows more space to be added as required but should be used with care. You do not want the transaction log to grow uncontrollably or you may consume the entire disk drive.

- **The transaction log can now be implemented across several files**   These files can be configured to grow automatically as well. The transaction log files are not striped; they are used one after another.

How the Transaction Log Works

SQL Server internally divides each physical transaction log file into multiple virtual files. The size and number of virtual files are decided dynamically by SQL Server when creating and extending log files. SQL Server tries to maintain a small number of virtual files for better efficiency during a database recovery. Too many virtual files can slow down recovery. When you create the log file, you can specify a size for the automatic growth increment. If you set this amount too low, SQL Server must extend the log file often, which may result in many virtual files. Therefore it is best to create your log files initially at the largest size to which you think they will ever grow, and to set the growth increment relatively large as well. This will avoid the overhead incurred from SQL Server having to automatically increase the size of the file.

The transaction log is a wraparound log. A logical log and physical log make this possible. When a database is created, log records are written starting at the beginning of the physical log, which at that time is also the beginning of the logical log, as shown in Figure 2-7. When records are truncated from the log file, the pointer for the beginning of the logical log is moved to where the end was, as shown in Figure 2-8. Records continue to be written from the new logical starting point until the end of the logical log reaches the end of the physical log. Now the logical log goes to the beginning of the physical log and continues writing, as shown in Figure 2-9. If the end of the logical log ever catches up to the beginning of the logical log, your log file has filled up. If automatic growth is enabled, your file will be extended by SQL Server. If not, you will get an error and have to manually dump or truncate the log.

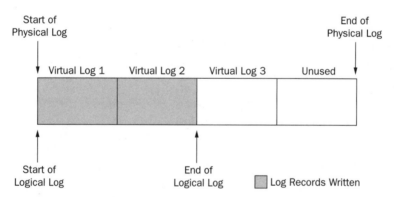

Figure 2-7 *View of the transaction log file with initial records written.*

The transaction log keeps track of when a transaction has committed. When a transaction issues a commit, the operation is not fully committed until a commit record has been written to the transaction log. Because changes to the database are not necessarily written to disk immediately, this log is the only means by which transactions can be recovered in the event of a system failure. If a database is damaged and must be restored from a backup, all the transactions that had performed some type of data modification must be replayed in order to recover the database to the point just before the failure. For this reason, the transaction log is critical. (See Chapter 15 for more specifics on backup and recovery.)

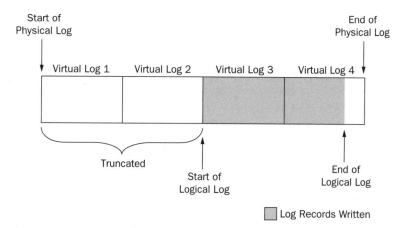

Figure 2-8 *View of the same transaction log file after a truncation.*

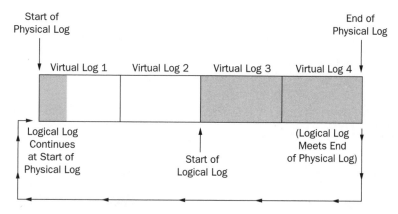

Figure 2-9 *View of the same transaction log file after the logical log wraps around.*

In the event of a system failure in which data files are not damaged, the current transaction log is used to recover the database because it is necessary to recover only those transactions that have not yet been written to disk. The number of pages that must be recovered depends on the number of modified (or dirty) pages in the database, which in turn is governed by the checkpoint interval. A checkpoint writes dirty pages to disk to reduce the time it takes to perform a recovery. Checkpoints and the checkpoint interval will be discussed in detail in the section "Checkpoints" later in this chapter.

Truncating the Transaction Log

Depending on the number of changes to your database, the transaction log can grow to be quite large. Because the transaction log is a finite set of one or more files, it will eventually be filled and therefore must be truncated periodically. Although it is possible to truncate the log without doing a log backup, we do not recommend doing so. The log backup is used to save the information contained in the transaction log that may be needed to recover transactions that occurred since the last database backup. The log is automatically truncated at the completion of a log backup.

> **Note**   The log can also be truncated without backing it up by setting the database option *trunc. log on chkpt* to TRUE for that database. However, after doing so you will not be able to back up the transaction log. This setting will make the database nonrecoverable and therefore is not recommended.

Checkpoints

A *checkpoint* is an operation of synchronizing the physical data files with the current state of the database cache by writing out all modified data pages in cache to disk. This assures you a permanent (on disk) copy of the data. SQL Server has a thread dedicated to checkpoints. Checkpointing will reduce the necessary recovery time in the event of a system failure in cases in which automatic recovery by SQL Server is possible.

The amount of time needed to recover the database is determined by the amount of time since the last checkpoint and the number of dirty pages in the buffer cache. Thus, decreasing the checkpoint interval (shown in the next section) will reduce the recovery time, but at a cost. The checkpoint process may incur a lot of overhead because of heavy writes if there are a large number of modified pages that must be written to disk.

The Checkpoint Process

The checkpoint process involves a number of operations, including the following:

- **Writing out all dirty pages**   A *dirty* page is one that has been modified in the buffer cache but not yet written to disk. A checkpoint operation has two phases. During the first phase, the checkpoint process marks all pages that need to be written. In the second phase, the checkpoint forces a write to disk of those marked dirty pages.

- **Writing a list of outstanding transactions to the transaction log**   This step gives SQL Server an idea of what transactions were currently in progress when the checkpoint was occurring. Thus the recovery process knows that it needs to go back further in the log than the checkpoint in order to recover those transactions.

- **Writing all dirty log pages to disk**   This step ensures that the log buffer has been flushed to disk.

- **Storing checkpoint log records in the database**   This step keeps a record of the checkpoint outside the transaction log, since the log may be backed up and truncated.

Checkpoints occur whenever you issue a CHECKPOINT statement, whenever you shut down SQL Server using a SHUTDOWN statement, whenever you shut down SQL Server using Service Control Manager, and periodically as specified by the checkpoint interval setting.

Configuring the Checkpoint Interval

The checkpoint interval (the time between the beginnings of two consecutive checkpoints) is determined by the *recovery interval* configuration parameter and the number of records in the transaction log rather than by the system time or size of the log. The more records in the transaction log, the shorter the checkpoint interval which means the checkpoint will automatically execute more often. As more changes are made, more records will be inserted into the transaction log; consequently, SQL Server will configure the checkpoint interval, to write those changes to disk more often. If few or no changes are made to the database, the transaction log will contain only a few records, and the checkpoint interval will be long. If your system experiences many changes to the database, the transaction log will contain many records, and the checkpoint interval will be short.

The checkpoint interval is defined by the SQL Server configuration option *recovery interval*. This parameter is set for an entire SQL Server system, not for each individual database, but checkpoints occur on a per-database basis. This parameter specifies the number of minutes that SQL Server should take to recover each database in the event of a system failure. The default value of 0 instructs SQL Server to determine the checkpoint interval for you—usually less than 1 minute. For systems that have a large amount of memory and a lot of insert and update activity, this default setting might cause an excessive number of checkpoints to occur. In that case, you might want to set the option to a larger value. If you can stand a 30-minute recovery in the event of a system failure, you will see better transaction performance because checkpoints will be initiated less often. Changing this parameter depends on your capacity to handle the resulting downtime and on the frequency of failures.

The *recovery interval* option can be changed in two ways: using Enterprise Manager or T-SQL. To set *recovery interval* from Enterprise Manager, in the left-hand pane right-click on the name of the server that you want to set this option for, and choose Properties from the context menu. The SQL Server Properties dialog box is displayed. Select the Database Settings tab and specify the desired recovery interval, in minutes, in the Recovery Interval Spin box.

To set *recovery interval* using T-SQL, use the *sp_configure* stored procedure, as shown here:

```
Lsp_configure "recovery interval", 1

GO
```

This option does not require SQL Server to be restarted to take effect. As noted earlier, however, the change will not become active unless you run the RECONFIGURE command. If you are sure of your change, enter the following T-SQL statements:

```
RECONFIGURE

GO
```

The RECONFIGURE command signals SQL Server to accept the configuration changes as the run value.

To ensure that the setting you have made is actually in effect, use the following T-SQL statement:

```
sp_configure "recovery interval"

GO
```

The output looks like this (note that the recovery interval has indeed been set):

```
name                      minimum maximum config_value run_value

_____          ____. ____. _____ ____.

recovery interval (min) 0         32767   1            1
```

Caution The *recovery interval* parameter is an advanced option and should be changed only after careful planning. Increasing the *recovery interval* setting will increase the time necessary to perform a database recovery.

Summary

In this chapter you have learned some of the basics of SQL Server architecture. By knowing how SQL Server works, you can better understand your system as a whole, and you will have a better foundation on which to build when learning how to tune your system. The following chapter will help you understand the characteristics of disk drives and different RAID levels and how to tune your I/O subsystem.

Chapter 3
Understanding the I/O Subsystem and RAID

The I/O subsystem is frequently the cause of performance degradation in an RDBMS system, for a number of reasons. Sometimes the application is efficient and the I/O subsystem is simply overloaded; other times excessive I/Os are not really necessary. Inefficient SQL statements can cause unnecessary table scans when an index lookup would work better. Too many users on the same system can overload the I/O subsystem. Running large batch jobs on an OLTP system can also cause severe performance problems. When the I/O subsystem is overloaded, the I/O latency (response time) will increase. The term *latency* refers to the amount of time that one component or process is idle waiting for another component to complete some operation. In this chapter we discuss various latencies, such as the I/O latency and subcomponents' latencies.

In this chapter we explore the I/O subsystem. We start with how a disk drive works and why it has fundamental performance limits. After discussing disk drives, we cover the various available RAID levels and their performance characteristics. In addition we show you how to identify and solve an I/O performance problem. Finally we present a number of I/O subsystem tips and recommendations.

Performance Characteristics of Disk Drives

The disk drive (also known as the hard disk) is one of the fundamental components of the computer system. Amazingly enough, the mechanics of disk drives have not changed much in the last 20 years. They are, of course, much more reliable and faster than they originally were, but fundamentally they have remained the same. From a performance standpoint disk drives are still one of the most important system components to tune. Of course you can't really tune a disk drive; however, by knowing its performance characteristics and limitations and configuring your system with those limitations in mind, you are in effect tuning the I/O subsystem.

Disk Drive Description

The data storage component of a disk drive is composed of a number of magnetic disk platters. These platters store the data magnetically in tracks, much like the tracks of a record (or CD, for those of you who don't remember records). The track in turn is made up of a number of sectors. As you get further from the center of the disk drive there are more sectors per track. Figure 3-1 shows a typical disk platter.

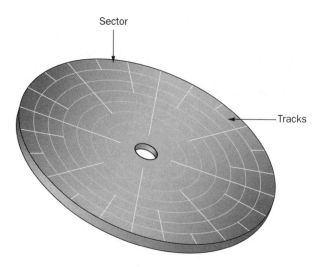

Figure 3-1 *Disk platter.*

Instead of having just one platter, a disk drive is made up of many disk platters stacked on top of each other, as shown in Figure 3-2. A magnetic head both reads data from the disk and writes data to the disk. Since there are many platters, there are also many disk heads, one per surface. These heads ride on top of an armature that moves in and out of the disk, much like the arm that holds the needle on a record player. These heads and armatures are all connected and move in sync; thus, all heads are over the same *X-Y* position on all platters at the same time. Because disks operate in this manner, it makes sense for all heads to read and write at the same time, and thus data is written and read from all tracks simultaneously. We say that data is stored in *cylinders* (see Figure 3-2).

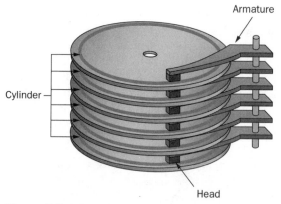

Figure 3-2 *The anatomy of a disk drive.*

Disk drives can be made up of as few as one disk platter or as many as six or even more platters. The density of the data on the platters and the number of platters determine the maximum storage capacity of a disk drive. In fact there are many disk drives that have identical mechanical properties, but the size is determined by the number of platters. A common product line of disk drives includes a 9-GB disk drive with three disk platters and an almost identical 18-GB disk drive with six disk platters.

Disk Drive Behaviors

Now that you have an idea of what makes up a disk drive, let's look at how it works. First you will learn about the rotational characteristics of the disk drive, and then you will learn how disk seeks fit into the performance characteristics of disk drives.

Rotational Latency

Many high-performance disk drives spin at 10,000 revolutions per minute (rpm). If a request for data caused the disk to rotate completely before it was able to read the data, this action would take approximately 6 milliseconds (ms), or 0.006 second. A rotational speed of 10,000 rpm equates to 166.6 rotations per second. This in turn translates to 1/166.6 seconds per rotation, or 6 ms per rotation.

In order for the disk heads to read a sector of data, that sector must be directly underneath the head. Since the disk drive is always rotating, the disk simply waits for that sector to rotate to this position. The time it takes for the disk to rotate to where the data is available is called the *rotational latency*. The rotational latency can be as long as 6 ms (if the disk has to rotate completely around), but on average it is around half of the maximum revolution time. For our 10,000-rpm example disk, the average rotational latency is approximately 3 ms.

When we begin to focus on the performance of disk drives, the rotational latency becomes important because this time contributes to the overall time needed for disk access. When you are choosing disk drives for your system, the rotational speed is thus an important factor to consider. As you have just seen, for a 10,000-rpm disk drive the rotational latency is around 3 ms. Older-generation disk drives on the market run at a rotational speed of 7,200 rpm. With this type of disk drive, one rotation takes 8.3 ms to complete, and the average rotational latency is about 4.15 ms. This may not seem like a lot, but it is 38 percent longer than the 10,000-rpm disk drive. As you will see later in this chapter, this amount can add a lot to your I/O times.

Disk Seeks

When retrieving data from a disk drive, the disk must not only rotate under the heads that will be reading the data, but the head must also move to where the data resides. The disk armature moves in and out between the disk surfaces in order to move the heads to the cylinder that holds the desired data. The time it takes the head to move to where the requested data resides is called the *seek time*. Figure 3-3 represents the concepts of seek time and rotational latency.

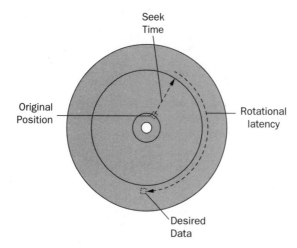

Figure 3-3 *Rotational Latency and seek time.*

The time it takes for a seek to occur depends mainly on how far the disk heads need to move. When the disk drives are accessing data sequentially, the heads need to move only a small distance, which can occur quickly. When disk accesses are occurring all over the disk drive, the seek times can get quite long. In either case, by minimizing the seek time you improve performance.

The seek time and the rotational latency both add to the time it takes for an I/O to complete, and thus they affect the performance of a disk drive. The rotational latency is usually around 3 ms for 10,000-rpm disks. The seek time of the disk varies depending on the size and speed of the disk drive and the type of seek being performed. Since data cannot be read until the seek has been completed, the rotational latency and seek time do not occur serially. The disk must first seek to the desired track, then the disk must rotate from wherever it currently is to the sector where the data is.

Track-to-Track Seeks

The *track-to-track seek time* is the time required to move between adjacent tracks. This type of seek is used when performing sequential I/Os. A typical 10,000-rpm, 9-GB disk drive has a track-to-track seek time of around 0.8 ms. As you can see, with a track-to-track seek time of 0.8 ms, the rotational latency of approximately 3 ms is a large factor in the disk drive performance. If the I/Os are submitted to the disk drive fast enough, the disk drive may be able to access adjacent tracks or even read or write an entire track at a time. However, this is not always the case. In some cases the I/Os are not requested fast enough and the sequential accesses each incur a disk rotation between them. Whether this happens typically depends on the design and speed of the disk controller.

Average Seek Time

The *average seek time* is the time it takes on average to seek between random tracks on the disk. According to the specification sheet of an average 10,000-rpm disk drive, the average seek time is around 6 ms. Since almost all the I/Os that are generated by a SQL Server system are random, your disk drives will be performing a lot of random I/Os.

The maximum seek time of a typical disk can be as long as 13 ms. The maximum seek time occurs from the innermost track of the platter to the outermost track or vice versa. This is referred to as a *full-disk seek*. But on average the seeks will not be full-disk seeks, especially if the disk drive is not completely full.

Disk Drive Specifications

In this section you will see how fast a disk drive can perform I/O operations based on what type of I/O is being done. In order to make these calculations you must know some information about the disk drive. Much of this information can be found by looking at the specification of the disk drive provided by the disk drive manufacturer. In this and earlier sections, we use specifications for a 10,000-rpm, 9.1-GB disk drive. Some of the specifications for this typical disk drive are given in Table 3-1.

As you will see, these specifications can be very useful in determining the performance of the disk drive.

Disk Drive Reliability

Disks are some of the few components in a computer system that are partially mechanical in nature. The disk drive spins at a high rate of speed and operates at a high temperature. Components include several motors and bearings that will eventually wear out. The disk drive specifications include a figure for mean time between failure (MTBF), which is an indication of how long a disk is expected to last on average. However, this figure is only an average. Some disk drives may last longer than others. A typical modern disk drive may have an MTBF of 1,000,000 hours, or 114 years. This is a long time; however, some disks will last much longer and some will fail immediately. The point is, this is a mechanical component and thus subject to wear and tear and eventual failure.

Table 3-1 Disk Drive Specification

Disk capacity	9.1 GB	Unformatted disk capacity
Rotational speed	10,000 rpm	Speed at which the disk is spinning
Transfer rate	40 MB/sec	Speed of the SCSI bus
Average seek time	5.2 ms (read), 6 ms (write)	Time it takes to seek (on average) between tracks during random I/Os
Track-to-track seek time	0.6 ms (read), 0.9 ms (write)	Time it takes to seek between tracks during sequential I/Os
Full-disk seek time	12 ms (read), 13 ms (write)	Time it takes to seek from the innermost sector to the outermost sector of the disk, or vice versa
Average latency	2.99 ms	Average rotational latency
Mean time between failures	1,000,000 hours	Average life span of the disk; some last longer, others shorter

Disk Drive Performance

The total time it takes for a disk operation to be completed is made up of a number of smaller time intervals:

- The seek time required to move to the track that holds the data
- The rotational latency required in order for that data to rotate under the heads
- The time required to electronically transfer that data from the disk drive to the disk controller

Thus, the time it takes for an I/O to be completed is the sum of the time intervals described here plus overhead incurred in the device driver and in Windows NT. Remember, the total time for a disk I/O mainly depends on whether the I/O in question is sequential or random. A sequential I/O is dependent on track-to-track seeks. Random I/O performance depends on the average seek time.

Sequential I/O

Sequential I/O consists of disk accesses of adjacent data in disk drives. Since the track-to-track seek time is much faster than random seeks, it is possible to achieve much higher *throughput* from a disk when performing sequential I/Os. To get an idea of how fast sequential I/Os can occur, let's look at an example.

With the disk drive described in Table 3-1 it takes approximately 0.8 ms to seek between tracks on a disk drive. Folding in the rotational latency of 2.99 ms, it will take approximately 3.79 ms per I/O. This would theoretically allow us to perform 264 sequential I/Os per second (since 3.79 ms occurs 264 times in a second). But with sequential I/Os, other factors come into play, such as the limitation for the transfer rate (40 MB/second is a common limitation) as well as OS components such as the file system and the device driver. Taking into account that additional overhead, the maximum at which a drive can sustain sequential I/O is around 250 I/Os per second (depending on how big the blocks of data are). As you will see in Part II, "Sizing and Capacity Planning," if you run a disk drive at more than 85 percent of its capacity, *queuing* will occur; thus, the maximum recommended I/O rate is 225 I/Os per second.

Random I/O

Random I/O occurs when data is accessed from different parts of the disk. This causes random head movement, and thus reduced performance. Again, let's look at the example disk described earlier. Instead of taking approximately 0.8 ms to seek between adjacent tracks on the disk, it is now necessary to seek to random tracks on the disk. This random seeking takes approximately 6 ms to finish (on average), which is 7.5 times longer than the track-to-track seek.

A typical random I/O takes approximately 6 ms (on average) for the disk to seek to where the data is held and an additional 2.99 ms in rotational latency, for a total of 8.99 ms. This gives a theoretical maximum of 111 I/O operations per second (since 8.99 ms can occur 111 times per second). As noted earlier, if you run a disk drive at more than 85 percent of its capacity, queuing will occur. Therefore, the maximum recommended I/O rate is 94 I/Os per second. Taking into account overhead in the controller, a rule of thumb is to drive these disk drives at no more than 85 I/Os per second.

When accessing a disk randomly, a normal disk latency (the time it takes to retrieve I/Os) is around 9 ms (8.99 ms). When a drive is accessed faster than it can handle, queuing will occur and the I/O latency (response time) will increase. As you can see in Figure 3-4, the closer the number of I/Os per second gets to maximum capacity, the longer the latencies get. In fact, once you reach 100 percent, queueing is guaranteed to occur and performance will degrade dramatically.

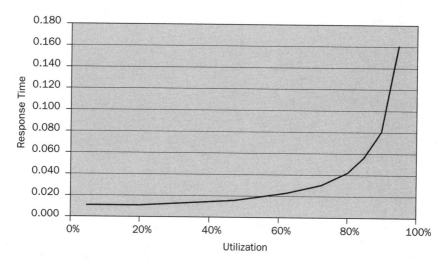

Figure 3-4 *The relationship between I/O latency and the utilization.*

As you will learn later, SQL Server is very sensitive to I/O latencies. When I/Os take excessive amounts of time to execute, the performance of SQL Server will degrade and problems such as blocking and deadlocks may occur. When a thread is waiting for an I/O, it may be holding locks. The longer the I/O takes to execute, the longer the locks are held, thus causing these types of problems.

Elevator Sorting

When random I/O operations are issued to disks, the heads must move in and out between the disk surfaces randomly, which causes latencies to increase. Many RAID controllers support *elevator sorting* to make random seeks more efficient. Elevator sorting is a method of making random I/O operations more efficient. If multiple I/Os are queued on the controller, they can be sorted to reduce head movement, much like the operation of an elevator.

Imagine if an elevator serviced floors in the order that people on the elevator pushed the buttons. The elevator might pass floors where it could more efficiently let people on and off. Just as an elevator is efficient about stopping at floors where it is needed, based on where it is, so do the elevator sorting algorithms achieve efficiency. If there is more than one I/O queued at a time, the controller uses an elevator sorting algorithm to choose the most efficient path (see Figure 3-5). Elevator sorting reduces overall disk seek times, although sometimes at the expense of individual seek times.

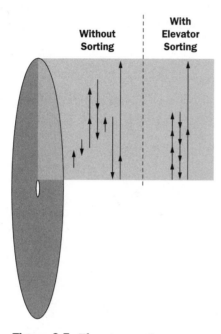

Figure 3-5 *Elevator sorting.*

As you can see, elevator sorting can make I/Os more efficient, thus resulting in improved performance. Even though the disk manufacturers and the controller manufacturers attempt to make I/O more efficient, the only real way to improve I/O performance is to live within the performance capacity of the I/O subsystem. By understanding the limits of the I/O subsystem and remaining within those limits, latencies will be reduced and SQL Server performance optimized. Some tips on how to do this are given in the next section.

Solving the Disk Performance Capacity Problem

So, how do we solve the problem of disk capacity? It is actually very straightforward. By following these guidelines you should be able to design a system that performs optimally.

- **Isolate sequential I/Os.** By allocating components that are sequential in nature to their own disk volume, their sequential nature can be maintained. The transaction log is an example of a sequentially accessed file. If you place more than one sequentially accessed file on the same disk volume, the I/Os will become random because the disk must seek between the sequential components belonging to different files.

- **Distribute random I/Os.** Since the I/Os are random in nature, the addition of more disk drives should lessen the loadon any one disk. By building a system with enough disk drives to handle the random I/O load, you should not experience any problems. Determining how many disks are necessary and how to configure them are topics addressed later in this chapter and in Part II, "Sizing and Capacity Planning."

Introduction to RAID

As you might imagine, it can become increasingly more difficult to manage a system as you add more and more disk drives. Instead of adding tens or hundreds of individual disk drives, many users prefer to use RAID (redundant array of inexpensive disks). RAID can be implemented by using software and existing I/O components, or by purchasing hardware RAID devices. This section introduces you to what RAID is and how it works.

As the name implies, RAID takes two or more disk drives and creates an array of disks. To the operating system this array appears as one *logical disk*. This logical disk is also known as a *disk volume*, since it is a collection of disks that appears as one disk to the user, the application, and even to Windows NT (if hardware RAID is being used). In many cases, however, this single logical disk is much larger than any disk you could purchase.

Not only does RAID allow you to create large disk drives, but many *RAID levels* (configurations) provide you with disk fault tolerance as well. *Fault tolerance* allows the RAID logical disk to survive (tolerate) the loss of one or more individual disk drives. The next few sections explain how this is possible and describe the characteristics of various RAID levels.

As mentioned earlier, RAID can be implemented by using software; in fact, Windows NT comes with RAID software. However, this chapter is mostly concerned with hardware RAID because of the additional features that it provides. The most common of these hardware RAID features is the controller cache.

Controller Caches

In order to improve I/O performance, many vendors offer a *controller cache*, which is RAM that resides on the disk controller itself. This cache serves two purposes:

- **Caching data to be written**   Since there is memory on the controller, it is possible for the controller to tell the OS (and subsequently SQL Server) that the I/O has completed as soon as it has been written to the cache, thus making logical write performance very fast. Of course, this data still must be written to the disk at a later time.

- **Caching read-ahead data**   Another use of the controller cache is to read data in addition to the data that was requested, in anticipation of that additional data being requested soon. If it is, the response time will be very fast. The operation that reads additional data is called *read-ahead* since it will read the next data on the disk, even if it is not currently requested.

As you will see later in this chapter, write performance can be very important, especially when using RAID level 5. In most cases the controller cache is of great benefit. There are, however, a few things to be careful of.

- Don't use write caching without a battery backup. Most caching controllers include a battery (or have it as an option). This battery helps retain data in the cache in the event of a power failure. Without the battery the data in the cache would be lost and the database could become corrupted.

- In rare situations in which the RAID array is run near capacity, write caching can actually hurt read performance because of the priority that writes are given within the controller in order to empty the cache.

Controller caches can enhance the performance of your disk array. By understanding the various RAID levels and their performance characteristics you will be better able to configure and size your system.

Internal vs. External RAID

There are two basic types of RAID controllers: internal and external, which refer to where the RAID logic lies in the configuration (see Figure 3-6). With most controllers the RAID logic resides on the controller card, which resides in the chassis that houses the computer system. This is referred to as an *internal* RAID system. In addition there is a second type of RAID controller in which the RAID logic resides in the cabinet that houses the disk drives. This is referred to as an *external* RAID controller. Each type of controller has its own properties and characteristics. However, these characteristics are not really pertinent to this chapter; these different types of controllers are presented only for completeness.

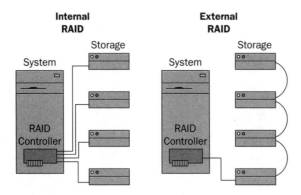

Figure 3-6 *Internal vs. external RAID.*

Storage Area Networks

One of the latest technologies on the market today is the *storage area network* (SAN). A SAN is basically a large external RAID system that shares the storage among several different systems (hence the term *network*). A SAN offers consolidation of storage and cost savings while allowing centralized management and centralized support.

The concept of a SAN is fairly straightforward. Whereas an external RAID system has a connection directly from the host bus adapter (HBA) to the external RAID subsystem, a SAN's connection from the HBA goes into a switch. This switch has multiple HBAs connected to it as well as at least one external RAID system. With this setup it is possible for all the systems on the SAN to access the RAID subsystem. The SAN system is shown in Figure 3-7.

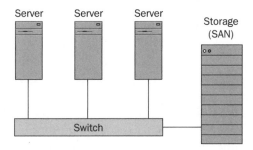

Figure 3-7 *SAN system.*

Common RAID Levels

Two or more disks can be combined into a RAID array. The main characteristic of a RAID array is that physical disk drives are combined to form a *logical disk drive*, that is, a virtual disk drive. To Windows NT (and to PerfMon), this logical disk drive appears as a single disk drive, even though it could be made up of many individual physical disk drives. In fact, a logical disk drive in Windows NT could appear to be many hundreds of gigabytes in size, even though 100-GB disk drives don't exist (yet!).

Striping

Most of the RAID levels that will be described here use *data striping*. Data striping combines the data from two or more disks into one larger RAID logical disk. Striping is accomplished by partitioning the data and then taking the first piece of data and placing it on the first disk, placing the second piece of data on the second disk, and so on. These small pieces are known as *stripes* or *chunks*. The size of the stripe is determined by the controller. Some controllers allow you to configure the stripe size, whereas other controllers have a fixed stripe size.

The combination of all the related chunks of data across all disk drives is also referred to as a *stripe,* as shown in Figure 3-8. Thus the term *stripe* can be used to describe the piece of data on a specific disk drive (that is, "the disk stripe") or to refer to the entire set (that is, "the RAID stripe"). Keep this in mind when RAID is being discussed.

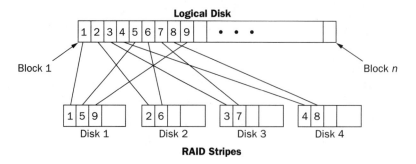

Figure 3-8 *RAID stripes.*

The other characteristics of a RAID array are determined by the RAID level itself. The *RAID level* is a term used to identify the RAID configuration type. One of the most important features of a RAID system is *fault tolerance*, which is the ability to continue functioning after a disk drive has failed. Fault tolerance is the primary reason that RAID controllers are used. Because your data is valuable, it must be protected against a disk failure. In this section you will learn about the most common RAID levels-how they work, what fault tolerance they provide, and how they perform. Some RAID levels are rarely used; only the most popular ones will be mentioned here.

RAID 0

RAID 0 is the most basic of the RAID levels. It offers disk striping only. A chunk (the size of which is defined by the controller) is created on each disk drive. A round-robin method is used to distribute the data across all the disks in the RAID 0 array in order to create a large logical disk. An illustration of RAID 0 striping is shown in Figure 3-9.

Although RAID 0 is considered a RAID level, it doesn't support any redundancy. Since there is no redundancy, there is no fault tolerance. In the event that any disk were to fail in a RAID 0 array, data would be lost. The loss of one disk of a four-disk array, for example, would be equivalent to losing every fourth word in this book. With this portion of the data missing, the entire logical disk is useless; thus the entire database on that logical disk is useless.

RAID 0 Recommendations

RAID 0 is not normally recommended for storing SQL Server data files. Since the data in the database is important to your business, its loss could be devastating. A RAID 0 array does not protect you against a disk failure, so we do not recommend using it for any critical system component, such as OS, transaction log, or database files.

> **Note** A disk drive is a mechanical component. The disk is spinning at a high rate of speed and operates at a high temperature. Because the disk is a mechanical component, it eventually will fail. Thus, it is important to protect your database against that failure by using fault tolerance on SQL Server data files.

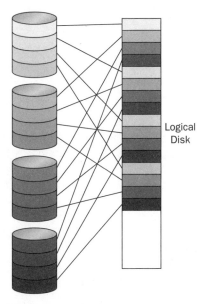

Logical
Disk

Figure 3-9 *RAID 0.*

RAID 1

RAID 1 is the most basic of the fault-tolerant RAID levels. RAID 1, also known as *mirroring,* creates a duplicate of your data disk. This duplicate contains all of the information that exists on the original disk. In the event of a disk failure, the mirror takes over; thus there is no loss of data. A representation of RAID 1 is shown in Figure 3-10. The data is all held on one disk (and stored in the identical form on its mirror), so there is no striping involved. Since RAID 1 uses the second disk drive to duplicate the first disk, the total space of the RAID 1 volume is equivalent to the space of one disk drive. Thus RAID 1 is costly in that you must double the number of disks without getting any additional disk space in return; however, you do get a high level of fault tolerance.

When data is written to a RAID 1 volume, the controller must write this data to both disk drives before the I/O is considered to be completed, because the system is not fault tolerant until both disks have the data. Once the data has been written to both disk drives, it can be recovered in the event of a failure in either disk. The latency involved in writing to the disk is the longer of the two disks writes; thus, if one disk takes longer to write than the other disk, the latency will be longer.

The fact that the write goes to both disks also figures into the capacity of the disk drive. When calculating how many I/Os are going to each disk drive in the array, you must multiply the number of writes by 2. Reads occur only on one disk. The reason that the disks

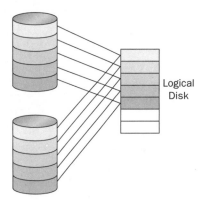

Figure 3-10 *RAID 1.*

may perform at different rates is that the heads on one disk may be positioned different-ly from the heads on the other disk. This happens because RAID 1 supports *split seeks;* thus, a seek may take longer on one disk than on the other.

Split seeks allow you to perform reads from either disk in a RAID 1 volume independently. Most vendors support split seeks in order to decrease read latency. By allowing two disks to perform reads, performance increases because the I/O load is distributed to two disks instead of one. However, since the disk heads are operating independently and they both must perform the write, the write latency becomes the longer of the two write latencies.

RAID 1 Recommendations

RAID 1 offers a high degree of fault tolerance, as well as good performance. Some rec-ommendations for using RAID 1 are as follows:

- Use RAID 1 when all the data fits on one disk drive.
- Use RAID 1 for your OS disk. It can be very time-consuming to rebuild an OS in the event of a failure. Since the OS usually fits on one disk, RAID 1 is a good choice.
- Use RAID 1 for the transaction log. Typically the SQL Server transaction log can fit on one disk drive. In addition, the transaction log performs mostly sequential writes. Only rollback operations cause reads from the transaction log. Thus you can achieve a high rate of performance by isolating the transaction log to its own RAID 1 volume.
- Use write caching on RAID 1 volumes. Since RAID 1 writes will not finish until both writes have been done, performance of writes can be improved through the use of a write cache. When using a write cache be sure that it is backed up by a battery.

As you will see later in this chapter, there are other fault-tolerant solutions that can be used when more than one disk is required. RAID 1 is great when fault tolerance is required and one disk is sufficient for all the data.

RAID 5

RAID 5 is a fault-tolerant RAID level that uses *parity* to introduce redundancy to the data. When the data is partitioned into stripes, additional parity bits are computed and stored on one disk in the stripe. If one disks fails, causing a stripe to be unavailable, the parity bits, along with the data stored on other disks in the RAID stripe, can be used to recreate the data on the failed disk drive in the stripe. Thus, a RAID 5 array can tolerate the loss of one disk drive in the array. The parity information is rotated among the different disk drives in the array as shown in Figure 3-11.

The advantage of RAID 5 is that the space available in this RAID level is equal to $N - 1$, where N is the number of disk drives in the array. Thus a RAID 5 array made up of 10 disk drives will have the space of 9 disks. This makes RAID 5 a very economical fault-tolerant choice.

Unfortunately, RAID 5 carries performance penalties. Additional overhead is involved in maintaining the parity. When writing to a RAID 5 array, both the target disk stripe and the parity stripe must be read and the parity calculated, and then both stripes must be written out. Therefore a RAID 5 write actually incurs four physical I/Os.

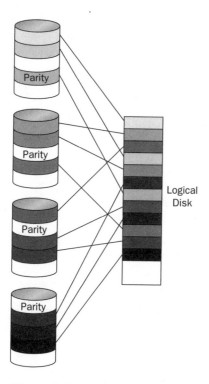

Figure 3-11 *RAID 5.*

Parity Explained

In RAID 5, parity is computed on all the data in all the stripes for all the disk drives. *Parity* is an additional piece of data that is computed by examining all the other bits and determining which value the parity bit must contain in order to create an even number for even parity, or odd number for odd parity. This parity bit, along with all the remaining bits, can be used to determine the value of a missing bit.

Let's look at an example of how parity works. For this example we will consider a RAID 5 system with five disk drives. Each disk drive is essentially made up of a number of bits, starting from the first part of the stripe on each disk to the end part of the stripe on each disk. The parity is basically created by looking at the individual bits from each disk drive and creating a bit parity.

In this example we will consider the parity to be even; thus, all the bits must add up to an even number. So, let's see how a parity works. If the first bit on the first disk drive is 0, the first bit on the second drive is 1, the first bit on the third drive is 1, and the first bit on the fourth drive is 1, then the parity can only be 1 in order for the sum of these bits to add up to an even number, as shown in Figure 3-12.

Think of the parity as being created on single bits. Even though the disk stripe contains many bits, it is by computing parity on the single bits that the data becomes recoverable. As you can see from Figure 3-12, the parity is actually created on individual bits in the stripes. Even though the disk drives are broken up into chunks or stripe pieces that may be 64 KB or larger, the parity can only be created in a bitwise fashion, as shown in the figure. Of course, the way in which parity is actually calculated is a little more sophisticated than shown here.

So, let's say for example that disk 3 failed. In this case, the parity bit plus all the other bits from all the other disk drives can be used to recover the missing bit from disk 3, since we know that they must all add up to an even number.

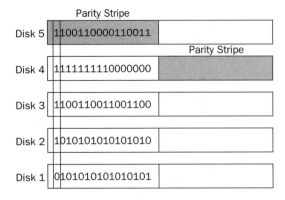

Figure 3-12 *Example: Computing a parity bit.*

Computing Parity

As you have seen, the RAID 5 parity is computed by finding the sum of the same bit on all the drives in the RAID 5 array and then creating a parity bit so that the result is even. Well, as you might imagine, it is very impractical for an array controller to read all the data from all the drives each time an I/O occurs. This would be very inefficient and slow.

Instead, when a RAID 5 array is created the data is initially zeroed out and the parity is reset. Once this process has been completed, you are left with a set of RAID 5 disk drives with no data but with a full set of parity. From this point on, whenever data is written to a disk drive both the data disk and the parity disk must first be read. The new data is compared with the old data and if the data for a particular bit has changed, the parity for that bit must change. The controller accomplishes this task with an XOR (exclusive OR) operation. Thus the array controller need read only the data disk and the parity disk, not all the disks in the array.

Once this operation has been performed, both disk drives must be written since the parity operation works on entire stripes. Therefore for each write I/O to a RAID 5 volume, four physical I/Os are incurred: two reads (one from data and one from parity) and two writes (back to data and back to parity). But with a RAID 5 array the parity is distributed, so usually this load is balanced among all the disk drives in the array.

RAID 5 Recommendations

Because of the additional I/Os incurred by RAID 5 writes, this RAID level is recommended for disk volumes that are mostly used for reading. Because the parity chunks are distributed among the different disks in the array, all disks are used for read operations. These characteristics lead to the following recommendations.

- Use RAID 5 on read-only volumes. Any disk volume that does more than 10 percent writes is not a good candidate for RAID 5.

- Use write caching on RAID 5 volumes. Since a RAID 5 write will not be complete until two reads and two writes have been performed, the response time of writes can be improved through the use of a write cache. When using a write cache be sure that it is backed up with a battery. However, the write cache is not a cure for overdriving your disk drives. You must still stay within the capacity of those disks.

As you can see, RAID 5 is economical, but at a performance price. You will see later in this chapter how high that price can be.

RAID 10

RAID 10 is a combination of RAID 0 and RAID 1. RAID 10 involves mirroring a disk stripe. Each disk will have an exact duplicate, but each disk will contain only a part of the data (see Figure 3-13). This configuration allows you to have the fault-tolerant advantages of RAID 1 and at the same time have the convenience and performance advantages of RAID 0.

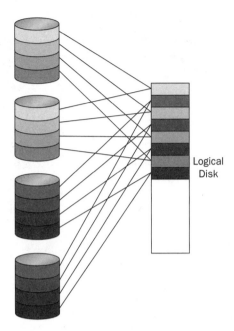

Figure 3-13 *RAID 10.*

As with RAID 1, each write operation will incur two physical I/Os, one to each disk in the mirror. Thus when calculating the number of I/Os per disk, the writes must be multiplied by 2. Similarly, the I/O operation is not considered to be complete until both writes have been done; thus, the write latency may be increased. However, most controllers support split seeks with RAID 10, just as they do with RAID 1, so the response time for reading is not increased.

RAID 10 offers a high degree of fault tolerance. In fact, more than one disk can fail and the array can survive. Of course, the loss of both sides of the mirror cannot be tolerated. If the mirror is split across disk cabinets, the loss of an entire cabinet can be tolerated.

RAID 10 Recommendations

RAID 10 offers a high degree of fault tolerance and is high performance. RAID 10 should be used when a large volume is required and more than 10 percent of the I/Os are writes. RAID 10 recommendations include the following:

- Use RAID 10 whenever the array experiences more than 10 percent writes. RAID 5 does not perform well with large numbers of writes.

- Use RAID 10 when performance is critical. Since RAID 10 supports split seeks, performance is very good.

- Use write caching on RAID 10 volumes. Since RAID 10 writes will not be complete until both writes have been done, performance of writes can be improved through the use of a write cache. Write caching is only safe when used in conjunction with caches that are backed up with batteries.

RAID 10 is the best fault-tolerant solution, but it comes at a cost. You must purchase twice the number of disks that are necessary with RAID 0. If your volume is mostly read, then RAID 5 may be acceptable.

Performance Comparison of RAID Levels

To properly configure and tune your RAID system you must understand the performance differences among the various RAID levels. By understanding how the RAID system works and how it performs under various conditions, you will better be able to tune your I/O subsystem. This section compares the different performance characteristics that were described earlier.

Read Performance

Read performance is not significantly affected by RAID controllers. When performing read operations on a RAID 0, RAID 1, RAID 5, or RAID 10 volume, you are able to take advantage of the performance provided by the total of all the disk drives in the system. Since random I/Os are typically the most problematic, they are covered here. You can maximize sequential performance by isolating the sequential I/Os to their own volume. Let's look at random read performance under the various RAID levels.

- RAID 0 volumes spread the data evenly among all the disks in the RAID array. Thus, random I/Os should spread out randomly among all the disk drives in the system. If we use the rule of thumb of 85 I/Os per second per disk drive (random I/O), a RAID 0 array of 10 disk drives should be able to handle 850 I/Os per second.

- RAID 1 volumes support split seeks, so for read operations both disk drives are used. Thus a RAID 1 volume can support twice the number of reads as a single disk, or 142 I/Os per second, before performance begins to suffer.

- RAID 5 arrays spread the data evenly among all the disk drives in the array. Even though one disk drive is used for parity in each stripe, all drives are typically used for reading because the I/Os are random in nature. Thus, as with the RAID 0 array, the read capacity is 85 I/Os per second times the number of disk drives in the array. Running at more than that will reduce SQL Server performance.

- RAID 10 arrays, like RAID 1, support split seeks. The read performance is therefore equivalent to the number of disk drives times 85 I/Os per second. Exceeding this limit will work, but may cause performance degradation.

As you can see, calculating the read capacity of a RAID array is fairly straightforward. By adding enough disk drives to support your I/O requirements and staying within these limitations, your performance should be excellent.

Write Performance

Write performance is dramatically affected by RAID controllers. Again, random I/Os are typically the most problematic, so let's look at random write performance under the various RAID levels.

- RAID 0 is the configuration most capable of handling writes without performance degradation, but at the price of no fault tolerance. Since RAID 0 does not mirror data or use parity, the performance of RAID 0 is simply that of the individual disk drives. Thus a RAID 0 array of 10 disk drives can handle 850 random writes per second.

- RAID 1 arrays must mirror any data that is written to the array. Therefore a single write I/O to the array will generate two I/Os to the disk drives. A RAID 1 array thus has the capacity of a single disk drive, or 85 I/Os per second.

- RAID 5 arrays are even more demanding on write I/Os. A write to a RAID 5 array actually generates two reads from the disks and two writes to the disks. Thus an I/O to a RAID 5 array generates four physical I/Os to the disks, making the write capacity of a RAID 5 array one-fourth the number of disk drives in the array.

- RAID 10 has the same characteristics as the RAID 1 array. Each write to the RAID 10 volume will generate two physical writes. Thus the capacity of the RAID 10 array is equivalent to the capacity of one-half the number of disk drives in the array.

As you can see, calculating the write capacity of a RAID array is a fairly complex operation. By adding enough disk drives to support your I/O requirements and staying within the limitations described above, you will keep the I/O subsystem from becoming a bottleneck. In the next section you will see how to calculate the number of I/Os per disk in various situations.

Disk Calculations

To determine how much load is being placed on the individual disk drives in the system, you must perform some calculations. If you are using a hardware RAID controller, the number of I/Os per second that is displayed is the number of I/Os that is going to the array. Additional I/Os that are generated by the controller for fault tolerance are not shown. In fact, Windows NT is not even aware that they are occurring, but you must be aware of them.

The following formulas can help you determine how many I/Os are actually going to each disk in the array.

RAID 0

Calculate the number of I/Os per disk drive in a RAID 0 array by adding up all the reads and writes to the array and dividing by the number of disks in the array, as follows:

I/Os per Disk = (*Reads* + *Writes*) / *Number of Disks*

RAID 0 presents a very simple and straightforward equation.

RAID 1

With RAID 1 the calculation becomes a little more complicated. Since writes are doubled, the number of I/Os per disk is equal to the number of reads plus twice the number of writes, divided by the number of disk drives in the array (which is two for RAID 1). The equation is as follows:

$$I/Os\ per\ Disk = [Reads + (2 * Writes)]\ /\ 2$$

RAID 1 is harder on writes, but offers a high degree of fault tolerance.

RAID 5

RAID 5 reads are distributed equally among the different disk drives in the array, but writes actually cause four physical I/Os to occur. To calculate the number of I/Os occurring on the individual disk drives, you thus must add the reads to four times the number of writes before dividing by the number of disk drives. The equation for RAID 5 I/Os is as follows:

$$I/Os\ per\ Disk = [Reads + (4 * Writes)]\ /\ Number\ of\ Disks$$

RAID 5 has a high level of overhead on writes, but offers fault tolerance.

RAID 10

The calculation with RAID 10 is the same as with RAID 1. Since writes are doubled, the number of I/Os per disk is equal to the number of reads plus twice the number of writes, divided by the number of disk drives in the array. The equation is as follows:

$$I/Os\ per\ Disk = [Reads + (2 * Writes)]\ /\ Number\ of\ Disks$$

RAID 10 is harder on writes, as is RAID 1, but offers a high degree of fault tolerance.

Choosing the Right RAID Level

Let's compare the different RAID levels directly. This may better help you to determine which RAID level is best for you. When comparing I/O performance across different RAID levels, one of the most important factors to consider is the read to write ratio. The different RAID levels perform comparably when performing reads; only the writes have different characteristics. You should also keep in mind whether fault tolerance is necessary for you. Finally you should be aware of the different costs involved (for the space you get). Table 3-2 summarizes the characteristics of the various RAID levels. As you can see, your best choice really depends on your requirements.

Table 3-2 RAID Levels

RAID Level	Performance	Fault Tolerance	Cost
RAID 0	Best	No fault tolerance	Most economical
RAID 1	Good	Good	Most expensive
RAID 5	Good reads	OK	Most economical
	Slow writes		Fault tolerant
RAID 10	Good	Excellent	Most expensive

Table 3-3 illustrates the differences between RAID 5 and RAID 10 at different read/write ratios. This table shows the load for 500 I/Os per second across 10 disk drives with varying read/write ratios. At about 90 percent reads to 10 percent writes, the disk usage is about even, but for higher ratios of writes RAID 5 incurs much more overhead.

Table 3-3 Comparing Disk Loads

Read/Write Ratio	RAID 5 I/Os*	RAID 10 I/Os†
100% reads; 0% writes	(500 + 0) / 10	(500 + 0) / 10
	50 I/Os per disk	50 I/Os per disk
90% reads; 10% writes	(450 + 200) / 10	(450 + 100) / 10
	65 I/Os per disk	55 I/Os per disk
75% reads; 25% writes	(375 + 500) / 10	(375 + 250) / 10
	87.5 I/Os per disk	62.5 I/Os per disk
50% reads; 50% writes	(250 + 1000) / 10	(250 + 500) / 10
	125 I/Os per disk	75 I/Os per disk
0% reads; 100% writes	(0 + 2000) / 10	(0 + 1000) / 10
	200 I/Os per disk	100 I/Os per disk

* [Reads + (4 * Writes)] / Number of Disks
† [Reads + (2 * Writes)] / Number of Disks

I/O Latencies and SQL Server

SQL Server is very sensitive to I/O latencies because of the concurrency of transactions within the SQL Server engine. Under normal conditions there are tens or hundreds of applications running against a SQL Server database. In order to provide for this concurrency, SQL Server has a complex system of row, page, extent, and table locks, as you will see throughout this book. When a piece of data or a SQL Server resource is locked, other processes will block, waiting for that data or resource to be unlocked.

When I/Os take excessive amounts of time to finish, the locked resources will be held for a longer period of time than normal. When this occurs the amount of blocking will also be increased, thus delaying other processing in the system. In addition, excessive blocking leads to higher chances of deadlocks. Thus, the longer the I/O takes to finish, the longer the locks are held and the greater the potential for problems.

The time for a query to finish processing will be significantly increased if an I/O subsystem is overloaded. Take, for example, a case in which long table scans are running on your system. It is not uncommon for these types of queries to read hundreds of thousands or even millions of rows in order to complete the task. If such a large table scan causes 1 million I/Os to be performed, the time difference between an optimal and suboptimal system can be dramatic. On average, 1 million I/Os at 10 ms each will take approximately 2.7 hours to complete. If your system has overloaded the I/O subsystem and each I/O is taking 40 ms, however, the time to complete the I/Os associated with this query will increase to 11 hours.

As you can see, SQL Server performance can be severely degraded by a poorly sized or poorly configured I/O subsystem. By designing your I/O subsystem to work within the capacity of the individual components, you will find that the performance of your database will be excellent. Some tips and recommendations are provided in the next section.

Guidelines for Configuring I/O Subsystems

This section presents a number of different tips and recommendations on how you can best utilize RAID controllers in your system. Some of these tips and recommendations have been mentioned earlier and some are new. We hope that they can help you to better configure and use your RAID array.

- Isolate the SQL Server transaction log onto its own RAID 1 or RAID 10 volume. I/Os to the transaction log are almost 100 percent sequential and almost 100 percent writes. The only time the sequential nature of the transaction log is disrupted is during a rollback operation. If the data needed for a rollback is no longer cached, the information must be read from the transaction log.

- Configure enough drives to keep the data file volumes at less than 85 I/Os per second per disk. This is accomplished by simply adding more disk drives to the array until you have enough. If the I/Os are random, and they usually are, the I/Os will spread out among all the disk drives in the array.

- Configure data file volumes as RAID 5 if write I/Os are less than 10 percent, and as RAID 10 if writes are greater then 10 percent of the total I/Os.

- Regularly monitor the number of I/Os per second per disk. If the disks are nearing their capacity limit, add more disk drives.

By following these guidelines and carefully monitoring your system you should be able to avoid performance problems.

Summary

In this chapter you learned the basics of I/O tuning. You learned how a disk drive works and what its limitations are, which gives you the knowledge to configure your system to work within those limitations. In addition you learned about how RAID controllers work, and about the various RAID levels. Knowing the characteristics of the different RAID levels will help you to configure your system to its best advantage. You also learned how a poorly tuned I/O subsystem can negatively affect SQL Server performance. I/O tuning is all about capacity. By working within the capacity of the various components, you can achieve excellent performance. In the next chapter, we will discuss how to measure and tune hardware, database layout, and SQL Server configuration parameters.

Chapter 4
Tuning SQL Server

Many aspects of your SQL Server system can be optimized, or tuned, to give your system better performance. Much of this book focuses on tuning your system in different areas, such as hardware, SQL Server configuration, database layout, SQL statements, SQL indexes, replication, backup and recovery, and more. This chapter discusses specific tuning issues involving hardware, database layout, and SQL Server configuration parameters.

First we describe ways to measure performance. Then we discuss how to tune your existing system hardware by determining if one or more of the hardware components is causing a bottleneck, which could be holding back the performance of the system. Although related in some ways, the information in this chapter is different from the chapters on capacity planning and sizing, which teach you how to decide on what type and how much hardware you will need in your system when you are initially building it. Here we focus on how you can determine if the hardware you currently have is sufficient for your needs and if it is performing optimally. We also discuss how to optimize your database layout using files and filegroups, in more detail than shown in Chapter 2. Finally we describe the most common SQL Server configuration parameters that may need to be adjusted from their defaults by the system administrator.

How to Measure Performance

The overall performance of a system can be generally measured according to transaction *response times,* that is, the time it takes to complete a query or task, which is also the time the user must wait for the task to finish and possibly return results. Slow (long) response times translate into bad performance and frustrated users, whereas quick response times mean better performance and happy users. You should talk with your users to get feedback on what is happening when they run transactions. But try to get specific and objective answers—sometimes the users do not know if their transactions should be running faster. They may be accustomed to a transaction taking two minutes to finish and therefore never complain about it, even though with some tuning the transaction might take only seconds to finish, allowing the user to get much more work done in a day.

You may encounter a transaction that does not finish within the same response time at each execution. For example, users may wait only 10 seconds for a query to finish the first time it is run, and another time they may wait 10 minutes. This difference is an indication you may have a performance problem, which may or may not be easy to resolve. The different response times for this same query may be related to the time of day when the query was run. For instance, if the query was first run at 7:30 A.M., before all the users logged into the system, and was run the second time at 10 A.M., when lots of processing was going on, then there was more contention for resources on the system in the second instance. Another possibility could be that a database backup was going on at the latter time, which causes a lot of read activity on the system and can slow down all user transactions.

Your system thus may show different levels of performance (good or bad) at different times of the day, according to heavy or light user activity. If a user query takes a relatively long time to finish, or more time than you think it should based on previous tuning experience (we've seen cases where a user transaction lasted 36 hours!), it is an indication that you may have a performance problem that could be resolved, and you should investigate what is going on in the system. Sometimes it is impossible to resolve a performance issue if you are limited in some way. For example, maybe you need more disks to handle the I/O needs of your system, but you cannot buy additional hardware because of budget limits. Be sure to include the costs for new and spare hardware in your budget calculations for the next quarter if you need hardware.

Another way to know if you have a performance problem is by simply monitoring your system on a regular basis. In this book you will learn what to look for when monitoring and some general guidelines on interpreting what you see. The main method for monitoring hardware performance that we discuss in this chapter is the Windows NT/2000 Performance Monitor. With the Performance Monitor, you can keep a log of the performance counters in order to view the data at a later time. The Performance Monitor also provides an excellent way of comparing performance data from different days and times to see how your system has evolved. (In other chapters of the book we discuss how to use SQL Server Enterprise Manager for other types of tuning.)

Before you decide that you have a hardware bottleneck, you should investigate your SQL statements, stored procedures, application code, database layout, and indexes. These other areas could also cause performance problems. If you have a query that is doing a table scan, for example, it could be causing much more disk I/O than if you had an index to cover that query. Later parts of this book discuss these topics in detail. The main point here is that you should not just look at one area of your system when tuning, such as the hardware only. You must look at each area and tune them together. You do not want to end up buying lots of hardware to support a badly written stored procedure that performs 100 times more I/Os than it should.

Tuning the Server Hardware

Hardware tuning involves several components of your system, of which the three most common that require tuning are the processors, disks, and memory. This section explains how to determine if one or more of those components causes a bottleneck, and how to solve the problem if you do find one. These methods will also help you determine if there is no real performance problem, in which case you do not need to add or upgrade hardware.

Many scenarios are possible. You may have a bottleneck in one component, fix it, and then find that doing so allowed more processing to be done on the system than was occurring before, which reveals that you have another bottleneck with the additional hardware, even though your throughput is better than it was originally. We give an example of such a case in the section "Tuning the Disk Drives." Let's start our discussion with a description of system processor architecture and how to tune processors.

Processor Architecture

Processors are also referred to as *CPUs*, although the CPU (central processing unit) is actually only a part of a processor unit. Each processor unit contains a CPU with a level 1 cache, possibly a level 2 cache, and a math coprocessor or other microprocessor chips designed for special functionality, as shown in Figure 4-1.

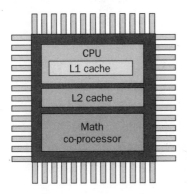

Figure 4-1 *Processor architecture.*

The level 1 (L1) cache is memory located within the CPU so that the CPU can access it quickly. It is relatively small: in the newer processors, it is 32 KB, of which 16 KB is used for storing instructions and the other 16 KB is used for storing data. This cache is the fastest memory access available to the CPU. The level 2 (L2) cache provides additional space for holding instructions. In some processors the L2 cache is located on the processor unit, and in other processors it is separate from the unit. The L2 cache normally comes in sizes such as 256 KB, 512 KB, 1 MB, and 2 MB.

When data or the next instruction is needed, the computer first checks the L1 cache to see if the needed data resides there, then checks the L2 cache, then system RAM. It is much faster to access the L1 or L2 caches than it is to read from the system memory. In turn, it is faster to read from RAM than from disk. For the rest of this chapter we use both terms, *processor* and *CPU,* to refer to the entire processor unit.

A system with one CPU is called *a single-processor system;* a system with more than one CPU is called a *symmetric multiprocessor (SMP) system*. In a single-processor system, only one thread at a time can execute on the CPU, and therefore only one task may be handled at a time. Multiple tasks must take turns using the CPU. With an SMP system, the CPUs can process threads in parallel, greatly increasing the processing capacity and speed, resulting in increased throughput. The CPUs all share the same system memory and must take turns accessing that memory by way of the memory bus, as shown in Figure 4-2. The more processors you have in a system, the higher the chances are of having collisions between the processors when they try to access the memory. The L2 cache is helpful in such a case. If the data is in the L2 cache, a processor will not have to access the system memory, thus avoiding collisions on the memory bus. Therefore, the more CPUs in your system, the more important a large L2 cache becomes.

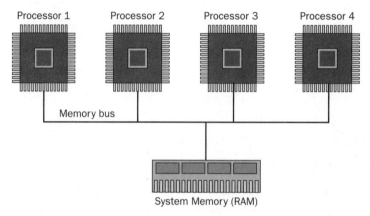

Figure 4-2 *Memory bus utilization with SMP.*

Although a large L2 cache can speed processing in all cases, it is particularly important in SMP systems. A system with a single processor will not have the same problem with collisions on the memory bus as in SMP systems, yet accessing data from the L2 cache will still prove faster than accessing the memory. Thus a large L2 cache helps performance, and does not hurt it.

Tuning the Processor

Whether you have one or more CPUs, the method of determining whether you have a CPU bottleneck is the same. First you must monitor the CPU activity on your system while work is being done. Make sure to monitor the system during all times of the day to determine if there are certain times when processing is heavier than other times so that you can configure your system to handle the heaviest load times. To monitor CPU utilization, use the Windows NT Performance Monitor and choose the following objects and counters to monitor:

- **Processor object, % Processor Time counter** Select all the processors by number that appear in the right-hand side of the window. This counter gives the processor utilization per processor.

- **System object, % Total Processor Time counter** This counter gives the average total processor time of all processors in the system.

A general rule is that if your processor utilization stays continuously at 80 percent or above, or if it peaks often at this rate, you may have a CPU bottleneck. See Part II of this book for more details on the capacity of CPUs. If you do detect a CPU bottleneck, adding more or faster processors to the system will improve performance. For example, let's say your system contains one CPU with a speed of 300 MHz, and you find that the CPU utilization is usually at 60 percent and often jumps to 90 percent for a period of about three to five minutes. In this case, you could benefit from adding a CPU to the system in order to have an SMP system with parallel processing capabilities, assuming there is an extra slot in your machine for a second CPU. If not, try exchanging the CPU for a faster one, perhaps a 500-MHz processor. The additional CPU will work in parallel with the original processor, or a faster processor will complete each task quicker. Both methods will improve performance, but the preferred method is to add another processor if possible.

As another example, let's say you have a system with four processors running at a speed of 400 MHz and an L2 cache of 512 KB. You find that CPU utilization is normally at 75 percent across the four CPUs, and at times the utilization hits 100 percent. This high utilization indicates a probable CPU bottleneck. You could try adding more CPUs if your system has the capacity; if not, switch the four existing CPUs for four faster ones, such as 500-MHz CPUs. Also, get a larger L2 cache on the processors, such as a 2-MB L2 cache.

When adding CPUs to your system, make sure that the operating system supports that number of CPUs. For example, different versions of Windows 2000 provide support for different numbers of CPUs. Make sure you get the right version for your system.

Tuning the Disk Drives

Every disk drive has certain characteristics that determine its speed for handling reads and writes of data. You cannot actually tune the disk itself; rather, you tune the type and number of disks on your system to better meet your I/O needs. Chapter 3 explained the internals of a disk drive and how it works. Reading that chapter should help you understand the concepts we discuss here concerning disk tuning.

The goal in tuning disk drives is to provide your system with the ability to process I/Os without experiencing long I/O latencies so that the disk subsystem is not a bottleneck and reads and writes do not slow transaction completion. The term *latency* refers to the amount of time that one component is idle waiting for another component to complete some operation; thus, I/O latency is the time it takes for the system to complete an I/O. In other words, you want your disks to achieve small (short) latencies. Small latencies ensure that you do not have a disk bottleneck. Latency is measured in milliseconds. This section teaches you some important concepts about disk drives, how to monitor your disks to determine the read and write latencies on your system, how to know if you have a bottleneck, and what to do if you have one.

Disk Drive Concepts

You should already understand the I/O capacity of a disk, which is the maximum number of I/Os (reads plus writes) that a disk is able to perform before the number of I/O requests waiting in the queue becomes so large that latencies become too long, slowing down performance. How to determine the I/O capacity of a disk was discussed in detail in Chapter 3, along with the importance of understanding how the different levels of RAID affect the actual number of physical I/Os that occur on a disk. (You will need to know that information for our examples later in this chapter.)

When the total number of I/Os that your system needs to perform exceeds the I/O capacity of the disk, each I/O will experience a longer wait time before it can be completed. An I/O request will have to wait its turn on the disk in a wait queue, causing a longer response time for the process that is waiting for the I/O request to finish in order to complete its task. Therefore, the essence of tuning disks is determining if you have sufficient disk speed and number of disks to efficiently handle the amount of I/O that is occurring on your system.

As a brief reminder from Chapter 3, disk drives are available in a number of sizes and speeds. The size is measured in gigabytes, and the speed is measured in revolutions per minute. In general, the faster the disk speed, the quicker the data can be accessed. The size of the disk determines how much data you can store on it. However, you never want to completely fill a disk with data. Once a disk hits 85 percent of its size capacity, it should be considered full. Part II explains the reasoning behind this size percentage limit.

Monitoring Disk I/O

Now let's learn how to monitor your disk activity using the Windows NT/2000 Performance Monitor. In order to allow Windows NT to collect data for the counters that we will be discussing, you must enable an option called *diskperf*. Type the following command at the DOS prompt:

```
Diskperf -Y
```

You must reboot your server in order for this option to take effect. To disable the *diskperf* option once enable, type `Diskperf -N` at a DOS prompt and reboot.

The following counters under the PhysicalDisk object are important for monitoring disk I/O:

- **Disk Reads/sec** The number of read operations performed per second on the selected disk (or disk array)
- **Disk Writes/sec** The number of write operations performed per second on the selected disk (or disk array)
- **Avg. Disk Queue Length** The average number of read and write requests that were queued on the selected disk during the polling interval
- **Avg. Disk Sec/Read** The average number of seconds it takes for a read from disk to be performed on the selected disk during the polling interval
- **Avg. Disk Sec/Write** The average number of seconds it takes for a write to disk to be performed on the selected disk during the polling interval

Select the disk or disks that you want to monitor from the Instance drop-down menu of the Add to Chart dialog box, as shown in Figure 4-3. The disk numbers you see listed there are the Windows NT disk numbers for the disks that you would see in Disk Administrator.

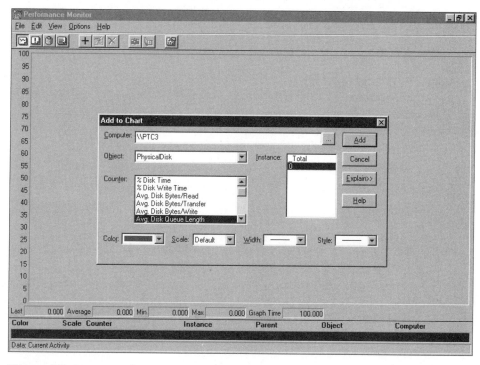

Figure 4-3 *Using Performance Monitor to select counters to monitor for the PhysicalDisk object.*

Finding Disk Bottlenecks

To illustrate how to use these counters to find disk bottlenecks, let's walk through some different system scenarios. Let's assume that the disks in these examples are 4-GB disks with an I/O capacity of 75 I/Os per second for random I/O. For our first example, let's assume you have a system configured with a RAID 10 array made up of four disk drives. That means that each drive has a mirror, so two drives are mirrored to the other two drives, as shown in Figure 4-4. The Windows NT disk number for this array is disk 2.

Figure 4-4 *Example with four disk drives configured as a RAID 10 array.*

Assume that when you use Performance Monitor to monitor the counters discussed earlier, you find the following figures for disk 2:

Disk Reads/sec	50
Disk Writes/sec	75
Avg. Disk Queue Length	1
Avg. Disk Sec/Read	0.006
Avg. Disk Sec/Write	0.008

We know that our drives can handle 75 random I/Os per second. To find out if we are breaking that limit, we can take the first two values given in the above list and calculate the total number of physical I/Os that are actually happening on the drives because of RAID 10, using the following formula:

[Reads + (2 × Writes)] / Number of Disks in Array = Total Physical I/Os per Disk

Remember that with RAID 10, reads can be serviced by a disk and its mirrored pair in parallel, and each write requires a physical write to a disk and its mirrored pair. Plugging in the values, we get

[50 + (2 × 75)] / 4 = 50 total physical I/Os per disk

Since 50 is well below the limit of 75 I/Os per disk per second, we do not have a bottleneck with these disks. Also note that the figures for seconds per read and per write are 6 msec and 8 msec, respectively. These low latencies also indicate that no bottleneck exists here.

Now let's look at this same example using different values for the counters:

Disk Reads/sec	120
Disk Writes/sec	150
Avg. Disk Queue Length	43
Avg. Disk Sec/Read	0.022
Avg. Disk Sec/Write	0.030

Plugging these new values into our formula, we get the following:

[120 + (2 × 150)] / 4 = 105 total physical I/Os per disk

The result, 105, is well above the limit of 75 I/Os per second; therefore we do have a disk bottleneck in this case. You can also see evidence of a bottleneck by simply looking at the figures for seconds per read and per write: the values should be under 20 msec to get the best performance from your drives. In this case, the figures are 22 msec and 30 msec, which indicate a bottleneck. Also note that the average queue length is 43, much higher than our previous example, which means that more I/O requests are waiting in the queue at one time.

To solve this disk bottleneck, you need to take the number of I/Os occurring and divide by the I/O capacity per disk, which will give you the minimum number of disks needed to support the amount of I/O. This calculation would look like the following:

[120 reads + (2 × 150 writes)] = 420 total I/Os
420 total I/Os / 75 I/Os per disk = 5.6 disks needed

Since it is impossible to have 5.6 disks, you should round up to 6 disks. Therefore, in this case you would need to add two more disks to the system.

For our next example, let's use a RAID 5 disk array of four disks that have the same I/O capacity as the disks in the previous examples and assume that random I/O will be performed on these disks. We will use the same number of reads and writes per second as the previous example, but change the other counters as shown:

Disk Reads/sec	120
Disk Writes/sec	150
Avg. Disk Queue Length	12
Avg. Disk Sec/Read	0.030
Avg. Disk Sec/Write	0.040

Just by looking at the values for seconds per read and per write, you should realize that there is a disk bottleneck. To calculate how many I/Os are going to each disk, you would use the following formula for RAID 5 (as shown in Chapter 3):

[Reads + (4 × Writes)] Number of Disks in Array = Total Physical I/Os per Disk

Plugging in our numbers, we get

[120 + (4 × 150)] / 4 = 180 I/Os per disk

Therefore, you would need to take the total number of I/Os occurring, which is the first part of the equation—[120 + (4 × 150)], or 720 I/Os—and divide that by the I/O capacity of the drive (75), as in the following equations:

120 reads + (4 × 150 writes) = 720 total I/Os
720 total I/Os / 75 I/Os per disk = 9.6 disks

Again you should round up to get a minimum of 10 disks needed.

What do we mean by the minimum number? It means that you need at least that many disks to support the current amount of I/O on the system. But after you relieve the current disk bottleneck, processes that were once waiting for I/O to finish will execute faster, allowing more processing to occur (if there is more to be done), which in turn can cause even more I/Os per second occurring on the system. This is not a bad thing! It just means that you may need to add even more drives to match the new performance of your system. In any case, the initial addition of disks will improve the performance.

This RAID 5 case requires more disks than our case using RAID 10 because each logical write in RAID 5 actually performs two physical reads plus two physical writes. As you can see, RAID 5 is not the best choice for systems performing a lot of writes. The general rule is that if more than 10 percent of a system's I/Os are writes, then RAID 10 is more efficient than RAID 5. But it can also be more expensive in some cases, so you must weigh the cost versus the performance gain according to your circumstances. If your system is performing less than 10 percent writes, it may be less expensive to use RAID 5 than RAID 10, (because you may need fewer disks) and the system could still perform well.

Tuning Memory

Now let's discuss the third major hardware tuning area—system memory. This includes physical memory tuning and SQL Server memory tuning. You want to have enough physical memory in the system to support SQL Server and any other applications, and you want to allocate as much of that memory as possible to SQL Server without overallocating it so that you avoid starving other applications of memory. (See Chapter 2 for details on how SQL Server uses its memory.) It is typically best to dedicate your server to SQL Server applications only, if possible. That allows SQL Server to use as much memory as possible in the system without having to share it with other applications.

To determine if you have enough physical memory in your system, you must consider several factors. You need to take all these factors into account before making a decision about how to tune your memory subsystem. You may need to add physical memory to the system, or you may simply need to adjust the SQL Server memory parameters to improve performance. You should monitor the following objects and counters through the Windows NT/2000 Performance Monitor (PerfMon):

- **Memory object, Available Bytes counter** The amount, in bytes, of available memory in the system that can be used by processes.
- **Memory object, Pages/sec counter** The number of pages per second that are paged out of memory to disk or paged into memory from disk.
- **SQLServer: Memory Manager object, Total Server Memory (KB) counter** The total memory size, in kilobytes, that SQL Server is currently using.
- **SQLServer: Buffer Manager object, Buffer Cache Hit Ratio counter** The percentage of data requests that were found in the data cache.
- **SQLServer: Buffer Manager object, Free Buffers counter** The number of free buffers available to SQL Server.
- **Process object, Working Set counter** The working set size (the size of memory recently touched by a process) in bytes on a per-process basis. Select the desired process to monitor in the Instance drop-down menu in PerfMon.
- **Process object, Page Faults/sec counter** The number of times a process references a page in memory that is not in its working set. If the page is still in main memory or being shared by another process, a page from disk will not occur; otherwise, it will.

Now let's discuss how to interpret these counters. If the value for the Available Bytes counter is very low, you should look at the other counters as well to determine whether you need to add physical memory. A low number of available bytes generally means that your system is too low on total physical memory, or it could mean that an application is not releasing memory as it should when it is finished using the memory. Realize though, that if there is enough free memory in the system, a process is not required to release its memory, which is also known as its *working set*. This working set is the amount of memory, in bytes, that the threads of a process have recently touched. Once free memory in the system goes below a certain threshold, Windows NT will trim working sets to free up some memory.

To find out if a process is holding onto its memory for too long when there is not a lot of free memory available (the value of the Available Bytes counter is low), thus starving other processes, monitor the Process object's Working Set counter for each process instance to determine how much memory each process has in its working set, and the maximum working set size it has used. If a process is no longer running but has not reduced its working set size (it remains at or near the maximum number of working set bytes), there may be a problem because that process is not releasing memory. If this is the case, you should consult with the software developer about fixing this problem before adding memory to the system. If there is no problem with an application holding onto memory, then continue to check the remaining memory counters.

To determine how much memory SQL Server itself is currently using, check the Total Server Memory (KB) counter of the SQLServer: Memory Manager object. This will show you whether SQL Server is hogging most of the memory in the system. The value may change as SQL Server allocates and deallocates memory, if it is configured for dynamic memory allocation.

Monitoring the Pages/sec counter is very important. (Paging is discussed in detail in Chapter 2.) Paging is a costly operation, so you want to reduce it as much as possible. If you see a high number of pages per second occurring, it could be because you are giving SQL Server too much memory and it is starving other applications of memory, causing them to page. In this case, add memory to the machine or reduce your SQL Server memory by lowering the *max server memory* value. To monitor which process is actually causing the paging, look at the Process object's Page Faults/sec counter for each process instance. But remember to look at the remaining counters (discussed below) before you reduce SQL Server memory, because you may cause SQL Server to perform worse.

You should also monitor the cache hit ratio for SQL Server. The *cache hit ratio* is the percentage of data pages that SQL Server requests that are found in the data cache, rather than being read from disk. For most applications (particularly OLTP), you want to achieve a cache hit ratio of 90 percent or more. In some applications, such as decision support, this may not be possible because the data and index pages are not reused often. To achieve this ratio when possible, you need to have enough memory dedicated to SQL Server so that its buffer cache (data cache) will be large enough to support the 90 percent cache hit ratio. If you have allocated as much physical memory as possible to SQL Server and have not reached the 90 percent cache hit ratio, add more physical memory and allocate more to SQL Server. If you can allocate more memory to SQL Server without adding physical memory (because there is still available memory for SQL Server to use), try increasing the *max server memory* parameter to allow SQL Server to take advantage of more memory. (This suggestion assumes that you do not already have the *max server memory* parameter at its default of 2,147,483,647 MB, which tells SQL Server to use as much memory as possible.)

Another indication of a lack of physical memory is if the number for the Free Buffers counter of the SQLServer: Buffer Manager object is consistently well below 5 MB, which is about 640 eight-KB pages. (The value is given in 8-KB pages.) If SQL Server cannot maintain 5 MB of free buffers as it is meant to, you are either running low on physical memory or allocating too much to SQL Server. If your cache hit ratio is not at 90 percent or higher, though, generally you need more memory in the system and you have not yet allocated enough to SQL Server. As you can see, you must take all of these Performance Monitor counters into consideration when forming a conclusion about your memory needs and how to tune memory.

On the other hand, you may have more memory than you need allocated to SQL Server. For example, let's say you have allocated a fixed amount of memory to SQL Server (by setting the *max server memory* and *min server memory* parameters to the same value and also setting *set working set size* to 1) or you have set the *max server memory* parameter to a number other than the default. You monitor the system and you see that the working set size for the SQL Server process is consistently less than the memory you have allocated to SQL Server (monitor the sqlservr instance of the Process object's Working Set counter). You should then be able to reduce the values for the appropriate memory parameters to free up memory for other processes.

Once you have made a change to your memory in some way, make sure to monitor the system again to see the effects. You may need to make more than one change before finally getting the system tuned well. As a general rule for all types of system tuning, try not to make too many changes at once, or you may never know which one actually made the difference. Even worse, one change could cause a great improvement in performance, while another change could degrade performance and therefore cancel out the effects of the improvement, and you would never know. Making one change at a time and monitoring it is preferable, but sometimes you are very sure that you need to change a couple of things at once. Either way, it is important to keep a record of each change and its effect on the system. Later, if you see the same problem again, you can review your notes to remember what works and what doesn't work to fix that problem, without having to repeat the same steps.

Optimizing Database Layout

The location and distribution of your data and log files are very important to the performance of your system. Two key guidelines for database layout are as follows: separate files that are accessed sequentially onto dedicated disks, and allow for parallel I/O by distributing data files across disks. This section gives you some general guidelines and concepts about database layout; the next section provides some examples of how to distribute your data across disks for improved efficiency by using files and filegroups. (See Chapter 2 for a detailed description of files and filegroups.)

Guidelines for Database Layout

SQL Server log files perform mostly sequential writes, and data files may perform either sequential I/O, random I/O, or both. As mentioned in Chapter 3, you should try to separate sequential I/O onto different disks from random I/O, as well as separating various sequential I/O files onto their own disks. Sequential I/Os can be performed much more quickly than random I/Os because the seek time on the disk platter is reduced greatly (see Chapter 3 for details).

If you place a data file that is accessed randomly on the same disk as a sequentially accessed data or log file, the sequential data can no longer be accessed sequentially on that disk—the random I/Os will interfere with the sequential I/Os, causing the disk read/write head to seek the platter in a random fashion. The same is true if you have two files that will be sequentially accessed on the same disk at the same time. One file's data accesses will interfere with the other file's accesses, resulting in neither file being physically accessed on the disk sequentially. Therefore, you should always place your log files on their own disks (since they are definitely sequential in nature), apart from all data files—whether those data files are accessed sequentially or randomly. This setup is optimal. Also, separate any sequentially accessed data files onto their own disks if possible, for the same reasons. Figure 4-5 illustrates a database disk layout for one log file and one large data file. This figure shows the log file on a RAID 10 disk array (or volume) and the data file on either a RAID 10 or RAID 5 disk array, for fault tolerance. You should always use some type of fault tolerance. For details on the different levels of RAID, see Chapter 3.

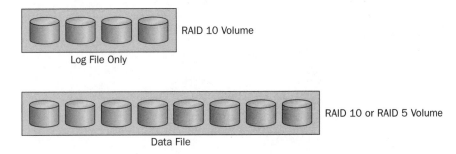

Figure 4-5 *An example disk layout for a log and a data file.*

Another general guideline when laying out your data files is that you should spread your data across as many disk drives as possible, to allow for more parallel disk access. For example, let's say your application needs to read and write more than one page of data at the same time, which is normally the case. If you have only one disk drive with the data file on it, then each read and write must wait in a queue for access to the disk drive in order to complete its I/O request. Each disk can generally satisfy only one request at a time, as shown in Figure 4-6. The exception is when your application is requesting multiple pages of sequential data, in which case multiple pages may be read at one time with one disk access.

Figure 4-6 shows four I/O requests waiting in the queue. Request 1 will be completed first. Request 2 will have to wait for request 1 to complete; then it will be completed. Request 3 must wait for requests 1 and 2 to finish before it can be completed, so it has a longer wait time, and so on. The more I/O requests sent to a disk, the longer the wait times grow for completing each I/O. This is one reason for needing multiple disk drives for your data. Note also that I/O requests may not be satisfied in the same order in which they were requested. Elevator sorting (see Chapter 3) may be used, whereby the I/O requests are sorted according to the location of the data on the disk platter so that they can be completed in an order that causes less disk head movement.

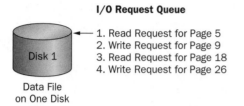

I/O Request Queue

Disk 1

1. Read Request for Page 5
2. Write Request for Page 9
3. Read Request for Page 18
4. Write Request for Page 26

Data File
on One Disk

Figure 4-6 *Several I/O requests to one disk must wait in the queue.*

Now to our point about distributing your data. By spreading the data across multiple disks, there is a high probability that the pages to be accessed will be located on two or more disks. Thus the I/Os can be completed simultaneously (in parallel) on the multiple disks, as shown in Figure 4-7. For this reason it is generally better to have more disks of a smaller size (such as 4 GB or 9 GB) to spread your data across than to have fewer disks of a larger size (such as 18 GB), as shown in Figure 4-8. This is of course assuming that all disks in consideration are of the same technology and speed (such as all 10,000-rpm Seagate disks).

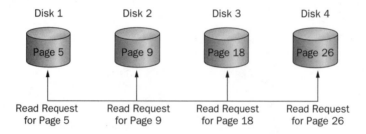

Disk 1 — Page 5 — Read Request for Page 5
Disk 2 — Page 9 — Read Request for Page 9
Disk 3 — Page 18 — Read Request for Page 18
Disk 4 — Page 26 — Read Request for Page 26

Figure 4-7 *Several I/O requests can be handled in parallel with multiple disks.*

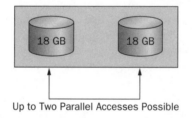

18 GB   18 GB

Up to Two Parallel Accesses Possible

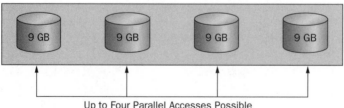

9 GB   9 GB   9 GB   9 GB

Up to Four Parallel Accesses Possible

Figure 4-8 *Comparison of parallel I/O using different sizes and numbers of disks.*

Now that you have learned the concepts behind separating log and data files and distributing data, we will present some examples using these techniques.

Examples Using Files and Filegroups

In order to specifically place your database tables and indexes on certain disk drives, you must create user-defined filegroups. A filegroup provides a way to logically group files together, as well as to isolate single files from the primary filegroup. The primary filegroup is created automatically by SQL Server when you create a database. All files go to the primary filegroup by default if you don't create other filegroups.

To avoid having database data on the same disk as your SQL Server system files and tables for the *master, model, msdb, tempdb,* and sample databases, you can create a user-defined filegroup on which to later create your tables and indexes. If you do not create a user-defined filegroup to place your data files onto, all the files you create will become part of the default (primary) filegroup. Thus, the primary data file will be used to hold user data as well as the system information because when you create your tables and indexes, they will be created across all the files in the primary filegroup, which includes the primary data file. This may be the effect you desire, but the recommended method is to separate your tables and indexes from the system tables. In this case, you need to create user-defined filegroups for your files. Figure 4-9 shows a simple example of one secondary data file apart from the primary filegroup that stores user data on separate drives. The figure shows a RAID 10 disk array for the log file; a RAID 1 array for the operating system files, SQL Server code, and system tables; and a RAID 10 volume for the user data tables and indexes.

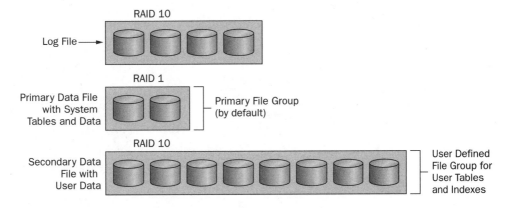

Figure 4-9 *Disk view with one user-defined filegroup.*

The example in Figure 4-9 shows a database layout that locates tables and indexes onto a user-defined filegroup that holds only one secondary data file. Now let's look at another example to demonstrate creating a user-defined filegroup that includes more than one secondary file. When you create a table or index on a filegroup with more than one data file, SQL Server uses a *proportionate fill strategy* to distribute the data between the files (see Figure 4-10). With this strategy, SQL Server fills each data file proportionately to its size. For example, if file1 is 400 MB and file2 is 100 MB, then SQL Server will allocate 4 extents of pages in file1 and 1 extent of pages in file2 to insert data into the files. In this way, file1 does not fill up faster than file2, or vice versa, and the data will be distributed proportionately between the files. Otherwise, you could end up with, for instance, one file completely full of data and the other file only one-fourth full, causing more I/Os to happen on disks holding the full file.

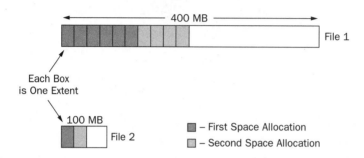

Figure 4-10 *Proportionate fill strategy.*

For another database layout example, let's say you have a larger disk subsystem with two RAID 5 volumes (or arrays) configured for data. In order to optimize the distribution of your data and to allow for more parallel I/O, you want to spread all your database tables and indexes, which will be accessed randomly, across both disk volumes. To do this, you can create a secondary data file for each volume and group them into one filegroup. Then you can create your tables and indexes on that user-defined filegroup, causing the data to be loaded or inserted into the tables in an even distribution across each of the disk drives of the two volumes (see Figure 4-11).

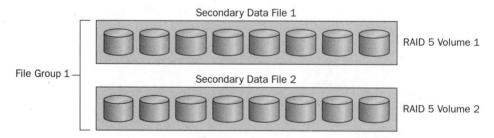

Figure 4-11 *Distributing data between two files within one filegroup*

Let's look at another scenario in which using filegroups to place data is necessary. Assume that you have a table, *TableS,* whose data will be accessed sequentially and another table, *TableR,* that will be accessed randomly. To take advantage of the performance benefits of sequential data access on the disk drives, you can place *TableS* on one set of disks and place *TableR* on a separate set. That way the random I/Os to *TableR* will not interfere with the sequential I/Os of *TableS*. As an example, you can create two separate filegroups with one file each, such as FilegroupS containing FileS, and FilegroupR containing FileR. Then you can create *TableS* on FilegroupS and *TableR* on FilegroupR (see Figure 4-12).

We have seen how using files and filegroups provides you with different methods to lay out your database more optimally on the disks. Now let's discuss tuning SQL Server behavior through its configuration parameters.

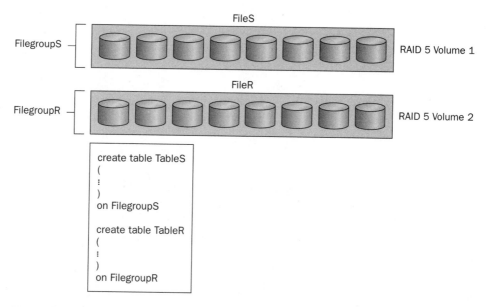

Figure 4-12 *Using filegroups to separate sequential and randomly accessed files.*

SQL Server Configuration Parameters

You can adjust several configuration parameters to affect the behavior of SQL Server. Compared with previous versions, SQL Server 7 requires less manual configuration because it can dynamically configure itself according to the current workload instead of limiting itself to fixed parameter settings. This section demonstrates how to configure the most commonly adjusted parameters for performance and explains how they affect the operation of your system. In most cases, changing these parameters will be unnecessary, but knowing what they are and what they do will allow you to make an educated decision concerning whether to modify them.

You can configure most of the parameters either through Enterprise Manager or with the T-SQL *sp_configure* command. To use Enterprise Manager, right-click on the name of the server you want to configure and then select Properties from the context menu. The SQL Server Properties window appears, with several tabs to choose from for configuring options. Later in this chapter we indicate which tab to use and how to configure the particular options that we discuss.

When using *sp_configure*, certain options are specified as advanced options. You must have another option called *show advanced options* set to 1 (enabled) in order to change an advanced option using *sp_configure*. It is 0 (disabled) by default. (You do not need to worry about this option when using Enterprise Manager to set advanced options.) To configure *show advanced options,* use the following statement:

```
sp_configure "show advanced options", 1
go
```

As we discuss the options, we will indicate which ones are advanced. In general, to set any option with *sp_configure,* use the following syntax:

```
sp_configure "option name", value
```

Also, we mentioned that most options can be set in either of two ways, but this is not true in all cases. Some options can be set only with *sp_configure* and not with Enterprise Manager. We will identify those options as well in the following sections.

Affinity Mask

The *affinity mask* parameter is used to specify which CPUs SQL Server can run on in a multiple-processor environment. The default value of 0 specifies that SQL Server determines the processor affinity. A nonzero value sets a bit mask defining the CPUs that SQL Server can run on. A decimal value of 1 (or a binary bit mask value of 00000001) indicates that only CPU 1 can be used, a value of 2 (or 00000010) indicates that only CPU 2 can be used, a value of 3 (or 00000011) indicates that CPU 1 and CPU 2 can be used, and so on. For example, to indicate that all processors in a four-processor system should be used by SQL Server, set this parameter to decimal 15 (binary bit mask 00001111).

The *affinity mask* parameter is an advanced option; therefore the *show advanced options* setting must be 1 in order to configure this using *sp_configure*. You can configure *affinity mask* using Enterprise Manager as well. Go to the Processor tab of the SQL Server Properties window, and in the Processor Control section, click the check box next to each CPU that you want SQL Server to use. Click Apply and OK to save the change. You must also stop and restart SQL Server for a change in this option to take effect.

Lightweight Pooling

The *lightweight pooling* option is used to configure SQL Server to use lightweight threads, or fibers. The use of fibers can reduce context switches by allowing SQL Server to handle scheduling rather than using the Windows NT or Windows 2000 scheduler. If your application is running on a multiple-processor system and you are seeing a large number of context switches, you might want to try setting the *lightweight pooling* parameter to 1, which enables lightweight pooling, then monitor the number of context switches again to verify that they have been reduced. The default value is 0, which disables the use of fibers.

The *lightweight pooling* parameter is an advanced option that can be set with *sp_configure* when *show advanced options* is set to 1. It can also be configured through Enterprise

Manager. Go to the Processor tab of the SQL Server Properties window. In the Processor Control section, check the box next to Use Windows NT Fibers to enable the option, or uncheck the box to disable the option. Click Apply and OK, then stop and restart SQL Server for the change in this option to take effect.

Locks

SQL Server 7 dynamically configures the number of locks used in the system. Use the *locks* option to set the maximum number of available locks, thus limiting the amount of memory SQL Server uses for locks. The default setting is 0, which allows SQL Server to allocate and deallocate locks dynamically based on changing system requirements. The maximum amount of memory that SQL Server will ever allow for locks is 40 percent of its total memory. We recommend that you leave the locks parameter at the default value of 0 and allow SQL Server to allocate locks as necessary.

The *locks* parameter is an advanced option and can be set only by using *sp_configure*. The new setting takes effect after stopping and restarting SQL Server.

Max Async IO

The *max async IO* option specifies the maximum number of outstanding asynchronous I/O requests that can be issued per data file. The default value of 32 specifies that 32 reads and 32 writes can be outstanding at any one time per file. You might want to increase this parameter, especially when the SQL Server data files reside on a high-performance RAID controller with multiple disk drives. RAID controllers usually perform well when there are multiple simultaneous I/Os because the I/Os can be spread among the disk drives in the array. The maximum setting for this option is 255.

The *max async IO* parameter is an advanced option that must be set using *sp_configure*. It cannot be set through Enterprise Manager. A change to this option requires SQL Server to be stopped and restarted in order to take effect.

Max Server Memory

SQL Server 7 dynamically allocates memory on an as-needed basis. To specify the maximum amount of memory, in MB, that SQL Server will allocate to the memory pool, you can set the *max server memory* option. SQL Server takes some time to release memory; therefore, if you have other applications that periodically need memory, you can set the *max server memory* option so that SQL Server leaves some memory free for the other applications.

The default value is 2147483647, which means that SQL Server will acquire as much memory as it can from the system, while dynamically allocating and deallocating memory as other applications need it. Dynamic configuration is the recommended setting. If you are going to change this setting, calculate the greatest possible amount of memory you can give to SQL Server by subtracting the sum of the memory needed for Windows NT plus memory needed for any non–SQL Server uses from the total physical memory.

The *max server memory* parameter is an advanced option, and thus the *show advanced options* setting must be 1 in order to configure this parameter using *sp_configure*. You can set it with Enterprise Manager by going to the Memory tab and adjusting the slide bar under Maximum (MB) while the Dynamically Configure SQL Server Memory radio button is selected. This option takes effect immediately, without stopping and restarting SQL Server. (If you choose to select the radio button next to Use a Fixed Memory Size, then you can force SQL Server to allocate the amount you set; SQL Server will not release that memory after it has been allocated—thus it is a fixed size. See "*Set Working Set Size*" below.)

Max Worker Threads

The *max worker threads* option specifies the maximum number of threads (or fibers if you have *lightweight pooling* enabled) that SQL Server can use for processing. The default setting is 255. In some cases, this number of threads may overload the system. If the maximum number of threads causes too many context switches, try reducing this value. If you do choose to modify this option, always change it in small increments and test the results, because a large change could greatly affect performance. If you adjust it in small increments, you have a better chance of finding the value at which performance starts to degrade and can adjust back in the other direction (increase or decrease worker threads).

The *max worker threads* parameter is an advanced option, and thus the *show advanced options* setting must be 1 in order to configure this parameter using *sp_configure*. It can also be set using Enterprise Manager. Go to the Processor tab, and under Processor Control set the number of worker threads you want in the box next to Maximum Worker Threads. This option takes effect immediately without stopping and restarting SQL Server.

Min Server Memory

The *min server memory* parameter specifies the minimum memory, in MB, that is to be allocated to the SQL Server memory pool. The default value is 0, which allows SQL Server to dynamically allocate and deallocate memory. This is the recommended setting. This parameter is useful in systems in which SQL Server may reserve too much memory for other applications. For example, in an environment in which the server is used for print and file services as well as for database services, SQL Server may relinquish too much memory to these other applications. In such a case, you might want to change the value of the *min server memory* parameter.

The *min server memory* parameter is an advanced option that can be configured using either *sp_configure* or Enterprise Manager. In the latter method, go to the Memory tab of the SQL Server Properties window and adjust the slide bar under Minimum (MB) while the Dynamically Configure SQL Server Memory radio button is selected. This option takes effect immediately without stopping and restarting SQL Server.

Set Working Set Size

The *set working set size* parameter specifies that the memory that SQL Server has allocated cannot be paged out for another application's use. When set to 1 (enabled), the memory that SQL Server allocates will be physical memory and cannot be swapped out even if that memory can be more effectively used by another process. The *set working set size* parameter should not be used when SQL Server is allowed to allocate memory dynamically. It should only be enabled in conjunction with setting *min server memory* and *max server memory* to the same value. In this way SQL Server will allocate a static amount of memory as being nonpageable.

This parameter is an advanced option. It can be set with *sp_configure* or with Enterprise Manager. For the latter method, go to the Memory tab, select Use a Fixed Memory Size, and set a fixed amount to be allocated. You must restart SQL Server for this setting to take effect.

Recovery Interval

The *recovery interval* option defines the maximum time, in minutes, that it will take the system to recover in the event of a failure. By setting this option, you are telling SQL Server that you want to wait only *recovery interval* minutes for the system to recover from a crash. SQL Server then uses this setting and a special built-in algorithm to determine how often to perform automatic checkpoints so that recovery will take only the specified amount of time. SQL Server determines the time to allow between running checkpoints according to how much work is happening in the system. If a lot of work is being done, checkpoints will be issued with less time between them than if the system was not doing much work, because the less work you perform, the less time it takes to recover from a crash. Also, the longer the recovery interval, the more time will be allowed between checkpoints.

Increasing the recovery interval may improve performance by reducing the number of checkpoints (this is so because checkpoints cause intense writes to disk, which may slow down user transactions for a few seconds), but with the side effect of increasing the time it takes for recovery. The default value is 0, which specifies that SQL Server will determine the interval for you—about a 1-minute recovery time. Increase the *recovery interval* parameter at your own risk. A value of 15 to 30 minutes is not unusual. The acceptable setting depends entirely on whether you can risk waiting 15 to 30 minutes for your database to recover in case of a system crash. The reason you might want to increase *recovery interval* is for the simple fact that we stated earlier—you will reduce the frequency of the disk I/O that each checkpoint entails, therefore allowing users more freedom in the I/O subsystem to perform their transactions without interruption.

The *recovery interval* parameter is an advanced option; therefore the *show advanced options* setting must be 1 in order to configure this using *sp_configure*. You can also set it using Enterprise Manager. Go to the Database Settings tab of the SQL Server Properties window and enter the number in minutes next to Recovery Interval (min). A change to this option takes effect immediately, without stopping and restarting SQL Server.

User Connections

The number of user connections to SQL Server no longer needs to be set using a configuration parameter—SQL Server can dynamically allocate connections as needed. Although user connections are dynamically configured by default, you can set a maximum value with the *user connections* configuration parameter. Use this parameter to specify the maximum number of simultaneous user connections allowed to SQL Server. You may want to set a maximum to avoid having too many connections to your system. The actual number of user connections allowed also depends on the limits of your application and the hardware in your system. SQL Server allows a maximum of 32,767 user connections, which is also the maximum value for the parameter. In most cases, you should not need to change the value for this option. It works well when left dynamically configurable by SQL Server.

The *user connections* parameter is an advanced option. It can be set using *sp_configure* or in Enterprise Manager. For the latter method, open the Connections tab of the SQL Server Properties window and enter the desired value in the Maximum Concurrent User Connections box.

Summary

In this chapter you have learned what performance is and how to measure it. You've also seen several important areas for tuning your SQL Server system, including tuning processors, disk drives, and memory; optimizing database layout; and adjusting SQL Server configuration parameters. But these areas of tuning are only the beginning. The rest of this book will teach you more ways to optimize your database server's performance. The next chapter shows you the new features of SQL Server 7 that make it more robust, optimized, and efficient than previous versions.

Chapter 5
New Features and Performance Enhancements

SQL Server 7 has undergone many architectural design changes from previous versions. These changes improve the efficiency, performance, and stability of SQL Server and reduce administration overhead for the DBA. This chapter discusses the new dynamic configuration features of SQL Server 7 and explains how they work. It also covers the major performance enhancements and other new features of SQL Server 7 that are not related to configuration.

Dynamic Configuration

One of the enhancements of SQL Server 7 is that it performs much more dynamic (self) configuration than before. Overall, you will find that SQL Server 7 is much easier to administer than previous versions. Certain configuration options now do not need to be set, but instead can be left at their default values, allowing SQL Server to appropriately configure them as needed. Here we show you which configuration options are dynamic by default and how SQL Server handles them if you choose to manually give them values.

Memory

You no longer have to set a specific fixed memory size for SQL Server to use for its memory pool (although you may still do so). SQL Server 7 has the capability to dynamically configure its memory pool size as needed. Recall from Chapter 2 that the memory pool consists of the system data structures, the buffer cache, the procedure cache, the log caches, and the connection contexts. SQL Server always dynamically configures the size of each of these sections within the memory pool as needed. Optionally, SQL Server can also dynamically configure the total size of the memory pool.

This section explains the three methods of memory pool configuration: letting SQL Server dynamically configure its memory pool size, limiting the memory pool to a range by setting a specific minimum and maximum size, and specifying a fixed size for the memory pool. The two parameters used to configure the memory pool size are *min server memory* and *max server memory* (see "SQL Server Configuration Parameters" in Chapter 4). In essence, SQL Server will not allow its memory pool size to fall below the *min server memory* setting, and it will not use more memory than the *max server memory* setting. With this in mind, let's discuss in more detail the three methods of configuring the memory pool.

Dynamic Memory Configuration

By leaving the two memory parameters at their default settings of 0 (MB) for *min server memory* and 2147483647 (MB) for *max server memory*, you allow SQL Server to dynamically configure its memory. Here is how it works. SQL Server periodically queries the system to determine how much physical memory is available. It constantly maintains at least 5 MB (plus or minus 200 KB) of physical memory free in an attempt to prevent Windows NT from paging. Therefore, as SQL Server needs space in the memory pool to handle its workload, it allocates memory to itself, but only up to the point at which the operating system still has 5 MB of free physical memory. At that point SQL Server stops allocating memory. If SQL Server does not need all the memory that is available, it will not take all of it: it takes only what it needs.

Once SQL Server has allocated some memory to itself, it maintains that memory in the memory pool even if the workload becomes idle. In an idle system, SQL Server does not release memory. However, if another application starts up and there is no longer 5 MB physical memory free, SQL Server releases memory from its memory pool to Windows NT/2000 in order to maintain 5 MB of free physical memory on the system, thus allowing the other application to use the released memory. When the other application has finished and released its memory, SQL Server recommits the memory (again leaving 5 MB of physical memory free) only if it needs more memory for its current workload.

Dynamic configuration is the recommended setting for SQL Server memory because it allows SQL Server to use as much memory as possible. It is the preferred configuration for a system dedicated to SQL Server. If you run other applications on the same system as SQL Server, however, you will want to consider trying one of the two options for memory management that are described next.

Limited Memory Range

You can manually set values for the *min server memory* and *max server memory* configuration parameters in order to limit the size of the memory pool (with a lower limit, an upper limit, or both). You may want to do this to accommodate other applications that need memory on the system.

If you set only the *min server memory* parameter to a value (for instance, to 500 MB) and leave the *max server memory* parameter at its default, SQL Server uses at least 500 MB and does not release memory to fall below the 500 MB size—no matter how much memory the other applications may demand. This scenario assumes there is enough physical memory in the system for SQL Server to reserve 500 MB while maintaining 5 MB of free physical memory. If there isn't this much memory available, SQL Server uses as much memory as possible. SQL Server also uses as much memory as needed above the minimum of 500 MB when there is available physical memory in the system, because there is no specified upper limit (*max server memory* was left at the default). You may want to set a minimum memory value for SQL Server so that other applications cannot steal too much memory from SQL Server, causing it to perform poorly.

If you leave the *min server memory* parameter at its default of 0 and manually set a value for the *max server memory* parameter (for instance to 1000 MB), SQL Server allocates memory as needed for the memory pool (as long as free physical memory is available on the system) up to a maximum of 1000 MB. SQL Server also releases memory if other applications require it, with no minimum amount reserved for itself (because *min server memory* is set to 0). You may want to set a maximum for SQL Server memory to ensure that enough memory is available for other applications to be able to start up without having to wait for SQL Server to release memory to them

You can manually set both *min server memory* and *max server memory* to specific values. Doing so allows you to determine the exact limits on both ends of the range—the least and the greatest amount of memory SQL Server can use. For example, you could set *min server memory* to 500 MB and *max server memory* to 1000 MB. SQL Server would then not allow its memory to fall below 500 MB, and also would not allocate more than 1000 MB to its memory pool. Again, you would want to set these ranges for SQL Server memory only if you have a system that is not dedicated to SQL Server, but runs other applications as well. The minimum of 500 MB ensures at least 500 MB for SQL Server to use, and the maximum of 1000 MB ensures that the available physical memory above 1000 MB will be left for other applications. On a dedicated SQL Server system, it is best to use the default values for the *min server memory* and *max server* memory parameters, which allows SQL Server to dynamically configure its memory pool.

Fixed Memory Size

Setting *min server memory* and *max server memory* to the same value causes SQL Server to use a fixed amount of memory of that size. You may want to do this if you have other applications running on the system, as mentioned earlier. With a fixed amount, SQL Server does not allocate and release memory dynamically; rather, it allocates and maintains the indicated amount.

Procedure Cache

The procedure cache area of the memory pool is where SQL Server stores execution plans for T-SQL statements and stored procedures. There is no longer a configurable parameter for the size of the procedure cache as there was in previous versions. SQL Server 7 dynamically configures the size of the procedure cache area within the memory pool as needed for optimal performance. This relieves the DBA from having to manually tune the procedure cache size.

The way in which SQL Server 7 uses the procedure cache has also changed from previous versions. The first time a stored procedure or T-SQL statement is executed, SQL Server compiles and saves the execution plan in the procedure cache. The execution plan consists of two components: the query plan and the execution context. The *query plan* is a read-only data structure that contains no user context information and can be used by many users in parallel. The *execution context* is a data structure that holds data specific to each user. This data structure can be reinitialized and used by another user once it is no longer being used by the first user. By allowing users to share query plans and reuse execution contexts, less space is needed in the memory pool for the procedure cache, leaving more space for the buffer cache, which can improve performance. (Earlier versions of SQL Server required separate copies of the compiled query plan for each user, necessitating more space for the procedure cache. You had to manually set a configuration parameter to indicate a percentage of space in the memory pool that would be dedicated to the procedure cache area.)

Locks

You no longer need to set the *locks* configuration parameter manually to determine the number of locks available for SQL Server use. If you leave the option at the default of 0, SQL Server dynamically configures locks based on system needs. If more locks are needed, SQL Server allocates more, although it will not dynamically allocate more than 40 percent of the total memory allotted to SQL Server. Also, if no free physical memory is left on the system because another application is using all available memory, SQL Server will not allocate more locks because the operating system would have to page the other application out to disk in order to free memory for locks. On the other hand, if allocated locks are not used for a certain period, SQL Server will deallocate them and release the memory for another use, such as for the buffer cache.

You may set the *locks* parameter to a specific number of locks, thus limiting the amount of memory SQL Server can use for locks. Do so with care, because you may get an error message from SQL Server stating that you have exceeded the number of available locks if the value is too low for your applications needs, in which case you must increase the value. Each lock requires 96 bytes of memory, so increasing the *locks* value may also require increasing the amount of total memory allocated to SQL Server. The best method is to allow SQL Server to allocate locks as needed by leaving the *locks* parameter at the default value.

User Connections

SQL Server can dynamically configure the number of user connections if you leave the value for the *user connections* parameter set to its default of 0. SQL Server adjusts the number of user connections automatically as needed, up to the maximum allowable value of 32,767. For example, if only 25 users are logged in, 25 user connection objects are allocated. If a user connection is not in use for a time, SQL Server will release the memory used by that connection. In most cases, you should not need to change the value for this parameter.

The actual number of user connections allowed depends in part on the limitations of your application(s) and hardware. You can use SQL Server Query Analyzer and the following T-SQL statement to determine the maximum number of user connections your system currently allows:

```
SELECT @@ MAX_CONNECTIONS
```

If you want to further limit the number of user connections allowed, you can set a specific value for the *user connections* configuration parameter. The value you set represents the maximum number of simultaneous user connections allowed on SQL Server. When you set this value, SQL Server does not allocate memory for the specified number of user connections right away, but rather allocates memory for the connections as needed until the maximum number of connections specified is reached. If more connections are requested at that point, SQL Server generates an error message saying that the maximum number of user connections has been reached. Note that each allocated user connection consumes about 40 KB of memory.

Open Objects

SQL Server dynamically adjusts the number of database objects allowed to be open at one time on the system if you leave the *open objects* option set to its default of 0. Database objects are tables, views, triggers, stored procedures, rules, and defaults. In most cases you should leave this option at its default. If you do choose to set this value, it indicates the maximum number of open database objects allowed on the system. If the maximum is reached and SQL Server needs more open objects, you will get a message that SQL Server has exceeded the number of open objects. Each open object consumes memory, so increasing the value of *open objects* may require increasing SQL Server memory as well.

Automatic File Growth

SQL Server 7 allows files to grow automatically when needed. This option is not a configuration parameter. Rather, when you create or alter a file, you can choose whether to allow SQL Server to automatically expand the file. We recommend that you choose automatic growth because it saves the administrator the burden of manually monitoring and increasing file space.

Here is how it works. A database file is created with an initial size. When that initial space is filled up, SQL Server increases the file size by a specified amount, called the *growth increment*. When this new space fills, SQL Server again allocates the amount of space specified by the growth increment. It will continue to expand the file as needed until the disk is full or until the maximum file size (if specified) is reached.

The maximum file size is just that—the maximum size to which a file is allowed to grow. This value is also specified at file creation but can be altered later. If there is no maximum size set for a file, SQL Server will continue to expand the file until all available disk space is exhausted. To avoid completely running out of space on the disk, set a maximum size for each file. If you do ever reach the maximum size, you can alter the database by adding a new file to provide more space.

We recommend that you use automatic file growth and provide maximum file sizes. When you create a database, allocate the largest size to which you think the files will ever grow, according to how much data you anticipate will be inserted over time. If you see that this initial space becomes filled and that automatic growth has taken place, you should reevaluate the space to determine whether more files or filegroups should be added.

Automatic Database or File Shrinkage

You can also allow SQL Server to automatically shrink your database or individual data and log files if you need the disk space for other data. Shrinking a database or file removes and frees unused pages. A database cannot shrink to less than its original size, but an individual file can do so. For example, suppose you created a database with an initial size of 100 MB, which then grew to 200 MB. When you perform the shrink operation, the database can shrink at most down to 100 MB. A file, on the other hand, can shrink to the smallest possible size that will hold the current data.

To shrink a database, use the *sp_dboption* stored procedure; to shrink a file, use the DBCC SHRINKFILE command. A file will not shrink smaller than the size necessary to hold the data no matter what size you specify with the DBCC SHRINKFILE command. See SQL Server Books Online for the syntax of these commands. Shrinking a database or file is done in the background and does not affect user activity. You can also use SQL Server Enterprise Manager to schedule periodic database shrinkage (under the General tab, select Shrink Database).

Improved Performance and Other New Features

Now let's discuss some of the major areas in which SQL Server 7 has been improved for performance. Chapter 2 discussed SQL Server architecture in general; here we focus on some of the same topics, but with an emphasis on improved performance.

Locking

One new feature of SQL Server 7 is support for full row-level locking, that is, the ability to acquire locks on a row in a data page or index page. Row-level locking is the smallest lock granularity that can be achieved. Prior to SQL Server 7, the smallest lock granularity was page-level locking. This new level of locking provides increased concurrency for many online transaction processing (OLTP) applications because while a single row on a page may be locked by one user, other rows on that same page remain accessible to other users at the same time. Row-level locking is especially useful when you are performing row inserts, updates, and deletes on tables and indexes.

In addition to the row-level locking feature, the entire locking management subsystem has been improved in SQL Server 7. Lock requests are completed faster and lock resources are adjusted dynamically. SQL Server 7 is also optimized to choose which type of lock to acquire on a resource—usually row-level locking for inserts, updates, and deletes, and page-level locking for table scans. SQL Server automatically chooses the most cost-effective locks when the query is executed, based on the characteristics of the database schema and the query itself. SQL Server also dynamically manages *lock escalation,* that is, the conversion of many fine-grained locks (such as page locks) into fewer, more coarse-grained locks (such as table locks). Lock escalation reduces the system overhead incurred when using a large number of fine-grained locks. You no longer need to set the lock threshold parameters (they no longer exist in version 7).

Transaction Log

The SQL Server 7 transaction log has been improved to be more robust and faster than before. The log is no longer a database table, but rather a separate file or set of files within the database, thus reducing the I/O overhead. The log cache is also managed separately from the buffer cache in the memory pool, as you have seen in Chapter 2. This allows for simpler, faster code within the database engine. Log data does not follow the same format as data pages. The data in the log is thus referred to as *log records* instead of log pages to differentiate it from data pages. The design allows for larger I/Os to the log than were possible in earlier versions.

Truncating the transaction log now takes only a few seconds. SQL Server simply moves a pointer in the log file to indicate the location of the logical start of the log records and deletes the unused log records. See Chapter 2 for details on how the transaction log works. You can also enable the automatic growth feature for log files so that SQL Server automatically increases file size as needed up to a maximum size, which you can also specify. Allowing automatic growth reduces the probability of receiving an 1105 error from SQL Server, which states that you have run out of log space.

Replication

Replication is a feature that is built in to SQL Server 7. It is based on the same publish/subscribe model as previous versions of SQL Server, but with many improvements that make it easier to set up, manage, monitor, and troubleshoot. Numerous wizards are available in Enterprise Manager to help you perform administrative tasks. These wizards prompt you for the information needed to set up the different components of replication and allow you to easily make changes to your replication schema through a graphical user interface (GUI).

In addition to the original types of replication (snapshot and transactional), a new type of replication is supported in SQL Server 7: merge replication. As you may recall from previous versions of SQL Server, snapshot replication takes a snapshot of the published data and refreshes the subscribers with that entire data set snapshot. Transactional replication replicates only changes to data (inserts, updates, and deletes) from the publisher by copying and running the same statements at the subscriber. New for 7, *merge replication* allows multiple server sites to make changes to replicated data; at a later time, these changes are merged to all sites involved in the merge replication. Basically, merge replication synchronizes data between the publisher and subscribers, all of which may update the data.

Note Merge replication does not guarantee transactional consistency. If you need to implement only one-way replication, you should not use merge replication.

An example situation in which merge replication is useful is when you have several employees who use laptops to make updates to their local databases (such as inserting new orders), which must then be replicated to the central database each night. At the same time, any updates made to the central database (such as an order marked as delivered) must be replicated to the local databases. Merge replication allows you to do this. If there is a conflict with a merge, such as a case in which the same row of data was updated in both the central database and in one of the local databases, merge replication uses conflict resolution criteria to determine which row is chosen. You can specify what the conflict resolution criteria should be. You can find information on how merge replication works in SQL Server Books Online.

Another new feature of replication is *immediate-updating subscribers.* In previous versions of SQL Server, all replication was one-way only: you could replicate data from the publisher to the subscriber, but could not replicate changes to that same data from the subscriber to the publisher. When you choose snapshot or transactional replication in SQL Server 7, you now have the option to allow immediate-updating subscriptions. Enabling this option means that a subscriber (as well as the publisher) is allowed to change replicated data as long as that change can also be immediately reflected at the publisher. This is achieved by using a two-phase commit protocol (a transaction that causes the change must commit at the publisher in order to be able to commit at the subscriber). In other words, the subscriber can perform inserts, updates, and deletes on published data only if it can perform a two-phase commit transaction with the publisher. If the two-phase commit succeeds, the publisher can propagate that change to all other subscribers through snapshot or transactional replication, according to the publisher's distribution schedule. This can be thought of as two-way replication.

This replication method is fairly simple because the immediate-updating subscriber does not need its own distribution database or a log reader. The immediate-updating subscriptions feature also guarantees transactional consistency. The immediate-updating subscriber can continue its activity while the updates are being trickled down from the publisher to any other subscribers. If you do not enable immediate-updating subscriptions, replication will work as before; that is, you can change replicated data on the subscriber, but those changes are not reflected back to the publisher.

These new features give the user more options for replication functionality. Also, the replication code has been completely rewritten in SQL Server 7 to provide improved performance. Replication schemas can get complicated, so be sure that you lay out your plan carefully before implementing it. Avoid replicating data that does not need to be replicated. Draw diagrams of which systems should be publishing and which should be subscribing, and try to come up with the simplest plan possible to get the right data replicated, thus reducing overhead and administration. See Chapter 14 for tips on how to tune replication for better performance.

Query Processing

The query processor for SQL Server 7 has been designed to support large databases and complex queries, such as those found in decision support systems, data warehouses, and online analytical processing (OLAP) applications. New execution strategies can greatly improve the performance of complex queries. For example, in addition to the nested loop join technique for queries that use joins, SQL Server 7 now supports hash join, merge join, and hash aggregation techniques, which scale well to large databases. SQL

Server 7 also has the ability to use index intersection and union techniques on multiple indexes in order to filter the amount of data before it retrieves rows from the database. The query optimizer now uses a much improved costing model and new techniques for selecting the most appropriate execution plan, therefore improving the quality of query plans and the speed of execution.

Another new feature of the SQL Server 7 query processor is that it uses sampling algorithms to automatically generate statistics about key distributions in indexes. These statistics are refreshed periodically to ensure that the query optimizer can continually create efficient execution plans. The distribution statistics indicate how likely it is that an index key value will identify rows in a table. Since this is done automatically, you no longer have to worry about manually updating index statistics.

Parallel query execution is another new feature designed to speed processing of queries over very large databases. It is available only on computers that have more than one processor. Allowing parallel query execution means that an individual query can be performed in parallel by using multiple operating system threads, up to a total of one thread per processor. A nonparallel query, on the other hand, can use only a single thread of execution. Complex queries that retrieve large amounts of data can be completed more quickly and efficiently by using parallel query execution.

Possible candidates for parallel processing are the WHERE clause in either an UPDATE or DELETE statement, SELECT statements (especially those with joins, aggregations, or unions), and the SELECT portion of an INSERT statement. Simple INSERT, UPDATE, and DELETE statements are executed serially. Not all of these candidates will be chosen for parallel execution, however. SQL Server automatically determines if a query is a good candidate for parallel execution by evaluating various factors such as how busy the processors are and whether there is sufficient available memory for the parallel processing; it also determines the best degree of parallelism to use (that is, the number of threads of execution).

To enable parallel query execution, set the *max degree of parallelism* configuration parameter. Valid values range from 0 to 32. The default of 0 indicates to use at most as many execution threads as the number of available processors. (A processor is not considered available if it was restricted from SQL Server use by changing the *affinity mask* parameter from its default.) Setting *max degree of parallelism* to 1 disables parallel execution. Setting it to a number greater than 1 restricts the maximum number of threads used in parallel query execution. If you set this parameter to a value that is greater than the number of processors in the system, the value is ignored by SQL Server (meaning that parallel execution is not available). The value is also ignored if you have a single-processor system. You should not need to change the value of this parameter in most cases.

Attaching and Detaching a Database

Another new feature of SQL Server 7 that may come in handy is the ability to detach and reattach a database from SQL Server. Over the course of operating SQL Server, circumstances may force you to reinstall the operating system and database software. (This sometimes happens if there appears to be a hardware problem, and the hardware support technicians tell you that you must first try reinstalling the software before they will come out and take a look at the hardware!) With SQL Server 7, you can do this without losing your database.

Before reinstalling any software, start SQL Server and run the *sp_detach_db* system stored procedure for each user database. This procedure detaches the specified database from the server without destroying the files in the database. The files can later be reattached to the server by using the *sp_attach_db* system stored procedure, specifying the name of the database and the names of the files in the database to attach. After detaching all the databases, you can reinstall your software and then reattach the databases; they will be as they were before you detached them. Another case in which you may need to detach and attach a database is to move it from one server to another. Please see SQL Server Books Online for the usage and syntax of these two stored procedures.

Checking Data Integrity

Several Transact-SQL DBCC (database consistency checker) statements can be used to verify the physical and logical consistency and integrity of a database. Most of these statements existed in previous versions of SQL Server, but have been improved in many ways in version 7. You no longer need to run these database checks on a regular basis, as was recommended for SQL Server 6.5. SQL Server 7 databases are more robust than in earlier versions because of two important architectural changes:

1. The database engine contains fail-fast logic that detects potentially harmful errors close to the time they originate. By detecting these errors early on, it is less likely that the errors will continue to occur long enough to cause problems in the database.

2. Database structures are now much simpler; therefore, they are easier to manage and less likely to have problematic errors.

The DBCC statements themselves have been improved to run faster as well. Complex database checks have been verified to run 8 to 10 times faster than before, and individual object checks have been seen to run over 300 times faster! SQL Server 7 also includes the option to allow DBCC statements to repair minor problems they may encounter, such as certain errors in the B-tree structures of indexes or errors in some of the allocation structures.

The following is a list of the available DBCC commands and a brief explanation of each. Commands that appeared in SQL Server 6.5 but are no longer used in 7 are mentioned as well. This list does not show all the options for each command. Complete documentation on the options and on how to run these commands can be found in the SQL Server Books Online.

- **CHECKALLOC** Checks the allocation and use of all the pages in the specified database. CHECKALLOC is a subset of CHECKDB. Usage: DBCC CHECKALLOC (*dbname*)
- **CHECKCATALOG** Checks for consistency within the system tables for the specified database. Usage: DBCC CHECKCATALOG (*dbname*)

- **CHECKDB** Checks the allocation and structural integrity of the specified database. This command catches and repairs any problems within the database allocation and tables. In fact, CHECKDB validates the integrity of everything within the database. Expect it to take some time to run. Usage: DBCC CHECKDB (*dbname*)

- **CHECKFILEGROUP** Checks the allocation and structural integrity of a specific filegroup in the database. Rather than running CHECKDB, you can use this command if you suspect that only a filegroup has been corrupted, possibly due to a hardware failure. Usage: DBCC CHECKFILEGROUP (*filegroup*)

- **CHECKIDENT** Checks the current identity value for the specified table. If necessary, it will correct it. Usage: DBCC CHECKIDENT (*table_name*)

- **CHECKTABLE** Checks the integrity of the table, index, text, ntext, and image pages for the specified table. This command is useful if you believe a specific table may be corrupt. Usage: DBCC CHECKTABLE (*table_name*)

- **DBREINDEX** Was used to reindex a table's indexes. This command is no longer supported. With SQL Server 7, use the DROP EXISTING clause with the CREATE INDEX command to accomplish this task.

- **DBREPAIR** Used to drop a damaged database. This command is not supported in SQL Server 7; use the DROP DATABASE command instead.

- ***dll_name* (FREE)** Unloads the specified extended stored procedure DLL from memory. Usage: DBCC *dll_name* (FREE)

- **HELP** Returns the syntax of a specific DBCC statement, thus allowing you to quickly get information about a command without having to refer to the SQL Server Books Online. The *dbcc_statement* name does not include the DBCC keyword (e.g., use CHECKALLOC instead of DBCC CHECKALLOC). Usage: DBCC HELP (*dbcc_statement*)

- **INPUTBUFFER** Displays the last statement sent to SQL Server by the user associated with the specified server process ID (SPID). Usage: DBCC INPUTBUFFER (*spid*)

- **MEMUSAGE** Provided a detailed report on memory usage. This command is no longer supported.

- **NEWALLOC** Same as CHECKALLOC. This command is no longer supported.

- **OPENTRAN** Displays information about the oldest active transaction in the database. This is useful for finding stalled or long-running transactions. Usage: DBCC OPENTRAN (*database*)

- **OUTPUTBUFFER** Displays the output data sent by SQL Server to the user associated with the specified server process ID. Usage: DBCC OUTPUTBUFFER (*spid*)

- **PINTABLE** Marks the table to be pinned. A pinned table does not relinquish itself from cache. In other words, all pages from that table that are placed in cache do not get ejected. This is useful for small tables that are infrequently used but require immediate access. Care should be taken in making sure that the memory used by the pinned table does not adversely affect other SQL Server processing. Usage: DBCC PINTABLE (*table_name*)

- **PROCCACHE** Displays information about the SQL Server procedure cache. This information can be valuable in assessing the effectiveness of the procedure cache and SQL statements. Usage: DBCC PROCCACHE

- **ROWLOCK** Used in SQL Server 6.5 to enable row locking. Row locking is now automatic within SQL Server 7, so this command is no longer supported.

- **SHOW STATISTICS** Displays statistics for the specified target (such as an index name) on the specified table. These are the statistics that are used by the SQL Server query optimizer. Usage: DBCC SHOW_STATISTICS (*table_name, target*)

- **SHOWCONTIG** Displays information about fragmentation for the data and indexes of the specified table. A heavily fragmented index should be rebuilt. A heavily fragmented table should be exported and imported back into the database. Usage: DBCC SHOWCONTIG (*table_name* [, *index_name*])

- **SHRINKDATABASE** Shrinks the size of the files associated with the specified database. The recommended method of performing this task is by using the *autoshrink* option of the *sp_dboption* system stored procedure, which enables automatic periodic shrinking for all database files. Usage: DBCC SHRINKDATABASE (*dbname* [, *percent*])

- **SHRINKFILE** Shrinks the size of the specified file, which can be either a data file or log file. Usage: DBCC SHRINKFILE (*filename* [, *target_size*])

- **SQLPERF** Provides information about the amount of space used by the transaction logs in all databases. This information is useful for capacity planning and sizing and for determining how often to perform transaction log backups so you do not run out of log space. Usage: DBCC SQLPERF(LOGSPACE)

- **TEXTALL** No longer supported in SQL Server 7. Instead, use CHECKDB to check the consistency of tables that contain text, ntext, and image columns.

- **TEXTALLOC** No longer supported in SQL Server 7. Instead, use CHECKTABLE to check the consistency of tables that contain text, ntext, and image columns. DBCC TEXTALL previously ran DBCC TEXTALLOC.

- **TRACEOFF** Disables the specified SQL Server trace flag or flags. Usage: DBCC TRACEOFF (*flag(s)*)

- **TRACEON** Enables the specified SQL Server trace flag or flags. Usage: DBCC TRACEON (*flag(s)*)

- **TRACESTATUS** Displays the status of the specified trace flag or flags. Usage: DBCC TRACESTATUS (*flag(s)*)

- **UNPINTABLE** Marks a previously pinned table to be unpinned. The table will now be treated like any other object in a cache; that is, its pages will be allowed to be released from the cache. Usage: DBCC UNPINTABLE (*table_name)*

- **UPDATEUSAGE** Reports and corrects inaccuracies in the *sysindexes* table. These inaccuracies may result in incorrect data being returned by *sp_spaceused*. Usage: DBCC UPDATEUSAGE (*dbname*)

- **USEROPTIONS** Returns the status of the options that are currently set for the current connection. This command works only for the current connection. Usage: DBCC USEROPTIONS

Backing Up and Restoring Databases

The backup and recovery strategy of SQL Server 7 has been improved in several ways. New methods are available for performing backups and restores, and both operations execute much faster than in previous versions. This section explains how backups and restores are now more efficient, and describes the different types of backup/restore strategies. Methods for tuning your backups and restores for better performance are found in Chapter 15.

How a Backup Works

For database backups other than the backup of the transaction log only, SQL Server assigns a reader thread to each disk device (or each file) that a database uses and assigns a writer thread to each backup device. The reader thread reads the data from the database file, and the writer thread writes the data to the backup device, which may be another disk or a tape device. You can increase the amount of parallel read operations by spreading your database across more files on more logical disk devices (thus allowing more reader threads to be used), and you can increase parallel write operations by creating more backup devices (thus allowing more writer threads to be used).

For transaction log backups, one reader/writer thread is assigned to each log backup device. Even if there is more than one log file, the log is logically one stream of data and is read sequentially by one thread. Therefore, adding more log files will not increase the speed of the backup, but increasing the speed of the disk device (such as by using RAID 10 disk striping across multiple disk drives) can improve read performance. To improve write performance, increase the number of backup devices to the point at which the write capacity reaches the read capacity of the disk device, making the disk device the bottleneck.

How a Restore Works

To restore a full or differential database backup, the database and transaction log files must first be created if they do not already exist. The contents of the files are initialized to 0. Multiple threads create and initialize the files in parallel, with one thread assigned to each disk device or file. Spreading the files evenly across logical drives allows for the best I/O performance. After the files are created, SQL Server copies the data from the backup devices into the files. One reader/writer thread is assigned to each backup device to read the data from the backup device and write it to a disk device. Thus, in this case more backup devices allow for more parallel operations and faster performance, up to the point at which there are so many backup devices and reader/writer threads that the disk device becomes the bottleneck because its capacity to accept data has been reached. Restoring an individual database file involves the same process, and again one reader/writer thread is assigned to each backup device.

To restore a transaction log backup, data is copied from the backup devices to the transaction log file. Again, the more backup devices you have, the more reader/writer threads are used. This will improve performance of the restore operation up to the point at which the disk device capacity for receiving data from the backup devices is reached. The only way to improve SQL Server's performance of the automatic recovery and rolling forward of transactions in a transaction log is to use a faster computer.

Full, Differential, and Log Backups

SQL Server 7 supports full database backups and transaction log backups, as did previous versions, as well as supporting a new type of backup known as a *differential database backup*. A full database backup backs up the entire database and its transaction log. A transaction log backup backs up only the transaction log. A differential database backup creates a backup of only the changes that occurred in the database since the last full database backup. By using all three of these backup types in combination, you can reduce the time it takes to restore your database in the event of a failure. Using differential backups together with transaction log backups ensures greater database security because if either the differential backups or the transaction log backups become unavailable or corrupted, you can rely on the other type of backup alone to restore your database.

One general backup strategy is to perform database backups at long intervals, differential backups at medium intervals, and transaction log backups at shorter intervals. For example, create a full database backup weekly at 11 P.M., a differential backup each night at 11 P.M., and transaction log backups hourly, as shown in Figure 5-1.

SUN	MON	TUE	WED	THU	FRI	SAT
-Log Backups Hourly	-Log Backups Hourly	-Log Backups Hourly	-Log Backups Hourly	-Log Backups Hourly	-Log Backups Hourly	-Log Backups Hourly
FULL DB BACKUP	-DIFF. DB BACKUP	-DIFF. BACKUP	-DIFF. BACKUP	-DIFF. BACKUP	-DIFF. BACKUP	-DIFF. BACKUP

Figure 5-1 *A backup strategy using full, differential, and transaction log backups.*

The main purpose of the differential backups is to avoid having to restore all the transaction log backups. To restore a database that used a backup strategy such as the one in Figure 5-1, you would first restore the full database backup, then the most recent differential database backup, and then only the transaction log backups that were created after the most recent differential backup. If you did not perform differential backups at all, you would have to restore every single transaction log backup after the full database backup was created.

For example, if a database using the schedule in Figure 5-1 crashed on Thursday morning at 10 A.M. and needed to be restored up to that point, you would first create another transaction log backup at that moment if possible. You would begin the restore process by restoring the full database backup from Sunday; then you would restore only the most recent differential backup (not all differential backups!), which was created on Wednesday night at 11 P.M.; finally you would restore all the transaction log backups that were performed since the differential backup on Wednesday night, including the last one you created at 10 A.M. Thursday. See Figure 5-2 for a chart of which backups to restore for this case. By using differential backups, you will avoid having to restore more than 72 log backups (all hourly log backups from Sunday night through Thursday morning), and the restore will occur much faster.

SUN	MON	TUE	WED	THU	FRI	SAT
FULL DB BACKUP			-DIFF. BACKUP	-Log Backups Up to Point of Crash at 10 A.M.		

Figure 5-2 *Restoring from a crash on Thursday morning.*

It is best to schedule your backup strategy to occur automatically on a regular basis without user intervention. Do this by creating a separate SQL Server job for each type of backup (full, differential, and transaction log) since they will occur on different schedules (weekly, nightly, and hourly). Be sure to check your job history details each day to see if the backups are succeeding.

File and Filegroup Backups

In addition to the new differential database backup, SQL Server 7 supports two other new types of backups: individual file and individual filegroup backups. These are useful if your database is too large to entirely back it up in one night. Instead, you can back up separate files or filegroups each night. Also, if only one file is damaged (due to media failure, for example), you do not have to restore the entire database, but can restore only that particular file or filegroup if it was backed up separately.

All files or filegroups that a table and its indexes span must be backed up together in order for you to be able to restore the table and indexes properly. SQL Server will generate an error message if any of these required files or filegroups are missing when you attempt to perform a file or filegroup backup. Also, you must perform a transaction log backup after each file or filegroup backup, since these backup types do not include a backup of the transaction log automatically. You will normally need to perform transaction log backups at short intervals, such as hourly, to avoid filling up the transaction log.

Let's say you have part of your files stored on filegroup_1 and the other part on filegroup_2. Each table and its indexes are stored together on the same filegroup, but the two filegroups are too big to allow backing up the entire database in the same night. Therefore, you could design a strategy to back up the two filegroups separately three times a week. Let's say you back up filegroup_1 on Monday, Wednesday, and Friday at 1 A.M., and back up filegroup_2 on Tuesday, Thursday, and Saturday at 1 A.M., as shown in Figure 5-3.

If only one of the filegroups is damaged due to a media failure on that filegroup, then you can recover your database by restoring only that one filegroup. So if filegroup_1 is damaged, for example, you restore the most recent backup of filegroup_1, then also restore all the transaction log backups performed since that backup. In the same manner, if filegroup_2 is damaged, you restore the most recent backup of filegroup_2, then restore all the transaction log backups performed since that backup.

SUN	MON	TUE	WED	THU	FRI	SAT
	Back Up Filegroup 1	Back Up Filegroup 2	Back Up Filegroup 1	Back Up Filegroup 2	Back Up Filegroup 1	Back Up Filegroup 2
	Log Backups	Log Backups	Log Backups	Log Backups	Log Backups	Log Backups

Figure 5-3 *A filegroup backup strategy.*

Caution To restore the entire database after a system crash when using file and filegroup backups as opposed to full and differential database backups, you must have a backup available for every file or filegroup in the database. You also must have available an unbroken chain of transaction log backups dating from the earliest file or filegroup backup through to the most recent file or filegroup backup. If any of these components is missing, you will not be able to restore your database!

In our example, if you had to restore your entire database at some point, you would restore the most recent backup of filegroup_1 and the most recent backup of filegroup_2, plus all the transaction log backups created since the earliest filegroup backup. For this reason, it is best to use the backup strategy described earlier that combines full, differential, and log backups. Such a strategy offers better security for a full database recovery.

Summary

This chapter covered numerous topics involving new features of SQL Server 7. It looked at the dynamic configuration options for SQL Server and how they work if you choose to manually configure them, and discussed automatic file growth and shrinkage. You learned about performance improvements in SQL Server locking strategy, the transaction log, replication, query processing, database consistency checks, and backup and restore processes. You also learned about the new types of backups available and how they work. In the following chapter, you will build on your knowledge by learning some of the new features of SQL Server Enterprise Manager and learning the ways to monitor performance with the Performance Monitor.

Chapter 6
Monitoring Performance with Enterprise Manager and the Performance Monitor

Microsoft SQL Server, in conjunction with Microsoft Windows NT and Microsoft Windows 2000, provides several graphical tools to assist you in monitoring performance of the database system. These tools allow you to monitor your system in either real-time or logging modes. This chapter discusses what information is available from two of the tools, how to monitor the system, and finally what the information means.

Enterprise Manager

SQL Server Enterprise Manager is part of the Microsoft Management Console (MMC). Though it is primarily an administrative tool, it can also provide some valuable information for performance monitoring and tuning. From Enterprise Manager, you can graphically display information about the currently running processes in SQL Server. You can identify blocked processes, locks, and general user activity. The performance data displayed is a snapshot of the current activity in the system. The performance information available in Enterprise Manager does not include any historical data, and there is no mechanism for logging the data.

Monitoring Current Activity

Enterprise Manager offers you an easy method for ad hoc viewing of the current activity on your system. To view this information, open Enterprise Manager and expand the appropriate Server Group, and then expand a server. Next expand Management and then Current Activity. When you click on Process Info, you see the current server activity in the details pane (see Figure 6-1). The data provided by the Enterprise Manager's Current Activity screen is a snapshot. To update the display, right-click on Current Activity and select Refresh. Doing so takes another snapshot of current system activity.

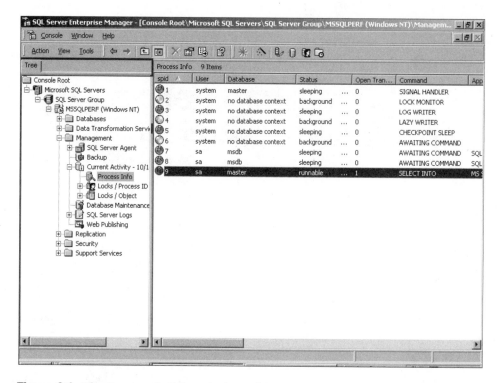

Figure 6-1 *The Current Activity window of Enterprise Manager.*

The Process Info pane contains a great deal of information about the current processes active on the system. Each row in the pane is identified with the *server process ID* (SPID). The SPID is a reference number that SQL Server uses to manage or interact with the session. It can be either an actual user session or another application that connects to the database. The Process Info pane contains the following information (you might need to scroll the pane to the right to see some fields):

- The SQL Server user ID associated with the SPID
- The database to which the SPID is currently connected
- The current execution state of the SPID
- The current command the SPID is executing
- The SQL Server application to which the SPID is connected
- The amount of time, in seconds, that the SPID has been waiting
- The reason the SPID is waiting
- The resource for which the SPID is waiting
- The SPID, if any, that is blocking the selected SPID

Using the Current Activity window will allow you to identify those user sessions that are blocking others or are being blocked themselves. If a session has a Wait Type of "blocked," check the value in the Blocked By column (found by scrolling the Process Info pane to the right) to determine which session is doing the blocking. You can then determine if the blocking process has acquired a lock on a resource that your session requires.

Displaying Locking Information

Enterprise Manager also provides you with a vehicle to display the current locking information for your system. To view a snapshot of the current lock activity, expand Management; then expand Current Activity. You can then expand Locks / Process ID to view the current locks for each connection, and Locks / Object to view the current locks for each object that is locked.

Finally, in the console tree, click the SPID or object you wish to view. The current locks for the SPID or object are displayed in the details pane. Keep in mind that this is a snapshot and may be outdated as soon as you view it, particularly in a system with a high transaction rate.

Performance Monitor

The Performance Monitor (PerfMon) is one of the most important tools available for monitoring and tuning SQL Server. The Windows NT or Windows 2000 platform provides the actual Performance Monitor application. PerfMon collects data via objects and counters. You can think of the object as the general category, whereas the counters are more specific. There is also an instance, where appropriate. For example, the % CPU counters are collected under the Processors object, and there is an instance for total processors as well as each individual processor. When you install SQL Server, several specialized objects and counters are installed for your use in Performance Monitor. The integration of these counters allows you to monitor system information, disk information, and SQL Server information simultaneously.

Performance Monitor consumes a small amount of CPU and disk resources on the system being monitored. On very busy systems, this overhead may be unacceptable, in which case you can run PerfMon from another computer to remotely monitor the system.

Performance Monitor allows you to monitor the system in one of two ways. You can watch the system in real time or you can log the information for later analysis. Regardless of which mode you choose, PerfMon allows you to view the data in two formats: graph mode or report mode. The graph mode (Figure 6-2) is useful for identifying trends in the data. The reporting mode (Figure 6-3) is extremely useful for objects and counters dealing with logical and physical disk I/O.

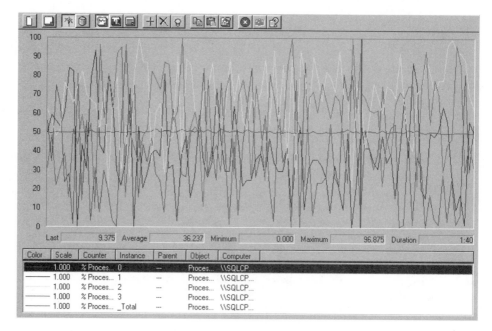

Figure 6-2 *A PerfMon graphical screen.*

\\SQLCPQ7K

Memory

Pool Nonpaged Allocs	38000.000
Pool Nonpaged Bytes	52355072.000
Pool Paged Allocs	37976.000
Pool Paged Bytes	26673152.000
Pool Paged Resident Bytes	24231936.000

Objects

Events	2010.000
Mutexes	184.000
Processes	54.000
Sections	526.000
Semaphores	270.000
Threads	444.000

Processor	_Total	0	1	2
% Processor Time	0.000	0.000	0.000	0.000

System

Context Switches/sec	254.995
File Read Bytes/sec	767.985
File Write Bytes/sec	0.000
Processes	43.000
Processor Queue Length	0.000
System Calls/sec	389.992
System Up Time	27048.563
Threads	428.000

Figure 6-3 *A PerfMon report screen.*

Logging Performance Data

Probably the most valuable aspect of PerfMon is its logging capability. It is often advantageous to capture PerfMon data for some interval and then analyze the data at a later time, possibly on a different machine. However, you need to be careful: the captured data is written to a log file, which can quickly grow very large. If this happens, you should consider increasing the sampling interval when logging performance data. Generally, 30 to 60 seconds is adequate to track all the counters and ensure that the data reflects the actual system state. If your sampling interval is too long, you may miss the peaks and valleys in the data, which may mislead you in your tuning efforts. If you have multiple megabytes of available storage on the monitored system, you can leave the interval at its default value of 15 seconds.

Note When using Performance Monitor in logging mode, you should not log the data over a network connection. It is much more efficient to log the data locally on the server itself. You can access the log file later from a remote system if needed. If you must log over the network, you should reduce the number of objects and counters to those that are the most critical.

To start logging information on Windows NT 4 using Performance Monitor, follow these steps:

Note The steps for logging are slightly different in Windows 2000. See the Windows 2000 Performance Monitor for more information.

1. Open Performance Monitor from the Administrative Tools in the Control Panel.
2. Select Log from the View menu.
3. Click the plus (+) button.
4. In the Add to Log dialog box, select the objects you wish to add to the log. When logging, you only need to select the object. All counters and instances are included. For this exercise, select Processor.
5. Click Add to add the selected objects, and then click Done to close the window.
6. From the Options menu select Log.
7. In the File Name field, enter the name and location of the file where the PerfMon data will be stored. For this exercise, type ProcessorMon.
8. Click Start Log to start logging.

When you have completed logging the desired data, perform the following actions to stop logging:

1. From the Options menu choose Log.
2. Click Stop Log.

After you have collected the information and stopped the logging process, you can use the following steps to load the logged data into the Performance Monitor:

1. From the View menu click Log.
2. From the Options menu, choose Data From and select the Log File option in the window that appears.

3. Use the browse (...) button to find the desired PerfMon log file. In this exercise, choose the file ProcessorMon you created earlier.

4. In the Data From dialog box, click OK to load the file.

5. From the View menu select Chart.

6. Use the plus (+) button to add objects and counters from the log file to the graphical display.

Occasionally you may want to localize the data in the log file to a particular time rather than looking at the entire file. This is easily accomplished in PerfMon, as follows:

1. After you have loaded your log file into PerfMon, from the Edit menu select Time Window.

2. In the Input Log File Timeframe dialog box, you may adjust the start and stop time of the graphical data by dragging the Start and Stop time indicators (see Figure 6-4).

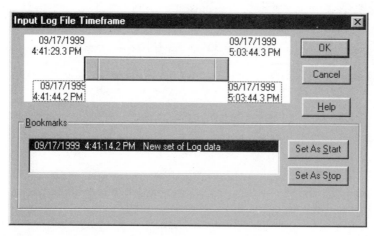

Figure 6-4 *The PerfMon Timeframe dialog box.*

Monitoring Disk Activity

Some of the most useful tuning counters in Performance Monitor are those dealing with disk activity. By default, you will be able to monitor the logical disk activity. The logical disk counters are associated with the logical drive letters assigned by the Windows NT Disk Administrator. If you are not using one of the RAID methods, these logical disk counters are adequate. If you are using some type of RAID, you need to consider using the physical disk counters.

The physical disk counters provide information when used in conjunction with the DiskPerf service. DiskPerf processes the information available at the physical disk level and passes it to the physical disk counters in PerfMon. DiskPerf can be enabled via one of two methods. From a Windows NT command line, type `diskperf-y` and press Enter. You will then be prompted to reboot your system to finish enabling DiskPerf. Alternatively, you can enable the service via the Services applet in the Control Panel.

An important consideration when enabling DiskPerf is the overhead required to monitor the physical I/O statistics. Windows NT 4 uses I/O Request Packets (IRPs) to monitor these statistics; these IRPs require an additional stack or structure in memory. Windows NT 4 has built-in functions that provide look-aside lists to improve performance of many of the paged and nonpaged memory pool allocations. The default size of the large IRP look-aside list allows for four stack levels in memory. When you enable DiskPerf, an additional stack level is required. This means that, by default, most large IRP list allocations will overflow this look-aside list and allocate the IRP from the nonpaged pool, which will cause an extra four spinlocks per I/O. (A *spinlock* is a tight loop the process executes while waiting to access the resource. Spinlocks are a necessity in multiprocessing systems, but they should always be kept to a minimum.) The extra spinlocks consume CPU resources that might better be reserved for your user work. Therefore, if you enable DiskPerf, increase the size of the IRP look-aside list by at least 1. The exact percentage of CPU you save will vary based on your system configuration and the number of I/Os your system is performing. To avoid the additional—and unnecessary—spinlocks, you should increase the number of large IRP look-aside lists by adding a key to the Windows NT registry.

Caution Modifying the registry can be potentially dangerous. You should always make a backup copy of the registry before you make any modifications.

To add the registry key, follow these steps:

1.   Click on Start and choose Run.
2.   Type REGEDT32 and click on OK. This will start the Windows NT Registry Editor.
3.   Click on HKEY_LOCAL_MACHINE to bring the window to the foreground.
4.   Expand System, then CurrentControlSet, then Control, and finally SessionManager.
5.   Select Edit, Add Key on the menu bar.
6.   Add a key with the name of I/O System.
7.   In the I/O System key, add a Value LargeIrpStackLocations with a Data Type of REG_DWORD.
8.   Enter 5 for the data.
9.   Shut down and restart your system in order for this change to take effect.

PerfMon Objects, Counters, and Instances

This section covers each of the SQL Server performance counters in detail. In addition to explaining what the counters mean, we explore how to tune and manage your system to ensure optimum performance.

Processor Object

The most obvious component to monitor and analyze is CPU utilization. The general processor information is contained in the Processor object. Your overall goal is to keep all the processors busy enough to maximize throughput, but not so busy that they become a bottleneck. A rule of thumb is not to push the CPU utilization over 90 percent for each processor you monitor. Peaks over 90 percent are acceptable, but an average utilization over 90 percent should be avoided.

A system with multiple processors lists an instance for each processor as well as a total instance for the entire system in the Instance window of the PerfMon Processor object. If you only have a single processor, you will see only one instance listed here.

The counters that you should monitor under the Processor object are as follows:

- **% Processor Time** The percentage of time that the processor is executing a non-idle thread. This value is calculated by subtracting the amount of time the processor was idle from 100 percent. It is an excellent indicator of overall system CPU utilization.

- **% Privileged Time** The percentage of processor time spent working in the privileged mode (that is, performing operating system functions and running drivers, such as I/O). This time includes the time in which the CPU (or CPUs) is servicing interrupts and deferred procedure calls (DPCs).

- **% User Time** The percentage of processor time spent working in user mode. This type of work is generated by applications. Generally, you want to maximize the % User Time value and minimize % Privileged Time.

- **% Interrupt Time** The percentage of time the CPU is busy servicing hardware interrupts. Many hardware components of a system, such as the mouse, network interface cards, or disk controllers, can issue processor interrupts. You will see interrupts occurring as part of normal Windows NT operation.

- **Interrupts/sec** The number of hardware interrupts per second that the processor is receiving and processing. It does not include the system DPCs, which are counted separately.

System Object

The System object and its associated counters measure aggregate data for threads running on the processor. Although you cannot examine a particular processor's workload or a particular thread's behavior with these counters, they provide valuable insight concerning overall system performance. The System counters are as follows:

- **Processor Queue Length** The number of threads in the processor queue. In other words, it is the count of threads waiting to run. There is a single queue for processor time even if your system has multiple processors. The counter tallies only the threads that are ready to execute but are still waiting, not those that are currently running.

- **Context Switches/sec** The combined rate at which all processors on the computer are switched from one thread to another. Context switches occur when a running thread voluntarily relinquishes the processor, is preempted by a higher-priority ready thread, or switches between user mode and privileged (kernel) mode to use an executive or subsystem service. It is the sum of Thread: Context Switches/sec for all threads running on all processors in the computer.

SQLServer: Buffer Manager Object

The Buffer Manager counters provide information about the memory buffers that SQL Server uses. These counters are as follows:

- **Buffer Cache Hit Ratio** The percentage of requests that reference a page currently located in the buffer cache. Having the page already in memory allows SQL Server to avoid requesting a physical I/O to be performed from the disk subsystem. Since accessing memory is relatively inexpensive compared with a physical I/O, a high buffer cache hit ratio increases system performance and throughput. If your system is well tuned, you should have a ratio of 80 percent or higher. If you have a low buffer cache hit ratio, you should allocate more memory to SQL Server. If you currently have all the existing memory allocated to SQL Server, you will need to increase the amount of physical memory on your system.
- **Cache Size (pages)** The number of pages in the SQL Server buffer cache. This number multiplied by 8 KB yields the amount of kilobytes in use.
- **Free Buffers** The number of free SQL Server memory buffers.
- **Page Reads/sec** The number of physical data page I/O requests per second.
- **Stolen Page Count** The number of pages that SQL Server was using for the buffer cache that have been given to another process on the system. Windows NT reallocates this memory to satisfy the requirements of other system components.
- **Page Writes/sec** The number of physical data page writes per second that have been issued by SQL Server.

SQLServer: Databases Object

The counters for the Databases object provide information about the SQL Server databases, including the amount of free log space available and the number of active transactions in the database. There is one instance of each counter for each database on a system. These counters include the following:

- **Log Flush Waits/sec** The number of database commits that are waiting for a log flush before they can continue
- **Percent Log Used** The percentage of the currently defined log space that SQL Server is actually using

SQLServer: General Statistics Object

The General Statistics object contains information about general serverwide activity. It has one counter:

- **User Connections** The current number of user connections on a system

SQLServer: Latches Object

This object's counters provide information about the latches in effect on the internal SQL Server resources. The counters are as follows:

- **Average Latch Wait Time (ms)** The average time, in milliseconds, that a latch request had to wait before it was serviced
- **Latch Waits/sec** The number of latch requests that could not be serviced immediately and were forced to wait for the resource to free up

SQLServer: Locks Object

The Locks object provides data about the individual lock requests made by SQL Server, such as lock timeouts and deadlocks. You will have multiple instances of these counters on your system. The counters are as follows:

- **Average Wait Time (ms)** The average amount of time, in milliseconds, that each lock request was forced to wait
- **Lock Timeouts/sec** The number of lock requests that timed out on your system
- **Lock Waits/sec** The number of lock requests that could not be satisfied immediately and required the calling thread to wait before being granted the lock
- **Number of Deadlocks/sec** The number of requests that resulted in a deadlock condition

SQLServer: Memory Manager Object

The Memory Manager object contains information about SQL Server's memory utilization, including the total amount of cache memory SQL Server is using. The counters under this object are as follows:

- **Memory Grants Pending** The current number of processes waiting for a workspace memory grant
- **SQL Cache Memory (KB)** The total amount of dynamic memory that SQL Server is using for the dynamic SQL cache
- **Target Server Memory (KB)** The total amount of dynamic memory that SQL Server is willing to consume
- **Total Server Memory (KB)** The total amount of dynamic memory that SQL Server is currently consuming

SQLServer: SQL Statistics Object

This object provides information about the SQL queries being executed on your system, including data on the number of query compilations and recompilations. It has the following counters:

- **Batch Requests/sec** The number of SQL batch requests that the server is receiving
- **SQL Compilations/sec** The number of SQL statement compilations that SQL Server is performing per second
- **SQL Re-Compilations/sec** The number of SQL statement recompilations that SQL Server is performing per second

Logical Disk Object

The Logical Disk object provides information regarding logical disk I/O performance. The logical disk counters are associated with the logical drive letters assigned by the Windows NT Disk Administrator. This object has the following counters:

- **% Disk Read Time** The percentage of elapsed time that the selected logical disk is busy servicing read requests
- **% Disk Write Time** The percentage of elapsed time that the selected logical disk is busy servicing write requests
- **% Disk Time** The percentage of elapsed time that the selected logical disk is busy servicing read or write requests, computed as the sum of % Disk Write Time and % Disk Read Time
- **% Idle Time** The percentage of time during the sample interval that the logical disk was idle
- **Avg. Disk Queue Length** The average number of both read and write requests that were queued for the selected logical disk during the sample interval
- **Avg. Disk Read Queue Length** The average number of read requests that were queued for the selected logical disk during the sample interval
- **Avg. Disk Write Queue Length** The average number of write requests that were queued for the selected logical disk during the sample interval
- **Avg. Disk sec/Read** The average time, in seconds, of a read of data from the logical disk
- **Avg. Disk sec/Write** The average time, in seconds, of a write of data to the logical disk
- **Avg. Disk sec/Transfer** The time, in seconds, of the average transfer from a logical disk
- **Disk Reads/sec** The rate of read operations on the logical disk
- **Disk Writes/sec** The rate of write operations on the logical disk
- **Disk Transfers/sec** The rate of read and write operations on the logical disk

PhysicalDisk Object

The PhysicalDisk object provides information regarding the physical disk I/O performance. Its disk counters are associated with the physical drives in the system and are activated only when you are running the DiskPerf service. The counters under this object are as follows:

- **% Disk Read Time** The percentage of elapsed time that the selected physical disk is busy servicing read requests
- **% Disk Write Time** The percentage of elapsed time that the selected physical disk is busy servicing write requests
- **% Disk Time** The percentage of elapsed time that the selected physical disk is busy servicing read or write requests, computed as the sum of % Disk Write Time and % Disk Read Time

- **% Idle Time** The percentage of time during the sample interval that the physical disk was idle
- **Avg. Disk Queue Length** The average number of both read and write requests that were queued for the selected physical disk during the sample interval
- **Avg. Disk Read Queue Length** The average number of read requests that were queued for the selected physical disk during the sample interval
- **Avg. Disk Write Queue Length** The average number of write requests that were queued for the selected physical disk during the sample interval
- **Avg. Disk sec/Read** The average time, in seconds, of a read of data from the physical disk
- **Avg. Disk sec/Write** The average time, in seconds, of a write of data to the physical disk
- **Avg. Disk sec/Transfer** The time, in seconds, of the average transfer from a physical disk
- **Disk Reads/sec** The rate of read operations on the physical disk
- **Disk Writes/sec** The rate of write operations on the physical disk
- **Disk Transfers/sec** The rate of read and write operations on the physical disk.

Memory

Memory is a very valuable resource in any system. Windows NT not only allows but encourages you to overcommit memory. Windows NT provides a transparent mechanism that allows applications to "believe" that they have more memory than is physically available on the system. As Windows NT processes applications, it pages (swaps) unused memory pages to a paging file on disk. Some paging is normal in most systems, but excessive paging can impair overall system performance. The following counters allow you to monitor system paging.

- **Page Faults/sec** The overall number of faulted pages handled by the processor per second. A *page fault* occurs when a process requires code or data that is not in its working set (its space in physical memory). This counter includes both hard page faults (those that require disk access) and soft page faults (where the faulted page is found elsewhere in physical memory.)
- **Page Reads/sec** The number of times the disk was read to resolve hard page faults. (Hard page faults occur when a process requires code or data that is not in its working set or elsewhere in physical memory and must be retrieved from disk.) This counter includes reads to satisfy faults in the file system cache (usually requested by applications) and in noncached mapped memory files.
- **Page Writes/sec** The number of times pages were written to disk to free up space in physical memory. Pages are written to disk only if they are changed while in physical memory, so they are likely to hold data, not code.
- **Pages/sec** The number of pages read from or written to disk to resolve hard page faults. It is a sum of the Page Reads/sec and Page Writes/sec counters.

What Does It All Mean?

Now that you have collected all this data, what does it tell you about your system? You should follow a sound methodology when analyzing the collected data. The tuning process can be tedious: changing one aspect of a system can and will affect other components. For example, increasing the buffer cache may decrease the physical I/Os required because more data can be cached. Therefore, you should identify an area of concern, address it, and then capture more data with PerfMon. This method will allow you to determine what impact your changes have made on overall system performance. With that in mind, let's go through the different components and PerfMon objects and see what they indicate about your system's performance.

Processor Object

The Processor object contains detailed data about processor utilization and I/O performance. When the percentage of privileged time is high on your system, it generally indicates that your system is experiencing a high number of system interrupts for I/O processing. This condition can be confirmed by looking at the Interrupts/sec counter for the processors. When you are experiencing excessive interrupts, you should examine the PhysicalDisk object's counters. Generally, excessive interrupts per second can be reduced by adding I/O bandwidth. See Chapter 3 for more information on I/O performance and tuning.

System Object

The next step is to investigate the Context Switches/sec counter of the System object. As stated earlier, a context switch occurs when the operating system or application is forced to change from executing one thread to executing another. You will always see some context switching on a multiprocessor system running multithreaded applications, but you should be concerned when these context switches are excessive. Generally, more than 10,000 context switches per second is considered excessive.

An easy way to alleviate the number of context switches is to enable fiber-based scheduling in SQL Server by setting the *lightweight pooling* configuration parameter to 1. (The *sp_configure* command allows you to change this scheduling parameter.) When you enable lightweight pooling, SQL Server schedules its own units of work within the Windows NT thread system and greatly reduces the number of context switches required. If after you set *lightweight pooling* your system is still experiencing excessive context switches, you can generally alleviate this condition by adding I/O bandwidth, which can be in the form of additional physical disks or additional disk controllers. Chapter 3 contains additional information on I/O bandwidth and throughput.

The Processor Queue Length counter of the System object should be monitored in conjunction with the Processor object data. When the Processor Queue value is greater than 2 per processor, you have a CPU bottleneck. You can alleviate this condition by adding more processors, installing faster processors, or reducing the workload on the system. Tuning your queries or improving your index strategy can accomplish this workload reduction. These approaches are discussed in Chapters 17 and 18.

SQLServer: Buffer Manager Object

The Buffer Manager object provides information about how SQL Server is utilizing the memory allocated to it. The Buffer Cache Hit Ratio counter shows you how many data pages that SQL Server requested were already resident in memory. When this value drops below 80 percent, you should consider allocating more memory to SQL Server. This can be accomplished in several ways: you can add physical memory to your system, or you can allocate more of the existing memory to SQL Server.

If your system is dedicated to SQL Server, that is, if you are not running any other applications on the system, you should set the SQL Server *max server memory* configuration option to the default of 2147483647. This value instructs SQL Server to allocate the maximum amount of memory that Windows NT will allow. If your Buffer Cache Hit Ratio is still low, you will need to add physical memory. If you have the *max server memory* parameter set to the maximum and you add physical memory to the system, SQL Server will consume it without any other configuration changes.

If your system is not and cannot be dedicated to SQL Server, you will have to balance the memory requirements of all running applications. The Cache Size counter allows you to monitor the number of 8-KB pages that SQL Server has access to. Watching this counter as you start additional applications will allow you to judge the impact of each application on SQL Server's cache.

In addition to the Cache Size counter, you should monitor the Stolen Page Count. This counter shows you how many 8-KB pages are being removed from the SQL Server data cache to satisfy the requirements of other applications on the system. To alleviate the impact of the lost pages on SQL Server, you can set the *sp_configure* option *min server memory* to some value other than the default of 0. This instructs SQL Server to initially request memory in the amount of the *min server memory* value and not to relinquish it to other applications. Be aware that this setting will probably negatively affect the other applications on your system. When they attempt to allocate memory, they may not be able to get all they request or require. This could cause Windows NT to page, which should be avoided. The only remedy for this latter condition is to add physical memory to your system.

If you are monitoring the Page Reads/sec counter of the Buffer Manager object, you will see high values until your system reaches a steady-state condition. As more pages are read into memory and then reaccessed as cache hits, the number of page reads will decrease. If this value stays consistently high, you may need to increase SQL Server's memory allocation, increase the physical memory on the system, or tune your queries.

In addition, a consistently low Free Buffers counter value indicates low memory on your server. You should add memory to your system to alleviate this condition.

SQLServer: Databases Object

The Databases object provides some basic information about the behavior of each database on your system. The most critical counter in this object is Log Flush Waits/sec, which indicates how many database commits are waiting for a log flush. In order to maintain the data integrity of a database page, the page cannot be written to disk until the log is flushed. After the log buffer has been flushed to the log file, the actual dirty database page can be written. When commits are waiting for log flushes, the log device is usually the bottleneck. This condition can easily be remedied by adding I/O bandwidth to your log devices.

SQLServer: Latches Object

A *latch* is a lightweight, short-term synchronization object that protects an action that does not need to be locked for the life of a transaction. When the relational engine is processing a query, it requests the storage engine to return a row each time a row is needed from a base table or index. While the storage engine is actively transferring the row to the relational engine, the storage engine must ensure that no other task modifies either the contents of the row or certain page structures such as the page offset table entry that locates the row being read. It does this by acquiring a latch, transferring the row in memory to the relational engine, and then releasing the latch.

When you have a high number of latch waits per second or a long average latch wait time, the system is generally experiencing a low cache hit ratio and is being forced to perform physical I/Os. This will ripple into an I/O bottleneck. The optimum way to alleviate this condition is to increase the physical memory on the system. If you cannot increase memory any further, you will need to increase the I/O bandwidth of your system.

SQLServer: Locks Object

SQL Server's data-locking mechanisms ensure data integrity for all queries and data accesses. Locks can be taken at the data row level, page level, or table level, or at all these levels. The Locks object provides data about how applications and queries are behaving and coexisting. The most critical counter to monitor here is Number of Deadlocks/sec. A *deadlock* is a condition in which two users or processes have locks on separate objects and each user or process is trying to acquire a lock on the object that the other user or process holds. SQL Server ends a deadlock by automatically choosing the user whose transaction will be aborted to break the deadlock; this user is called the *deadlock victim*. SQL Server rolls back the deadlock victim's transaction, notifies the user's application with error message 1205, cancels the user's current request, and then allows the transactions of the other users to continue.

Do not confuse deadlocking with normal blocking. When one transaction has a lock on a resource that another transaction wants, the second transaction waits for the lock to be released. Since, by default, SQL Server transactions do not time out, the second transaction is blocked, but not necessarily deadlocked. When your system experiences a deadlock, you need to examine what each user is attempting to do. Tools such as SQL Server Profiler and SQL Server Query Analyzer, both discussed in later chapters, will aid you in determining how to restructure your queries to minimize deadlocking. Several methods for avoiding deadlock scenarios are outlined here.

- **Access objects in the same order.** If all transactions execute concurrently, you should strive to access the different database objects in the same order. Though not always possible, this technique makes deadlocks less likely to occur. For example, if two concurrent transactions obtain a lock on the *Supplier* table and then the *Part* table, one transaction is blocked on the *Supplier* table until the other transaction finishes. After the first transaction commits or rolls back, the second continues. No deadlock occurs. Figure 6-5 illustrates this data access. Using stored procedures for all data modifications can standardize the access order.

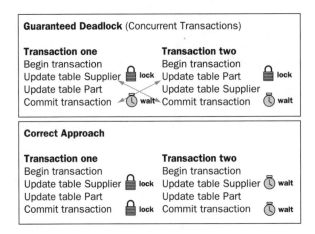

Figure 6-5 *Avoiding deadlocks.*

- **Avoid user interaction in transactions.** You should avoid writing transactions that include user interaction because users tend to be slow in responding to requests for feedback, such as a prompt for a parameter requested by an application. For example, if a transaction is waiting for user input and the user goes to lunch, or even home for the weekend, the user holds up the transaction, thus preventing its completion. This degrades system throughput because any locks held by the transaction are released only when the transaction is committed or rolled back. Even if a deadlock situation does not arise, other transactions accessing the same resources are blocked, waiting for the transaction to finish.

- **Keep transactions short and in one batch.** Deadlocking typically occurs when several long-running transactions execute concurrently in the same database. The longer the transaction, the longer the exclusive or update locks are held, blocking other activity and leading to possible deadlock situations. Keeping your transactions in one batch minimizes network round-trips during a transaction and reduces delays in completing the transaction and releasing locks.

- **Use as low an isolation level as possible.** Though it is sometimes difficult, you should determine if your transaction can run at a lower isolation level, for example, Read Committed rather than Serializable. A transaction implementing the read committed level is able to read data previously read, but not modified, by another transaction without waiting for the first transaction to finish. Using a lower isolation level, such as Read Committed, holds shared locks for a shorter duration than a higher isolation level such as Serializable, thereby reducing locking contention.

You should always monitor the counters for average wait time and the number of lock waits per second, although these events are not as important as deadlocks. You will always encounter locking on your system; the secret is to minimize the number of lock waits and the amount of time spent waiting. By following the recommendations for deadlocking just given, you can also minimize the number and duration of locks.

SQLServer: Memory Manager Object

The Memory Manager object provides some useful data about how SQL Server is managing its allocated memory. As each process executes on the database, it requests and is granted memory resources. Monitoring the Memory Grants Pending counter allows you to determine how many users or processes are waiting for memory grants. When SQL Server is starved for memory, the Memory Grants Pending value increases because more users or processes are waiting for memory. You can alleviate this condition by increasing the amount of memory allocated to SQL Server or by increasing the amount of physical memory on your system.

SQLServer: SQL Statistics Object

The SQL Statistics object provides valuable insight into how your queries and transactions are behaving. The Batch Requests/sec counter shows you how many SQL batches the server is receiving. A SQL *batch* is a group of one or more SQL statements that are sent to the server at one time. Passing several SQL statements to the server at one time is beneficial to performance. When you submit statements in a batch, SQL Server can compile them into a single execution unit, which allows SQL Server to process the statements more efficiently.

The Logical and PhysicalDisk Objects

Since the counters for the Logical and PhysicalDisk objects are similar, we cover them together. Depending on your actual I/O system configuration, you will want to monitor either the logical or physical disk counters. If you are using a RAID I/O disk subsystem, the physical disk counters will provide more meaningful data. In other cases, the logical disk counters will suffice.

You can gain much insight from the volume of data in the disk counters. We cover the most important counters in this chapter. The first counter to investigate is Avg. Disk Queue Length, which monitors the average number of both reads and writes queued for a particular disk. If you are running a RAID subsystem with multiple hard drives in a single volume, this number is the total for all drives in that volume. For example, if you have seven drives in a volume, and there are on average nine queued requests, approximately 1.28 (9/7) requests are queued to each drive. A general rule of thumb is to keep the average number of queued requests at two or less per disk. When this counter's value exceeds 2, your system will be in an I/O bound state. You can alleviate this by adding more disks for the data or by increasing the relative speed of the disks.

Another important set of counters are Avg. Disk sec/Read, Avg. Disk sec/Write, and Avg. Disk sec/Transfer. The average disk seconds per transfer is an aggregate of the seconds per read and the seconds per write. The seconds per read, write, or transfer are also referred to as the *disk latency* and are an indication of how long the disk is taking to respond to requests. Latency is covered in more detail in Chapter 3. You generally want to strive to have a value for Avg. Disk sec/Write of 12 msec or less. If you have a disk controller that has write caching enabled, you generally will see times at or below 4 msec per write. If your disk seconds per write are consistently above this range, you will need to increase the number of disks holding the data or use faster hard disks.

The same general rules apply to the average disk seconds per read. Read times of 11 to 15 msec are adequate for most systems. If your SQL statements tend to access the data sequentially, you should investigate the use of a disk controller that provides a read cache along with the write cache. This will allow the system to read additional rows for each read requested by the server. If the next read request is for this additional data, it will be serviced from the cache rather than from the relatively slower physical disk. If your data access is not sequential, read caching is not beneficial and in fact may degrade the overall system performance.

The last group of logical and physical disk counters we will discuss are those monitoring the number of actual reads, writes, and transfers per second. The Disk Transfers/sec counter is the aggregate of both read and write values. The rule of thumb for disk transfers is to strive to have no more than 60 to 80 I/Os, or transfers, per second per disk. As before, if you have a RAID disk subsystem, you need to divide this number by the total number of physical disks that make up the logical disk in question. The formulas for calculating the actual number of I/Os per second per drive depend on the type of RAID being used (see the "Disk Calculations" section in Chapter 3).

Memory

Windows NT attempts to maximize memory utilization based on the demands applications place on it. As more is demanded of the memory subsystem, Windows NT will start paging. Paging occurs in one of two forms: soft or hard. *Hard paging* (also called *hard page faults*) means that Windows NT uses the page file on disk to resolve memory references. Hard paging is expensive since it involves both disk and CPU resources. *Soft paging* is slightly different. It means that a user or process in an application has requested memory pages that are physically in memory, but are not part of the application's working set. Most processors today can handle a large amount of soft paging. However, hard paging will cause significant delays.

Hard paging is easily detected using the PerfMon counters. The best indicator of hard paging is the Pages/sec counter. When this value is consistently greater than 0, your system is experiencing hard paging. (You will occasionally see some paging even on a well-tuned system because Windows NT performs general housekeeping and memory optimization.) If you are allowing SQL Server to dynamically adjust memory, you can add memory to the system or remove other applications that are competing with SQL Server for memory in order to reduce the hard paging. If you have manually set the *max server memory* parameter, you may need to lower that value, add memory to the system, or remove other applications competing for memory resources.

Soft paging is a little more difficult to monitor. Since there is no specific counter for soft page faults, you will need to calculate this value. The number of soft page faults per second is derived by subtracting the counter value for Pages/sec from the value for Page Faults/sec. Soft page faults frequently occur when SQL Server first accesses its data pages. These should not be any concern for overall system performance.

If you wish to know if SQL Server is causing the soft paging, you should monitor the Page Faults/sec counter for the Process object. If this value is similar to the number of pages per second, then SQL Server is causing the soft page faults.

Summary

In this chapter you learned how to use two of the graphical tools available to assist you in your tuning efforts. You have seen how to use Enterprise Manager to identify which SQL Server process or user is blocking other processes. You have also learned how to work with the Windows NT Performance Monitor. The Performance Monitor contains a wealth of performance data that you can use to monitor and tune your system. You have explored what the Performance Monitor data means and what you can modify on your system to ensure the optimum use of all components. The next chapter looks at another useful tool for tuning: SQL Server Profiler.

Chapter 7
Using SQL Server Profiler

Debugging a performance problem always starts with determining where the root of the problem is. In many cases the root cause of a problem is ineffective SQL statements. This chapter teaches you how to determine which SQL statements may be using excessive resources. In addition it shows how to decompose SQL statements in order to determine which resources are being used. Gathering this information allows you to more effectively tune your system.

When looking for SQL statements to tune, start with the ones that are using the most resources or the ones that are executed most often. Tuning a SQL statement that occasionally runs for a short time will not affect the overall performance of the system, whereas tuning a SQL statement that uses a large amount of system resources will have a noticeable effect on system performance. By narrowing down the candidate SQL statements to the 10 or 20 that are most likely to affect the system, you can more effectively use your time.

The chapter begins with an overview of SQL Server Profiler's functions and capabilities. Next it covers how to invoke and use SQL Server Profiler, including how to use the built-in filters and how to create your own filters. This material is followed by instructions on how to analyze Profiler data. We provide several sample scenarios that show how the Profiler can be used to debug performance problems. The chapter ends with a brief explanation of how SQL Server Profiler can be used to capture, replay, and debug SQL statements.

SQL Server Profiler Overview

SQL Server Profiler is a graphical tool that is provided as part of Microsoft SQL Server's tool set. This tool provides a mechanism for DBAs to monitor SQL Server *engine events*, that is, events that occur within the SQL Server engine itself. These events include the following:

- Cursor events
- Errors and warning messages
- Locks acquired or released on SQL Server objects
- Login events, such as connects, disconnects, and failed attempts
- Remote procedure call (RPC) batch status
- Start or end of a stored procedure
- Start or end of a SQL statement within a stored procedure
- Start or end of a SQL batch
- T-SQL SELECT, INSERT, UPDATE, and DELETE statements

The Profiler works by setting up *traces* (also called *trace filters*). A trace, or trace filter, is a set of stored events that will be profiled. Several predefined traces are provided with the Profiler; you can also create your own, as you will see later in this chapter.

The predefined trace definitions provided with SQL Server Profiler are well organized and work well under many different cases. By taking advantage of them, you can save yourself a lot of work. These traces are as follows:

- **TSQL**   Collects T-SQL statements in the order in which they were submitted. The result is a list of T-SQL statements and the time each was issued.

- **TSQL (grouped)**   Collects data similar to that gathered by the TSQL trace just described, but the resulting data is grouped by which user submitted the T-SQL statements.

- **Stored procedure counts**   Counts the number of stored procedures that have been run. The results are grouped by the stored procedure name, and the number of times a procedure was executed is displayed.

- **TSQL + Stored procedure steps**   Displays the stored procedure as well as the T-SQL commands within that stored procedure. The results are ordered by time.

- **TSQL by duration**   Displays the T-SQL statements that have been issued as well as the time it takes for those T-SQL statements to execute. The time is displayed in milliseconds.

- **TSQL for Replay**   Provides detailed information on the T-SQL statements that have been issued. The intent of this trace is to provide data that can be used to replay T-SQL statements in SQL Server Query Analyzer.

Some of these predefined traces can be very useful. The TSQL By Duration trace can help you determine which SQL statements are taking the most time to execute. This gives you a place to start looking for problem queries.

Caution The Profiler can use significant system resources, thus causing a performance problem itself. The more events you trace, the more overhead you use.

In addition to tracing SQL Server engine events, SQL Server Profiler can be used to debug SQL statements. The Profiler has the capability to single-step through SQL statements, as well as the ability to capture and replay someone else's SQL statements.

Using the Profiler

You invoke SQL Server Profiler via the Start menu by selecting Programs, then Microsoft SQL Server 7.0, then Profiler. Once the Profiler has been invoked the application will launch, but profiling will not begin until you define the events that you want to profile. The initial screen has no panes open within it, and nothing is being profiled; thus, you will see a blank screen.

SQL Server Profiler consists of seven drop-down menus:

- **File**   Used for creating, opening, closing, and modifying the properties of trace filters or SQL scripts.

- **Edit** Used for clearing trace windows, finding text strings, and copying data.
- **Replay** Used for manipulating SQL statements when running in SQL debug mode. Statements can be started, single-stepped, paused, and manipulated from here.
- **View** Used to manipulate the Profiler environment, such as which toolbars are visible.
- **Tools** Used to gain easy access to SQL Server tools such as the Create Trace Wizard as well as external tools such as Enterprise Manager and the Query Analyzer.
- **Window** Used to control the windowing environment of the tool.
- **Help** Used to invoke online help regarding both the Profiler and T-SQL.

In addition to the drop-down menus, the Profiler has a number of icons that you can use to perform functions such as trace manipulation, windowing, and tool invocation. Once you get used to the icons they are very convenient.

Setting Trace Options

At some time during your use of SQL Server Profiler, you will want to modify the trace options. These options are available by selecting Options from the Tools menu. Doing so brings up the General tab of the Trace Options dialog box, as shown in Figure 7-1.

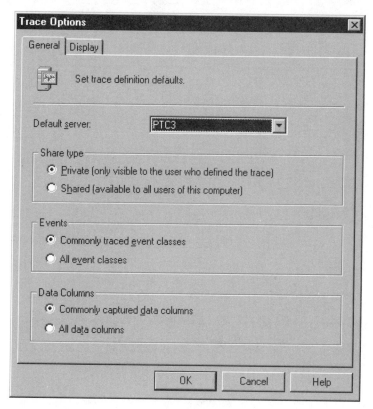

Figure 7-1 *The General tab of the Trace Options dialog box.*

From this screen you should set the default server name, which is the server that will be selected for all traces by default. Setting a server name here will save you a lot of time that would otherwise be devoted to individually modifying the trace properties. Once you have selected the default server, you can also select whether the trace is private (available only to you) or shared (available to others) on the server from which the trace is run. In addition you can specify the number of events and data columns that are added to traces by default. I prefer to leave the default options of Commonly Traced Event Classes and Commonly Captured Data Columns selected.

Once you have finished setting options in the General tab, you should review the options that are set in the Display tab. One of the main options here is the ability to specify when tracing starts, as shown in Figure 7-2. I prefer to uncheck the Auto-start Trace When Created box so that traces start when I am ready, but this is up to your own personal preference.

You can specify the number of lines to display in the trace window, as well as the number of lines to buffer. Typically the default values are sufficient for your needs. The last option allows you to set the font types. This may be useful for some types of monitors.

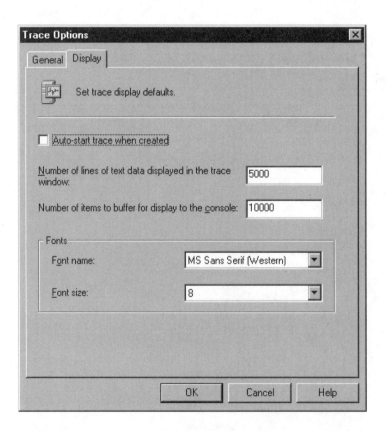

Figure 7-2 *The Display tab of the Trace Options dialog box.*

Once you have set the trace options, you are ready to begin running traces. The next section shows how to run the predefined traces; later you will learn how to modify those traces as well as how to create your own trace filters.

Running Traces

In order to start profiling you must either run an existing trace or create a new trace and run it. To run an existing trace, pull down the File menu and choose the Run Traces option. This brings up the Start Selected Traces dialog box (Figure 7-3), from which you can run one of the predefined traces or one of your stored traces.

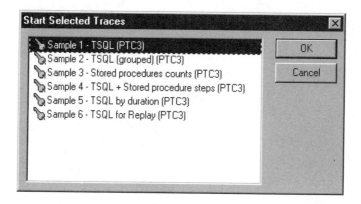

Figure 7-3 *The Start Selected Traces dialog box.*

Selecting a trace from the Start Selected Traces dialog box opens the trace window, as shown in Figure 7-4 (on the next page). This window consists of two panes: an overview and a details pane. The overview pane allows you to see all the events that have been run, with one event per line. Clicking on an event line brings up more information in the details pane.

The information presented in the trace window will vary according to the trace you choose. The different traces filter and present events according to how you have configured the trace filter.

Predefined Traces

This section provides detailed information on how the Profiler works by walking through the predefined trace filters.

TSQL

The TSQL predefined trace collects T-SQL statements in the order in which they have been submitted. This information is very similar to the data that was provided by the Trace utility in SQL Server 6.5. The information can be used to help you view the activity on the system. This activity can then be correlated with other events on the system, such as deadlocks or other system problems.

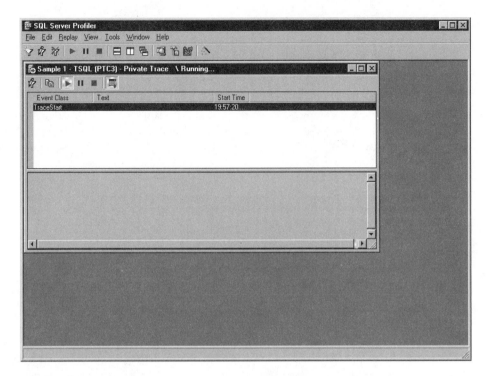

Figure 7-4 *The Trace window in SQL Server Profiler.*

The TSQL trace is invoked by selecting TSQL from the Run Traces menu. The initial screen that appears contains two panes: the summary pane and the details pane (see Figure 7-5). I always prefer to maximize this screen, unless I am doing several traces at once. If your system is busy you will immediately see information being displayed in the Profiler, as shown in Figure 7-5.

Viewing the data collected by the TSQL predefined trace is very simple. All that is displayed is the Event Class (type of event), the SQL statement text, and the time that the statement began execution. Expanding each line in the summary pane simply displays the SQL text in the details pane.

This predefined trace is good for monitoring system activity. Since only a small amount of data is saved, you will be able to save space and still collect a few days' worth of traces. This data can be used to find problem SQL statements as well as to provide a record of what SQL statements were run.

TSQL (Grouped)

The TSQL (Grouped) trace collects data similar to that gathered by the TSQL trace just described, but the resulting data is grouped by the application name and login name of the user who has submitted the SQL statements. This information can be very useful

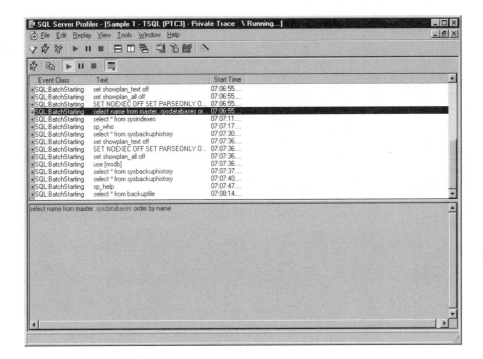

Figure 7-5 *Running the TSQL predefined trace.*

when looking for a problem that specific users have reported, such as a few users who are experiencing deadlocks.

When this trace is enabled you are presented with a screen that is similar to the screen in the previous example. Again, once the trace is opened it immediately begins collecting data, as shown in Figure 7-6 (on the next page). Initially you only see a list of applications that have connected to SQL Server. When you expand the Application Name row by clicking on the + box, you are then able to drill down to first the Windows NT user name and then the SQL Server user name, as shown in Figure 7-6. Finally, you will be able to drill down to the list of SQL statements that a particular user has run through a particular application.

The TSQL (Grouped) trace is very useful for debugging a set of SQL statements that were invoked by a single user running a third-party application. By filtering the events in this manner, you can view both the order and the syntax of the SQL statements that an application has used. Furthermore, by checking the timestamps for when the SQL batches started, you can get a fairly good idea of how long each step in the application is taking. Keep in mind that delays may be caused by the application as well as by slow-running SQL statements.

In order to more accurately measure the time it takes to run each SQL batch, you can modify the trace by adding the SQL:BatchCompleted event. An example of this is shown in Figure 7-7.

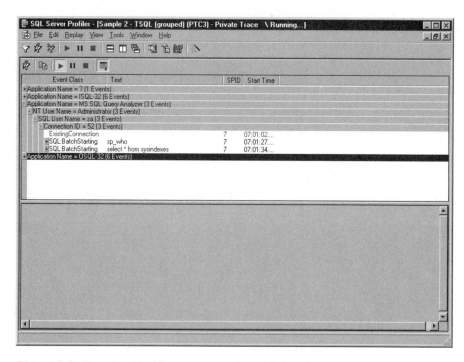

Figure 7-6 *Running the TSQL (Grouped) predefined trace.*

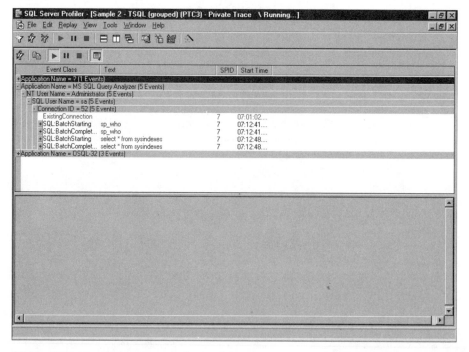

Figure 7-7 *The TSQL (Grouped) predefined trace with the SQL:BatchCompleted event added.*

If your goal is to find long-running SQL statements within a specific application, this method can be extremely useful. By capturing the beginning and ending times of the SQL statements, you can easily browse through the data to find the SQL statements that take the longest time to run. This gives you a good starting point for tuning the application.

Stored Procedure Counts

The Stored Procedure Counts trace keeps track of the number of stored procedures that have been run. The results are grouped by the stored procedure name, and the number of times each was executed is displayed. This is a very simple trace, as shown in Figure 7-8. Knowing the number of times that various stored procedures run can be useful in determining which stored procedures are good candidates for tuning. Since you may not have time to analyze and tune all stored procedures, focusing on the most heavily used stored procedures is a good strategy.

When tuning an application, we usually look for SQL statements that run for a very long time. It is also good to look for SQL statements or stored procedures that are run repeatedly. The frequency with which a stored procedure is run is a major consideration for the total amount of resources that it is using. An inefficient stored procedure that is constantly run is a very good candidate for tuning.

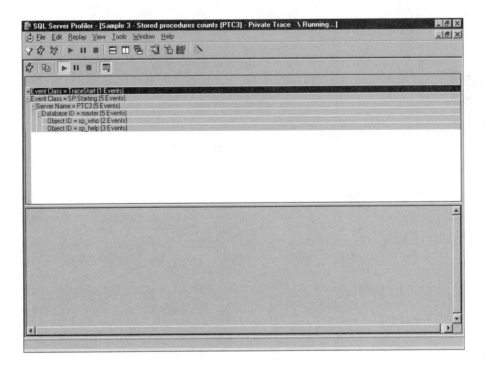

Figure 7-8 *The Stored Procedure Counts predefined trace.*

TSQL + Stored Procedure Steps

The TSQL + Stored Procedure Steps trace displays a stored procedure as well as the SQL commands within that stored procedure. The results are ordered by the time that the event started (see Figure 7-9). This trace is very similar to the TSQL trace, but with an additional column that shows which stored procedure is calling each SQL statement. This information can be very useful when debugging stored procedures, especially those that call other stored procedures.

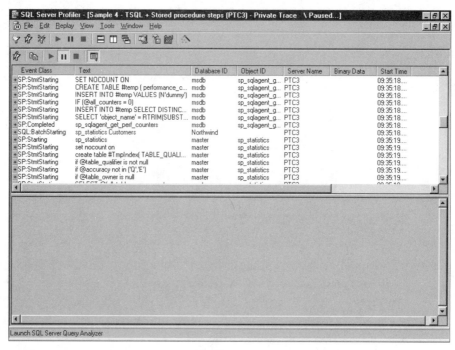

Figure 7-9 *The TSQL + Stored Procedure Steps predefined trace.*

Before the Profiler was available it was very difficult, and sometimes impossible, to determine which SQL statements were using excessive resources. In SQL Server 6.5 the SQL Trace facility displayed only the SQL statement itself. But by using the TSQL + Stored Procedure Steps predefined trace you can easily track the problem SQL statements once you know from which stored procedure they are being run. With this tool the job of identifying these problem SQL statements is much more manageable than before.

TSQL By Duration

The TSQL By Duration trace displays the T-SQL statements that have been issued, as well as the time (in milliseconds) that it takes for those T-SQL statements to execute. Figure 7-10 shows a sample screen generated by running this trace. This predefined trace allows

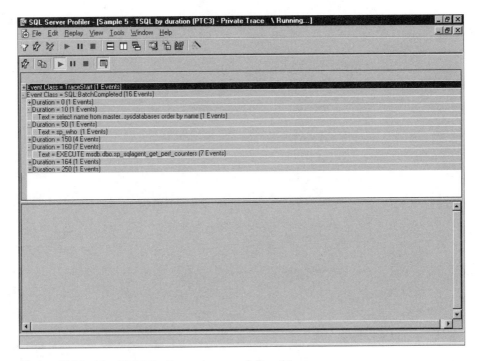

Figure 7-10 *The TSQL By Duration predefined trace.*

you to identify specific SQL statements that take an excessive amount of time so that you can focus your tuning efforts on them.

In order to get useful data from this trace you must first expand the SQL:BatchCompleted event. Here you will see a list of time intervals as well as the number of times that a specific SQL statement has run in those time intervals, as shown in Figure 7-10. Once you have identified the long-running SQL statements by time, you can expand the Duration event in order to see the SQL statement itself.

TSQL For Replay

The T-SQL For Replay trace provides detailed information on the T-SQL statements that have been issued (see Figure 7-11 on the next page). The intent of this trace is to provide data that can be used to replay SQL statements that have been run on the server. These SQL statements can be rerun on this or another server.

This trace is somewhat useful for capturing a set of SQL commands for replay. However, if you have more than one user connecting to this server, the SQL commands will be intermingled when captured, thus making the results useless. To correct this situation, you can change the filter properties to trace only the single user ID you desire. How to modify filters is described in the next section.

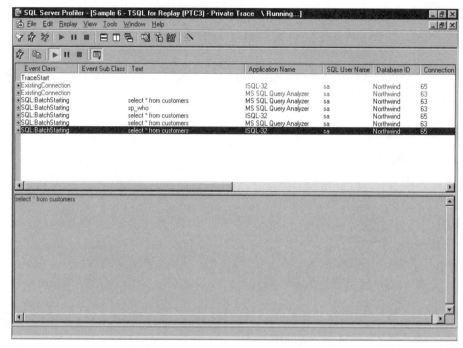

Figure 7-11 *The TSQL For Replay predefined trace.*

Modifying Trace Properties

Once a trace has been invoked, you can modify the trace filter by selecting Properties from the File menu. The Trace Properties dialog box appears, with the General tab displayed (see Figure 7-12).

From the General tab you can perform the following operations:

- **Select a trace** The trace specified in the Trace Name list box is the trace whose properties will be modified. By default the trace that is currently active appears here.
- **Select a SQL Server** The SQL Server name specified in the list box is the name of the system from which the Profiler will gather data.
- **Save profile data** You can save trace data to a file or a SQL Server table, as described next.

Saving Trace Data

Trace data can either be saved to a file or to a table within SQL Server itself. To save profile data to a file, check the box next to Capture To File. You can then select a valid Windows NT pathname by clicking on the folder icon. From here the Save As dialog box allows you to browse and select the filename. By saving profile data to a file, you can either view the trace in the Profiler again or replay the trace.

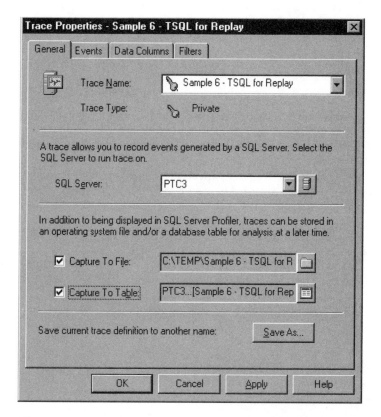

Figure 7-12 *The General tab of the Trace Properties dialog box.*

To save profile data in a SQL Server table, first check the box next to Capture To Table and then click on the table icon. The Capture To Table dialog box allows you to choose the SQL Server system, database, owner, and table name. Trace data saved to a table can be either viewed in the Profiler again or replayed. Capturing the data to a table keeps it secure within SQL Server for easy recovery. For long-term traces this is probably the better option. For example, if you want to continuously run a trace that logs unsuccessful login attempts, it would probably be a good idea to save this data in a SQL Server table. The data is managed under SQL Server and can be viewed and manipulated with SQL commands.

Tip   If you are using the Capture To Table option, do not use the default table name that is presented to you in the dialog box, since it may contain SQL Server keywords. If you use the default name with predefined trace 5, TSQL By Duration, or trace 6, TSQL For Replay, you would then need to remember to use SET QUOTED_IDENTIFIER ON in order to manipulate the resulting tables because both table name descriptions include SQL Server keywords: BY and FOR.

Adding or Deleting Events in an Existing Trace Filter

The next tab in the Trace Properties dialog box is the Events tab (Figure 7-13), which is the core of the Profiler. From this tab you can add or delete events in a trace filter. The set of events being monitored is what provides you with useful trace information. The Events tab is made up of two windows. The left window, Available Events, is a list of events that can be monitored but have not been selected. The right window, Selected Events, is a list of events that have been selected for monitoring. Double-clicking an event that is listed in the Available Events window selects that event for monitoring and moves it to the Selected Events window. Double-clicking an event that is listed in the Selected Events window removes that event from the list of monitored events and places it back in the Available Events window. The Add and Remove buttons can also be used to move events from one window to another.

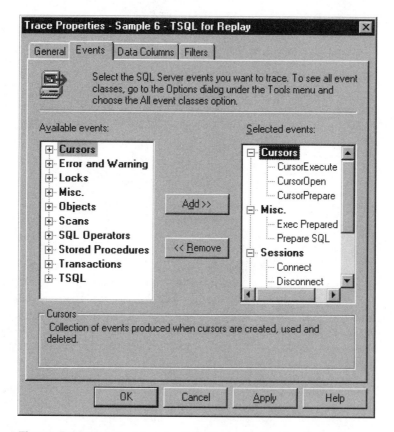

Figure 7-13 *The Events tab of the Trace Properties dialog box.*

The events available for monitoring are split into categories based on their general application within SQL Server. These categories are as follows:

- **Cursors** The trace events in this category are related to cursor processing, such as CursorOpen, CursorClose, CursorExecute, CursorPrepare, and CursorUnprepare. If you are interested in who is using what cursor and when, these events will tell you.

- **Error and Warning** These events display error and warning messages. Some of these events, such as ErrorLog and EventLog, display messages that are being written to their respective logs. Other events, such as Missing Column Statistics and Missing Join Predicate, are messages that are normally given to the user running the SQL statement.

- **Locks** The Locks events display information about lock problems that are occasionally experienced in SQL Server. The events are Locks:Deadlock and Locks:Deadlock Chain. If you have ever tried to debug deadlocks, you will really appreciate these trace events.

- **Misc**. The Misc. category includes various unrelated events, namely, Execute Prepared SQL, Execution Plan, Login Failed, Prepare SQL, Service Control, and Unprepare SQL. Of special use is the Execution Plan trace event, which shows you the execution plan of the SQL statements that are being run. Another useful trace event is Login Failed, which can be used to track failed login attempts.

- **Objects** The event traces in this cateogry allow you to monitor which database objects are being accessed and by whom. This trace category is made up of the Object:Closed, Object:Created, Object:Deleted, and Object:Opened events.

- **Scans** This category consists of the Scan:Started event, which gives information on table scans.

- **Sessions** The Sessions category is selected by default when a new trace is created. This category provides session information through the Connect, Disconnect, and ExistingConnection events.

- **SQL Operators** This trace category provides information on the various SQL operators that are being run. It is made up of the Delete, Insert, Select, and Update events.

- **Stored Procedures** The Stored Procedures category provides information on the use of stored procedures and is made up of the SP:Completed, SP:Starting, SP:StmtCompleted, and SP:StmtStarting trace events.

- **Transactions** This category allows you to collect transactional information and consists of the DTCTransaction and SQLTransaction events.

- **TSQL** This category contains traces related to T-SQL execution. It is made up of the RPC:Starting, RPC:Completed, SQL:BatchCompleted, SQL:BatchStarting, SQL:StmtCompleted, and SQL:StmtStarting events.

By selecting the best traces and collecting the most relevant information for your particular needs, you can tune your system quickly and effectively. Too little information will leave you without enough data to solve the problem. Too much information will overwhelm you and take an excessive amount of time to sift through.

Modifying the Data Columns

The next tab on the Trace Properties dialog box is the Data Columns tab (Figure 7-14). From this tab you can add or delete columns in a trace filter. The left side of this tab is the Unselected Data pane, and the right side is the Selected Data pane. By double-clicking or by using the Add and Remove buttons, you can move columns from one side to the other, thus selecting or deselecting those columns.

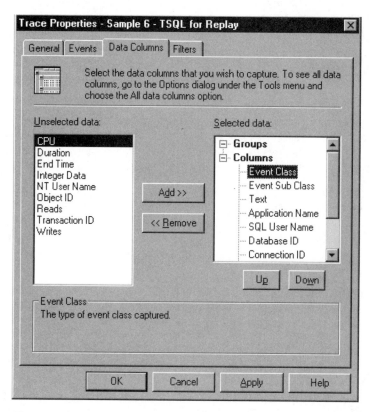

Figure 7-14 *The Data Columns tab of the Trace Properties dialog box.*

The choices within this tab allow you not only to select which columns are displayed for each event, but also to select how that data is sorted and grouped. These choices allow you to sort and group data in a manner that is most useful for your purposes.

The Selected Data side of the tab has two main branches into which data can be placed: Groups and Columns. The Groups branch is used to hold columns that you wish to group together. The Columns branch specifies the order of the selected columns. You can move a column up and down within a branch and between the Groups and Columns branches by selecting its name and clicking the Up and Down buttons.

Grouping is useful for separating specific data, such as NT User Name and SQL User Name. Such a separation is done in the TSQL (Grouped) predefined trace. Separating the data into groups can remove a lot of confusion. If you have ever used the SQL Server 6.5 Trace utility you will really appreciate this new feature.

Once the data has been grouped, it will then appear in columns in the order specified by the names in the Columns branch. This order can be modified to suit your own tastes. By creating a trace filter that is exactly what you need, additional analysis work can be minimized.

Further Filtering Trace Data

The next tab in the Trace Properties dialog box is the Filters tab (Figure 7-15). From this tab you can add filtering criteria to your event tracing. This is useful in a number of cases in which you wish to include or exclude events of specific types.

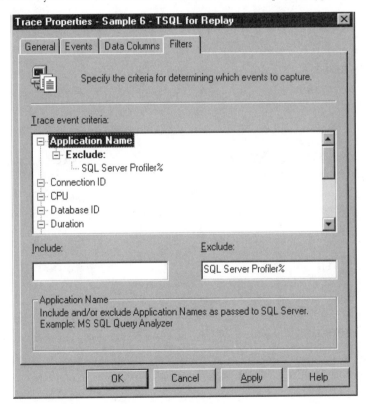

Figure 7-15 *The Filters tab of the Trace Properties dialog box.*

Items that can be added to a filter include the following:

- **Application Name** Allows you to specify which application to include or exclude from the trace. This is great if you wish to include the Profiler itself (excluded by default) or if you want to exclude the events generated by the SQL Server Agent.

- **Connection ID** Allows you to specify a connection ID that you want to trace. You can thus hone in on a specific job.

- **CPU** Allows you to specify the minimum and maximum amounts of time (in milliseconds) that a job must run in order to be logged in the Profiler.

- **Database ID** Allows you to specify the ID of the database that you want to monitor.

- **Duration** Allows you to specify the minimum and maximum amounts of elapsed time (in milliseconds) that the job must run in order to be considered a valid event. This is very useful if you are searching for those long-running jobs.

- **NT User Name** Allows you to specify a Windows NT user name to trace or to exclude from tracing.

- **Object ID** Allows you to specify one or more object IDs to monitor. You can also exclude system objects in this screen.

- **Reads** Allows you to specify a minimum and maximum number of logical reads that an event must have in order to be included in the trace. This option is useful for finding those resource-consuming jobs.

- **Server Name** Allows you to specify server names to include or exclude.

- **SQL User Names** Allows you to specify which SQL Server user names to include or exclude from tracing.

- **Text** Allows you to include or exclude events that contain a particular piece of text. This can be useful for specifying a specific table, or command to include, such as insert, update, delete. Multiple entries should be seperated by a ; (semicolon) and wildcards are designated by the % (percent sign).

- **Writes** Allows you to specify a minimum and maximum number of logical writes that an event must have in order to be included in the trace. This option is useful for finding those resource-consuming jobs.

As you can see, there is a great deal of additional filtering that you can apply to your traces. By adding filtering criteria it is possible to configure traces to find the specific events that you are looking for. Later in this chapter you will see how to generate specific trace filters based on specific tasks.

Creating Trace Filters

Creating your own trace filter is fairly straightforward. You can use either of two methods: manual creation or the Create Trace Wizard.

The Manual Method

To create a trace manually, select New and then Trace from the File menu. This action invokes the Trace Properties dialog box that you saw in the last section. The only difference is that this trace is starting out from scratch (see Figure 7-16). From the General tab, you will need to fill in the Trace Name list box and select whether this trace is private (trace data is only available to you) or shared (trace data is available to others).

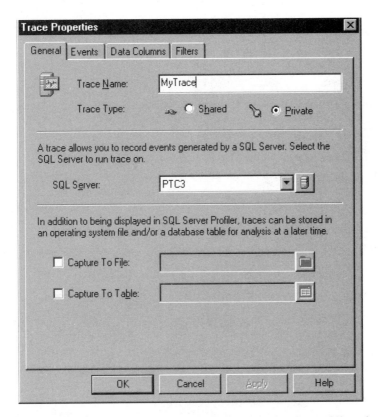

Figure 7-16 *The first step in creating a new trace is to fill in the General tab of the Trace Properties dialog box.*

Once you have selected a name for the trace, it is necessary to select events from the Events tab. When creating a new trace, you start out with only the default events (from the Sessions and TSQL groups) showing in this tab. In order to create the trace filter that suits your needs you should carefully select the events you want. We present some guidelines on event selection in the "Sample Scenarios" section.

Once you have selected all the events that you wish to capture, switch to the Data Columns tab. Here you can create the groups and select the column ordering that you wish to use. Grouping is important if you want to be able to distinguish events that have been generated by different users and different applications. The column order will help you distinguish between different events. Create the groups and column orders that make sense to you. After all, you are the one who has to interpret the data.

Once you have selected all the data columns, switch to the Filters tab. Depending on what your goals are for this trace filter, add filtering criteria as needed. For example, if your goal is to monitor a single application, filter for that application. Reducing the amount of data that is captured will make interpreting this data easier.

The Create Trace Wizard Method

In addition to creating trace filters manually you can easily create them using the Create Trace Wizard. The wizard is invoked by selecting Create Trace Wizard from the Tools menu. You will be greeted with the Welcome screen, as shown in Figure 7-17.

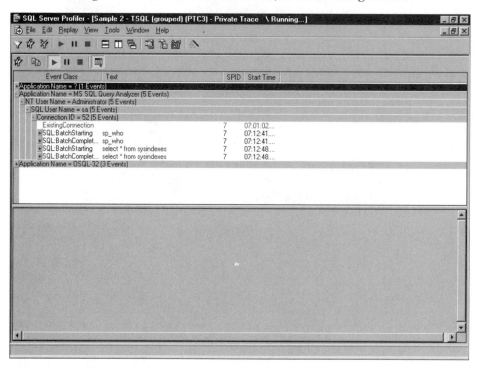

Figure 7-17 *The Create Trace Wizard's Welcome screen.*

Click the Next button to move to the Identify the Problem screen (Figure 7-18), where you have two options to set. The first is the name of the SQL Server that you want to run the trace against. By default this is the SQL Server to which you are currently connected. The second is a drop-down list that prompts you for the type of problem you wish to trace.

Selecting the drop-down list gives you a list of problems for which the wizard can create traces (see Figure 7-19). You can choose only one problem per trace. In SQL Server 7 the list is composed of the following choices:

- **Find the worst performing queries** If you choose this option you will be queried for the database name to be traced and the minimum duration of queries to be captured.
- **Identify scans of large tables** If you choose this option you will be queried for the database name to be traced and whether you want to capture trace data for all tables or only specific tables.
- **Identify the cause of a deadlock** If you choose this option you will be queried for the database name to be traced.

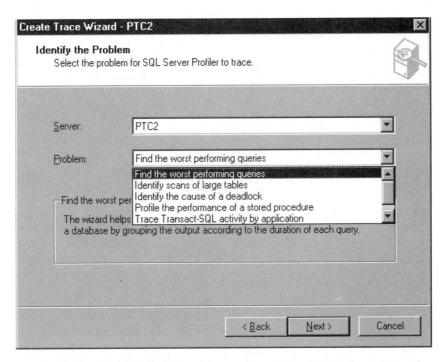

Figure 7-18 *The Identify the Problem screen of the Create Trace Wizard.*

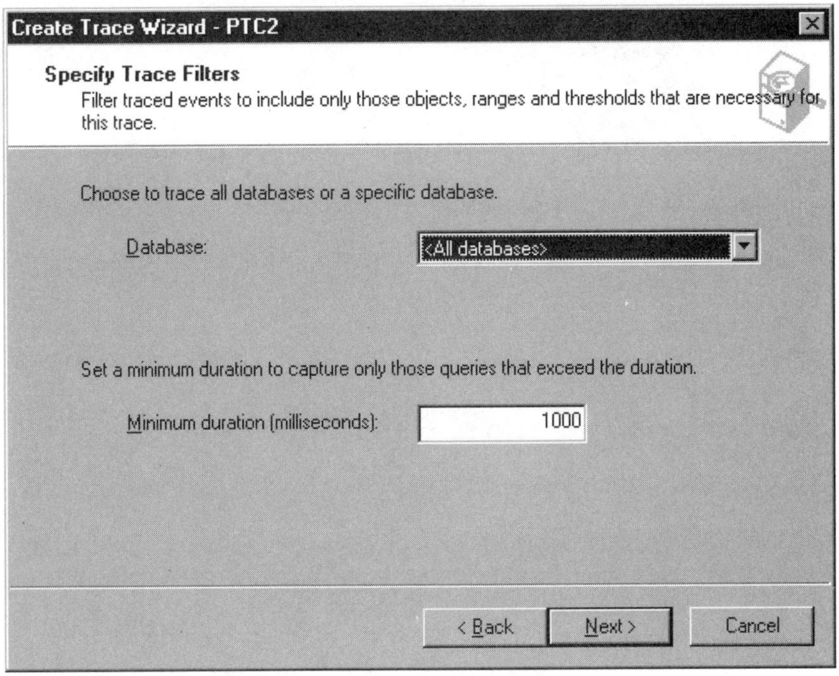

Figure 7-19 *The list of problems that the wizard can trace.*

- **Profile the performance of a stored procedure**   If you choose this option you will be queried for the database name to be traced and whether you want to trace all stored procedures or just specific ones.
- **Trace Transact-SQL activity by application**   If you choose this option you will be queried as to whether you want to trace all applications or only specific applications.
- **Trace Transact-SQL activity by user**   If you choose this option you will be queried as to whether you want to trace all users or specific users.

Once you have chosen the type of trace that you want to create, click the Next button to proceed to the Specify Trace Filters screen (see Figure 7-20). This screen will vary depending on what you selected in the previous step.

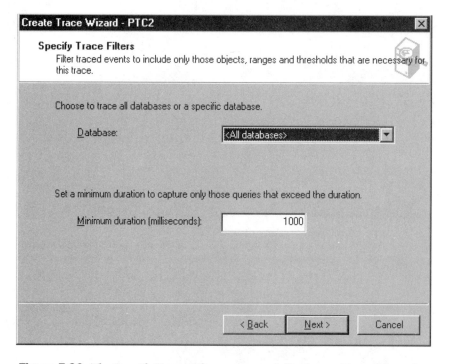

Figure 7-20 *The Specify Trace Filters screen of the Create Trace Wizard.*

You may see an additional Specify Trace Filters screen, depending on what you selected as the problem type. This additional screen is shown in Figure 7-21. This and allows you to specify further filtering.

Once you have finished selecting filters, the Completing the Create Trace Wizard page allows you to verify your choices before actually creating the trace. You also name the trace filter in this screen (see Figure 7-22).

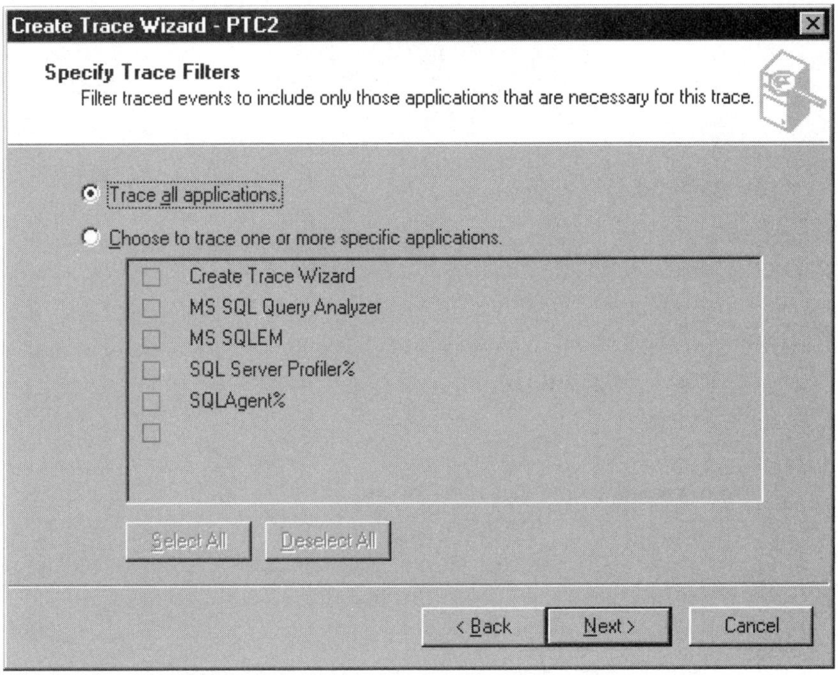

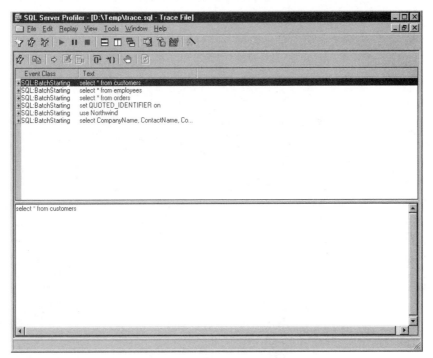

Figure 7-21 *The second Specify Trace Filters screen.*

Figure 7-22 *The Completing the Create Trace Wizard page.*

After you click the Finish button, the new trace is created and immediately starts running. The wizard is an easy way to create traces, but is somewhat inflexible. If you find that you can't create a trace you want using this method, remember that you can always take an existing trace filter and modify it for your own use.

Analyzing Profile Data

Analyzing profile data involves reading through page after page of saved data. This data can be quite voluminous. Therefore, any reduction of data that can be achieved through the Profiler's filtering capabilities will help.

The basics of analyzing and interpreting profile data involve understanding the data that your trace saved. Regardless of which event you trace, the information includes a set of data as specified in the Data Columns tab of the Trace Properties dialog box. This data contains information such as the following on connections, transactions, SQL statements, and stored procedures:

- **Type of event** What types of events occurred. Examples of events are the beginning or completion of SQL batches, and the establishment or termination of connections.
- **Connection information** Which user was connected, where that user was connected from, and details about the user connection.
- **Object information** What object was accessed during this operation.
- **SQL text** What the actual SQL statement executed was.
- **Resource information** How long the event took and how many resources were used during the event. This is the key information that is gathered by the Profiler.

Interpreting the data that is gathered by the Profiler is very important. Let's look at a list of the data that is gathered and what this information means. You can modify the properties of the trace and add or remove data columns depending on whether you want to view specific data. Some of these data columns are selected by default for all event classes. These default columns are highlighted in italics in the following list.

- *Application Name* The name of the client application that was used to run this specific event. Every connection to SQL Server must be via some sort of application. This information can help you track down an application that is using excessive resources.
- **Binary Data** The binary data is specific to the event class that is being monitored. With some events this data further specifies the event; for example, the binary data for Locks:Acquired displays the lock ID. In other cases the Binary Data column does not hold any information.
- *Connection ID* The ID that SQL Server has assigned to the connection. This number is assigned when the connection is established, and is released when the connection is dropped. Sometimes events are triggered by system processes. In that case a connection ID may not be present.
- *CPU* The amount of CPU time, in milliseconds, that was used by the event. This data could be either valuable or useless, depending on the event. Events such as ExistingConnection and Disconnect will sometimes show very high CPU values;

however, this data will not help you at all in terms of finding resource consumers because this value represents a cumulative CPU count for the connection rather than an individual measure of resource consumption by a particular SQL statement. In other cases, the CPU counter can be valuable.

- *Database ID* The ID of the database that is currently being used.
- *Duration* The amount of elapsed time, in milliseconds, for the event. This is useful for a high-level overview of system performance, since this represents the response time of the users (such as a user clicking a button).
- *End Time* The time that the event ended.
- *Event Class* The type of the event that is being shown.
- **Event Sub Class** The subtype of the event that is being shown.
- **Integer Data** Like the binary data, integer data is also specific to the event class that is being monitored. With some events this data further specifies the event. In other cases the Integer Data column does not hold any information.
- *NT User Name* The Windows NT or Windows 2000 user name.
- **Object ID** The ID of the object that has been accessed via this event.
- **Reads** The number of logical reads that have been performed by this event. This value does not represent the number of physical reads. The number of physical reads cannot be determined within the Profiler.
- *Server Name* The name of the SQL Server that is being traced.
- *SQL User Name* The SQL Server user name of the connection that has caused the event.
- **SPID** The server process ID of the process that has caused the event.
- Start Time The start time of the event. This column can be useful if you are tracing a certain event or set of events that caused performance degradation within a specific time frame. The Start Time and End Time columns can be used to locate specific events.
- **Text** The text value of the event (if applicable). This is the actual text of a SQL statement.
- **Transaction ID** The system-assigned transaction ID of the transaction that has initiated the event.
- **Writes** The number of logical writes that have been performed by this event. This value does not represent the number of physical writes. The number of physical writes cannot be determined within the Profiler.

Analyzing the profile data involves taking the information from these columns and extracting the data relevant for the type of work that you are doing. Selecting the best grouping for the columns can enhance your ability to interpret the data. You will start to get a better feel for using the Profiler in the next section, in which a few different scenarios are presented and the resulting data analyzed.

Sample Scenarios

This section provides some examples of how SQL Server Profiler can help you debug performance problems on your system or simply act as a SQL Server monitor. We hope that these scenarios give you a better idea of how to use this tool and give you some ideas for creating your own traces.

Looking for Long-Running SQL Statements

Long-running queries may be an indication of a poorly tuned system, a poorly written application, or simply a job that does a lot of work. In any case, finding and tuning these long-running SQL statements will improve the performance of that job, and perhaps the performance of the system in general, by relieving some of the processing load from the server.

Recommended Trace Events

The best way to find long-running queries is to use the following counters and to group by the Duration column.

- **TSQL, SQL:BatchCompleted** How long the execution of the SQL batch took to complete. This indicates the latency of the transaction step.
- **TSQL, RPC:Completed** When the remote procedure call has been completed. The duration value of this event will indicate how long the RPC has run.

This type of trace will be created if you select "Find the worst performing queries" in the Create Trace Wizard.

Looking for Resource Consumers

A trace that looks for applications or users that consume excessive resources can be a useful tool for the DBA. This type of trace should look at SQL statements that consume both CPU and I/O resources. Which one you are most concerned with will be determined by how your system is running.

Recommended Trace Events

The best way to find the excessive resource users is to select the following events to monitor, and group by either CPU, Reads, or Writes, depending on whether you are most concerned with I/O or CPU usage.

- **Sessions, Connect** The Connect event is useful for logging the time at which connections have been made to SQL Server and seeing how much resources the connections used.
- **Sessions, Disconnect** This event works in conjunction with the Connect event. Here you can track when sessions disconnect from SQL Server.
- **Sessions, *ExistingConnection*** This is useful for displaying connections that already exist when the Profiler is started.
- **TSQL, SQL:BatchCompleted** This event shows how long the SQL batch has taken to be completed. The CPU, Reads, and Writes data columns will indicate the resources used by this event.

- **TSQL, RPC:Starting** This will identify the beginning of the RPC. The CPU, Reads, and Writes data columns will indicate the resources used by this event.

This type of trace can help identify the heavy resource consumers and thereby give you a starting point for tuning the applications.

Using the Profiler to Detect Deadlocks

Depending on what your users are doing, deadlocks may or may not be a problem in your system. If many deadlocks are occurring, the problem can sometimes be severe. Therefore, identifying the cause of deadlocks can be essential to improving performance.

Recommended Trace Events

When using the Profiler to look for the cause of deadlocks, the following events, grouped by Event Class, should be included in the trace definition:

- **TSQL, RPC:Starting** The time the RPC began
- **TSQL, SQL:BatchStarting** The SQL batch that is running
- **Locks, Lock:Deadlock** The event of the deadlock itself
- **Locks, Lock:Deadlock Chain** The sequence of events leading up to the deadlock

By being able to identify the cause of the deadlocks in the system you will better be able to solve the problem. This type of trace will be created if you select "Identify the cause of a deadlock" in the Create Trace Wizard.

Using the Profiler as a System Log

In addition to using SQL Server Profiler as a debug tool for solving specific problems, you can use it to monitor and record general SQL Server usage. When using SQL Server Profiler as a system log, it is often better to save the data to a database table rather than a file because you can create stored procedures or SQL statements to more effectively query the data when it is in a table.

In order to set up the Profiler to act as a system monitor you must think about which events you want to monitor. These events will provide information that you can later use to determine system activity.

Recommended Trace Events

When using the Profiler as a system monitor the following events should be included in the trace definition:

- **Sessions, Connect** The Connect event is useful for logging the time at which each connection has been made to SQL Server. This can give you a good idea when activity begins on the system. It is also useful for finding connections that constantly are reconnecting or those that never disconnect.

- **Sessions, Disconnect** This event works in conjunction with the Connect event. Here you can track when sessions disconnect from SQL Server.
- **Sessions, ExistingConnection** This is useful for displaying those connections that already exist when the Profiler is started.
- **Error and Warning, ErrorLog** It is always a good idea when using the Profiler as a system monitor to include messages that go into the error log.
- **Error and Warning, EventLog** It is also a good idea to include messages that go into the event log.
- **Misc., LoginFailed** The LoginFailed event will alert you to excessive failed login attempts that could indicate a security problem.

Under normal conditions this type of trace will not consume excessive system resources and is safe to run continuously.

Debugging SQL Statements

In addition to tracing events within SQL Server, the Profiler can debug transactions or stored procedures by capturing and replaying SQL statements. You can replay SQL statements in single steps, as within a debugger, and analyze the individual steps. The function of the Profiler is similar to that of other Microsoft development tools. This section provides a brief overview of how to capture and replay SQL statements and how to single-step through those statements.

Capture and Replay

If you have access to the stored procedure or application source code that you want to debug, it is not really necessary to capture the SQL statements. However, often it is difficult to determine exactly what variables are being passed to the stored procedure or which path is being taken within a stored procedure. In these cases, as well as when the application in question is proprietary and source code is not available, it is necessary to capture the SQL statements within SQL Server Profiler.

You can use any of the predefined trace definitions to capture a SQL statement, or create your own definition. Note that the TSQL events SQL:BatchStarting and RPC:Starting must be present in order to capture enough information to save and replay SQL scripts.

Single-Stepping

Once you have captured a SQL script (or you have a SQL script that has been written for your application), it is a simple matter to run it. When you open the SQL script, the controls available within SQL Server Profiler change; icons and controls for running the SQL statements become visible (see Figure 7-23).

Initially, the Profiler will have two frames open within it. The top frame contains the event and text, and the lower frame contains the SQL statements. You can click on an event in

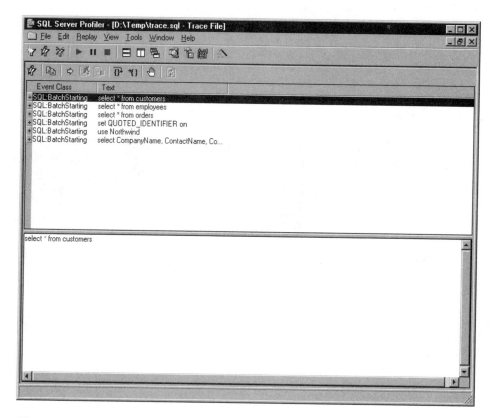

Figure 7-23 *Running a SQL script.*

order to view the entire SQL statement, or you can expand the event by clicking on the + icon next to the event. Once you start running the SQL statements, a third frame containing the results of the steps will appear, as shown in Figure 7-24 (on the next page).

From here it is an easy matter to single-step through the stored procedure or SQL statements. If conditionals are used, you will be able to view the path that was taken and see the values that have been assigned to variables. This allows you to easily debug complex SQL statements and stored procedures by seeing what is happening while they are running.

In addition to single-stepping through the stored procedure, you have the ability within the Profiler to set breakpoints. Thus, the Profiler allows you to perform the following actions with SQL scripts or stored procedures:

- **Run** You can run the entire SQL script.

- **Run to breakpoint** By setting breakpoints in certain areas you can avoid having to single-step through the entire file.

- **Single-stepping** You can run SQL statements one at a time.

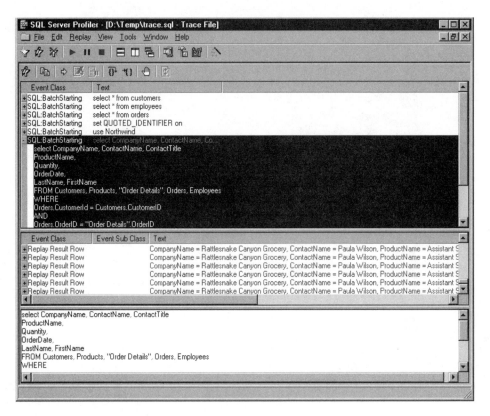

Figure 7-24 *Single-stepping through a SQL script.*

- **Run to cursor** By simply clicking on an event, you can run to where the cursor is currently pointing.
- **Pause execution** You can momentarily pause execution of SQL statements (by hitting the Pause Traces button) and then resume as needed.
- **Stop execution** You can stop execution at any time and resume at a later time.

The Profiler thus provides many of the same features you will find in a debugger. These features allow you a lot of flexibility and ease of use in debugging problem stored procedures or SQL statements.

Summary

This chapter has provided an overview of SQL Server Profiler, one tool that can be used to help determine what the performance problem is, which is a task that may be as difficult—or more difficult—than actually solving the problem. SQL Server Profiler is a powerful tool for this task and can be used in conjunction with other tools and methods that you will learn about in this book.

To become proficient at using the Profiler you should take the time to experiment with it. Create your own trace filters or use the predefined filters and see how they work. Then analyze the trace data and see what types of information it provides. By practicing you will become more comfortable with the Profiler and your skills will improve.

Part II
Sizing and Capacity Planning

Chapter 8
Modeling for Sizing and Capacity Planning

A *model* is a mathematical construct used to understand a physical system to which it is analogous. This chapter examines the principles and variables involved in modeling system capacity. First, however, we provide some background on capacity planning itself.

Introduction to Sizing and Capacity Planning

The discipline of capacity planning is usually thought of as having two forms: preconfiguration capacity planning and postconfiguration capacity planning.

Preconfiguration Capacity Planning

Preconfiguration capacity planning, or *sizing*, involves anticipating the hardware requirements necessary to process your workload within a specified time, as spelled out in either the service level agreements (SLAs) or other such agreements.

SLAs are the most common form of agreement used to establish the conditions of operation as agreed to by all organizations involved in the operation and performance of the system in question. The SLAs are outlined as a result of meetings among these groups to ensure performance and smooth operation of the system. An example of an SLA would be to specify that the workload item or transaction in question should execute within a certain response time, say, 5 seconds. Another example is that no more than 85 percent of memory will ever be used, leaving 15 percent free space at any time so that page faulting won't get out of hand. Such specifications are agreed upon by the users, the operations group, the applications analysts, and the performance group (and also persons responsible for capacity planning, if a separate capacity planning group does not exist) to ensure that the agreed upon conditions are always met. If a violation is recorded, it usually means that a failure or overload of a resource has taken place somewhere in the system.

In preconfiguration capacity planning, there is usually no real performance data to work with since the system has not yet been designed, so you must use whatever other information is available. Results will vary depending on the accuracy of this information.

Postconfiguration Capacity Planning

Postconfiguration capacity planning is a complex and ongoing performance study of hardware and software resource consumption on a system that is already set up and processing. You perform postconfiguration capacity planning so that your organization can adequately prepare for workload growth in relation to system resources. These studies are primarily established to provide capacity data to the system manager, DBA, and operations manager pertaining to their system's growth. These persons use this data to justify system alterations designed to maintain the level of system performance defined in the SLAs.

Capacity planning studies offer other highly useful features, including the ability to perform predictive analysis on the historic data to project where the system's capacity is heading. The capacity planner can also project "what if" scenarios (predictive analysis) on workloads. In a common postconfiguration capacity planning study scenario, you perform the analysis using historical performance data stored in a database. Through this analysis, you can project trends in the normal growth of CPU utilization (the amount of time a CPU is busy during an observation period), disk usage, memory usage, and network usage. You will also be able to project sudden rises in CPU, disk, and memory utilization caused by the addition of new users onto the system. These studies can be extremely detailed and can involve profiling the activities of specific users or types of users (such as accounts payable personnel) to predict exactly what kind of resource consumption would take place if you added these users and workload. This predictive analysis gives the system manager ample time to obtain the necessary hardware before the new users are added to the system, thus averting any degradation of system performance or response time.

You can also obtain tuning information through postconfiguration capacity planning studies. For example, adding users will result in more database table accesses. The number of tables that users access, and how often they access them, can be monitored and tracked. This information can be useful in determining whether relocating some of these tables to different disk drive arrays will prevent a potential bottleneck in the disk subsystem. In this and the following three chapters, we look at how to perform both types of capacity planning functions and examine their similarities and differences.

History of Capacity Planning, Benchmarking, and Simulations

In the early years of multiple-user computers, the concepts of capacity planning and performance were not widely understood or developed and were mostly the province of consulting firms who specialized in the field. By the early 1970s, a sizing project for such a firm consisted of finding customers who were running an application that "ran like" the target customer application. Finding these customers was difficult, and matching companies or organizations and their application use was even more challenging.

Emergence of System Simulation and Benchmarking

In the mid-1970s, customers and application suppliers developed an analysis methodology that consisted of running a specific benchmark or workload to guess at the optimal initial size of a machine. This process involved building an application similar to that of the customer in question and running it on similar hardware to gather performance statistics. These statistics were then used to determine the best size machine to meet the customer's needs. This process also enabled "what if" scenarios to be run with the benchmark to determine what size machine would be required if more users, application processes, or data were added to the system. The one drawback to this process was its expense. The early benchmarks, originally developed to simulate customers' usage patterns, began to be used mostly by system vendors as marketing tools to sell systems and to compare the relative performance of competing hardware offerings.

During this period, analysts were developing methods of predicting usage of resources on an existing system. On the surface, this process seemed less challenging than preconfiguration capacity planning, but it proved to be just as difficult because tested methodologies did not exist, nor were there tools available to collect the necessary data. Scientists such as Dr. Jeffrey Buzen, a pioneer in capacity planning, were still developing theories on usage and determining how to perform calculations to model usage.

Evolution of Benchmarking Standards

By the 1980s, the early benchmark simulations had evolved into standard benchmark loads, such as the ST1 benchmark, the TP1 benchmark, and the Debit/Credit benchmark, but the emphasis was on finding the fastest-performing hardware for promotional usage instead of on developing a standard application workload that could be used to size and maintain systems. Customers still could not use these benchmark offerings for system hardware comparisons because their situations were different. Customer demand led to the formation of a computer industry consortium, the Transaction Processing Performance Council. The council specified standardized transaction loads for over 45 hardware and software manufacturers. These benchmarks could often show the relative capabilities of hardware and database software; unfortunately, they were not useful for sizing an application workload.

At the same time, client/server computing and the use of relational database technology was maturing, and the need for predicting the initial size of a system and its capacity maintenance requirements was growing. Most modern applications are now written based on client/server architecture. Servers are typically used as central data storage devices, and the user interface is primarily run locally on a desktop machine or on a remote Web site. This cost-effective strategy for using expensive server processing power takes advantage of the GUIs to which customers are accustomed. Because servers running database applications are heavily utilized, these servers are now the focus for most sizing projects and capacity planning studies.

Sizing and Capacity Planning for Small to Average-Size Systems

To date, the application simulation benchmark remains the most common method for sizing servers, and the collection of historical performance data and the use of capacity planning techniques on this data are still the most accurate ways of predicting the future use of a machine. Although the process is expensive and time-consuming, organizations can achieve a fairly significant degree of accuracy if they simulate the exact usage of the server. However, because large projects may require a multimillion-dollar investment on the part of the organization or the system vendor, only the largest organizations can usually gain access to systems for this kind of testing. Clearly a method is required to perform in-depth, accurate system sizing and capacity planning for small to average-size systems. For such systems, some easy calculations and a general knowledge of system usage are all you need to be able to size and predict the usage of a system to within 10 percent accuracy. The method and calculations for the procedure will be covered in this chapter and in Chapters 9, 10, and 11.

Modeling Principles for Sizing and Capacity Planning

Like any structured science, capacity planning has rules that must be adhered to. In this section we look at the rules that govern the maximum allowable values of some parameters, such as CPU utilization and queue length, that affect the performance of a system. We use the knee of the curve theory to model these parameters.

Queuing Theory and the Knee of the Curve

Queuing theory states that utilization has a direct effect on queues, and because queues are directly related to response time (in fact, queue length is part of the response time equation), utilization thus has a direct effect on response time.

Consider the following analogy. Suppose you go to the supermarket at 3:00 A.M. You pick up the items you require and then go to the cashier for checkout. At this time in the morning there is no one in front of you, so the utilization of that cashier is 0 percent and the queue length (objects, or in this case people, in front of you) is also 0. Your response time for completing the shopping transaction will be equal to your service time because there is no one in front of you. This means that your service time (in this case the time it takes you to complete the transaction of being checked out and paying for the groceries) is all the time it will take you to complete this task.

Now consider this scenario at 5:00 P.M., a much busier time for a supermarket. You come to that same cashier, only now there are eight people in front of you. Your response time for completing the shopping transaction now is equal to the sum of individual service times of all the people in front of you (some people have three items to check out, whereas others have many more items) plus your own service time. In the second case the utilization of the cashier was much higher at 5:00 P.M. than at 3:00 A.M., which had a direct effect on queues and therefore on your overall wait or response time.

When we look at computer systems, we find that a CPU whose utilization in a steady state is above 75 percent has drawbacks. Such a CPU will cause queues to grow exponentially. From the performance perspective, we much prefer *linear growth*, or the even, incremental growth of utilization, as shown in Figure 8-1.

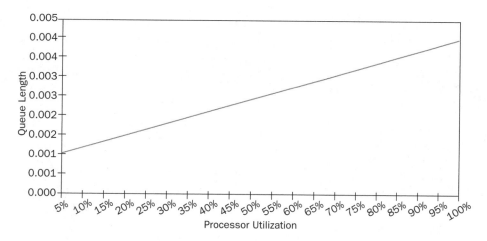

Figure 8-1 *Graph of linear utilization growth.*

This even, incremental growth does not take place in CPUs with utilization factors over 75 percent. In such a system, a point is reached at which the growth becomes *exponential*, rising geometrically and straight up to infinity. The point at which this occurs is known as the *asymptotic* point or the *knee of the curve*. Figure 8-2 depicts this type of growth. Notice that at about 75 percent utilization the curve that indicates the growth of the queue length goes from linear growth to asymptotic growth (or growth that appears on the graph to go straight up).

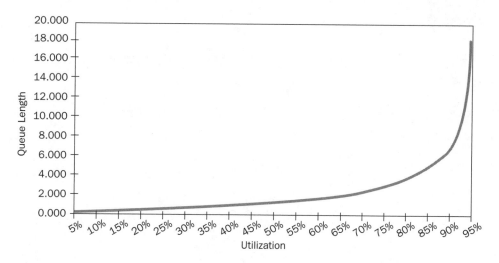

Figure 8-2 *Graph of exponential queue length vs. utilization growth.*

Figure 8-3 illustrates that utilization has a direct effect on the response time. Notice that the curve in this graph is the same as that in the queue length graph. This is why you never want to run your CPUs in a steady state of over 75 percent utilization. This is not to say that you can never run your CPUs above 75 percent utilization for short periods of time, but the longer you do, the more negative impact you will see in terms of queue lengths and response time. The relationship among utilization, queuing length, and response time is one of the most important ones of sizing and should be considered when selecting the number and size of CPUs your system will require.

For example, assume that you are sizing a system. During this sizing you calculate that your system will produce anticipated total processor utilization factors of 180 percent. It would be better to buy three CPUs that will run at about 60 percent, keeping the utilization 15 percent under the knee of the curve, than to have two CPUs running at about 90 percent, which would make the utilization 15 percent over the knee of the curve.

The knee of the curve principle also applies to other facets of your system, such as disks, although these components do not have the same knee of the curve as processors. The knee of the curve for disks tends to be at 85 percent utilization, as opposed to 75 percent for processors. This utilization figure applies to the size and I/O capability of the disk drive in question. For example, a 9-GB disk should not store more than 7.6 GB of data at any given time. Observing this limit will allow for growth and, more important, will help keep down response times. A disk that is at full capacity will have longer seek times, therefore adding to your overall response time.

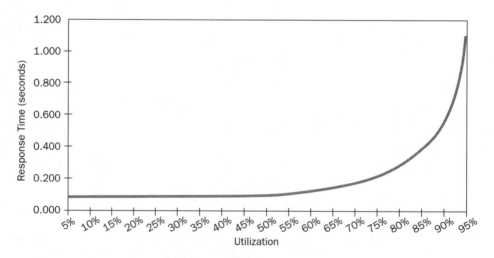

Figure 8-3 *Graph of response time vs. utilization growth.*

By the same principle, if a disk drive has an I/O capability of 70 I/Os per second, you would not want to have a constant I/O arrival rate of more than 60 I/Os per second in a steady state of operation. By following this principle you can minimize your overall response times because you will not enter a situation of using your processors or disks at maximum utilization. You will thus get the most out of your system and will have a reserve capacity for peak utilization periods.

Atomic Demand Modeling and Queue Modeling

A model of a computer system is simply a group of equations that calculate the utilization of certain parts of the system (CPU or disk) and other statistics. These equations yield information that is useful for maintaining a well-running system. *Atomic demand modeling* is the technique of identifying elements of a system and performing calculations on those components to produce statistics such as CPU utilization, that show the demand on each resource that is used in a workload. It is called *atomic* demand because it separates each part of the workload to find each component's statistics. This means that each part or component has a separate set of equations that produces statistics for that component.

When you group resources together to perform certain functions, you form a *service chain*. Modeling a service chain is known as *queue modeling*. Consider that a transaction involves not only a database, but also many different machines such as a client, network, and other servers, all of which have components such as CPUs, memory, and disks that the transaction might use. All these resources can be broken down to their respective components and then modeled.

Service Chains

A *service chains* is a collection of resources that are used in the processing of a transaction or service. One can see the importance of understanding service chains in relation to response times because the total response time is the sum of all the service times in the service chain. Indeed, SLAs cannot exist without identifying and observing the service chain. When a transaction is requested, and the response time of that transaction exceeds the time agreed to in an SLA, it is very important that all resources involved in processing the transaction come under close scrutiny and performance observation. In this way the system management staff will have advance notification of any failures that will result in violation of an SLA.

The first thing a system manager must do is identify the components of the service chain. Figure 8-4 illustrates a typical service chain. In this example, the workload flow starts at the client, then proceeds through the network, then through a network router to the server (which could be an application server), then to the database server, where the desired information is retrieved; finally, the information is sent back to the client via the reverse path. The complete response time for this transaction is the sum of all the service times of the individual components of the service chain during the round-trip.

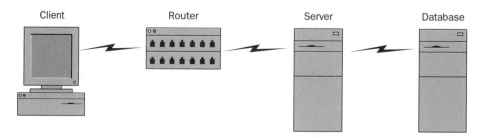

Figure 8-4   *A typical service chain.*

After identifying these components, the system manager should arrange to have them monitored by the Performance Monitor and should also collect historic performance data to produce capacity planning reports on their activities. In this way the system manager can be kept aware of any increases in activity that may violate certain service level agreements. The historic performance data can be used to predict trends that show growth and thus can alert the system management staff as to when the system will need additional resources to maintain the service level agreements.

Mathematics for Modeling

You will begin to understand a system's workload when you can see what kinds of events take place during execution. The effects of execution can be revealed and understood by the statistics that you gather on the various components. These statistics are the results of calculations that are performed by the Performance Monitor's report generator or by a spreadsheet that a performance analyst uses to track capacity. This section discusses the types of statistics that are gathered and how to interpret them.

Understanding the Basic Model Set

You begin the job of modeling system capacity by gathering certain information on the system in the form of independent variables. *Independent variables* are inputs to equations that calculate system statistics such as CPU utilization or CPU queue length. These inputs are not usually calculated but instead are either directly selected by the user or returned to the user by a reporting mechanism such as the Performance Monitor.

The three independent variables for the basic model of system capacity are observation time (T), busy time (B), and completions (C). Observation time (the amount of time the system is observed) is selected by the analyst performing the study. Busy time (the time the system was active during the observation period) is returned to the user by the monitoring mechanism. Completions (the number of transactions that were completed during the observation period) is a value returned to the analyst by a transaction monitor.

With just these three independent variables, you can calculate the six different dependent variables of the basic model. A *dependent variable* is the result of a calculation that is either directly or indirectly dependent on the independent variables.

Given the values of the three independent variables, you can calculate the following information:

The utilization of the CPU	$U = B / T$
The transaction throughput of the system	$X = C / T$
The average resource service time	$S = B / C$
The transaction capacity of the system	$Cp = 1 / S$
The average resource queue length	$Q = U / (1 - U)$
The average resource response time	$R = (Q * S) + S$

Now that you understand the equations, let's look at the vital statistics that can be gathered using the three independent variables. Figure 8-5 provides an example of such data. The independent variables in this example are as follows: we observed the system for 43 seconds (T), during which there were 96 completed transactions (C), and the system was actually busy processing the workload for 31 seconds (B). From this information we can calculate that the utilization (U) was at 72.09 percent, and the average transaction throughput (X) was 2.23 per second. The average service time for these transactions (S) was 0.32 second, and the average system queue length (Q) was 2.58. Transactions were completed in an average time of 1.15 seconds (R), and the system capacity (Cp) was 3.125 transactions per second. A quick analysis of these values would indicate that the CPU utilization was just under the recommended maximum value based on the knee of the curve model.

```
T = 43 Seconds

C = 96 Seconds

B = 31 Seconds

U = 31/43 = 72.09% util
X = 96/43 = 2.23 trans per sec
S = 31/96 = .32 sec
Q = .7209/.2791 = avg q 2.58
R = (2.58 * .32) + .32 = 1.15 sec
Cp = 1/.32 = 3.125 trans per sec
```

Figure 8-5   *An example of calculating system statistics.*

The Utilization Law

There are two ways to calculate the percentage of utilization. We saw the first method earlier, namely, the equation $U = B / T$. Because not all performance monitors return the time in seconds that a CPU was busy, there is another way to determine utilization. We can derive this law algebraically, as follows:

*Utilization = Throughput * Service*

This equation is known as the *utilization law*.

If we apply the utilization law and use the values calculated in Figure 8-5, we can derive the value for utilization as follows:

$$U = X * S$$

$$B / T = (C / T) * (B / C)$$

$$31/43 = (96/43) * (31/96)$$

$$0.72093 = 2.23256 * 0.32292$$

$$0.72093 = 0.72093$$

$$72.09\% = 72.09\%$$

As you can see, the derivation $B / T = (C / T) * (B / C)$ is depicted, proving that the utilization law calculation $U = X * S$ produces the same results as the utilization equation $U = B / T$. Plugging in the values from Figure 8-5, this derivation is as follows:

$U = B / T$, or 31 busy seconds / 43 observed seconds

$X = C / T$, or 96 transactions completed / 43 observed seconds

$S = B/ C$, or 31 busy seconds / 96 transactions completed

Both sides of the equation yield the same result: 72.09 percent utilization.

Arrival Rates and Queues

The arrival rate (Ar) is another independent variable that an analyst might find useful. This value can reveal queue sites within a system or service chain. Let the variable A equal the number of arrivals per second at a resource site. Then the equation for arrival rate is as follows:

$$Ar = A / T$$

Suppose that we have 96 transactions arriving at a resource site per second, a 43-second observation period, and a throughput of 2.32. We calculate the arrival rate as follows:

$$Ar = 96 / 43 = 2.23 \; arrivals \; per \; second$$

We thus find that the arrivals are equal to the throughput of 2.23 per second. Figure 8-6 shows the arrival rate vs. throughput rate for this system. Because the arrival rate for this system is the same as the throughput, queues will not accumulate at this site.

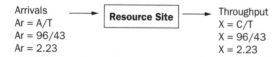

Figure 8-6 *Arrival rate and throughput rate for an example system.*

On the other hand, if transactions were delivered in batches at the arrival rate of 125 arrivals per second (and the original completion value of 96 was maintained), the model would give us these results:

$$Ar = 125 / 43, \text{ or } 2.91 \text{ per second}$$

$$X = 96 / 43, \text{ or } 2.23 \text{ per second}$$

$$Ar - X = 2.91 - 2.23 = 0.68$$

In this example there is a queue buildup of 0.68 transaction overlap per second. This simple study mathematically reveals a queue site so that proper action can be taken.

End-to-End Response Time

So far we have discussed the model of an individual system's resources. We can now begin to assemble a larger, multitier model. When we consider response time, we do not think in terms of the single site's response time but of all the resources that make up the service chain for that transaction. So the first step in determining end-to-end response time is identifying the components that make up the service chain.

One way to determine this would be to list or draw the service chain to find all the resource sites of a transaction. For example, assume that there is a client machine, a network, an application server, and a database server. You could designate these components as follows (see Figure 8-7 on the next page): Transaction = new transaction, Client = client machine, Network1 = the network over which this load is traveling to the application server, ApServ = application server, Network2 = the network over which this load is traveling to the database server, and DbServ = database server.

After you identify the service chain, you execute a performance measurement in order to retrieve the values of the independent variables. When this has been accomplished you can then determine the end-to-end response time for the transaction. The complete response equation is as follows (the Σ symbol indicates summation):

$$R = \Sigma \, Ri = \Sigma \, [(Q_i * S_i) + S_i]$$

Figure 8-7 depicts the conceptual path that the data in our hypothetical service chain takes to complete a transaction. The transaction starts off at the client machine, which is running a 0.861-second response time. The execution path travels through Network1, to the application server, then through Network2 until it reaches the database server. The request is not yet satisfied. After the data is retrieved, it must then travel back through Network2 to the application server for further processing and formatting, through Network1, and finally back to the client machine.

Now you can calculate the end-to-end response time for this transaction:

$$R_{\text{Client}} = (3.1 * 0.21) + 0.21 = 0.861$$

$$R_{\text{Network1}} = (1.23 * 0.023) + 0.023 = 0.05$$

$$R_{\text{ApServ}} = (2.8 * 0.43) + 0.43 = 1.634$$

$$R_{\text{Network2}} = (2.56 * 0.034) + 0.034 = 0.121$$

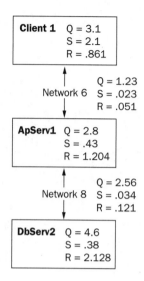

Figure 8-7 *A service chain and the computation of the end-to-end response time.*

$$R_{DbServ} = (4.6 * 0.38) + 0.38 = 2.128$$

$$(Ri = R_{Client} + R_{Network1} + R_{ApServ} + R_{Network2} + R_{DbServ} + R_{Network2} + R_{ApServ} + R_{Network1} = 6.599$$

The total end-to-end response time is thus 6.599 seconds. If this transaction were under a service level agreement, the SLA should be set at 8 seconds, giving the management team a 1.4-second margin of safety.

The next thing you do is establish the model with the above numbers, knowing at that point that the response time will be 6.599 seconds for the service chain. After this is done, you need to identify a performance monitoring configuration to measure the service chain and to set alert thresholds at the various model values (for example, Client queue length greater than 3.1, or ApServ service time greater than 0.43). If these values are exceeded, you will know that an SLA has been violated and where the problem is located.

Developing a Conceptual Model

We are now ready to develop a basic conceptual model of a service chain for a transaction. Remember that not all transactions or workloads need to be profiled in this manner, but certainly the transactions that are under SLAs should. If you are intending to use this information for determining the capacity of critical systems, then these workloads should also be profiled. An example of this conceptual model report is shown in Figure 8-8.

In this figure you can see how a conceptual model of a service chain is developed. The information derived from it is valuable for understanding the present usage and for forecasting future usage. The statistics in Figure 8-8 tell us that the client machine is overuti-

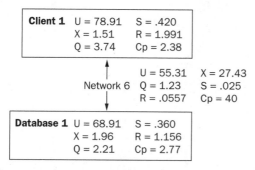

Figure 8-8   *The conceptual service chain model.*

lized and has high queue lengths. This indicates that there is not much room for future growth on this machine. At $U = 68.91$, the database server has some room for growth in CPU utilization; however, the queue length is 2.21, which is over the limit and may indicate performance problems. Network1 has a sufficient reserve capacity. At this point the managing staff must decide whether the queue length on the database server will cause unacceptable response times for users or violate SLAs.

Remember that this is a conceptual view of a record for a service chain within a performance database. We recommend that you collect this data on a regular basis, at an interval of one record per day. With this data you can report on how the individual system or service chain is growing, and can predict how the machine will be performing in the future. You can even perform "what if" sizing scenarios on this data to see what will happen to the system if you add more transaction completions to each segment in order to model the effects that additional users would have on the system.

Summary

This chapter covered the basic concepts and techniques of system modeling. With this basic information, you can perform capacity planning for systems within a service chain. Understanding the basic model is essential for preconfiguration capacity planning. The principles presented in this chapter, such as the knee of the curve theory, govern the sizing process. In the next chapter we will see how these principles affect the number of CPUs, the number of disks, and the amount of memory needed to process your workload in an acceptable time frame while allowing for additional growth and maintaining SLAs.

More Info: For additional reading on advanced modeling topics, see *Probability, Statistics, and Queueing Theory* by Arnold O. Allen (Boston: Academic Press, 1990).

Chapter 9
Sizing the Database and Application Servers

The most important phase of any system's development is the preconfiguration planning. Many systems turn into maintenance nightmares because the sizing phase of the development was either overlooked or performed haphazardly. All the tuning in the world won't solve your problems if the hardware is inadequate to perform the task. This chapter discusses the factors to consider when sizing your system so that you can avoid this fate.

Preconfiguration Capacity Planning

The area of capacity planning known as preconfiguration capacity planning has many facets. Memory, disks, and CPUs are usually the focal points for this planning, but there is more to consider. How will the system be configured in terms of disk fault tolerance? Will this system have a database residing on it? Will the application reside on this main system, or will the application reside on another system?

Any sizing scenario must ask this basic question: how will the system be used? There are many types of workloads. For example, many information systems retrieve data but don't allow writing data to the database interactively. These systems update the database in a batch mode. Some systems that are interactive, on the other hand, might do as many writes as they do reads to the database. Deciding what a system will be doing will certainly result in vastly different configurations based on the expected workload. This section covers the factors to be considered in any basic preconfiguration capacity planning.

Transaction Processing Types

One of the first things to decide is what type of system you will need based on the workload type. This is usually answered by determining what type of transaction is being processed. For example, consider a server that performs only database functions; in terms of its workload, we need to consider only reads and writes. In fact, any transaction can be broken down into database or file reads and writes. When a SELECT or an UPDATE statement is executed, the database server interprets the statement as a series of read and write operations. Broken down to this atomic level, a database server mostly processes I/Os. You thus should select a system that can handle both the type and volume of transactions you expect, and the I/Os those transactions will generate. In contrast, if a system is going to perform application functions such as accounts payable, it is not concerned as much with the retrieval of the basic information as it is with what it does with the data once it gets it.

These two systems would have different configuration requirements for carrying out their respective tasks. The database server would have a large data farm in which to store the data and carry out I/O functions; the application server, on the other hand, would not need this data storage capacity.

In either case the sizing question that needs to be resolved is what type of transaction will be processed. The two main transaction types are online transaction processing and decision support.

Online Transaction Processing (OLAP)

The OLTP transaction is a workload unit that is usually expected to run in a short period of time because it deals with the database in real time or in online mode. In other words, many of these transactions update the database constantly, based on the most current information available, so that the next user can rely on that information being current. For example, in an order entry system, all the information pertaining to inventory is kept in tables spread across a disk system, and the database is on line. Any user has access to the database information. Database tables, such as *Item Table* or *Stock_Level_Table*, need to have the most current information on the types and quantity of the items that are sold. When an order for a certain quantity of a specific item is received, you can thus access the database tables to find out whether the item is available, and the quantity of the item in stock, to prevent overselling of an item.

Decision Support

The second type of transaction is decision support. Such a transaction is usually complex and read intensive. Little writing to the database occurs. A decision support system (DSS) usually provides information to management staff to help them make business decisions—for example, decisions about business growth, levels of stock on hand, and so on. The U.S. Air Force uses a DSS to inform high-level personnel about the current status, location, and weaponry of its jet fighters, bombers, and personnel. A system such as this needs certain characteristics, such as massive processor power and usually a large database capacity.

Unlike an OLTP system, a DSS limits the time spent processing requests rather than limiting processor utilization. Indeed, most DSS queries will utilize a processor at 100 percent until query completion. In an OLTP system, throughput of transactions is commonly measured in transactions per second (TPS) or transactions per minute (TPM), but in DSS processing, throughput is usually measured in queries per hour (QPH). Decison support stresses completing as many whole queries as possible, whereas OLTP stresses completing as many transactions as possible—without regard to how many queries are actually completed. The same principles of configuration apply to both OLTP and DSS processing: you don't want to overload the system in terms of size or I/O.

Peak Utilization vs. Steady-State Processing

A major consideration of sizing is the time frame for processing requests. During a typical sizing session, the analyst will eventually come across the time frame or duration of processing, which is not to be confused with the response times of individual transactions. Rather, it is the amount of time during the day, week, or even the year that processing times are the slowest. Peak utilization is when utilization of the machine and its various components is at the maximum.

As an example, let's walk through a sizing scenario of an automatic teller machine (ATM) system. During the planning session the information needed is mainly how many transactions will be processed, what these transactions consist of in terms of reads and writes, and how long the system is processing them. Figure 9.1 shows the arrival rate of transactions at a popular bank's ATM, graphed over a 24-hour period. Notice the uneven arrival rates, which are indicative of OLTP transactions. In this case let's say that a total of 250,000 transactions will be completed during a working day (which is 24 hours), and 150,000 of them will be taking place during the hours of 11:00 A.M. and 2:00 P.M. (during most people's lunch break), representing the peak utilization period for that day.

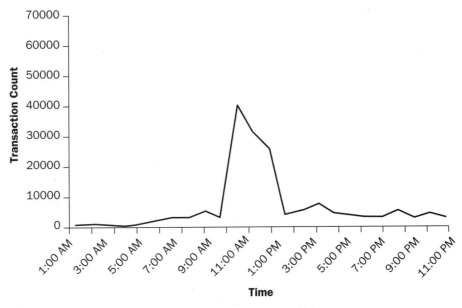

Figure 9.1 *The utilization for transactions at an ATM.*

In Chapter 8 we defined the equation for arriving at throughput as Throughput = Completions/Time. In this scenario, we have identified the peak utilization period as between 11:00 A.M. and 2:00 P.M. (or 10,800 seconds), and the transactions that need to be completed during this time interval as 150,000. Thus, the throughput rate during this time is 150,000/10,800, or 13.88 transactions per second. The system in question would therefore have to be capable of at least 13.88 transactions per second. By building a system that can handle this peak period load, we can handle the worst part of the processing day. During the rest of the day, the system should experience satisfactory processing utilization and response times.

When you cannot define the peak utilization period, precapacity planning is usually accomplished by estimating the transaction activity expected during steady-state processing. You know the maximum number of transactions you expect to complete in a processing day, and you know the length of your processing day, so you can calculate the average transactions per unit time.

In our example scenario, suppose we have the information that a total of 250,000 transactions will be completed during a working day, which is 24 hours, but we don't know the arrival rate of these transactions. We can use the same equation to determine the throughput: Throughput = 250,000/24 hours (86,400 seconds). The throughput is thus equal to 2.89 transactions per second. However, since we don't know the actual arrival rate for these transactions, we should size the system with a built-in reserve capacity. *Reserve capacity* refers to a certain portion of system processing power left in reserve to accommodate the more stressed workload periods.

Single-Tier vs. Multitier Systems

A *single-tier system* is one in which all components reside on the local machine. This architecture is basically a stand-alone system. The configuration is usually a large mainframe type, with the user interfaces, database, and applications all working on the single system. This type of system usually needs more attention from system administrators, in particular in the area of performance tuning and capacity planning, because there is more possibility of the various components contending for the same resources. A stand-alone system can have severe performance problems because of the queuing factor. These systems are also more complicated to maintain than their multitier counterparts. However, they are still popular because of their sheer processing power.

A *multitier system* is two or more systems linked together to perform workload processing. These configurations are less expensive than their single-tier counterparts because they can be composed of an inexpensive desktop system, a smaller server-type system (such as one of the popular multiprocessor Intel solutions) for the database, possibly another server for the applications (although most of the popular applications reside on the user interface system or the desktop system), all connected by a network.

This solution, also known as a *client/server* solution, is probably the most frequently selected because of its ease of use and low cost per transaction. These solutions are relatively inexpensive in comparison with the much larger mainframes, are extremely space efficient, and do not require housing in a special computer room. The multitier system is also much less expensive to maintain than the mainframe counterpart. Currently, the majority of users select these systems rather than single-tier systems because they are user friendly and are productive when configured correctly.

Page Faulting

To help size memory, we use the principle of page faulting. Page faults are normal system occurrences and are used to retrieve data from the disk. If a system needs a certain code page and it is in memory, a *logical I/O* event occurs: the data is read from memory and the transaction that needed the data is processed. However, what if the code page or data page is not in memory? In this case the system must perform a *physical I/O* to read the needed page from the disk. This is accomplished via page faulting.

A system issues a page fault interrupt when a needed code page is not in its working set in main memory. The page fault causes another part of the system to perform a physical I/O and retrieve the data from the physical disk. A page fault will not cause the page to be retrieved from disk if that page is on the standby list, and hence already in main memory, or if it is in use by another process with which the page is shared.

There are two types of physical I/Os: user and system. A *user physical I/O* occurs when a user transaction asks to read data that is not found in memory. A simple data transfer from the disk to memory occurs. This transfer is usually handled by some sort of data flow manager combined with disk controller functions. A *system physical I/O* occurs when the system requires a code page for a process it is running and the code page is not in memory. The system issues a page fault interrupt, which prevents processing until the required data has been retrieved from disk. After this retrieval, processing continues. Both physical I/O conditions will prolong response time because the retrieval time for data found in memory takes several microseconds (millionths of seconds) whereas physical I/Os can take up to several milliseconds (thousandths of seconds). Since page fault activities cause physical I/Os, and physical I/Os prolong response time, you will achieve better system performance by minimizing page faults.

Three types of page faults can occur in a system:

* **Code address faults**   If the system is executing operating system code and the next code address is not in memory, the system will issue a page fault interrupt to retrieve the next code address from the disk. The transfer of the code data from the disk to memory requires a single physical I/O.

* **Code page faults**   If the system is executing any other code and the next code page is not in memory, the system will issue a page fault interrupt to retrieve the next code page from the disk. Again, the transfer of the code data from the disk to memory requires a single physical I/O.

* **Page fault swap**   In the case of a data page that has been modified (known as a *dirty* page), a two-step page fault known as a *page fault swap* is used, causing the system not only to retrieve the new data from disk but also to write the current data in memory to the disk. This two-step page fault requires two physical I/Os. If swapping occurs often enough, it can be the single most damaging factor for response time.

When estimating the minimum memory requirement for a new system, always try to anticipate the total memory that you will need to process the workload by finding the memory
specifications of all processes (including the operating system and database engines) that will
run on your system. And don't forget about page faults. To maintain a system's memory, information about page fault activity should be collected and stored as part of the performance
database. Predictive analysis (covered in Chapter 11) should be performed on this data to project when in the future you will require additional memory. A comfortable margin of available
memory (at least 10 percent, if not more) should be maintained for peak utilization.

Disk Requirements of the Database Server

When sizing a database server, you must consider everything that the server is going to
do. As in every type of sizing, you must consider the functionality, the amount of users,
and the transactions that will result because of your workload. You should consider the
load on memory, CPUs, the disk farm, and the network in order to design an adequate
system with a space for growth. This section concentrates on the database itself to determine the adequate amount of disk drives required to support a workload. Chapter 10 covers how to determine adequate CPU, memory, and network resources, as well as how to
calculate the processing performance of these elements.

RAID Fault Tolerance

Most computer companies today provide fault tolerance through the support of RAID
technology. (See Chapter 3 for a discussion of RAID.) Remember that the most commonly
used RAID levels are as follows:

* **RAID 0**   Single disk drive
* **RAID 1**   Mirrored disk drive
* **RAID 5**   Multiple disk drives, data striping

Because RAID 0 requires a single disk or set of disks, it has a single point of failure—in
other words, if the disk drive fails, you will lose the data on that disk drive and therefore
the entire database. Figure 9.2 depicts two RAID 0 configurations. The first, a single-disk
configuration, shows the single point of failure, which is the primary disk. A RAID 0 configuration can also be made up of multiple disks, all of which are potential single points
of failure. When the disk controller sets up this kind of RAID 0 configuration, there is no
redundancy of the data stripe and therefore no data fault tolerance.

RAID 1 provides a mirror image of the database disk drive. If a disk drive fails, you have a
backup data drive complete with all the data that was on the failed disk drive. If you specify RAID 1, users get the added benefit of *split seeks* (discussed in Chapter 3), which
enable the system to search both drives simultaneously, greatly accelerating search speed
and thereby reducing transaction response time.

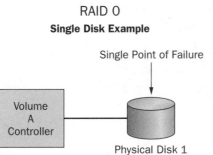

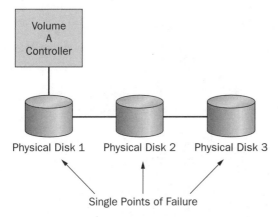

Figure 9.2 *RAID 0 single-disk and multiple-disk configurations.*

The choice of RAID level directly affects the number of disk I/Os because different RAID levels alter the number of writes to the disk. For example, RAID 1 requires twice as many writes as RAID 0. If the user describes a transaction as having 50 reads and 10 writes and wants to use RAID 1, the number of writes increases to 20.

Figure 9.3 shows two different RAID 1 configurations using single and multiple disks. In any RAID 1 configuration there are twice the number of disk drives as in a RAID 0 array. The benefit of the RAID 1 configuration is that it offers the fastest possible recovery from a physical disk failure.

If a RAID 0 configuration has two designated disk drives, a comparable RAID 5 configuration would have three disk drives. A RAID 5 configuration includes a parity stripe that contains information about the data on the other two drives, which can be used to rebuild a failed disk's data. This database protection scheme comes with a performance cost as well as a dollar cost. Each write under RAID 5 adds twice the number of reads and twice the number of writes for each transaction processed because each transaction must be written to two disks, and the parity stripe must be read, altered to incorporate the new data, then written. This redundancy lengthens the transaction response time slightly.

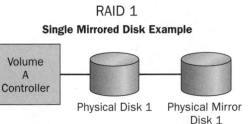

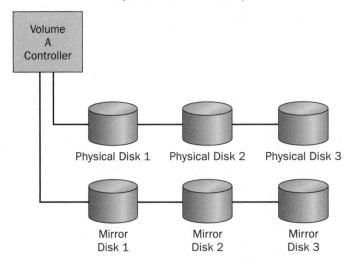

Figure 9.3 *Single and mulitple RAID 1 disk configurations.*

Figure 9.4 depicts a normal RAID 5 configuration before and after a disk failure. After a failure the parity is used to rebuild the failed disk's data. In this example, physical disk 2 has failed. The system recovers from this failure by rebuilding physical disk 2's data on the online spare disk.

Rules for Database Disk Drives

One of the most frequently asked questions in sizing pertains to the number of disk drives required to support a workload. The most common response to the answer is "How come so many drives are required?" Many people are surprised at how many disk drives they need for their database because they think in terms of the database size only and do not take into account the amount of I/Os that the workload will cause. In addition, the I/Os caused by the use of RAID arrays are often forgotten or overlooked.

RAID 5

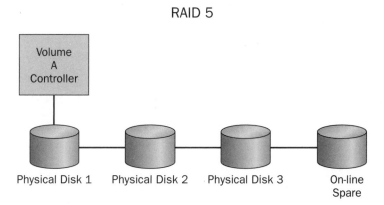

Recovery After a Failure

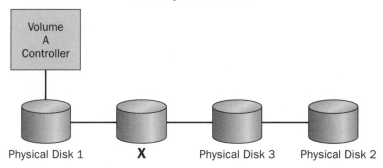

Figure 9.4 *RAID 5 disk configuration.*

A positive feature of having additional disk drives is that this setup provides more access points to the data, so you are less likely to encounter the bottlenecks that might occur had you used fewer drives. For example, suppose you have a database system that is 10 GB large and is generating 140 I/Os per second. Using the 85 percent rule for disk space utilization discussed in Chapter 8, you would need one 12-GB drive to accommodate the size of the database.

Now look at the drive requirement from an I/O point of view. If the disk drives were rated at 70 I/Os per second, the utilization rule would yield 59.5 I/Os per second. At this rate it would take three disk drives to accommodate the number of I/Os per second based on using only 85 percent of the I/O capacity of each drive. Therefore, since I/O capacity analysis yields the greatest result, which is three disk drives, we should use three 4-GB drives (a total of 12 GB, as we calculated earlier), each rated at 70 I/Os per second. This will give us a capacity of 180 I/Os per second; at 140 I/Os per second, we will be using 78 percent of that capacity.

> **Note** When sizing a disk subsystem, always apply the 85 percent utilization rule to both the size of the database and the number of I/Os per second that users will generate. Use whichever criterion results in the larger number of drives. Remember that too many I/Os per second on the disk drives will cause bottlenecks and therefore prolonged response times.

File Structures, Queries, and the Resulting I/Os

In database sizing, it is necessary to anticipate the number of I/Os that will be generated based on the amount and type of transactions that will be processed. This information is necessary not only to size the database in terms of number of disks, but also to calculate the CPU utilization and other necessary statistics. So where do you begin? The first stage of any sizing is to know the questions to ask and who to ask. For this information it is necessary to enlist the database administrator and the person who is writing the application queries or transactions. Figure 9.5 shows the most basic block diagram of a record in a table called *Customer*. This information will help in analyzing the transaction I/Os.

Figure 9.5 *Block diagram of a table layout.*

After the diagrams have been created, you can start to think about the transactions that will be used in this workload system. There are a few issues that you must take into account before you proceed. If you are creating the queries, remember that certain techniques are more efficient than others. When issuing a query to find a customer record, for instance, it is better to structure the query to request the customer record by a unique key such as the customer number. For example, you might want to use a query similar to this one:

```
SELECT CUST NUM, NAME FROM CUSTOMER
WHERE CUST NUM = "1235687"
```

This strategy will reduce the amount of reads necessary to retrieve the required record.

Another thing to take into account is the amount of table joins that are created by the query. The more joins there are, the more reads are necessary to gather the data you are requesting. Figure 9.6 depicts a typical table join. In this case the customer table is joined to the order table; the actual link is at the "O.N.," or order number. The type of query shown in Figure 9.6 will return the existing customer record and all order records for that customer. This means that if there were 25 past orders for that customer, 26 records will be returned.

Select C.Phone, C.Name, O.Item
From Cust C, Order O
Where C.Ordnum = O.Ordnum
And Cust.No = "12345"

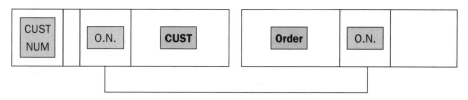

Figure 9.6 *A example of a table join.*

Figure 9.7 shows a typical table join and the expected returned records. In this case the query resulted in a return of five records: one customer record and four order file records. You may be saying to yourself that this is too easy and that there must be something hidden in all this, and you would be correct. In the previous case the number of reads would not be simply five, since additional reads are taking place just to find this information. You figure out the true number of reads and writes that will occur by using values known as *index factors.* These take into account the hidden or behind-the-scenes reads and writes that take place as a result of executing a query involving joins.

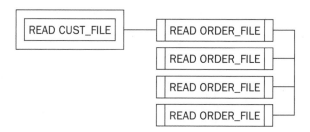

Figure 9.7 *The results of a table join: the returned records.*

Figure 9.8 depicts the index values to use for calculating the total number of reads and writes associated with a transaction. When calculating the number of reads on a random-type query such as OLTP, we use a higher value because the likelihood of the record being in cache is not as good as when performing sequential reads and writes.

Index–Factors -

    6 – Random Access

    4 – Random Insert or Update

    3 – Sequential Access

    2 – Sequential Insert or Update

Calculate Reads -

    Rows * Index Factor

Calculate Writes -

    Σ Updates

    Σ (Inserts * 2)

    Remember Each Write is an Implied Read

Figure 9.8 *Index factors to calculate the number of reads and writes generated by a query.*

Let's use the index factors to calculate the average number of reads and writes for a simple transaction. Assume that the example system is an order entry system. Let's see how we can ascertain the average number of reads and writes for a transaction of inserting a new order. The New Order transaction consists of the following elements:

Phase 1: Two random row selections with data retrieval

Phase 2: One random row selection with retrieval and update

Phase 3: Two row insertions

We can now apply the index factors and calculate the number of disk accesses. The results are shown in Table 9.1.

Table 9.1 Average Number of Reads and Writes for a New Order Transaction

	Number of Rows	Index Factor	Total Reads	Total Writes
Element 1	2	6	12	0
Element 2	1	6	6	1
Element 3	2	4	8	4

The total number of I/Os for our example transaction is thus 26 reads and 5 writes (assuming a RAID 0 configuration). The last thing you must do is figure out the RAID differential for this transaction. In this case using RAID 5 would result in 36 reads and 10 writes (see the equation in "RAID Fault Tolerance"). These calculations must be performed for each transaction in the workload.

Sizing the Database Disk Farm

When sizing the database disk farm, or finding the required total number of data disks (disks that have only database files on them and not system or database log files), you must have certain information, which is gathered during the interview process. One of the most important pieces of information is the estimated size of the database. This in itself can determine the size of the disk farm: if this value is larger than the total number of I/Os that are expected per second, then it will be the size of the disk farm (see "Rules for Database Disk Drives" earlier in this chapter). In our example sizing, suppose that the expected total size of the database is 38 GB. Applying the 85 percent rule of disk usage, this implies that we will need to have twelve (rounded to the next whole value) 4-GB drives to store the database of this size.

Let's apply all the information that we learned so far to a simulated sizing situation. The system in question is an order entry system that is composed of the transactions listed in Table 9.2. In this example, we are using a RAID 0 configuration.

Table 9.2 Transactions and I/Os for a Sample Order Entry System

Transaction Name	Reads*	Writes*	Transaction Count
New Order	77	36	865
Repeat Order	84	41	325
Order Status	56	0	255
Shipping	204	0	205
Items	1200	0	865

*The values for reads and writes are for a single transaction in a RAID 0 configuration.

The next piece of information you need is the time factor for processing the workload. In this case the working day has been defined as 6 hours (21,600 seconds). With this piece of information we can begin to figure out what the disk farm should look like. First we must calculate the total I/Os that are generated by this workload (see Table 9.3).

Table 9.3 Total IOs for the Sample System's Workload Using RAID 0

Transaction Name	Total Reads	Total Writes
New Order	66,605	31,140
Repeat Order	27,300	13,325
Order Status	14,280	0
Shipping	41,820	0
Items	1,038,000	0
Total	1,188,005	44,465

So far, we assumed a RAID 0 configuration. In reality, you need to find out what the actual RAID level for a database will be. The most frequently used RAID configuration for the database disk drives is RAID 5, so let's now use that type here. We will calculate the effect the RAID factor has on the totals. In this case the total number of reads will increase to 1,276,935 and the total number of writes will increase to 88,930. This yields a total transaction I/O count of 1,365,865.

To find out how many I/Os per second this total count gives, we will assume the 6-hour processing time (21,600 seconds). In this simulation the I/Os per second turn out to be 63.234 or, rounded to a whole value, 63 I/Os per second. We can now calculate that the total number of disk drives required to process the I/O load is one 4-GB drive. A typical 4-GB drive has an I/O capacity of 70 I/Os per second. When compared with the required amount of disk drives for space (twelve 4-GB drives), we find we need more disk drives to accommodate the size than we would based solely on the I/O activity. Thus, the disk farm for this system should be twelve 4-GB drives.

Sizing the Application Server

Sizing the application server is somewhat easier than sizing the database server. In this case you have to choose the processing model. There are three possibilities: the single-tier model; the client/server multitier model; and the client/server, application server, and database server multitier model.

Single-Tier Model

In a single-tier model the application resides on the same system as the database. In this case the first thing to determine is how you will lay out the configuration. In some single-tier systems it is possible to segregate the database from the application. In most cases this will be necessary because the database activity would interfere with the application activity. For example, if an application request screen is running on the same processor as a database disk process, they will interfere with each other's operation. While the request is being processed, the request screen will freeze because the database disk process is running, taking up the CPU time until the request is processed. If the database disk process is running on another processor, the request screen will go on to another user request while the database is retrieving the first request. As you can see, configuration has a lot to do with the sizing of the single-tier system. If you size your system correctly but configure the processors incorrectly, you could find yourself overloading some processors, while others do very little work.

Multitier Model

In the multitier configuration, usually a single user has an application running on the client machine, and in this case the only thing to be concerned about is the size of the application and the utilization factors. Most of the popular Microsoft applications have this information available. Because this configuration has single-user clients, you don't have to worry about queuing on the client machines. Queuing will occur when you have multiple requests going through the system at once. In this case the queuing will take place on the database server or the network, not the client machine.

Another usage of the multitier system is the application server. In this configuration there is a client, but this client does not run the application, only the interface to the system. A separate application server processes the application code and the requests. This can cause queuing on the application server when multiple requests come in. The amount of threads created to process the requests from different users of the application can also cause high CPU utilization factors and high memory usage. The memory can be overutilized because of the number of code and data pages these additional threads entail.

Another factor to be considered is the number of users that will connect to this machine. Each user will have an interface process, known as a *shadow process,* which will increase CPU utilization and memory usage. Multitier application servers are usually deployed as a part of a security system in which the administrators do not want users to have copies of the application on the individual client machines. A well-known user of this configuration is the military.

Summary

This chapter explained the factors that you must take into account to size a system correctly. These factors include the types of transactions being processed, the amount of time the system spends processing, the RAID level being used, and the number of I/Os generated by typical transactions. Using this information, you are now ready to size a system correctly.

The next chapter uses these principles to demonstrate the actual application of this method of sizing. It demonstrates not only how to determine the amount of hardware and software that will be required to process your workload, but also how to calculate and obtain the statistics for the processing characteristics of the proposed system.

Chapter 10
Methods for Sizing a System

Preconfiguration capacity planning seems complicated on the surface, but it follows logical rules. Most analysts who perform this task have their own methods. Obviously, the most accurate method is a reliable benchmark in which the actual workload is run on a system and performance statistics are gathered to produce an accurate picture of the workload's effect. This method not only allows for accurate estimation of the hardware necessary to carry out the processing, but also allows you to play "what if" scenarios with the workload to predict sudden elevated levels of utilization caused by increasing the number of users on the system, and to predict where those elevations will occur. This method presupposes that the application workload has been written and is totally functional and that the database is, or can be, built to carry out the testing. When these criteria are met, the only task left is to load and run the tests.

Although the benchmark method is the most accurate for building a system, its use is limited by several factors. An obvious problem for benchmark sizing is that the expense is usually far beyond what a small business is prepared or able to pay. Thus benchmark sizing exercises are usually confined to large organizations that have the funds for this function. Another problem is that the workload and database must be developed to the point at which they can be placed on a system and processed.

Fortunately, another method for sizing can be used to estimate the hardware requirements for processing a workload. This method of sizing, which I call statistical hardware estimation, relies on having a complete application and database design schema and uses the following conditions for the target system:

- The steady-state CPU utilization is less than 75 percent.
- The cache hit ratio is at least 90 percent.
- No disk drive exceeds 85 percent utilization of space or I/O activity.
- The server runs only a database.
- The distribution of disk I/Os is even across all drives.
- The number of disk controllers is sufficient to meet the demand of the workload.

The logic behind these conditions was covered in depth in Chapters 8 and 9. We will assume these conditions hold for the target system and use them to figure out the capacity for the CPU.

Sizing the Processor

Let's focus on sizing a database server. Predicting the capacity of a CPU on a database server is not as complicated as you might think. Remember that a database server is processing only transactions. The application is running on a client machine, so application sizing does not enter into the equation. The server will be processing requests in the form of read and write operations—that is, it will be processing I/Os. So the task at hand is to determine how many I/Os will be generated by the transactions and in what time frame they need to be completed. You need to know how many transactions the system will be required to process and the definition of either the working day (in hours) for this system or the peak utilization period. As we've seen, it's always preferable to size for the peak utilization period because it represents the worst-case scenario. Unfortunately, in most cases this information will not be available.

To gain a deeper understanding of the transactions that a system will be processing, you need access to the transaction anatomy (profile), which will help you determine the numbers of reads and writes (I/Os) that the transaction will generate and enable you to calculate the anticipated CPU utilization. The techniques for anticipating the number of I/Os caused by a transaction are covered in Chapter 9.

The single most important part of any sizing is obtaining the information about the workload and the environment in which this workload will be processed. You gather this information from interviews with the database designer, application designer, management, and the system administrator.

The Interview Process

The interview process can yield the bulk of the information you need for sizing the CPU. The essential data you require concerns the I/Os for a database server: what type of transactions, how many of each transaction, and how many I/Os these transactions will cause. The application designer can provide pertinent information about the nature of the transactions. The database designer can provide information pertaining to the tables and the indexes that will be affected by these transactions. Other factors that you must consider are the amount of time these transactions will be processed and the fault tolerance of the database disk drives.

Let's look at an example interview scenario. A company is developing an order entry system for sales that they wish to deploy in a few months. The company has limited funds for a system to process the online and telephone orders that are to be placed. They want an accurate estimation of the hardware requirements for processing this workload within certain time limitations. At a meeting with the database administrator you learned that the database size will be 30 GB. This estimation includes the index tables and the temporary files that the database will use. The database administrator also provided the schema of the database and the number of tables that will be used. There will be five main tables, the largest of which will be 3 GB.

The application developer has determined that this order entry system will consist of five main transactions and has calculated that the number of reads and writes (at RAID 0) are as given in Table 10-1. The application developer and the system administrator have determined that they require fault tolerance, but they would like to be economical. This requirement is best fulfilled by a RAID 5 selection for fault tolerance. The additional I/Os generated by fault tolerance equipment must also be considered when sizing the CPU (see Chapters 3 and 9).

Table 10-1 Transaction I/Os for Sample Order Entry System with RAID 0

Transaction Name	Reads*	Writes*	Transaction Count
New Order	93	29	1100
Repeat Order	72	33	431
Order Status	64	1	250
Shipping	67	1	250
Items	1800	1800	1100

*The values for reads and writes are for a single transaction.

The only piece of information that is left to determine is the working day for this workload. The management would know this information. In this case the working day is 8 hours. At this point you can begin to determine the CPU requirement for this particular workload.

Note   For an existing system, you can profile transactions by running each of the transactions separately and using Performance Monitor to track the number of I/Os generated. This information can be used to adjust the speed, type, and number of CPUs in use.

Calculating CPU Utilization

Once you have determined the total number of reads and writes caused by transactions and added the I/Os caused by the RAID level you have selected, you have all the information you need to calculate the CPU utilization. The following formula is used to determine the CPU utilization of a proposed system:

*CPU Utilization = Throughput * Service Time*

where Throughput is the number of I/Os, and Service Time is the amount of CPU time per I/O. This formula simply states that utilization is the total number of I/Os the system processes (throughput) multiplied by the time it takes to perform each task (service time).

To determine the capacity of a specific processor, perform the following steps to account for every transaction that will be processed as part of this workload set:

1. Calculate the total number of reads that will be going through the system by using the following formula:

    *Total Reads = Σ (Reads per Transaction with RAID * Transaction Count)*

    From the interview information (see Table 10-1) and the equation for I/O increases with RAID 5 (see "Disk Calculations" in Chapter 3), you can calculate the total number of reads for each transaction. These results are summarized in Table 10-2. Plugging these values into the formula yields the following:

    *Total Reads = Σ Reads per Transaction with RAID 5 * Transaction Count)*
    = 166,100 + 59,478 + 16,250 + 17,000 + 5,940,000
    = 6,198,828

Table 10-2 Total Number of Reads for Sample Order Entry System with RAID 5

Transaction Name	Reads	Transaction Count	Reads per Transaction
New Order	151	1100	166,100
Repeat Order	138	431	59,478
Order Status	65	250	16,250
Shipping	68	250	17,000
Items	5400	1100	5,940,000
Total			6,198,828

2. Determine how many of these reads will be physical I/Os and how many will be logical I/Os (memory reads) by using the following formulas:

    *Total Logical Reads = Total Reads * Cache Hit Ratio*

    Total Physical Reads = Total Reads – Logical Reads

    We have calculated the total number of reads to be 6,198,828 under RAID 5. Using these equations and the criterion of a 90 percent cache hit ratio yields the following figures: the logical read count is 5,578,945 (rounded), and the physical read count is 619,883 (rounded).

3. Convert the total number of each read type to reads per second by using the following formulas:

    Logical Reads per Second = [(Total Logical Reads / Work Period) / 60] / 60

    Physical Reads per Second = [(Total Physical Reads / Work Period) / 60] / 60

    From the interview process you know that the work period is set at 8 hours. With this information you can now determine the logical read rate:

Logical Reads per Second $= [(5,578,945 / 8\ hours) / 60] / 60$
$= 5,578,945 / 28,800\ seconds$
$= 193.71$

The physical read rate is determined in the same way:

Physical Reads per Second $= [(619,883 / 8\ hours) / 60] / 60$
$= 619,883 / 28,800\ seconds$
$= 21.52$

4. Calculate the amount of CPU utilization for each of the read functions by using the following formulas:

Logical Read Utilization = Logical Reads per Second * Logical Read CPU Time

Physical Read Utilization = Physical Reads per Second * Physical Read CPU Time

These formulas allow you to calculate the cumulative service times for each of the read functions. The calculation for the logical read utilization is as follows:

Logical Read Utilization $= 193.71$ * *Logical Read CPU Time*
$= 193.71 * 0.0001$
$= 0.0194$
$= 1.94\%$

The calculation for physical read utilization is as follows:

Physical Read Utilization $= 21.52$ * *Physical Read CPU Time*
$= 21.52 * 0.002$
$= 0.043$
$= 4.3\%$

The total read utilization for this proposed system would thus be 6.24 percent CPU utilization.

Note   The formulas here use 0.0001 second for the logical read CPU time (service time) and 0.002 second for the physical read CPU time, which are the values for a 200-MHz Pentium processor. The service times will vary depending on the type and speed of the target CPU.

5. Calculate the total number of writes that will be going through the system by using the following formula:

Total Writes = Σ (Writes per Transaction with RAID * Transaction Count)

Using this formula and the equation for I/O increases with RAID 5, we can now derive the information in Table 10-3 regarding the write activity. Plugging these values into the equation for total writes gives us the following:

Total Writes $= 63,800 + 28,446 + 500 + 500 + 3,960,000$
$= 4,053,246$

Table 10-3 Total Number of Writes for Sample Order Entry System with RAID 5

Transaction Name	Writes	Transaction Count	Writes per Transaction
New Order	58	1100	63,800
Repeat Order	66	431	28,446
Order Status	2	250	500
Shipping	2	250	500
Items	3600	1100	3,960,000
Total			4,053,246

6. Now find the number of writes per second that will be passing through the system by performing the following calculation:

   Writes per Second = [(TotalWrites / Work Period) / 60] / 60

   For the example system, the writes per second can be calculated as follows:

   Writes per Second = [(4,053,246 / 8 hours) / 60] / 60
   = 4,053,246 / 28,800 seconds
   = 140.74

7. Determine the total CPU utilization involved in processing the writes by performing the following calculation:

   CPU Write Utilization = Writes per Second * Write CPU Time

   Using the numbers that have been previously calculated yields the following for CPU write utilization:

   CPU Write Utilization = 104.74 * Write CPU Time
   = 104.74 * 0.001
   = 0.1047
   = 10.47 %

Note This formula uses 0.001 second for the CPU write time. For these calculations a 200-MHz Pentium processor was used. The actual service times will vary depending on the type and speed of the target CPU.

8. Calculate the total CPU utilization for the transactions by using the following formula:

   Total Utilization = Logical Read Utilization + Physical Read Utilization + Write Utilization

   The CPU utilization is thus calculated as follows:

   Total Utilization = 1.94% + 4.3% + 10.47%
   = 16.71%

   This value represents a steady-state utilization.

9. Finally, calculate the total number of processors that will be required for this workload, using the following formula:

Total CPUs = CPU Utilization / Number of CPUs

where Number of CPUs is a number that will bring the total utilization below 75 percent. In the example system, the processor count would be set to one CPU because the utilization is already below 75 percent.

Calculating System Statistics

Your calculations pertaining to CPU utilization also allow you to determine other information about the system. Recall from Chapter 8 that knowing utilization allows you to calculate such statistics as the system's throughput, capacity, and average queue lengths and response times. This section provides examples of these calculations.

I/O Throughput

The I/O throughput is calculated by the following formula:

I/O Throughput = Total I/Os / Work Period

If we apply this formula to the previous values for the example system, we find the following:

I/O Throughput = 10,252,074 / Work Period
= 10,252,074 / 28,800 seconds
= 356 (rounded)

The I/O throughput is thus 356 I/Os per second

System Capacity

Calculate the capacity of the system by using the following formula:

System Capacity = 1 / Average Service Time

where

Average Service Time = Work Period / Completions

In the example system the average service time would be calculated as follows:

Average Service Time = Work Period / Completions
= 28,800 / 10,252,074
= 0.00281

Given this value, system capacity is calculated as follows:

System Capacity = 1 / Average Service Time
= 1 / 0.00281
= 355.87 per second

Note The system capacity is usually calculated as Capacity = $1/S$ (where S is service time), and the service time is calculated as S = Busy/Completions. The calculation above uses the work period as the busy time. This calculated capacity is the minimum capacity of this system. The actual system would probably have a higher throughput capacity. This example calculation is meant to give you an idea of the way capacity calculations work.

Queue Length and I/O Response Time

Calculate the queue length of the system by using the following formula:

$$Q = U / (1 - U)$$

where Q is queue length and U is CPU utilization.

For the example system we will use the estimated figure of 16.71 percent utilization for the single CPU.

$$Q = U / (1 - U)$$
$$= 0.1671 / (1 - 0.1671)$$
$$= 0.2$$

The response time per I/O if a single-processor system were used for the example order entry system would be calculated as follows:

$$Response\ Time = (Queue\ Length \bullet Service\ Time) + Service\ Time$$
$$= (0.2 \bullet 0.00281) + 0.00281$$
$$= 0.003372\ second$$

Note Remember that the expected service time is the average time per I/O without any queuing at all. Response time is the service time and the queue time combined.

Transaction Response Times

The last thing to calculate is the expected transaction flow (not I/O flow) in terms of the expected response times for each transaction. For the example system we will use the figures compiled in the previous transaction tables, which are summarized in Table 10-4.

Table 10-4 Summary of Transactions in the Sample Order Entry System Using RAID 5

Transaction Name	Reads	Writes	Transaction Count
New Order	151	58	1100
Repeat Order	138	66	431
Order Status	65	2	250
Shipping	68	2	250
Items	5400	3600	1100

A transaction's response time can be derived by following the steps given below.

1.   Calculate the number of physical reads and logical reads for the transaction:

Logical Reads = Transaction Reads • Cache Hit Ratio

Physical Reads = Transaction Reads – Logical Reads

In our example, we can calculate the following for the New Order transaction:

Logical Reads   = 151 • 0.90
               = 136

Physical Reads = 151 – 136
               = 15

2.   Calculate the service time for the reads of the transaction:

Read Service Time = Total Logical Read Service Time + Total Physical Read Service Time

where

Total Logical Read Service Time = Logical Read Service Time • Logical Reads

and

Total Physical Read Service Time = Physical Read Service Time • Physical Reads

In our example of the New Order transaction, the calculation would be as follows:

Read Service Time = (0.0001 • 136) + (0.002 • 15)
                  = 0.0136 + 0.03
                  = 0.0436

3.   Calculate the service time for the writes of the transaction:

Write Service Time = Transaction Writes • Service Time

In the case of the New Order transaction, this would be the following:

Write Service Time = 58 • 0.001
                   = 0.058

4.   Calculate the total transaction service time:

Transaction Service Time = Read Service Time + Write Service Time

In our example of the New Order transaction, this calculation would be as follows:

Transaction Service Time = 0.0436 + 0.058
                        = 0.1016

5.   Calculate the response time for the single-processor system you decided was to be used for this workload:

Response Time = (Queue Length • Service Time) + Service Time

In our example of the New Order transaction, this would be as follows:

Response Time = (0.2 • 0.11016) + 0.1016
= 0.12192 second

Note This procedure must be performed for each transaction in the workload system. The sum of the transaction response times is the transaction flow for the system.

Sizing Memory

When performing capacity planning for memory, you need certain pieces of information, including the number of concurrent users who will be on the system, the type of transaction workload, and, of course, the type of operating system. You must also take into account the desirable cache hit ratio and page faulting. You would typically start the sizing process by interviewing the database designer, the DBA, and management personnel. In our example situation, you are sizing a database server, so information pertaining to the memory usage of client applications does not affect database server size.

Note For the purposes of these calculations, a small database is defined as less than 50 GB, a medium-sized database is 55 to 150 GB, and a large database is greater than 150 GB.

Let's consider the example system. The first piece of information that you will need is the number of concurrent users. For the example system, you learn that on average, 200 concurrent users will be on the system at any given time. You will thus need 100 MB of memory just for the users.

Note Generally, you should allow 500 KB of memory for each user to accommodate the shadow process.

Next you need to know the operating system that will be used. In this case, the operating system is Windows NT, which uses about 20 MB of memory. (Windows 2000 uses about 64 MB.) This brings your total memory use up to 120 MB so far. The next piece of information you need is the size of the database executable that you are going to use—in this case, SQL Server, which is 5.5 MB. The total memory required is now 125.5 MB.

The final piece of information you need is the size of the database processing area. This area consists of two elements: the log area and the database cache. The log area holds the information about write activity that is taking place. This area, sometimes called the *audit trail*, is extremely important because if a system failure occurs during the processing of a transaction, the data stored here will be used to restore the "before" image of the database, that is, the database state as it was before the failure occurred. Thus audit trails enable you to roll back partially complete transactions caused by a disk failure.

Note A good rule of thumb for sizing the log is to use 500 MB for a small database, 1 GB for a medium-sized database, and 2 GB for a large database.

The other element in the database processing area is the database cache. All the data processed by your system will pass through it. The larger the database cache, the greater your cache hit ratio. Obviously, you want the highest cache hit ratio you can achieve. A cache area that is too small will cause physical I/Os to occur because the system must access the disk to retrieve data not present in the cache. These physical I/Os increase the response time of the transaction.

To calculate the required cache size, use the following formula:

*DB Cache Size = DB Cache Block Size * DB Block Elements*

where DB Cache Block Size is the block size for SQL Server (which is 8192), and DB Block Elements is the number of blocks placed in cache.

Note   No set cache size can guarantee a 90 percent or better cache hit ratio. A good rule of thumb is to use a cache size of about 300 MB for a small system, 750 MB for a medium-sized system, and 1 GB for a large system. Systems with very large databases (around 300 GB) can require as much as 3 GB of cache to achieve the desired cache hit ratio.

From the information you've collected so far, you can calculate the minimum amount of memory you need. The following formula is commonly used for calculating minimum memory:

Minimum Memory = System + User Memory + DB Process Area

where

System = Operating System + SQL Server Database

*User Memory = Concurrent User Count * Memory per User*

DB Process Area = Log Area + DB Cache Size

*DB Cache Size = DB Cache Block Size * DB Block Elements*

The equations above can be used for calculating the minimum memory required for normal operation of OLTP applications. For example, consider a system that uses 300 MB for the database cache, 500 MB for logs, 20 MB for the OS, and 5.5 for SQL Server. Let's further assume that there are five users, each requiring 20 MB. Using the equations above, we can arrive at the minimum memory requirements as follows:

DB Cache = 300 MB

DB Process Area = Log Area + DB Cache Size
= 500 MB + 300 MB
= 800 MB

*User Memory = Concurrent User Count * Memory per User*
*= 5 * 20 MB*
= 100 MB

$$System = Operating\ System + SQL\ Server\ Database$$
$$= 20\ MB + 5.5\ MB$$
$$= 25.5\ MB$$

$$Minimum\ Memory = System + User\ Memory + DB\ Process\ Area$$
$$= 25.5\ MB + 100\ MB + 800\ MB$$
$$= 925.5\ MB$$

In an OLTP application system, you should check the cache hit ratio when the system is installed. A high cache hit ratio will help ensure that your system has excellent response time and performance.

Note   The target cache hit ratio for your system should be as close to 100 percent as possible and not less than 90 percent.

Sizing the Disk I/O Subsystem

Now that you have sized the memory and the processor, it's time to size the disk I/O subsystem. Sizing this part of the system is easy because you have already calculated most of the required parameters. First you need the total number of I/Os that will be processed through the system. You already have this information from the processor sizing. Second you need the size of the database. This information can be provided by the database designer; in our sample system, the database is 30 GB. When you are sizing the disk subsystem, it is important to realize that you are sizing for either the size of the database or the number of I/Os per second, whichever yields the greater number of disk drives (see "Rules for Database Disk Drives" in Chapter 9).

Let's take a detailed look at how to calculate the proper number of disk drives for your system. You need to store four major components: Windows NT, SQL Server, log files, and the database itself. To determine the total number of drives your system requires, calculate the number of drives you need for each component, then add the numbers together.

Operating System Disks

First you need to calculate the number of disk drives needed to support the Windows NT operating system and the SQL Server database. Usually, you will want these disk drives to be a separate volume using a RAID 1 configuration (mirrored disk drives) for the fastest possible recovery. The number of disk drives may vary depending on size, but usually the Windows NT operating system and the SQL Server database system can fit on a single disk. Our simple calculation would look like this:

$$Operating\ System\ Disks = OS\ DB\ Disks * RAID\ Factor$$

where OS DB Disk is the number of disk drives for the Windows NT operating system and SQL Server, and RAID Factor is the number of RAID drives.

In this case, the result would be 2 for mirrored disk drives. (Windows NT and SQL Server are on one disk, and that disk is mirrored in a RAID 1 volume). We do not recommend setting the operating system volume to RAID 5 or RAID 0. You must have at least two initial disk drives to use RAID 5, so you wouldn't be saving any disk space, and you will want the fastest possible recovery for the operating system and the database executable.

Log File Disks

Next you should calculate the number of disk drives needed to support your system's log files. This depends largely on the total number of writes per second your transactions will cause, which was calculated during the processor sizing. For example, consider a workload that resulted in 1,500,000 writes using a RAID 0 volume. This would result in 52.08 I/Os per second, and would require only one disk drive at RAID 0. If we now switch to the recommended RAID 1 level, we're looking at 3,000,000 writes over an 8-hour period, or 104.17 writes per second (remember that using RAID 1 results in twice as many writes per transaction as RAID 0), but they are going to twice as many disk drives.

To calculate the number of drives needed, use the following formula:

$$Log\ Disk = (Writes\ per\ Second\ /\ Max\ Disk\ I/O) + RAID\ Factor$$

where

$$Writes\ per\ Second = [(Total\ Writes\ /\ Work\ Period)\ /\ 60]\ /\ 60$$

$$Max\ Disk\ I/O = Maximum\ I/Os\ per\ Disk\ *\ 85\%$$

RAID Factor is the number of extra disk drives needed to support the desired fault tolerance. If we use the ceiling of 85 percent utilization for the number of writes allowed on a disk drive that has a capacity of 70 I/Os per second, we would have the following calculation for the workload described above:

$$Log\ Disk = (Writes\ per\ Second\ at\ RAID\ 0\ /\ Max\ Disk\ I/O) + RAID\ Factor$$
$$= 52.08\ /\ 59.5$$
$$= 0.88\ (without\ RAID\ consideration)$$

The Log Disk value should be rounded up to the next whole integer: this system would need one disk drive for the logs at RAID 0. Because we want to use RAID 1, that number should be doubled (the drives will be mirrored). Thus, at RAID 1 this system will need two disk drives for the logs.

Database Disks

The final step is calculating the number of disk drives that will be required for the database. Remember to calculate the number of drives required based on both the size of the database and the number of I/Os per second, and to use the larger of the two numbers of drives.

Size Criterion

To determine the number of disk drives that are required to accommodate the database size, use the following formula:

*Disks for Size = [DB Size / (Max Disk Size * 85%)] + RAID Factor*

where DB Size is the database size in bytes, Max Disk Size is the maximum disk size in bytes, and RAID Factor is the number of extra disk drives needed to support the desired fault tolerance. For example, the number of 12-GB disks needed for a 30-GB database using RAID 1 would be calculated as follows:

*Disks for Size = [30 GB / (12 GB * 0.85)] + RAID Factor*
   = (30 / 10.2) + RAID Factor
   = 2.9 (rounded up to 3 disks, without RAID)

The drives must be mirrored for RAID 1, so you would need six 12-GB drives to accomodate the size of this database. If this example were for RAID 5, you would require only three disk drives to accomodate the size of the database (plus one drive as an online spare if necessary).

Note   A RAID 5 level is recommended for database drives.

I/O Criterion

The number of disk drives required to accommodate I/Os can be drastically different from the number of drives required to accomodate the database size, as we saw in an earlier simplified example in Chapter 9. The I/O requirement may thus cause you to revise your recommendation concerning the size of the disk subsystem. To calculate this value, follow these steps:

1. Calculate the total number of read I/Os that will be going through the system by using the following formula:

    *Total Reads = Σ Reads per Transaction with RAID * Transaction Count)*

2. Determine how many of these read I/Os will be physical reads and how many will be logical reads by using the following formulas:

    *Total Logical Reads = Total Reads * Cache Hit Ratio*

    Total Physical Reads = Total Reads – Logical Reads

3. Convert the total number of physical reads to reads per second by using the following formula:

    Physical Reads per Second = [(Total Physical Reads / Work Period) / 60] / 60

4. Calculate the total number of write I/Os that will be going through the system by using the following formula:

    *Total Writes = Σ Writes per Transaction with RAID * Transaction Count)*

5. Calculate the total number of physical I/Os per second by using the following formula:

Total Physical I/Os per Second = (Total Physical Reads + Total Writes) / Work Period (in seconds)

6. Calculate the total number of database disk drives by using the following formula:

Num DB Disks = [Total Physical I/Os per Second / (Max Disk Capacity • 85%)] + RAID Factor

where Max Disk Capacity is the maximum disk I/O capacity per second and RAID Factor is the number of extra disk drives needed to support the desired fault tolerance.

Sizing Example

Getting back to the original example order entry system, you have the information to calculate the number of disk drives that will be required to process the workload. In the case of the operating system, you would need to calculate the following:

*Operating System Disks = OS DB Disk * RAID Factor*

Considering that the disk space requirements are small for the operating system (Windows NT) and the SQL Server database engine, two 2-GB disk drives would suffice for this load.

For the log file space, you can use the following calculation. Remember to round up to the next integer value:

Log Disks = (Writes per Second / Max Disk I/O) + RAID Factor

In the example system's case, the equation would look as follows:

Log Disks = (70.37 RAID 0 Writes per Second) / 59.5) + RAID Factor
= 1.18 (without RAID consideration)

Rounded up, the result is two disks before considering the desired RAID level. For the example order entry system, you would need four 4-GB disk drives because of the large number of writes associated with this workload and the selection of RAID 1.

The final calculation regarding the I/O subsystem needed to handle the order entry workload is the number of database disk drives. For this calculation you use the following equation:

Disks for Size = [DB Size / (Max Disk Size 85%)] + RAID Factor*
= 30 GB / 10.2 GB
= 2.9 disks (without RAID consideration)

For the example system (a 30-GB database using RAID 5), you thus need four 12-GB disk drives to support the size of the database: three disk drives for the database, and one disk drive for the online spare. Most new servers are equipped with the hot pluggable feature that allows for dispensing with the online spare disk drive. The database can easily fit on a single disk array. Not taking the I/Os involved in the order entry system into account, its size would require a comparatively small amount of disks.

Now you must calculate the number of disk drives required to support the amount of I/Os required to process this workload:

$$Num\ DB\ Disks = [Total\ Physical\ I/Os\ per\ Second\ /\ (Max\ Disk\ Capacity * 85\%)]\ +$$
$$RAID\ Factor$$
$$= (162.26\ RAID\ 5\ Physical\ I/Os\ /\ 59.5)$$
$$= 3\ disk\ drives\ for\ I/O\ capacity\ without\ RAID\ consideration$$

To factor in the RAID disks for RAID 5, you must decide how many disks will make up the arrays and how many controllers are going to be used. You can obtain information on array disk maximums and controller capacity from the various hardware vendors.

The final quantity of disk drives for the order entry system would be as follows:

- Three 12-GB disk drives for I/O capacity without additional RAID disk consideration
- Four 4-GB disk drives for the log activity
- Two 4-GB disk drives for the operating system and SQL Server database system

The final estimated system configuration is as follows:

- One CPU (at least 200 MHz).
- Six 4-GB disk drives.
- Three 12-GB disk drives without online spare
- About 750 MB for the cache area and 125.5 MB for the users, the operating system, and database, or 900.5 MB total minimum memory (using the rule of thumb from the "Sizing Memory" section of this chapter). In this exercise it would be wise to round the memory to 1 GB.

The difference between sizing a database server and an application server is that in the latter case you must take into account how many applications (or copies of an application) will be running simultaneously and make sure that there is enough memory for them. The application server will generally require more memory and fewer disk drives than the database server.

Summary

Sizing a server, be it a database server or an application server, is a long process, but if you use the calculations explained in this chapter it is not a complicated one. Remember that the process explained in this chapter not only gives you information pertaining to the amount of equipment that will be required to process your proposed workload but also offers statistics about the system you are creating. If the information that you obtain from the interview process is essentially correct, then this method should result in a rewarding sizing experience and a system that is within a reasonable percentage of its optimal size. Remember to account for initial growth of the workload, database, and memory. This will buy you time to start a stringent capacity planning and data collection process so that you are aware of future growth.

The next chapter will cover the postconfiguration capacity planning process of data collection and analysis in detail. This process, diligently followed, allows users, administrators, and management to know the current capacity of their system and to plan for additional capacity.

Chapter 11
Capacity Planning

Capacity planning refers to complex, ongoing performance studies of hardware and software resource consumption on an existing system. These studies are established to maintain the service level agreements (SLAs) that have been agreed upon by management staff and system administrators and to make sure the performance of the system in question is stable. SLAs (discussed in Chapter 8) are set up to ensure that a certain amount of reserve capacity is available to maintain the response times of critical activities under peak load conditions.

Capacity planning studies offer another outstanding feature, namely, the capability to perform "what if" scenarios on workloads. In a typical capacity planning study, the person performing the task uses historic performance data stored in a database to project trends in the following areas:

- CPU utilization
- Disk usage
- Memory usage

The analyst is also able to project sudden rises in CPU, disk, and memory utilization caused by the addition of new users to the system.

In the past the discipline of capacity planning was mostly concerned with large mainframes because of the expense of the hardware. The analysts who performed the task commanded high wages for their expertise. Over the years, more people have become acquainted with this discipline, and there is a growing demand for this practice to be used on the smaller servers that are so prevalent in today's market. Smaller businesses, which make up a significant portion of today's computer industry, want the ability to plan for the future growth of their systems and to avoid any surprise growth in the utilization of computer resources that could lead to lengthened response times for workload completions.

Capacity planning studies can be extremely detailed and in most cases involve profiling the activities of specific types of users. This information is valuable for performing "what if" scenarios in which you add simulated users (such as people who perform general ledger functions) to the system workload scenario to predict exactly what kind of resource consumption will occur. This prediction gives a system manager ample time to obtain the necessary hardware before the actual new users are added to the system, thus averting any degradation of system performance or response time.

This chapter explains the practice of capacity planning and shows how to perform capacity planning studies that will give you the advantage of seeing the future of your computer's resource consumption.

Performance Tuning vs. Capacity Planning

The differences between capacity planning analysis and performance tuning analysis involve what is collected and how often this information is collected. Different Performance Monitor counters are useful for each type of analysis. When tuning a system, you are looking for anomalies that will cause your system to perform less than acceptably. Generally, you concentrate on one area of the system at a time, such as the disk subsystem or CPU, and collect short-term data concerning that area. In a capacity study, you are analyzing trends in resource consumption for workloads on your system. You therefore collect a sampling of data that is representative of the processing of your entire system over a long period of time.

For example, suppose your objective is to tune the disk subsystem of your system. The goal is clear: you want an equal distribution of I/Os to the disk drives in order to avert a bottleneck that might hamper performance. The first thing to do is to take a measurement of the disk subsystem to find out which disk or disks are bearing the majority of the workload in terms of I/O. You set up the measurement by defining the counters that you want the Performance Monitor to collect. The set of counters selected for monitoring is known as a *measurement configuration.* In this case, you would want to collect PhysicalDisk statistics such as I/O and disk utilization counters.

After collecting the data, you typically graph the activity to visually review the resource consumption of the various disk drives. Figure 11-1 displays the collected data in a graph that shows the I/O distribution among the disk drives. Disk F is doing most of the work in this case. You next would take a look at the tables on this disk and move one or two of the more frequently used tables to a lesser-used disk, such as disk G, to even out the distribution. In performance tuning, the basic rule of thumb is to change one thing at a time and then measure the results of that change. If you proceed this way you can easily back out of the change and revert to the original system configuration.

Figure 11-2 illustrates the change in I/O distribution caused by relocating some tables. The objective of this tuning exercise is to get the graph as flat as possible by distributing the load among all the disks, so this change was beneficial. Systematic table relocation will eventually result in a tuned I/O subsystem.

In a capacity study, the objective is clear: you want to study trends in workload resource consumption on your system. The method is also clear: collect a representative sampling of data over a long period of time to track these trends. What is unclear is what will need to be fixed in terms of additional hardware. For example, suppose an ongoing study has been in progress for five months. You are tracking the I/O usage of your system after you have tuned it in the performance tuning example just described. You now produce a graph that shows the monthly average growth of I/O usage on disk F (see the solid line in Figure 11-3 on page 198).

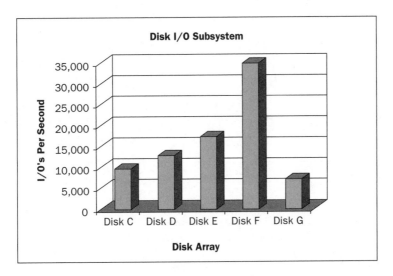

Figure 11-1 *A performance graph of an untuned I/O subsystem.*

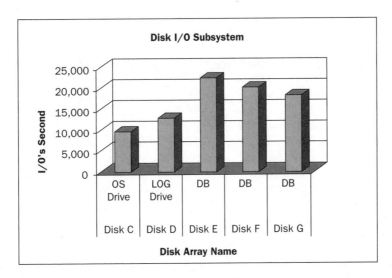

Figure 11-2 *A performance graph of the example I/O subsystem after relocating some tables.*

In October, when the study began, disk F had a usage of 21,897 I/Os per second. This has grown to 29,132 I/Os per second in February 1999. You can now project when the I/O usage of disk F will exceed its maximum limit of 40,000 I/Os per second. The dotted line in Figure 11-3 indicates the projected growth from February through August 1999, when it is predicted that the disk will be at its maximum I/O capacity.

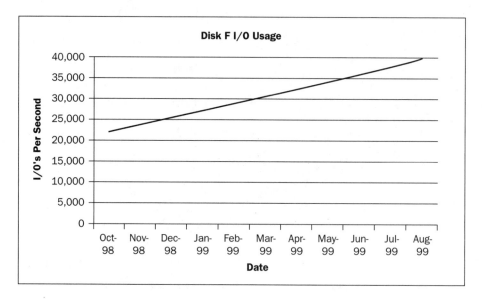

Figure 11-3 *A capacity study graph of I/O usage on disk F (solid line = actual usage; dotted line = projected usage).*

Studies that are part of capacity planning differ from performance tuning in terms of the length of the study and the concentration of data collection. In performance tuning, as in the example discussed earlier, you concentrate on one area of the system at a time—in this case, the disk I/O subsystem. In a capacity study, you collect data that is representative of the entire system. Another difference is the counters that you select to analyze. Some counters are clearly for tuning purposes, such as the Cache Size counter of the SQLServer: Buffer Manager object, which is used to adjust cache size to obtain a desired cache hit ratio. You generally would not collect this data for capacity planning purposes because once you have set this counter, the value will not change unless you manually change it. In contrast, counters such as Processor: % Processor Time will change as your system either grows or shrinks in usage. A good rule of thumb for capacity planning is to select counters that reflect system usage.

Now that you have a little background as to what capacity planning is and how these studies can help you in planning for your system's growth, we can proceed with how to perform these studies. The first rule of capacity planning is that you should have a well-tuned system on which to perform the study. If you perform a capacity study on a system that is not tuned, you will not get a clear picture of the resource growth because the resources might be used unevenly. Some resources will seem to have reached their capacity when others still have room for growth. You should run system components at close to the same level as others in their group. For example, all disks should be similar in terms of utilization, free space, and I/O traffic; otherwise, you will have to upgrade one disk array at one point in time and then another possibly not long after that. If the components are balanced to begin with, they will all need upgrades at around the same time, thus avoiding multiple downtimes.

Data Collection

Microsoft has an excellent performance monitoring and data collection tool called Performance Monitor. This tool can be used for either performance tuning or for capacity planning. Remember that the differences between the two types of studies are what counters are selected and how long the measurement periods are. Another difference is the length of the interval over which the counter values are averaged. The PhysicalDisk: Disk Reads/sec counter will show the average disk reads per second for an hour's usage at a time if you select an interval of 1 hour, or over the last 3 hours if you select that interval length. A good collection interval for a capacity planning study is 8 hours. This interval can be easily stored in daily averages that represent usage for workloads. Some people prefer an interval of 1 hour, but whatever interval you choose should be averaged for daily usage. When more data is collected, you can average it into weekly snapshots. For granularity purposes, it is better to have a year's data in weekly segments than in monthly segments.

The first thing to do in a capacity planning study is to select the counters that are relevant to the system being studied. The combination of counters is important for painting an accurate picture of the system's usage. For example, on a database server you will want to collect information pertaining to the whole system, but will clearly want to concentrate on the database activity and physical disk activity. A very basic measurement configuration for a database server is shown in Figure 11-4.

The counters selected in this configuration give a good statistical picture of the resource utilization of this server; they cover all the major resource areas (memory, disks, and CPU) while concentrating on the disk I/O subsystem. Notice the physical disk information that is being collected. The Avg. Disk sec/Read and Avg. Disk sec/Write counters indicate how long an average read or write takes—information that is used in sizing (see Chapter 10). Other important information is provided by the % Disk Time counter, which indicates the utilization of the disk drives that make up the drive array. The SQLServer counters give information on the current cache hit ratio, how many transactions per second the database is processing, and how many users are connected to the database currently.

It is better to overcollect counters than not have the information at all. Most people start off with a more elaborate measurement configuration than the example shown in Figure 11-4 and pare it down as they learn from experience what information they really do not need. The following lists describe counters that are useful for capacity planning, categorized by the type of machine being analyzed and the area of analysis. Usually more than one counter from each category should be selected to have a complete capacity planning view of the systems you want to analyze.

Basic Database Server Measurement Configuration	
Memory	Available Bytes
Memory	Page Faults/sec
Network Interface	Bytes Total/sec
Network interface	Current Bandwidth
Network Interface	Bytes Sent/sec
Network interface	Bytes Rec/sec
Physical Disk	% Disk Time
Physical Disk	Avg. Disk sec/Read
Physical Disk	Avg. Disk sec/Write
Physical Disk	Current Disk Queue length
Physical Disk	Disk Reads/sec
Physical Disk	Disk Writes/sec
Processor	% Processor Time
Processor	Processor Queue length
Server	Server Sessions
SQL Server: Cache Manager	Cache Hit Ratio
SQL Server: Databases	Transactions/sec
SQL Server: General Statistics	User Connections
System	File Read Operations/sec
System	File Write Operations/sec
System	Processor Queue length

Figure 11-4 *A basic measurement configuration for a database server.*

Counters for All Machines

The counters in this section are useful for capacity planning on all types of machines: clients, database servers, or application servers. The counters are categorized by the type of data they return.

CPU data (Processor object)

- **% Privileged Time**   The percentage of time the operating system was busy.

- **% Processor Time**   The percentage of time the processor was busy, using the equation B/T (see Chapter 8). If the observation period was 1 hour (T) and the processor was busy 30 minutes (B), then the CPU was busy 50 percent of the time. Remember to measure all CPUs in the system.

Memory data (Memory object)

- **Available Bytes**   The amount of free space in memory. This value is a snapshot, not an average; it will need to be averaged for a day's usage.

- **Page Faults/sec**   The number of page faults per second for code pages and data pages, averaged over the interval period.

- **Pages/sec**   The number of actual pages being moved from disk to memory or back to disk. Only data pages are written back to disk when they are modified. Code pages do not get modified.

Network data (Network object)

- **Bytes Received/sec**   The number of bytes received by this system per second, averaged over the interval period.

- **Bytes Sent/sec**   The number of bytes sent by this system per second, averaged over the interval period.

- **Bytes Total/sec**   The total number of bytes sent and received by the system per second, averaged over the interval period. This counter's value is the sum of the Bytes Received/sec and Bytes Sent/sec counters.

- **Current Bandwidth**   The current size of the line.

User activity (Server object)

- **Server Sessions**   The number of user sessions currently going on within the server.

Disk I/O subsystem data (PhysicalDisk object)

Note   To use PhysicalDisk counters, you must be logged on as *Administrator*.

- **% Disk Read Time**   The percentage of time that the disk was busy performing a read function. This counter is useful if you want to know how much of the overall disk time is spent reading. You may consider this counter optional if you are measuring % Disk Time.

- **% Disk Write Time**   The percentage of time that the disk was busy performing a write function. This counter is useful if you want to know how much of the overall disk time is spent writing.

- **% Disk Time**   The percentage of time that the disk was busy performing read or write functions. This counter is necessary for capacity planning studies and should be collected for every disk array within the system. The % Disk Time value is the sum of the % Disk Read Time and the % Disk Write Time counters.

- **Avg. Disk Queue Length**   The actual disk queue for read and write operations. This counter is necessary for capacity planning studies. A disk queue of 2 is the maximum desirable value for this counter.

- **Avg. Disk sec/Read**   The average time (in milliseconds) a read operation takes. This time is important because prolonged read and write operations indicate an overutilized disk.

- **Avg. Disk sec/Write**   The average time (in milliseconds) a write operation takes. This time is important because prolonged read and write operations indicate an overutilized disk.

Counters for Database Servers

There are a number of specialty counters for dedicated servers. Some of the more important counters for database servers are listed here.

- **Cache Hit Ratio (SQLServer: Cache Manager object)**   The percentage of time that a record was found in cache. The recommended cache hit ratio is 90 percent or more.

- **User Connections (SQLServer: General Statistics object)**   The number of users that are connected to this database.

- **Transactions/sec (SQLServer: Databases object)**   The number of transactions started for the database. These transactions come in the form of requests from client machines that are serviced by the database.

- **Data File(s) Size (KB) (SQLServer: Databases object)**   The cumulative size of the data files that reside on a disk array. This counter is useful for tracking disk usage growth for capacity planning studies.

- **Percent Log Used (SQLServer: Databases object)**   The percentage of the log that is used. This counter is helpful for tracking log growth in capacity planning studies.

The complete list of SQL Server counters can be found by activating Performance Monitor and clicking the add counter icon (+). Doing so brings up the Add Counters dialog box (Figure 11-5). To access a specific set of counters, select the appropriate object from the Performance Object drop-down menu. The various counters associated with the object (in this case, SQLServer: Databases) are displayed in the left pane of the Add Counters dialog box.

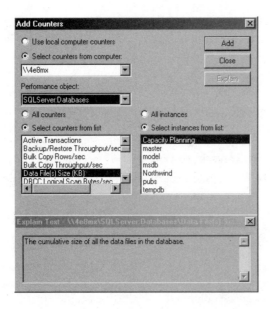

Figure 11-5 *The Performance Monitor's Add Counters dialog box.*

Selecting a counter from the list and clicking the Explain button brings up a definition for that counter in the Explain Text area. PerfMon also displays the kind of counter the selected entity is. The counter selected in this example is Data File(s) Size (KB). Notice that the box on the right has Capacity Planning highlighted to indicate that the purpose of this counter is capacity planning.

Counters for Web Servers

The Web server specialty counters can be found under the Web Service object.

- **Anonymous Users/sec**   The connection activity for the Web service per second, averaged over the interval period.

- **Current Connections**   The number of current active connections to the Web server. This counter is useful for tracking user activity on the server.

- **Connection Attempts/sec**   An activity counter that shows the number of attempts to connect to this server.

- **Total Anonymous Users**   The total count of users that established a connection with this Web service since the service was started. This counter combined with the Anonymous Users/sec counter is useful for seeing trends in user activity.

Counters for Application Servers

The counters that are particularly informative for performing capacity planning on application servers can be found under the Process object.

- **% Processor Time**   The percentage of processor time that the process selected for monitoring (the instance) has used in the system.

- **Elapsed Time**   The time, in seconds, that the process instance has been running. This counter is useful for tracking activity trends over long periods of time. It is also useful for "what if" scenarios, to see what will happen to CPU utilization if you add more application users.

- **I/O Data Operations**   The number of read and write operations that are generated by the process instance. This counter is useful for keeping track of I/O activity for application types, as well as for analyzing "what if" scenarios concerning user-generated I/O activity.

Service Chains

Service chain monitoring is similar to single-node monitoring, except that you collect data on several machines. For example, suppose you want to track the complete workload for a general ledger system. You will need to collect data from the client machine, the application machine (the process will either be on the client machine or on the application server), the network, and the database server. This data collection process encompasses three, and possibly four, different elements and a variety of counters. The data that this collection of counters supplies is useful in "what if" scenarios. Monitoring service chains also allows you to compile utilization data on these chains that can be used for maintaining SLAs and predicting future growth of the services.

Data Analysis

The aim of performing capacity planning studies is to maintain the performance you have achieved during performance tuning. To do this, you must first build a capacity planning database by taking repetitive measurements each day at the same time for a period of weeks or months. Then you must create reports that use the historic capacity planning data to see what the current performance is and to determine how to maintain the same performance in the months to come. This process is known as *predictive analysis*. When performing predictive analysis, the more data points you have, the more accurate the prediction will be. If you want to project usage of a CPU for three months, make sure you have at least that much historic data.

For ease of analysis, export the performance data into a Microsoft Excel spreadsheet or SQL Server database. For our purposes we will look at the data within an Excel spreadsheet. Suppose that you have collected several counters for capacity analysis of a database server named System1. Figure 11-6 shows a simple format for storing the counter data in Excel that lends itself to sorting by any of the counters and to producing graphs. Any format that you use should include the configuration of the system as a reference.

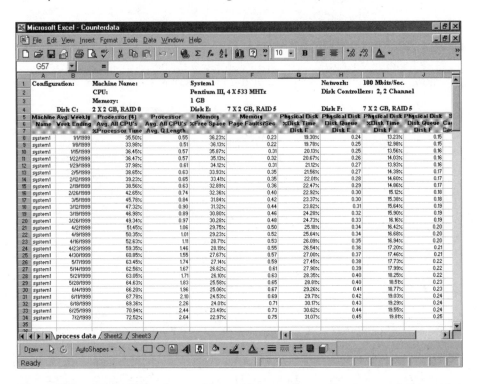

Figure 11-6 *A Microsoft Excel spreadsheet with example capacity data ready for analysis.*

Historic Data Reporting

Historic data reporting is exactly what it sounds like—reporting on the past activity of the system. In the preliminary analysis of such a report, you look for trends such as growth (or lack of growth) associated with a system component, such as a gradual or radical increase in CPU utilization, I/Os per second, file size, number of transactions, memory use, or number of users. At this point you are looking for components that will need additional analysis, such as predictive analysis or *correlative analysis* (performing "what if" scenarios on the data to see how changes in one variable affect another). A good place to start the preliminary analysis is with the utilization counters, which show the overall usage of the system. If you see a growth trend in system utilization, it usually (but not always) indicates that the entire machine is in a growth trend.

The first report you produce for System1 is CPU (processor) utilization. First you produce a graph tracking the utilization of the processors for the last six months. Figure 11-7 shows the historic data collected from January 1, 1999, through July 2, 1999. Note that the values on the Percent Utilization axis of this graph range from 0 to 75 percent, not 100 percent. This is because the 75 percent knee of the curve is the maximum steady-state utilization (see "Queuing Theory and the Knee of the Curve" in Chapter 8). If you look at the graph itself, you can see that a growth trend has been taking place since the beginning of the data collection period. The utilization is growing on almost a weekly basis.

Note If you are collecting information on individual processors in a multi-processor system, you should have a column in your data format for averages of the individual entities. This will give you a system average of CPU utilization so you can look at the system as one utilization value (which represents all CPUs in the system). This perspective makes analysis much easier.

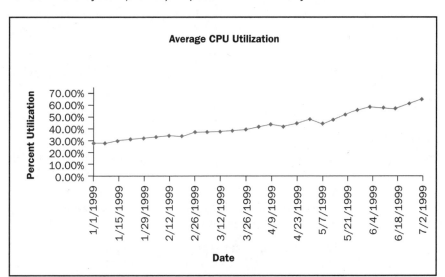

Figure 11-7 *CPU utilization graph for a six-month period.*

When you notice a growth trend such as this, the next logical step is to find other counters that are on the rise. One of the most damaging problems in system performance is a long CPU queue, which is tracked by the Processor Queue Length counter. It thus will be prudent to produce a graph for this counter. If you see a Processor Queue Length value of 2 or more, you must adjust the system (either by removing processes or adding CPUs) to shorten this queue length. Figure 11-8 shows the graph produced for this counter. As with the processor utilization, there is a growth trend since the date of the first collection in January. This comes as no surprise because you will almost always see a growth trend in the CPU queue length when there is a growth trend in CPU utilization.

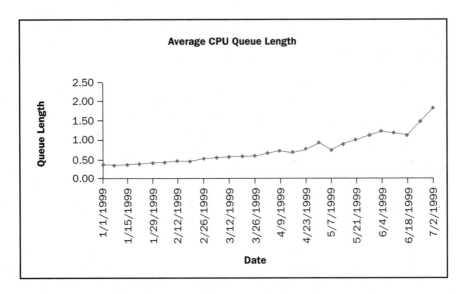

Figure 11-8 *The graph of the Processor Queue Length counter for a six-month period.*

You should then proceed to graph all the counters that you selected for collection. After producing these graphs, the next type of analysis that you should perform for this system is predictive analysis because of the growth trends noticed in this phase of the capacity planning analysis.

Predictive Analysis

When consistent growth trends are observed, it is logical to want to know when your system will hit the maximum values so that you have time to order equipment if necessary or perform fine tuning to the system before SLAs are violated. Microsoft Excel makes this kind of analysis easy to perform. You have already produced graphs such as Figures 11-7 and 11-8 for the historic counter data. The next step is to project the data into the future.

In the case of CPU utilization, you want to know when the maximum steady-state utilization of 75 percent will be attained. The steps to follow are the same as for any projection in Excel:

1. Go to the graph on which you wish to perform predictive analysis.
2. Right-click on the graph line; the Trendline dialog box will appear (see Figure 11-9).
3. Select the trendline type. In this case you will want a simple linear trend. This type of trend is useful for seeing how long it will take for an event to happen.
4. In the the Options tab, set the appropriate options. As you can see in Figure 11-10, the Options tab allows you to select forecasting and to specify how many units into the future you would like to project (in this case units equates to days). For this analysis, we selected 130 days.
5. Click on the OK button. The graph will then be completed, dates will be adjusted, and you will see exactly when you will exceed the selected boundary.

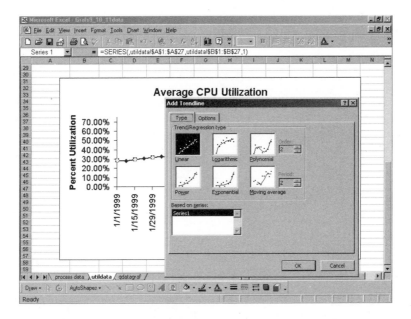

Figure 11-9 *Selecting the trendline type in Microsoft Excel to produce a graph of projected growth in CPU utilization.*

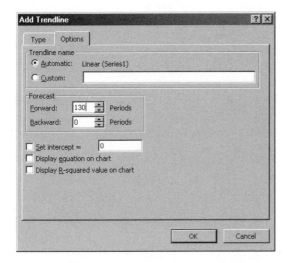

Figure 11-10 *The Options tab in the Add Trendline dialog box.*

The graph in Figure 11-11 clearly shows that the CPU utilization will reach the maximum steady-state utilization of 75 percent sometime in the middle of October. This information will give you plenty of time to avert any sudden violations of service level agreements.

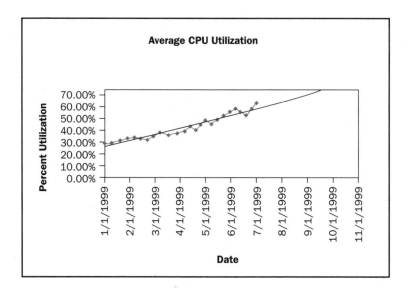

Figure 11-11 *The completed trendline graph for CPU utilization (squares = actual data points; solid line = projected utilization).*

Next you want to determine when response times will start to noticeably reflect this utilization increase. Usually response times start to show sudden rises long before the utilization hits its maximum projected increase; you can see this trend by considering the rise in queue lengths. Figure 11-12 shows the same actual data points as Figure 11-11 but with a logarithmic trendline that takes into consideration the queue lengths. As you can see, before the processors reach their projected mid-October milestone of 75 percent utilization (as we expected based on a linear rise in utilization), there is an exponential rise in queue length in the beginning of September. Thus users will see the effects of the rise in CPU utilization at that earlier point. All counters that show a growth trend should be graphed using linear and exponential trendlines so you can prepare for the increases.

Correlative Analysis

Correlative analysis is used to perform "what if" scenarios on the data to see how changes in one variable affect another. Taking the previous example of CPU utilization, one of the options for this system is to move some of the utilization from its CPUs to another machine. If you kept track of processes that were running on this system, you can predict what rate of growth these processes will have and what effect removing some of them will have.

Figure 11-13 depicts the system CPU utilization broken down by process. Here three processes—process 1, process 2, and process 3—make up the total utilization of System1. You can see that process 2 rose in utilization around April 23, 1999, and has been increasing from that point on. Moving this process to another machine should reduce the total utilization of System1.

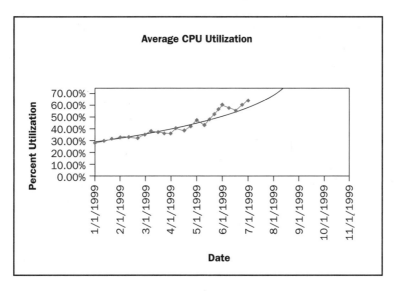

Figure 11-12 *Predicted logarithmic increases in queues.*

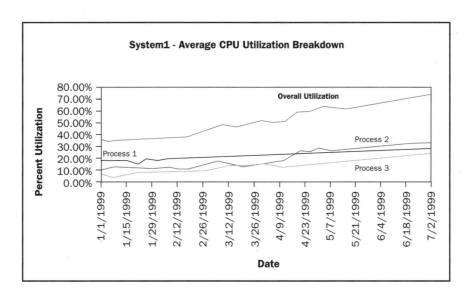

Figure 11-13 *Average utilization broken down by process.*

Figure 11-14 shows the reduction of utilization in System1 after removing process 2 from the running processes. You can see that this reduction will extend the amount of time before the system reaches the maximum utilization. At this point you can produce another graph showing this time extension more precisely.

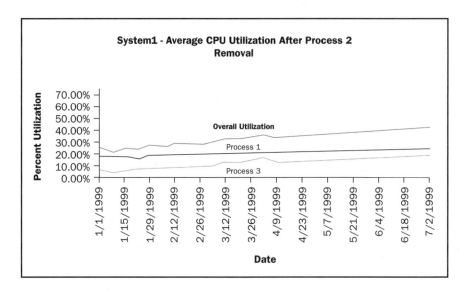

Figure 11-14 *Average utilization after removal of process 2.*

Service Chain Reporting

Service chain reporting can show the cost that workloads have on systems in terms of utilization and resource consumption. Service chain measurements and analysis span more than one system and involve multiple machines, such as a client machine, a database server, and sometimes a Web server. When analyzing a service chain, it is important to remember that the information can be viewed in two ways: as an average utilization spread over a couple of machines or as a series of individual utilizations.

For example, if you view the workload utilizations spread out across three machines as being 12 percent on the client machine, 18 percent on the application server, and 22 percent on the database server, then the service chain has an average 17.33 percent utilization. This calculation can give a misleading view of the situation. In this case it would be wiser to view the information as three separate entities rather than as a whole, especially if you are trying to determine what effect adding a certain number of more specific types of users to a system will have.

For example, suppose the data just described represents the usage for a general ledger workload. There are presently four users. This would imply that each user places 3 percent utilization on the client machine, 4.5 percent utilization on the application server, and 5.5 percent utilization on the database server. If you were to add two more users engaged in performing general ledger activities, you would be adding 6 percent utilization to the client machine, 9 percent to the application server, and 11 percent utilization to the database server. The final effect of all six users on the various systems would be as follows:

Final client machine utilization	18%
Final application server utilization	27%
Final database server utilization	33%

When performing "what if" scenarios on service chains, remember that the workload is usually spread out across multiple machines. Thus you must measure all aspects of the workload on the various machines, including processes and user activity.

Summary

Capacity planning can open up a new world of knowledge concerning the systems that you are using and for which you are responsible. This information can truly make you the master of this domain in terms of understanding the workload and being able to avert overutilization and violation of SLAs. Through historic data analysis and predictive analysis, you can foresee the future growth of a system due to normal usage. Correlative analysis allows you to manipulate processes and users within systems for tuning purposes and see the results of these adjustments without actually performing the changes.

Part III
Configuring and Tuning the System

Chapter 12
Online Transaction Processing Systems

Online transaction processing systems, or OLTP systems, are the traditional backbone of database processing. OLTP-style systems encompass everything from small single-machine systems processing 1 or 2 transactions per minute to massive clustered mainframe systems processing over 30,000 transactions per second. Throughout this spectrum, however, the concepts for designing an OLTP system remain the same.

In this chapter we look at the characteristics of an OLTP system as well as the different components of the system. In addition, we explore database design for OLTP systems and look at transaction monitors and what they can provide for your system.

What Is an OLTP System?

The industry generally defines an OLTP system as a system that represents the state of a particular business function at a specific point in time. An online transaction processing database is typically characterized by having large numbers of concurrent users who actively perform transactions that change data in real time. Although individual requests by users for data tend to reference few records, many of these requests are made at the same time. Common examples of these types of databases are airline ticketing systems and banking transaction systems. Maintaining data integrity is the primary concern in this type of application.

To maintain data integrity, OLTP systems rely on the transactional ACID properties of the database platforms. ACID is an acronym that stands for the following properties:

- **Atomicity** A transaction's changes to the state of the database should be *atomic* in nature; that is, either all the transaction's changes happen or none of them happen. If any step fails, no other steps should be completed. For example, a banking transaction may involve two steps: taking funds out of your checking account and placing them into your savings account. If the step that removes the funds from your checking account succeeds, you want to make sure that the funds are placed into your savings account or put back into your checking account.

- **Consistency** A transaction should leave the database in a consistent state. The actions of the transaction, taken as a group, should not violate any of the integrity constraints imposed by the database platform. In our banking transaction example, when you move funds from your checking account to your savings account, the account balances should be consistent and reflect the transaction's effect on your checking balance and your savings balance.

- **Isolation**   Modifications made by concurrent transactions must be isolated from the modifications made by any other transactions. A transaction either sees data in the state it was in before another concurrent transaction modified it, or it sees the data after the second transaction has completed, but it does not see an intermediate state. Isolation is discussed further in Chapter 19. For example, if you are talking to an airline ticket agent to reserve the last available seat on a flight and the agent begins the process of reserving the seat in your name, another agent should not be able to tell another passenger that the seat is available.

- **Durability**   Once a transaction is successful (that is, it commits), all its changes should survive a system failure.

A good illustration of the ACID properties of an OLTP system is to picture a cash withdrawal from an ATM system. The ATM withdrawal transaction is considered atomic if it updates your account information when it dispenses the cash. It is considered consistent if the money disbursed by the ATM machine is the same as the debit made to your account. The withdrawal adheres to the isolation property if the ATM program is unaware of other programs concurrently reading and writing your account information. Finally, the ATM transaction is considered durable if once the transaction is complete, or committed, your account balance accurately reflects the withdrawal even if the ATM machine or communication lines were to fail.

When analyzing the performance of an OLTP system, you need to take into account the entire system. OLTP systems generally include a server or servers being accessed by multiple clients directly. In a *two-tier system,* this access is direct. A *three-tier system,* on the other hand, inserts some type of transaction manager between the clients and the servers. In both cases, the tiers are connected via some type of network, which could be a local area network (LAN), wide area network (WAN), or the Internet. If you focus on only one of the tiers rather than analyzing the entire system, you may not be able to realize all the performance gains of which your system is capable.

Guidelines for Designing OLTP Systems

You should keep in mind several basic guidelines when looking at the design of your OLTP systems with the intent of optimizing performance. Though the following concepts may seem basic, they can benefit performance if you adhere to them.

OLTP and Decision Support Workloads

Often an organization needs to support both its online business requirements and some decision support or data mining requirements. Each of these workloads has different needs that are often in conflict with each other. The easy answer is to move the decision support data into a separate database in order to maximize the performance of each workload. The decision support database can be physically on the same system as the OLTP database, provided you have enough I/O capacity to support both workloads.

Separating the databases brings up some issues. You need some type of mechanism to keep both databases in sync. If you do not require real-time data in the DSS database, you can back up the OLTP database regularly and then restore it to the DSS database. This process introduces some lag into the currency of the data on the DSS system. If you require real-time data for your DSS database, then you should explore the replication features of SQL Server 7, which we cover in detail in Chapter 14.

Data Placement and Filegroups

One of the biggest concerns in an OLTP system is maintaining good I/O performance. Because OLTP systems generally have a large number of users accessing and modifying data in a random pattern, balancing I/O is critical. You should spread your data across as many physical disk drives as possible in order to eliminate potential I/O bottlenecks. The easiest way to spread data in SQL Server 7 is to use filegroups.

Placing data in multiple files and filegroups improves database performance by allowing a database to be created across multiple disks, multiple disk controllers, or RAID systems. For example, if your computer has four disks, you can create a database that comprises three data files and one log file, with one file on each disk. As data is accessed, four read/write heads can simultaneously access the data in parallel, which speeds up database operations. The following code provides examples of the creation of multiple files and filegroups for a database:

```
CREATE DATABASE SALES
ON PRIMARY
(          NAME            = SALES_ROOT,
           FILENAME        = 'C:\SALES_ROOT.MDF',
           SIZE            = 8MB,
           FILEGROWTH      = 0),
FILEGROUP  REGIONAL_DATA_FG
(          NAME            = REGIONAL_DATA_1,
           FILENAME        = 'E:\REGIONAL_DATA_1.MDF',
           SIZE            = 400MB,
           FILEGROWTH      = 0),
(          NAME            = REGIONAL_DATA_2,
           FILENAME        = 'F:\REGIONAL_DATA_2.MDF',
           SIZE            = 400MB,
           FILEGROWTH      = 0),
(          NAME            = REGIONAL_DATA_3,
           FILENAME        = 'G:\REGIONAL_DATA_3.MDF',
           SIZE            = 400MB,
           FILEGROWTH      = 0),
```

(continued)

(continued)

```
FILEGROUP    CITY_DATA_FG
(            NAME             = CITY_DATA_1,
             FILENAME         = 'H:\CITY_DATA_1.MDF',
             SIZE             = 600MB,
             FILEGROWTH       = 0),
(            NAME             = CITY_DATA_2,
             FILENAME         = 'I:\CITY_DATA_2.MDF',
             SIZE             = 600MB,
             FILEGROWTH       = 0)
LOG ON
(            NAME             = SALES_LOG,
             FILENAME         = 'D:\SALES_LOG.LDF',
             SIZE             = 1000MB,
             FILEGROWTH       = 0)
```

You can place data where you want by creating tables on specific filegroups. Doing so improves performance because all I/O for a specific table can be directed at a specific disk. For example, a heavily used table can be placed in one file on a particular filegroup located on one disk, and other, less heavily accessed tables can be placed in files on another filegroup located on a second disk. The following code shows example SQL statements for allocating a table to a single file and filegroup:

```
CREATE DATABASE SALES
ON PRIMARY
(            NAME             = SALES_ROOT,
             FILENAME         = 'C:\SALES_ROOT.MDF',
             SIZE             = 8MB,
             FILEGROWTH       = 0),
FILEGROUP    CUSTOMER_DATA_FG
(            NAME             = CUSTOMER_DATA,
             FILENAME         = 'E:\CUSTOMER_DATA.MDF',
             SIZE             = 200MB,
             FILEGROWTH       = 0),
FILEGROUP    BRAND_DATA_FG
(            NAME             = BRAND_DATA,
             FILENAME         = 'F:\BRAND_DATA.MDF',
             SIZE             = 150MB,
             FILEGROWTH       = 0)
LOG ON
(            NAME             = SALES_LOG,
             FILENAME         = 'D:\SALES_LOG.LDF',
             SIZE             = 800MB,
             FILEGROWTH       = 0)
```

```
GO
CREATE TABLE CUSTOMER
(
.

.

.
) ON CUSTOMER_DATA_FG
GO
CREATE TABLE SOFTDRINKS
(
.

.

.
) ON BRAND_DATA_FG
GO
CREATE TABLE FRUITDRINKS
(
.

.

.
) ON BRAND_DATA_FG
GO
```

SQL Server 7 writes data to filegroups using a proportional fill strategy across all the files defined in a filegroup (see "Filegroups" in Chapter 2). If you have enabled the automatic growth option for the database, SQL Server automatically expands one file at a time in a round-robin fashion to accommodate more data as soon as all the files in a filegroup are full. For example, suppose that a filegroup comprises three files, all set to automatically grow. When space in all files in the filegroup is exhausted, only the first file is expanded. When the first file is full and no more data can be written to the filegroup, the second file is expanded. When the second file is full and no more data can be written to the filegroup, the third file is expanded. If the third file becomes full and no more data can be written to the filegroup, the first file is expanded again, and so on.

The following code shows two different techniques for specifying file growth:

```
CREATE DATABASE SALES
ON PRIMARY
(          NAME          = SALES_ROOT,
           FILENAME      = 'C:\SALES_ROOT.MDF',
           SIZE          = 8MB,
           FILEGROWTH    = 0),
```

(continued)

(continued)

```
FILEGROUP    CUSTOMER_DATA_FG
(            NAME            = CUSTOMER_DATA,
             FILENAME        = 'E:\CUSTOMER_DATA',
             SIZE            = 200MB,
             FILEGROWTH      = 50MB,
FILEGROUP    BRAND_DATA_FG
(            NAME            = BRAND_DATA_FG,
             FILENAME        = 'F:\BRAND_DATA',
             SIZE            = 200MB,
             FILEGROWTH      = 20%)
LOG ON
(            NAME            = SALES_LOG,
             FILENAME        = 'D:\SALES_LOG.LDF',
             SIZE            = 500MB,
             FILEGROWTH      = 0)
```

The first technique is to specify the file growth size as a specific value. In this example, the CUSTOMER_DATA file will grow 50 MB at a time, provided there is adequate space on the E drive. The alternative technique is to specify file growth as a percentage of the current file size. In the example, the BRAND_DATA file will grow by 20 percent, provided there is adequate space on the F drive.

Here are several recommendations to keep in mind when using files and filegroups:

- Almost every database will work just fine with a single data file and a single transaction log file. For performance reasons, you should not put the transaction log file on the same physical disk or disks as your data files. This will isolate the transaction log I/Os from those accessing your data drives.

- If you choose to use multiple files, you should create additional filegroups for the additional files and use these filegroups as the defaults for your data. This allows you to reserve the primary file for system tables and objects only.

- To maximize your system's performance, create your files or filegroups on as many available local physical disks as possible, and place objects that compete heavily for space in different filegroups.

- Place different tables used in the same join queries on different filegroups. Doing so makes parallel disk I/O searches for joined data possible, which will improve your system's performance.

- Place heavily accessed tables, and the nonclustered indexes belonging to those tables, on different filegroups. This will improve performance, again because files located on different physical disks allow parallel I/O to occur.

Tuning OLTP Transactions

A good philosophy for OLTP systems is to strive to make your transactions as short as possible. This minimizes the duration of the locks that the query acquires and improves overall data concurrency and performance. We cover this concept in more detail in Chapter 17.

You should also avoid free-form user input fields in your transactions. If your transactions take input that is in an unpredictable form, it will be difficult, if not impossible, to predict the span and amount of data the query will access. Limiting user input to a finite set of well-defined values will aid in your tuning efforts.

Another technique you should use in your OLTP transactions is to attempt to execute a single stored procedure for the entire transaction. This minimizes the system context switches and allows you to process as much data as possible in a single context. Chapter 17 discusses the use of stored procedures.

One often overlooked technique for OLTP transactions is to place all the references to frequently accessed tables at or near the end of a transaction. This allows you to minimize the duration of the locks held on these popular tables. This technique is often not possible to use, but it is something you should strive to accomplish.

Controlling Data Content

Several strategies regarding the data of your database can improve performance of your OLTP system. For example, you should limit the amount of redundant data in your database. Reducing the redundancy of your data speeds up the data updates your transactions perform. This in turn improves overall system concurrency and throughput.

Note   Redundant data is advisable in some instances, such as when you are trying to limit the impact of joins on your queries. Such instances tend to be rare. See Chapter 19 for more information on joins.

Generally, OLTP systems require little or no historical or aggregate data in their online tables. Data that is rarely referenced should be archived in separate databases or moved out of the heavily updated tables and into tables containing just historical data. This strategy keeps tables and indexes as small as possible and will improve your transactions' performance.

Database Backup

The nature of an OLTP system is one of continuous operations. This generally means that the system must be available twenty-four hours a day, seven days a week. Downtime can be tolerated, but it must be kept to an absolute minimum. With this in mind, SQL Server 7 allows you to back up your databases even while they are being used. Doing so will consume system resources, so you should still schedule the backup process to occur when your system has the lowest utilization in order to minimize the impact the backup process has on your end users.

The decisions you make regarding the redundancy of the data in your database can also affect backup duration and performance. If you are able to reduce the amount of redundant information in your tables, you will likely get a performance boost for your queries as well as reduce the time required to back up the databases. This logic also applies to the historical and aggregate data that you move out of the online database.

Indexes

One of the most common misconceptions concerning OLTP systems is that more indexes are better. Actually, you should avoid overindexing tables. Each index you create must be updated each time a row is added or an indexed field is modified. When you define too many unnecessary indexes, the system can start to thrash as it updates a large amount of index data.

If the number of indexes on a table grows to four or five, you will generally see some performance degradation. When you insert a single row into the database, the system performs one data page write as well as one or more index page writes for each index on that table. For example, if you were to define six nonclustered indexes on a table, the system would perform a minimum of 7 writes to the database just to insert one row. If you do an update-in-place, the overhead is even higher. With those same six nonclustered indexes, this procedure generates up to 13 writes to the database because an update-in-place is actually a delete operation immediately followed by an insert operation.

Note You should use the SQL Server Index Tuning Wizard to design your indexes. See Chapter 18 for more information on indexes and Chapter 16 for information on the Index Tuning Wizard.

OLTP Tuning

Tuning an OLTP system can be compared to juggling several chainsaws while blindfolded. It can be done, but you must be aware of everything going on in your system. It is generally advisable to begin your attack on one area that you suspect is a bottleneck. Make a change and gauge its effects, then change something else, and so on, until you are satisfied with the system's performance. Typically, once you alleviate the initial problem, you may notice another bottleneck that had been masked by the impact of the first bottleneck. Depending on the state of your system, the tuning process may involve several iterations through bottlenecks. Keep attacking them one at a time and you will be able to bring your server to a fully tuned state. In this section, we examine the most common areas in which OLTP performance tuning can help prevent and eliminate bottlenecks.

Memory Subsystem or Data Cache

In any environment, not just OLTP, optimizing memory utilization can go a long way toward improving system performance. Memory configuration also affects the behavior of other components of your system. For example, a small data cache forces SQL Server to access the disk subsystem more frequently, which may produce an I/O bottleneck. A good, simple rule of thumb is to throw as much memory at the problem as you can afford. If allowed via configuration parameters, SQL Server will expand its data cache to consume all the additional memory. This allows SQL Server to maintain frequently accessed pages in memory to ensure quick responses. Chapter 6 contains more information on monitoring memory and data cache utilization.

Pinning Tables

SQL Server provides a technique to guarantee that a table remains in the data cache until the system is restarted. If you have small, frequently accessed tables, you can issue a SQL command instructing SQL Server not to flush the table out of memory. The rows in the table are not pinned until after the first access. In other words, they are not preread from disk and stored in memory. The following code provides examples of the SQL statements used to pin tables in memory:

```
SP_TABLEOPTION "WAREHOUSE", "PINTABLE", TRUE
GO
SP_TABLEOPTION "REGION", "PINTABLE", TRUE
GO
```

Pinning tables is a powerful method for holding frequently accessed data in the data cache, but it comes with a cost. The data cache consumed by the pinned table(s) cannot be used for any other data. That memory is effectively off limits for reuse. If you were to pin a large table, you could consume excessive amounts of data cache and severely degrade performance.

Network Subsystem

Generally, the network subsystem is not much of a concern in OLTP systems. A major characteristic of OLTP systems is the generation of a large number of small network packets. The overall amount of data transmitted between the client and the server is small. This is even more evident if you use stored procedures in your application, because in that case intermediate result sets need not be transmitted back to the client.

Page and Row Locking

SQL Server 7 allows you to specify the locking escalation to use on your indexes. By default, SQL Server 7 implements row-level locking. If a row-level lock cannot be acquired, SQL Server will attempt a page-level lock, and finally a table-level lock. You may override this escalation behavior by disallowing row or page locks. Depending on your application and stored procedures, you may want to have particular indexes that never allow a row-level lock to be acquired. As with pinning tables, you need to use some caution with this option.

The following code shows some examples of specifying lock escalation:

```
SP_INDEXOPTION "CUSTOMER", "AllowPageLocks", FALSE
GO
SP_INDEXOPTION "BRAND", "AllowRowLocks", FALSE
GO
```

The first example sets *AllowPageLocks* to FALSE for the index *CUSTOMER*, which instructs SQL Server not to attempt a page-level lock on that index. The order of lock escalation will thus be row, then table. The next example sets *AllowRowLocks* to be FALSE for the index *BRANDS*. The lock escalation will thus be page, then table. Chapter 2 discusses locking and lock escalation in more detail.

I/O Subsystem

After the data cache, probably the most critical component of an OLTP system is the disk or I/O subsystem. Chapter 3 discussed many different concepts regarding I/O subsystem performance. For OLTP performance, the critical concepts are utilization of caching controllers and ensuring sufficient I/O capacity on the physical disk drives.

Caching controllers are ideally suited for use in OLTP environments. Because OLTP systems do a great deal of updates and inserts, the ability to cache the write operations is a great benefit. With a write-caching controller, the application can issue an I/O request for a write and then immediately return to do other work because the caching controller will store the information in its on-board cache and immediately inform the application that the write has been completed. If you are not write caching, the application must wait until each write request has been successfully written to the physical disk, which can significantly delay the application. Again, Chapter 3 has more information on caching controllers.

The other area of concern is the I/O capacity of your physical drives. Different disk drives service I/O requests at different rates. An average disk drive can handle roughly 60 random reads and writes, or I/Os, per second. Your disk drives may be slower or faster. You can improve disk access by putting multiple physical drives in a RAID set. For example, if you put six drives, each with a capacity of 60 I/Os per second, into a RAID 0 array, you can expect to get about 360 I/Os per second from that array. You should utilize DiskPerf along with the Performance Monitor to determine the number of physical reads and writes your application is generating. Chapter 6 contains details and examples of how to capture this information.

Once you have captured the data on the performance of your physical drives, you should look for areas where the values are exceeding the rated capacity of the drives, as well as for areas where they are far below the rated capacity. You can then move some data from more frequently accessed drives to the less frequently accessed drives to achieve a semblance of system balance.

Transaction Monitors

Multiple-tier applications were considered leading edge a few years ago. Today they are more commonplace due to the widespread use of transaction monitors (TMs). Transaction monitors allow you to move some or all of the business logic away from the server and onto a middle tier of application servers. Off-loading the business logic from the database server allows you to maximize that server's data handling capabilities, because vital system resources will not be consumed for handling connections and other mundane functions. This latter type of work can be placed on one or more application servers, which are generally not as large and costly as the main database server.

Figure 12-1 shows how a three-tier environment works. The middle tier is where the transaction monitor resides. It controls the communications between the application program and the database. The users or clients communicate with the application program on the application server. To exploit this connectivity, you must develop code to run on the client system that connects the client to your application, handles the data transfer, and coordinates the processing between the client system, the application server, and the database server. Fortunately, the developers of TM products provide application programming interfaces that assist in the development of the three-tier applications.

Several transaction monitors are on the market today. You can find offerings from Microsoft (Microsoft Transaction Server), BEA Systems (Tuxedo), and IBM/Transarc (Encina), as well as others. You should ensure that the transaction monitor you choose provides the following features and functions:

- **Performance**   The TM should service each client request on demand rather than batching them for delayed processing.
- **Security**   Because you have split the application up, the TM must maintain security contexts at all times to prohibit access to sensitive or confidential data. A client must be authenticated prior to processing the client's request.
- **Scalability**   Ideally, the TM should be able to grow as the number of users or requests grows. This includes growth across multiple application server platforms.
- **Directory services**   The TM you choose should include an internal directory. This directory is critical in enabling ready access to clients, servers, and databases.

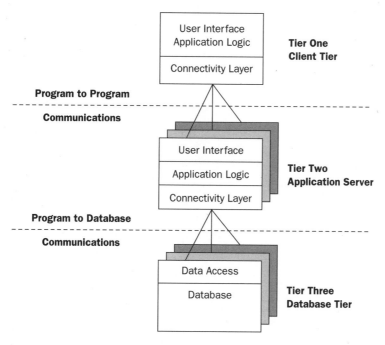

Figure 12-1 *A three-tier application.*

- **Recovery**   Failures can and will occur. A TM must be able to quickly recover from failures and restart itself. The recovery process should attempt to recover as much of the client's work as possible and must leave the data in a consistent state. Another feature in recovery is the ability for the work to be handled by another TM in the event of extended downtime of the original TM.

Summary

In this chapter, we have taken a look at what makes up an OLTP system. OLTP systems share general characteristics and are the most common type of system encountered today. We also explored several OLTP design philosophies that will assist you in developing your OLTP environment. In addition, we looked at the major areas of concern in OLTP performance and discussed three-tier architecture and transaction monitors. The next chapter discusses tuning issues that arise with online analytical processing systems.

Chapter 13
Data Warehouses and Data Marts

Data warehouses and data marts are databases designed to allow users to perform business analysis and generate reports using historical business data. The designs for such databases can range from very simple to extremely complex; frequently, complex data transformations must be performed on the data before it is loaded into the database. This chapter defines the characteristics and use of data warehouses and data marts. It also discusses techniques used in designing them, as well as techniques for tuning your system for the type of analytical queries that you run on these databases.

Note This chapter does not attempt to teach you how to build a data warehouse or how to decide what data to put in it, nor how to transform that data to be useful. Microsoft tools such as DTS and OLAP Services can be used to help you transform and query your data. These topics are very important and should be investigated further before you begin building your data warehouse.

Definitions and Characteristics

A *data warehouse* is a database that typically contains selected historical business data of an organization. This type of database is designed specifically to assist decision support and online analytical processing (OLAP) applications. No OLTP-type transactions are run on a data warehouse. A data warehouse is generally a large database, or will eventually grow to be very large. It may store up to ten years of historical data, for example. An organization typically uses a data warehouse to extract data summaries, such as top 50 product sales by region, monthly revenue per region, special offer success, seasonal trends, and so forth.

Note You should generally not modify the data in a data warehouse. Doing so would invalidate the historical information and defeat the main purpose of the data warehouse—to keep a record of business history for analysis. The only modifications that might need to occur are ones that update any initially incorrect data that was loaded into the data warehouse.

A *data mart* is similar to a data warehouse but typically holds only a subset of the entire organization's data, targeted at a smaller subset of users or functions. The information in the rest of this chapter applies to both data warehouses and data marts; therefore, whenever we refer to a "data warehouse," we mean either a data warehouse or a data mart.

The data warehouse is designed to avoid the problems you would encounter when trying to run decision support, analytical, or reporting queries on an OLTP system. OLTP systems provide up-to-date data that is constantly being updated, inserted, and deleted. Such a system stores the business transactions as they are actually occurring. An OLTP system has many concurrent users actively performing short queries that read, insert, and modify data. A decision support system, on the other hand, performs analytical queries that are read-only and that could be very time-consuming. *Read-only* means that these queries do not modify (update, insert, or delete) data in any way; they only read data from the database.

As more data is inserted into a database and it grows in size, most queries, including OLTP and decision support queries, take longer and longer to finish because there is more data to sift through or retrieve. The contention for resources, such as locks, becomes greater and will undoubtedly slow down the response times, which is less than desirable. Performing OLTP and decision support on the same system can cause major contention and slow performance greatly. For example, a decision support query may require a table scan and lock a large table, which would cause a normally quick OLTP task to wait a long time before being able to update a page in that table. Normally, there is high activity from the OLTP users, and only a few decision support reports are generated. Therefore, it is best to separate OLTP and decision support applications onto different machines for performance reasons.

The simplest way (not necessarily the best way, as you will see later) to separate your data onto more than one system involves copying the OLTP database(s) to another system; this may be done using backups and restores, data transfer methods, or data replication. We will consider this exact copy (no data transformations occur) of the OLTP database to be a simple data warehouse. You can then execute all the reporting queries on the data warehouse system only (see Figure 13-1). Once data has been stored in the data warehouse system, you may want to periodically purge that historical data from the OLTP system. This will free up disk space and leave less data for the OLTP queries to sort through, thus improving response times—possibly by a large factor. For example, you may need to have only one year's worth of data on the OLTP system, but you need to eventually store up to five years of historical data on the data warehouse system. Once you have more than one year of data on the OLTP system, such as one year and one month (and assuming that all the data in the OLTP system is already stored in the data warehouse), you could purge (or delete) the data that is older than one year from the OLTP system.

Figure 13-1 *A simple data warehouse configuration.*

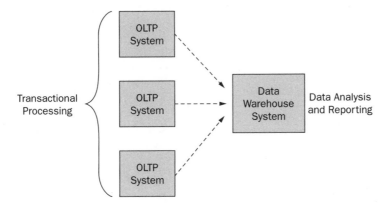

Figure 13-2 *Multiple OLTP systems participating in a simple data warehouse.*

One problem with this method of simply copying the database as it is on the OLTP system is that you will be using the same database schema on the reporting system as on the OLTP system. The OLTP database schema is most likely not optimized for a decision support application. For example, if store managers from every region want to get reports on the monthly sales per region, the monthly data will have to be summarized every time the report query is run on this database schema. This would be very inefficient and slow. Another problem with the simple method occurs when you have multiple heterogeneous OLTP systems from which to collect data for your data warehouse, as shown in Figure 13-2. The data may even be in different formats across the multiple systems.

To manage a complex system of this type, you need a more complex configuration for your data warehouse, using tools such as Data Transformation Services, which installs automatically with SQL Server, and OLAP Services, which is a separate installation option on your SQL Server CD-ROM. We will not discuss these tools in great detail in this book. This chapter focuses on describing database designs for data warehouses and on how to tune your hardware and SQL Server for the data warehouse.

Designing a Data Warehouse

The basic components of a data warehouse are fact tables and dimension tables. These components can be used in different designs, such as the popular star schema and snowflake schema. This section provides examples of each.

Fact Tables

Fact tables are tables in a data warehouse that store historical business data. They contain information that describes a specific event, or transaction, such as a bank deposit, a product sale, or an order. They may also contain aggregations of data, such as the total money withdrawn per month from all banks or the total monthly sales per region. Existing data is not usually updated in the fact tables; rather, new data is inserted periodically.

A fact table typically holds numeric data rather than character data. For example, it may contain such fields as region ID, salesperson ID, item ID, and customer ID. A fact table has many foreign keys that correspond to the dimension tables, described in the next section. Figure 13-3 shows a fact table for an example customer/sales data warehouse.

SalesTable
RegionID SalespersonID ItemID CustomerID Amount of Sale

Figure 13-3 *A sample fact table.*

The fact tables hold the majority of important information in the data warehouse. Therefore, they will make up the bulk of the database in terms of both size and activity. As you might imagine, a fact table could consist of millions of records and could use over a terabyte of disk space.

Dimension Tables

Dimension tables are used to refine the data contained in the fact table, or to describe it in more detail. The data is therefore typically character data. Whereas a fact table has such fields as region ID, salesperson ID, item ID, and customer ID, the dimension tables hold information such as the region name, salesperson name, the item description, and customer names and addresses. An example of a dimension table that stores detailed customer information is shown in Figure 13-4. Each dimension table stores rows of data with the character information needed to describe the corresponding fields in the fact table in more detail.

CustomerTable
CustomerID FirstName LastName Address City State Zip Phone

Figure 13-4 *A sample dimension table.*

The relationship of the two tables necessitates foreign key constraints from the fact tables on the dimension tables. For example, you would not want a customer ID to be allowed into the fact table if there were no corresponding row for that customer (with the customer name, address, phone number, etc.) in the dimension table. A foreign key constraint in this case will ensure that a row with a customer ID that does not already exist in the dimension table is not allowed to be inserted into the fact table.

By separating detailed information from the fact tables, you reduce the amount of data that must be scanned in the fact table, thus improving query performance. Unlike fact tables, the data in dimension tables may need to be updated at times, such as when a customer address changes; however, it will have to be changed in only one place—in the dimension table—rather than in the many rows of the fact table where that customer ID may exist.

Dimension tables are smaller and have fewer rows of data relative to the fact table—perhaps hundreds of rows as compared with thousands. The dimension table holds only one row of data per customer, for example, whereas the fact table may have many rows of data that record various transactions for that same customer ID. Now let's take a look at the two most efficient database schemas for data warehouses and see how the fact and dimension tables are related in each one.

Star Schema

The *star schema* is the most popular design technique for data warehouses. This schema consists of a single fact table surrounded by multiple dimension tables that hold denormalized data describing the facts in the fact table. Each of the dimension tables has a field that corresponds to a field in the fact table. Figure 13-5 (on the next page) shows a sample star schema for a sales scenario. The customer ID field in the *Sales* fact table has a corresponding customer ID field in the *Customer* dimension table. Similar corresponding field relationships exist for the region ID, salesperson ID, and item ID fields in the fact and dimension tables. Fields in the fact table that link to a dimension table are referred to as *dimensional keys*. If you imagine a fact table surrounded by dimension tables, as in this figure, you can see how it resembles a star.

Implementing the star schema helps reduce the number of disk reads during query processing. The queries can first analyze the data in the smaller dimension tables, then index into the fact table by using one of the dimensional keys, thus reducing the number of rows that must be scanned in the fact table. If you use Microsoft OLAP Services to help you query your data warehouse, the star schema is the recommended database design.

Snowflake Schema

A *snowflake schema* is a variation of the star schema. It involves dimension tables that join to other dimension tables before being joined to the fact table. The schema thus resembles a snowflake, as shown in Figure 13-6. This schema could involve more than one layer of dimension table joins before joining to the fact table. The reason for having more dimension tables is to get the data into a more normalized form and therefore possibly reduce disk reads in the same manner as mentioned earlier. The type of schema you implement, star or snowflake, will depend on the type of information you need in your data warehouse.

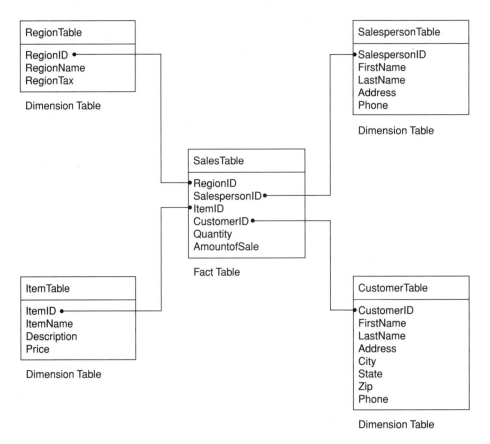

Figure 13-5 *A star schema.*

Tuning a Data Warehouse

This section looks at several areas that can affect the performance of your data warehouse system: the amount and type of hardware in the system, the choice of RAID levels, and the physical layout of your database. Chapters 3 and 4 discussed RAID levels and CPU, disk, and memory tuning in general. Here we focus on tuning issues specific to the data warehouse, based on the fact that a data warehouse consists normally of read-only data. You can perform certain optimizations to improve performance for a read-only database.

Hardware

In general, you must be sure that you have enough hardware for your data warehouse system so that it will run efficiently. Specifically, you need enough CPUs, disk drives, and memory. See Chapter 4 for details on how to tune an existing system for hardware, or see Part II for details on capacity planning and sizing for a system that is being newly designed.

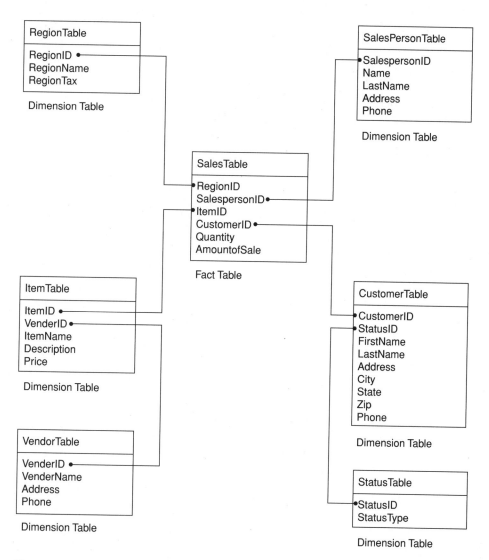

Figure 13-6 *A snowflake schema.*

Having multiple CPUs (SMP) in the data warehouse system is preferable in most cases. Multiple CPUs allow SQL Server to process more than one thread of work at a time. You may also benefit from SQL Server's parallel processing feature, which allows a single query to be processed by more than one thread in parallel. This feature is new for SQL Server 7; you will need to experiment with this option to see if it helps your system.

You can enable parallel processing by setting a configuration parameter called *max degree of parallelism*. The values for this parameter can range from 0 to 32. Set it to the number of CPUs in the system or less. Setting it higher will not allow more threads of parallel execution, because you can have at most one thread per CPU. If left at the default of 0, SQL Server will use the number of available CPUs. To disable parallel query processing, set this value to 1. Leaving the parameter at its default value is usually good for SMP systems; for single-processor systems, this value is ignored.

The number of disk drives in a data warehouse system should be determined by I/O capacity. You need to have enough drives to spread the data across so that each disk drive is performing a low number of reads—much fewer than the I/O capacity for that disk. This allows your disks to perform quickly and provides room for growth. As your database grows, and more data must be read to complete queries, you should continually monitor your disk I/O rates and I/O latencies to determine at what point you may need to add disk drives to the system. If the disk drives exceed their I/O capacity, thus causing I/O requests to wait a long time in the I/O queue, you will see a decrease in performance.

For system memory, the general rule is the more the better. The more memory you have to allocate to the SQL Server data cache, the better chance you have of finding needed pages in cache. The cache hit ratio will probably never get up to the normally desired value of 98 to 99 percent, as found in OLTP systems. It may be as low as 10 percent because of the nature of decision support queries. One query may run only once a day; therefore, it may not be likely that the data for that query will be found in cache. Other queries that follow that particular query may require totally different data pages, and thus may not find their pages in cache for the same reason. The cache hit ratio may thus be lower for a decision support system than an OLTP system.

RAID Levels

You may remember from previous chapters that you should always use fault tolerance for the data on your disk drives. Fault tolerance allows for data recovery if a disk drive goes bad. The most common choices are RAID 1, RAID 10, and RAID 5. See Chapter 3 for details on each of these RAID levels.

Let's talk a little about the log files first. Since your log files are critical for recovery in case of system failure, you should always use RAID 1 or 10 (mirror or striped mirror) on your log disks. These two RAID levels can provide a higher degree of fault tolerance than RAID 5. In addition, RAID 5 (which uses data parity for fault tolerance) is not a good choice for log files because by nature they perform almost all sequential writes (few reads), and RAID 5 is a horrible performer in cases where more than 10 percent of the I/Os are writes.

For the disk drives that hold your data warehouse data files, you could choose either RAID 10 or RAID 5. Either level will provide you with fault tolerance, and since your I/Os will be mostly reads, RAID 5 will perform well. (RAID 5 is also cheaper because you will not need as many drives as with RAID 10.) However, there is a benefit to using RAID 10 in this case as well. When you have a disk mirrored to another disk, both disks have a copy of the same data. Therefore, when performing reads, the disk controller can read the data from either one of the mirrored disks. (See Figure 13-7 for a diagram of this scenario.) If one read is occurring on one of the disks, another read can be serviced in parallel on the other disk in the pair. Thus reads with RAID 10 can be more efficient than with RAID 5. In the read-only data warehouse system, using RAID 10 can improve performance.

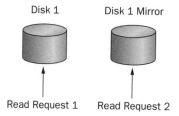

Figure 13-7 *Mirrored disks performing reads in parallel.*

Another point to consider if you want to use RAID 5 is what happens when you load new data into the data warehouse. If that load consists of a lot of data, and heavy writes occur for a long period of time, RAID 5 may slow down the loading process because for each logical write that SQL Server requests, there will actually be four physical I/Os to disk (two reads and two writes). If your loading time must be fast, you may be better off using RAID 10.

Database Layout

You may also remember from previous chapters that you should generally attempt to spread data across as many physical disk drives as possible. This configuration allows the system to achieve more parallel disk I/Os. This guideline applies to a data warehouse system as well: you should spread your database files across as many drives as possible, allowing for more parallel reads (and writes when loading new data) to occur. You can achieve this goal by creating user-defined filegroups to direct your data onto specific logical disk volumes, as discussed in Chapter 4.

Summary

We have covered some basic concepts of data warehouses and data marts in this chapter. We described the most popular techniques used in designing data warehouses—the star schema and the snowflake schema—and offered tips on how to optimize different areas of your system for the data warehouse. The next chapter discusses how to optimize your data replication systems.

Chapter 14
Tuning Replicated Systems

SQL Server 7 provides an improved system for replicating data. To take advantage of this replication system, you must understand how to configure, monitor, and tune the replication components as well as the underlying SQL Server system. This chapter takes you through the steps necessary to properly design a replication system with performance in mind. We discuss how to use the Performance Monitor counters to monitor the SQL Server replication components. In addition we explain what can be tuned and how to tune a system for replication.

Replication Overview

Microsoft SQL Server replication is based on the publish and subscribe metaphor. This metaphor uses the concept of publishers, distributors, and subscribers. A *publisher* is a database that makes data available for replication. A *distributor* is the server that contains the distribution database. A *subscriber* is a server that receives replicated data and stores the replicated database.

The publisher distributes a *publication*, which is a collection of one or more articles. An *article* is a group of data to be replicated; it can be an entire table, certain columns, or certain rows. The distribution can be either a push distribution or a pull distribution. A *push distribution* is one in which the data is pushed from the publisher regardless of whether a subscriber has asked for it. A *pull distribution* is one in which the subscribers request data on a regular basis.

Types of Replication

SQL Server 7 offers three different types of replication, which offer varying degrees of data consistency within the replicated database as well as different levels of overhead. The possible types of replication are snapshot, transactional, and merge.

Snapshot Replication

Snapshot replication is the simplest and most straightforward of the replication types and involves taking a picture, or snapshot, of the database and propagating it to the subscribers. The advantage of snapshot replication is that it does not involve continuous overhead on the publishers and subscribers. The disadvantage is that the database on the subscriber might not be current, since it is only current to the point at which the snapshot was taken. In many cases this type of replication is sufficient and efficient, such as when the data in question is not modified and need be replicated only occasionally. You can easily handle applications such as phone lists, price lists, and item descriptions by snapshot replication because you can update these lists once per day during off hours.

Snapshot replication works via the Snapshot Agent, which takes a snapshot of the entire database. This snapshot is copied to the distributor and at a later time is used to create the subscribing database. This snapshot is usually used to create the initial database for transactional replication.

Transactional Replication

You can use *transactional replication* to replicate both tables and stored procedures. With transactional replication the changes made to articles are captured from the transaction log and propagated to the distributors, which later pass them on to the subscribers. Transactional replication makes it possible to keep the publisher and subscriber at almost exactly the same state; thus, it is used when it is important for all the replicated systems to be kept current.

Transactional replication works by reading the transaction log and replaying transactions that have been used to update, insert, or delete data from the database. Once a transaction has been logged in the transaction log, a log reader process takes that transaction and copies it into the distribution database. This log reader process either runs continually or on a regularly scheduled basis, depending on how you have configured transactional replication. Once the transactions have been put into the distribution database, they are replayed on the subscribing systems; again, the frequency is based on how you have configured replication. Later in this chapter we discuss how to configure replication for optimal performance.

Merge Replication

Merge replication is similar to transactional replication in that it keeps track of all the changes made to articles. However, instead of propagating transaction changes, merge replication periodically transmits changes to the database. These changes can be batched and sent as necessary. Merge replication is designed to allow both the publisher and subscribers to make changes to the database. These changes eventually propagate to all subscribers to the merge replication; multiple systems can thus be kept synchronized.

Replication Tuning Basics

In general, tuning replication is the same as tuning any other type of SQL Server system. However, the replication systems have some special attributes that you need to address. These performance attributes are determined based on the type of replication that you are doing and are addressed a little later in this chapter. There are, however, some things you can do to improve replication systems in general.

- Filter data in order to reduce the amount of published (replicated) data. By reducing the amount of data that is replicated, you can reduce network traffic as well as minimize the amount of storage needed. The goal is to replicate the minimum amount of data necessary.

- Separate log files. Each database that is replicated should have its log files on a separate disk volume. This will maximize the performance of the transaction log as well as maximize replication performance. We address this topic in more detail in the section "Tuning for Transactional Replication" later in this chapter.

- Run snapshots for snapshot and transactional replication at off-peak times. Because snapshot replication uses a large amount of resources all at once, careful scheduling can reduce its effect on the system.

- Tune distribution based on need. The distribution process should run as infrequently as possible. Distribution that is constantly running creates high overhead on the system.

These are just general guidelines for replication. As you will see later in this chapter, each replication type has its own specific tuning considerations.

The Distributor

Before getting into the various replication types, let's first look at the distributor. The distributor is a SQL Server database that is used as a repository of replication data. This data is held in a SQL Server database for several reasons, among which are the following:

- **Performance**   The job of the distributor is to acquire, hold, and then distribute data—a job description that fits SQL Server perfectly.

- **Reliability**   SQL Server supports a high level of recoverability. By means of the transaction log, SQL Server is able to recover from system failures without losing any data.

- **Ease of use**   SQL Server replication communicates directly with the distributor via SQL Server communications protocols; thus, setting up and configuring the distributor is easy with SQL Server Enterprise Manager.

Because the distributor uses a SQL Server database to process replication information, you must configure and tune the distributor as with any other SQL Server database. The default distribution configuration may work for smaller replication systems, but you will most likely want to configure the distributor manually based on the amount of work being done on your specific system.

Configuring the Distributor

The SQL Server Replication Wizard does not place the SQL Server transaction log and data files optimally by default. We recommend that you do not choose the default location for the distribution database. Instead, manually configure the distribution database within the Configuring Publishing and Distribution wizard. Depending on the frequency of modifications to your database, the amount of activity in the distributor can be quite high. Because the distributor is a SQL Server database, all modifications to the distributor must be logged in the distributor's transaction log.

Keeping these facts in mind, you should configure the distribution database and log to be large enough to perform the work required and fast enough to perform it efficiently. Here are a few guidelines for achieving these goals:

- Use a RAID controller on the distribution database system. By using a hardware RAID controller, the fault-tolerance activities will be performed in hardware, which is more efficient than using software RAID.

- Configure the distribution database's transaction log on a RAID 1 volume. The transaction log should be isolated to allow for the higher performance that is achieved with sequential I/Os.

- Configure the transaction log to be large enough so that it is not necessary to constantly back it up. Depending on your needs, it may be possible to run all day without backing up the transaction log; you can then perform that task at night.

- Never run in "truncate log on checkpoint" mode. The distribution database is critical to replication and must be safeguarded from system failures.

- Configure the distribution database on a RAID 1 or RAID 10 volume. RAID 5 is not appropriate because of the high number of writes to the distribution database.

- Configure the distribution database to be large enough to hold extra replication data. If a subscriber were to fail, you may have to hold several days' worth of replication data if you are using transactional or merge replication.

- Tune the distribution database as you would any other SQL Server database.

By correctly configuring the distribution database in the beginning you may be able to avoid costly performance problems later.

Configuring the Distributor with Enterprise Manager

To configure the distributor using Enterprise Manager, use the Create Publishing and Distribution Wizard to create publishing and distribution. When you get to the Use Default Configuration screen, select the Yes option. This option allows you to set the distribution database name and location manually rather than accepting the defaults. You can enable publishing, create publications as well as subscribers, and specify where the distribution database resides (see Figure 14-1). The ability to specify this location allows you to properly configure the distribution database as recommended in the guidelines given earlier, which is the most important aspect for enhancing performance.

Unfortunately, you can set only the location of the distribution database, not its size, in the wizard. To modify the size of the distribution database, you must select that database in Enterprise Manager. If you prefer changing the location and size simultaneously, you can use the *sp_adddistributiondb* stored procedure.

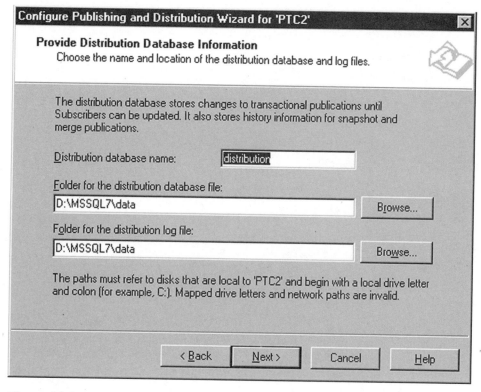

Figure 14-1 *The Provide Distribution Database Information screen.*

Configuring the Distributor with *sp_adddistributiondb*

The system stored procedure *sp_adddistributiondb* allows you to create the distribution database by hand, which is useful when you want to specify the size and location of the database and its transaction log. Creating the distribution database via the stored procedure is also handy for reusability. Once you have created a script that creates the distribution database, you can use it on different systems or to recreate the distribution database in the event of a system reconfiguration.

Note   Before you can create the distribution database, you must create the distributor. This is accomplished using the system stored procedure *sp_adddistributor* with the distributor's system name as the parameter.

The syntax for the *sp_adddistributiondb* stored procedure is shown in SQL Server Books Online. The following example illustrates the process of creating a distribution database using stored procedures:

```
sp_adddistributor Dash
```

Executing this procedure initializes the system named Dash as a distributor. You can now create the distribution database and specify its properties as follows:

```
sp_adddistributiondb
@database=dist,
@data_folder='C:\mssql7\data',
@data_file='dist.mdf',
@data_file_size=10,
@log_folder='C:\mssql7\data',
@log_file='dist.ldf',
@log_file_size=2,
@min_distretention=0,
@max_distretention=72,
@history_retention=96,
@security_mode=0,
@login='sa',
@password='',
@createmode=0
```

This code will create the *dist* database, which uses the file C:\mssql7\data\dist.mdf for the data file and C:\mssql7\data\dist.ldf for the transaction log. The data file is 10 MB and the transaction log is 2 MB. The other parameters are self-explanatory. This method allows you to script creation of the distribution database and thus easily repeat the process as necessary.

Monitoring the Distributor

You monitor the distributor via the Windows NT Performance Monitor. SQL Server adds a number of objects to the Performance Monitor when SQL Server replication is present. These objects are discussed in subsequent sections on the specific types of replication.

The most important object to monitor in the case of the distributor is the SQLServer: Replication Dist. object. This object provides the following counters:

- **Dist: Delivered Cmds/sec**   The number of commands per second delivered to the subscriber. This value gives you a good idea of how much replicated data is being sent to the subscriber.

- **Dist: Delivered Trans/sec**   The number of transactions per second delivered to the subscriber—another value that indicates how much replicated data is being sent to the subscriber.

- **Dist: Delivery Latency**   The average amount of time between when a transaction is delivered to the distributor and when it is applied to the subscriber. This value can give you some insight into how backed up the distributor is.

Although these counters give you some indication of how the distribution process itself is doing, tuning the distributor really comes down to tuning the SQL Server database. Things to look for on the distributor include the following:

- **High CPU usage**   Are one or more CPUs running at high rates (greater than 75 percent) for long periods of time?
- **I/O bottlenecks**   Are I/O rates too high? Look for I/Os per second and seconds per I/O in the Performance Monitor, as described in Chapter 6. Do not exceed recommended I/Os per disk drive and beware of I/O latencies that are too high.
- **SQL Server problems**   Are SQL Server response times too high? This can be determined by running test queries against the distribution database and monitoring response times.

The distributor is a key component in the replication system and thus should be well tuned. The next section provides some tips on how to do this.

Tuning the Distributor

As mentioned earlier, the distributor is tuned in basically the same manner as any other SQL Server systems, for the most part. However, there are a few differences that you should keep in mind. When snapshot replication is running (including the initial snapshot for other replication types), a large number of I/Os will occur at one time. Because so much data is being written to the distributor, the I/O subsystem may become overloaded. If this is the case, the time it takes to perform the snapshot will increase. Therefore, it is a good idea to specifically monitor the system during the snapshot.

Performance of the distributor can be enhanced by proper sizing, although as you have seen earlier in this book, sizing is not always an easy task. It generally is a good idea to give the distributor a little extra capacity. The distributor is the link between the publishers and the subscribers; therefore, you should carefully configure it so that it is not a bottleneck. Here are some tips for tuning the distributor:

- Tune the I/O subsystem. The distributor requires sufficient I/O performance capacity, just as with any other SQL Server system.
- CPU power is not usually a problem. In most cases the types of operations a distributor performs are not extremely CPU intensive. It is, however, advisable to use a multiprocessor system with at least two CPUs in order to allow concurrent operations to take place.
- Tune Windows NT. Typically, not much Windows NT tuning is necessary. However, there are a few things you can do, such as to configure the Server service to maximize throughput for network applications. Doing so will set the memory system to favor applications over file services. (You configure this within the Network utility, contained in the Control Panel.) Also, remove any services that won't be used, such as IIS and FTP services.
- Tune SQL Server, using the techniques and guidelines given within this book.

By properly configuring and tuning the distributor, replication will be enhanced.

Tuning for Snapshot Replication

Snapshot replication differs from the other replication methods in that the entire task of replication takes place at once. With transactional and merge replication, an initial snapshot is propagated to the subscribers and then replication is constantly applied to those systems. Snapshot replication is a full refresh of the database and is therefore much more straightforward. This section shows you how to configure and tune a snapshot replication system for excellent performance.

Attributes of Snapshot Replication

Because snapshot replication copies an existing database and propagates it to the distributor and then to the subscriber, the limiting performance factor in this process is the system's ability to move large amounts of data. Factors that can limit this ability include the following:

- **I/O performance on the publisher**   Because the database (either in whole or in part) is copied from the publisher, the performance of the I/O subsystem on the publisher could be a limiting factor. The snapshot task is more I/O intensive than CPU intensive; thus, CPU power is not usually a factor.

Note   If the I/O capacity is available, you may want to leave the database snapshot on the publisher itself. This will reduce the network overhead associated with copying the snapshot to the distributor. However, we only recommend this when there is sufficient I/O bandwidth such that the performance of the publisher is not adversely affected.

- **I/O performance on the distributor**   The distributor receives large amounts of data at one time, and at some later time distributes that data. A slow I/O subsystem here will bog down snapshot replication.

- **I/O performance on the subscriber**   The distributor attempts to distribute a database or subset of a database to the subscriber in one shot. If the I/O subsystem is inadequate, replication performance will suffer.

- **The bandwidth of the network connecting the publisher, distributor, and subscriber**   Because large amounts of data are being transferred, the network can easily become a bottleneck. This is especially true if you will be performing replication over a WAN. If the network is a problem, your alternatives are to suffer the performance degradation or upgrade your network. Running snapshots only at off hours may minimize this problem.

Properly sizing and configuring the snapshot replication system can reduce the effect of these factors and improve performance.

Configuring for Snapshot Replication

As you have just seen, it is important to configure the publisher, distributor, and subscriber with sufficient I/O capacity to absorb the load of the replication. Because the snapshot is distributed as a data file rather than as commands that have been generated from within the database, it is not necessary to tune SQL Server on the distributor for snapshot replication. When the snapshot is generated, the data is extracted from the database and a snapshot file is created. This file is stored (either on the distributor or in the location you specified during configuration) as a normal Windows NT or Windows 2000 file external to the distribution database; the distributor is used only to keep track of the snapshot file, not to store it. Thus the overhead on the distribution database during snapshot replication is very low.

You can specify some configuration choices that make a great deal of difference to the performance of snapshot replication. Here are some guidelines for configuring snapshot replication:

- Configure sufficient I/O capacity on the publisher, distributor, and subscriber.
- Configure the distributor to keep the snapshot on the publisher system.
- Configure the distributor and publisher to reside on the same system.
- Increase the number of bulk copy program (BCP) threads.

Let's look at each of these configuration guidelines in more detail.

Configure Sufficient I/O

Because a large amount of data is copied at one time, a slow disk subsystem will slow down the entire replication process. Thus, you should enhance the performance of the I/O subsystem. As with any SQL Server system, the transaction log should be located on its own RAID 1 volume for data protection. The data files should be located on one or more RAID 10 or RAID 5 volumes. The RAID level that you use depends on whether you are configuring the publisher, the distributor, or the subscriber.

Configuring the I/O Subsystem on the Publisher

Whether you should use RAID 5 or RAID 10 for the data files on the publisher depends on the read/write ratio of that data volume. As mentioned in Chapter 3, any disk volume that experiences more than 10 percent writes is not a good candidate for RAID 5 because of the excessive overhead associated with RAID 5 writes. Such a disk volume should use RAID 10 instead. To determine whether you can use RAID 5, monitor the system and track the number of writes versus reads. In either case, the I/O subsystem should be properly sized as outlined in Part II.

Configuring the I/O Subsystem on the Distributor

Since the snapshot actually stores a file on the distributor for snapshot replication rather than using the SQL Server database, you must make sure that the snapshot location has sufficient I/O capacity to absorb a large number of writes. Thus, the snapshot location is more suited for RAID 10 than for RAID 5. As you will see later in this section, in some cases locating the snapshot on the publisher may be more efficient.

Configuring the I/O Subsystem on the Subscriber

The subscriber will experience a large number of writes during snapshot replication. If the database is large, this process can take a significant amount of time. The performance of the snapshot can be enhanced by using a RAID 10 volume rather than RAID 5 because RAID 5 performs poorly for large numbers of writes.

Note   When configuring the I/O subsystems for snapshot replication, the size of the database should be considered. A snapshot replication that replicates only a few hundred rows and takes only a few seconds can easily work on any RAID level.

Set the Snapshot Location

Since snapshot replication copies the entire article to the distributor and then copies the entire article to the subscriber at a later time, it is possible to remove the distribution system from the replication process. The distributor is still used, but it can be configured to store the snapshot on the publisher. This will cut down on network activities.

You can set the snapshot location within the distributor by invoking the Configure Publishing and Distribution Wizard. Click the Publishers tab; you will see a screen similar to the one shown in Figure 14-2. You can set the distribution properties by clicking on the properties button, which is denoted by an ellipsis (...). This invokes the Properties screen, similar to the one shown in Figure 14-3. From here you can configure the snapshot to be located on the system on which the snapshot is generated. If you do so, make sure that this location has enough I/O capacity to handle the additional load that is generated by propagating the snapshot.

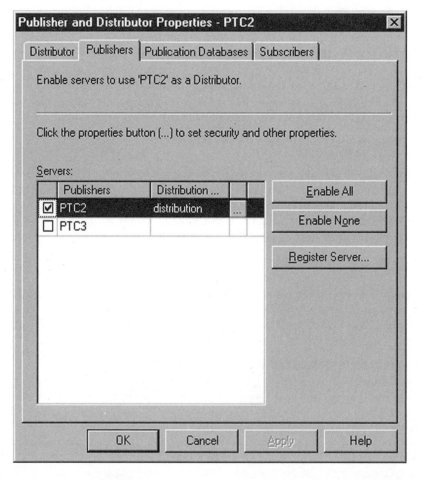

Figure 14-2 *The Publishers tab of the Configure Publishing and Distribution Wizard.*

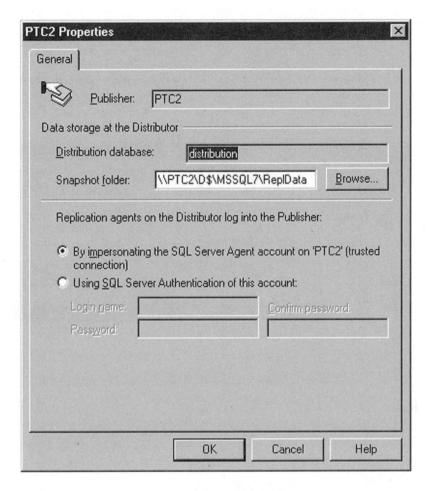

Figure 14-3 *The Properties screen for distribution.*

Note: When you configure the snapshot location on the distributor, you are doing so for all publications. Do not use this configuration if you are servicing more than one publisher system with this distributor.

Configure the Distributor and Publisher on the Same System

In cases in which all you are doing is snapshot replication, you can easily configure the publisher and distributor to be on the same system. This will cut down on network traffic because no extra network copy need be sent to the distributor. However, if performance on the publisher is an issue, you are better off keeping the snapshot on a remote distributor and letting the distributor handle the distribution overhead.

Increase BCP Threads

Performance can also be enhanced by increasing the number of BCP threads that are used for the snapshot process. This can be done through Enterprise Manager. Expand the Replication Monitor icon, then Agents, and then the Snapshot Agents folder within the console window in Enterprise Manager. Right-click on the desired publication and select Agent Profiles. This invokes the Snapshot Agent Profiles dialog box (see Figure 14-4).

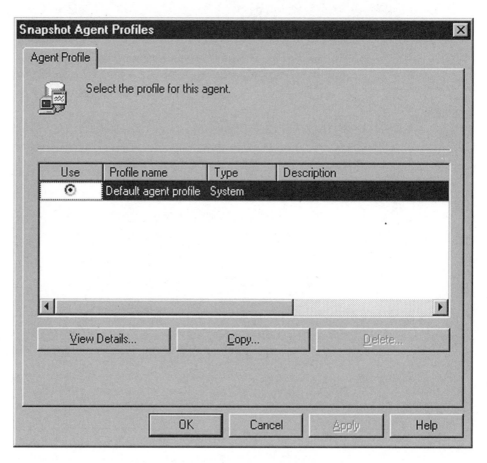

Figure 14-4 *The Snapshot Agent Profiles dialog box.*

In this dialog box, click Copy. This creates a copy of the agent profile, which you can then modify. You can increase the value of the *MaxBcp Threads* parameter in the Replication Agent Profile Details dialog box (see Figure 14-5). Once you have made your changes, name the profile and click OK. This saves the profile; you then select that profile from the Snapshot Agent Profiles dialog box for use in snapshot replication.

Once you have finished configuring your system for snapshot replication, you can begin the process of monitoring it, along with further tuning of the system as necessary.

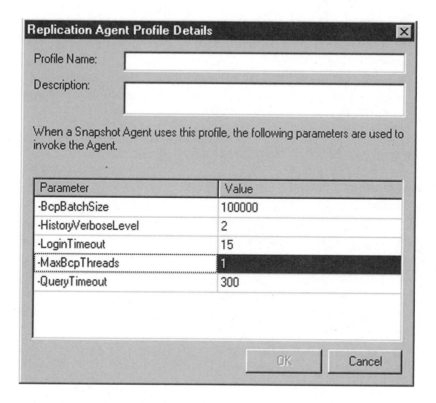

Figure 14-5 *The Replication Agent Profile Details dialog box.*

Monitoring the Snapshot System

Monitoring the snapshot system is done via the Windows NT Performance Monitor, using the following objects:

- **SQLServer: Replication Agents**   This object displays a count of each type of agent that is running.

- **SQLServer: Replication Dist.**   This object's Dist: Delivery Latency counter provides information on distribution latency.

- **SQLServer: Replication Snapshot**   This object provides information on snapshot performance.

- **PhysicalDisk**   The counters under this object are very useful since many performance problems related to snapshot replication are I/O related.

- **Processor**   This object provides information on the system processors.

- **System**   This object gives you a good overview of the entire system.

These counters will give you a fairly good idea of how things are going, but snapshot replication can occur quite quickly, so don't blink. Things to watch for include the following:

- **I/O bottlenecks** Are I/O rates too high? Look for I/Os per second and seconds per I/O. Follow the guidelines presented in Chapter 3 and throughout Part II to determine what is too high.

- **Network bottlenecks** It is difficult to find a network bottleneck, but you may be able to determine if you have one by calculating the network throughput and comparing that with the snapshot replication time.

By looking for I/O and network problems and solving them if they exist you will be able to improve the performance of snapshot replication.

Tuning the Snapshot System

Tuning the snapshot system usually just involves proper configuration, as mentioned previously. The critical things to look for during snapshot replication are I/O and network problems. To determine if you are network bound, you should look at the performance of the network and then determine if that network is sufficient for your replication needs. Let's look at an example.

Suppose you have a database that is 5 GB. In a 10BaseT network, there is a maximum bandwidth of 10 megabits per second, which is approximately 1 MB per second. Thus replicating this database will take the following amount of time:

$$[5 \ GB * 1024 \ (MB/GB)] \ / \ 1 \ (MB/sec) = 5120 \ seconds, \ or \ 1.4 \ hours$$

In contrast, a 100BaseT network can perform the same replication in 8.3 minutes. A Gigabit Ethernet network can do this same task in 51 seconds. The network comparison is summarized in Table 14-1.

Table 14-1 Comparison of Performance Times for Snapshot Replication with Various Network Speeds

Network Speed	Time (for 5-GB database)
10BaseT	5120 seconds (85.3 minutes, or 1.4 hours)
100BaseT	516 seconds (8.3 minutes)
Gigabit Ethernet	51 seconds

As you can see, the size of your network really does count. By performing calculations like this you can get a good idea of how fast the replication should take. If these tasks are taking much longer, you probably are experiencing a bottleneck somewhere else. How to find and solve these bottlenecks is covered throughout this book.

Tuning for Transactional Replication

Transactional replication is different from snapshot replication in that each individual transaction is replicated from the publisher to the distributor and then to the subscriber. This is accomplished by the Log Reader Agent reading the transaction log as described in the next section. Transactional replication is initially set up using a snapshot, as in snapshot replication; however, once this snapshot has been completed, replication is continuous.

Attributes of Transactional Replication

Transactional replication starts with a snapshot that is copied to the distributor and then to the subscriber. Once the snapshot has been completed, the Log Reader Agent reads the transaction log of the publisher either on a continual basis or on a regular schedule, depending on how you configure the Log Reader Agent.

On the publisher the only additional overhead comes from the reads being performed on the transaction log. The Log Reader Agent itself runs on the distributor and connects to the publisher in order to read the transaction log. These transactions are then placed into the distribution database on the distributor and are eventually sent to the subscribers. Factors that can limit transactional replication include the following:

- **I/O performance on the publisher's transaction log**   The transaction log on the publisher is read to determine what changes have been made to the database. Because the transaction log is now being read as well as being written, the sequential nature of the transaction log may be disrupted. This may cause a bottleneck if the I/O subsystem is not carefully configured.

- **Performance of the distributor**   Depending on how much replication is being done and how many publishers are using the distributor, there may be a performance problem at the distributor. Earlier in this chapter you learned how to configure and tune the distributor; all that information applies here.

- **Performance of the subscriber**   Depending on what activity is occurring on the subscriber, there may be a performance problem here. If this happens, you need to tune your SQL Server in the usual way.

Reducing the effect of these factors through proper sizing and configuration of the systems involved will improve performance.

Configuring for Transactional Replication

Tuning the publisher, distributor, and subscriber mainly involves proper configuration of these component's I/O subsystems. There are, however, some configuration choices that can make a great deal of difference for the performance of transactional replication. Here are some guidelines.

- Configure sufficient I/O capacity, following general I/O capacity guidelines. In addition some specific I/O changes should be made on the publisher because of the added overhead it experiences.
- Tune the commit batch size on the distributor.
- Tune the Log Reader Agent.

Let's look at each of these configuration guidelines.

Configure Sufficient I/O

You can enhance the performance of the entire replication process by configuring sufficient I/O capacity. As with any SQL Server system, the transaction log should be located on its own RAID 1 volume for data protection. The data files should be located on one or more RAID 10 or RAID 5 volumes. Unlike with the snapshot replication, there are only minor I/O considerations for the publisher, distributor, and subscriber in transactional replication. Those considerations are described here.

Configuring the I/O Subsystem on the Publisher

In general the publisher should follow normal SQL Server configuration guidelines as described throughout this book. In addition to the normal configuration guidelines, you may need to increase the I/O capacity of the transaction log. Normally it is recommended that the transaction log be configured on a RAID 1 volume. If necessary (depending on how busy your system is) you may need to use more disk drives in a RAID 10 volume. RAID 5 is not appropriate for the transaction log.

Configuring the I/O Subsystem on the Distributor

The distributor should be configured so that the distribution database has its transaction log on a dedicated RAID 1 disk volume. This allows the distribution database to achieve maximum transaction log performance, thus improving the overall performance of the distributor.

Configuring the I/O Subsystem on the Subscriber

Transaction replication does not call for any special I/O configuration on the subscriber. Simply follow general sizing and configuration guidelines as described throughout this book.

Tune the Commit Batch Size on the Distributor

The commit batch size on the distributor determines how many replication transactions are committed in a single batch. While the distribution database is being updated, locks are held on the distribution tables. Increasing the batch size allows more rows to be committed at a time, thus increasing the time that locks on those rows are held. By decreasing the batch size, fewer rows will be committed at a time, thus decreasing the time that the locks on those rows are held and giving other processes a chance to access the distribution database.

The commit batch size allows you to perform a trade-off. By using a smaller batch size, locks will be held for shorter times but will occur more often. A larger commit batch size is more efficient because more rows are committed at a time, but the total lock time will be increased. For example, if the batch size is small you may have to allocate 10 locks for 1 ms each. A much larger commit size may allow you to do the entire commit in 7 ms. Thus the cumulative lock time is much longer, but the time that an individual lock is held is much shorter.

If there is a large amount of activity on the distribution database from several different sources (that is, the publisher and several subscribers), you may want to try reducing the batch size. If the Log Reader Agent is running on a periodic schedule and has a lot of transactions to insert into the distribution database, you may benefit from a larger batch size. There may actually be no need to change it, but if you do, compare the results obtained from both increasing and decreasing the batch size in order to determine which is better.

You can configure the commit batch size through Enterprise Manager. Expand the Replication Monitor icon, then Agents, and then the Distribution Agents folder within the console window in Enterprise Manager. Right-click on the appropriate Distribution Agent and click Agent Profiles. This invokes the Distribution Agent Profiles dialog box (see Figure 14-6).

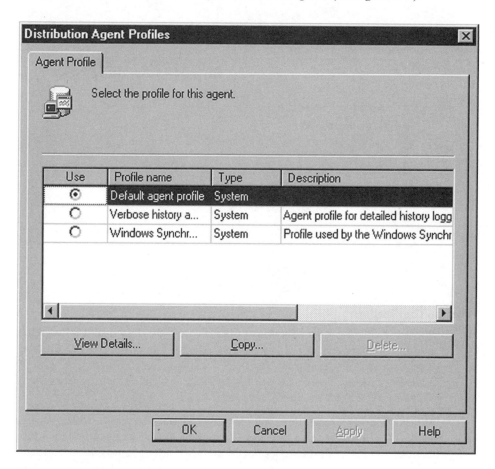

Figure 14-6 *The Distribution Agent Profiles dialog box.*

In this dialog box, select a profile and click Copy. This creates a copy of the selected agent profile, which you can then modify. You can change the *CommitBatchSize* parameter in the Distribution Agent Profile Details dialog box (see Figure 14-7). Once you have made your changes and named the profile, click OK. This saves the profile; you then select that profile from the Distribution Agent Profiles dialog box for use in transactional replication.

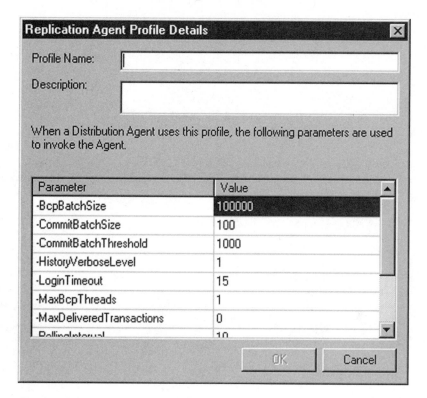

Figure 14-7 *The Distribution Agent Profile Details dialog box.*

Tune the Log Reader

By configuring the log reader you may be able to reduce its effect on the publisher's transaction log. There are several ways to make the log reader process more efficient. One way is to use a caching controller for the log drive volume. Because the Log Reader Agent reads from the log drive, a cache on a controller will allow the read from the cache, rather than causing a random I/O to occur.

Another way to tune the log reader is to modify the frequency with which it runs. The log reader can run on a continuous basis or can be configured to run periodically. Configuring the periodic frequency of the log reader agent is done via the polling interval parameter. On a system that is not experiencing a lot of update activity, it may be acceptable for the log reader to run continuously; however, on systems in which the transaction log is busy, configuring the log reader to run less frequently can improve performance of the publisher. This is so because reads from the transaction log tend to randomize the otherwise sequential I/Os. If the publisher does not read from the transaction log as frequently, the transaction log I/Os will be allowed to remain mostly sequential.

Yet another way to make the Log Reader Agent more efficient in heavily used systems is to increase the read batch size. This parameter specifies how transactions are read from the transaction log and copied to the distributor. In addition, it may be useful to increase the batch size when increasing the polling interval. If you increase the read batch size on the Log Reader Agent, we recommend that you increase the commit batch size on the distributor to correspond to the new read batch size.

You can configure the Log Reader Agent through Enterprise Manager. Expand the Replication Monitor icon, then Agents, and then the Log Reader Agents folder within the console window in Enterprise Manager. Right-click on the appropriate Log Reader Agent and select Agent Profiles. This invokes the Log Reader Agent Profiles dialog box (see Figure 14-8).

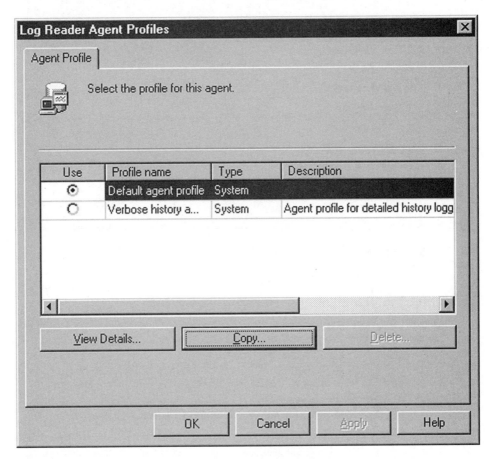

Figure 14-8 *The Log Reader Agent Profiles dialog box.*

In this dialog box, highlight a profile and click Copy. This creates a copy of the selected agent profile, which you can then modify. You can change the *PollingInterval* parameter as well as the *ReadBatchSize* parameter in the Log Reader Agent Profile Details dialog box (see Figure 14-9). Once you have made your changes and named the profile, click OK. This saves the profile; you then select that profile from the Log Reader Agent Profiles screen.

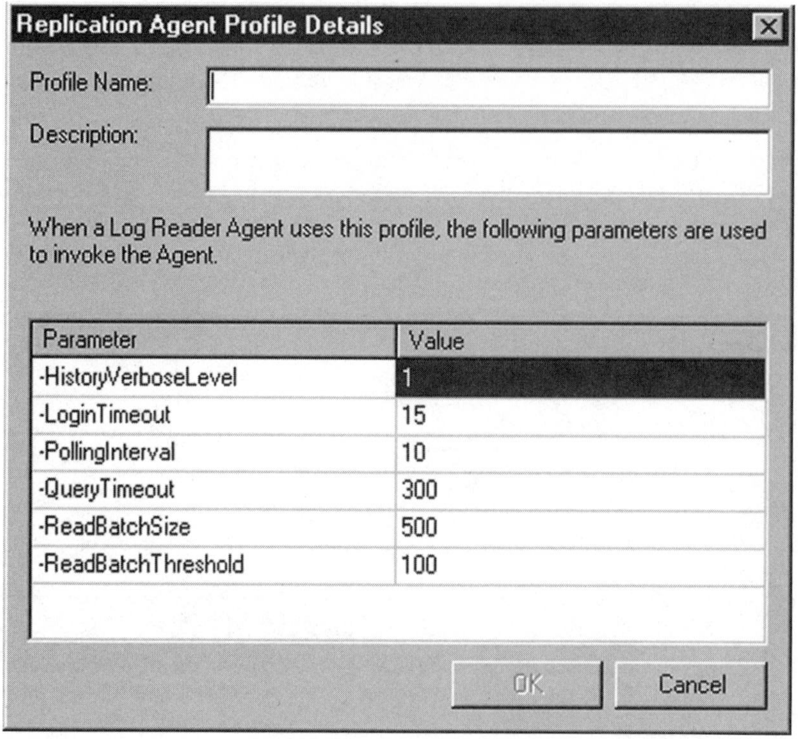

Figure 14-9 *The Log Reader Agent Profile Details dialog box.*

Monitoring the Transactional Replication System

As with the other replication types, monitoring transactional replication is done via the Windows NT Performance Monitor. Use the following objects:

- **SQLServer: Replication Agents** Keeps track of the number of each type of agent that is running.

- **SQLServer: Replication Dist.** Provides information on distribution latency. Long latencies can be a sign that the distributor is overloaded.

- **SQLServer: Replication Logreader** Provides data on log reader activity and latency. Look for long latencies, which can be an indication that there is a problem reading the transaction log on the publisher. Also watch the number of delivered transactions per second. If this value is high, you may need to add more I/O capacity to the disk volumes that hold the transaction log.

By using the Windows NT Performance Monitor to monitor these values, you can sometimes determine if there is a performance problem in the Log Reader Agent or in the distributor. This PerfMon data provides a lot of valuable information, but may not always identify problems.

Tuning the Transactional Replication System

The main steps in tuning the transactional replication system are to properly configure the system and monitor it as discussed earlier. In addition, after the system is in production and you can monitor it, you may need to modify the read batch size and the polling interval. The default value of 10 seconds is usually pretty good for the latter. Shortening the polling interval causes transactions to replicate faster, at the expense of more overhead on the transaction log. Lengthening the polling interval reduces the overhead on the transaction log, but leaves transactions in the log longer before they are replicated.

In update-intensive systems you may need to increase the read batch size. This will allow the Log Reader Agent to read more transactions at a time from the transaction log. By increasing this value and leaving the polling interval at 10 seconds, you will be able to replicate more transactions with less added overhead.

As with snapshot replication, it is necessary to monitor the capacity of the network and increase it if necessary. If your system appears to be performing well (that is, CPU and I/O usage are within their capacity limits) but the replication process seems to be taking too long, you may have a network problem. Unfortunately, network problems cannot be diagnosed via PerfMon; you will need to use a network monitor such as SMS (System Management Server). Look for network usage near the capacity of the network card.

In addition to these tuning guidelines, remember that the publisher, distributor, and subscribers are SQL Server systems just like any other SQL Server system. Thus, follow the tuning guidelines given throughout this book when dealing with these components.

Tuning for Merge Replication

Unlike transactional replication and snapshot replication, merge replication is not a one-way replication. Modifications can be made on either the publisher or any number of subscribers. Another difference is that whereas transactional replication is external to the normal operations of SQL Server (it is performed by reading the transaction log), merge replication uses internal triggers that are created on the replicated tables in order to track changes to them.

Attributes of Merge Replication

As is the case for transactional replication, merge replication begins with a snapshot, but since the snapshot only occurs once it is not important to tune it. The merge system creates tables both on the publisher and distributor in order to perform replication. In addition a new column holding a unique row identifier is added to every replicated table so that the replication agent can effectively track changes. Since merge replication is bidirectional, this column is used to note that a row has been replicated. Without this column, an insert done for replication would then be replicated back to the originator and would ping-pong back and forth (which is why transaction replication cannot function bidirectionally).

When a row is inserted or modified, the trigger marks that row as needing replication. When the Merge Agent runs, it collects all the marked rows and sends them to the distributor for replication. At the same time, the Merge Agent modifies any rows on the publisher that have been modified on the subscriber system or systems. In this manner, two-way replication is accomplished.

Configuring for Merge Replication

As with transactional replication and snapshot replication, the I/O subsystem and network are very important for merge replication. In addition to configuring sufficient I/O, you can improve merge replication by configuring the merge batch size. Increasing the batch size so that there are fewer, larger batches will cause replication to be more efficient. In addition to the merge batch size, you may want to tune the initial snapshot replication as described earlier. I/O configuration and the other considerations are described here.

Configure Sufficient I/O

You can enhance the performance of the entire replication process by configuring sufficient I/O capacity. As with any SQL Server system the transaction log should be located on its own RAID 1 volume for data protection. The data files should be located on one or more RAID 10 or RAID 5 volumes. As with transactional replication, merge replication causes only minor I/O considerations for the publisher, distributor, and subscriber.

Configuring the I/O Subsystem on the Publisher

In general the publisher should follow normal SQL Server configuration guidelines as shown throughout this book. Unlike transactional replication, no additional load is put on the transaction log, so just follow normal tuning guidelines.

Configuring the I/O Subsystem on the Distributor

You should configure the distributor so that the distribution database has its transaction log on a dedicated RAID 1 disk volume. This will allow the distribution database to achieve maximum transaction log performance, thus improving the overall performance of the distributor.

Configuring the I/O Subsystem on the Subscriber

Because merge replication is multidirectional, the subscriber and publisher are tuned similarly. Follow the general sizing and configuration guidelines as discussed throughout this book.

Configure the Merge Batch Size

In busy systems it is possible to improve the performance of merge replication by configuring the merge batch size. The merge batch size determines how many changed rows are copied to the distributor at a time. By increasing the batch size, fewer and larger batches will be sent, which may be more efficient.

You can configure the Merge Agent through Enterprise Manager. Expand the Replication Monitor icon, then Agents, and then the Merge Agents folder within the console window in Enterprise Manager. Right-click on the Merge Agent you want and select Agent Profiles. This invokes the Merge Agent Profiles dialog box (see Figure 14-10).

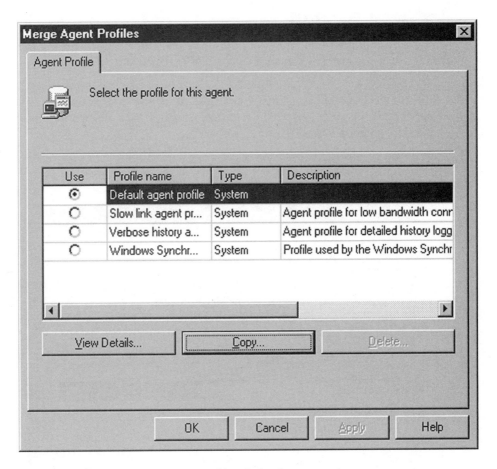

Figure 14-10 *The Merge Agent Profiles dialog box.*

In this dialog box, highlight a profile and click Copy. This creates a copy of the selected agent profile, which you can then modify. The Merge Agent Profile Details dialog box is shown in Figure 14-11. Here there are a number of parameters that you can configure, including the following:

- **BcpBatchSize**   The number of rows to be sent. Increasing this parameter will increase the number of rows that are copied in a single bulk copy operation. Depending on your network and I/O subsystem, this could increase performance or may not help at all. In some cases, decreasing the batch size may increase performance. Determining the best value for this parameter requires some trial-and-error testing.

- **DownloadGenerationsPerBatch**   The size of the generation batch download. This is essentially the change information for merge replication. Increasing this parameter will enhance performance for systems in which large numbers of rows are modified at a time or in which frequent updates are done.

- **UploadGenerationsPerBatch** The batch upload size. This is essentially the change information. As with the download batch size, increasing this parameter will enhance performance for systems in which large numbers of rows are modified at a time or in which frequent updates are done.

You should document your changes to these parameters and any performance improvements or degradation that result from these changes. This information will enhance further configuration and tuning.

Once you have made your changes and named the profile, click OK. This saves the profile; you then select that profile from the Merge Agent Profiles dialog box.

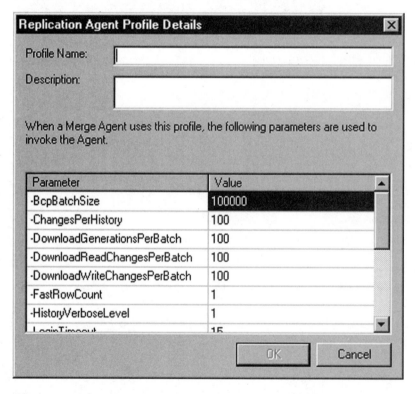

Figure 14-11 *The Merge Agent Profile Details dialog box.*

Monitoring the Merge Replication System

You monitor merge replication via the Windows NT Performance Monitor, using the following objects:

- **SQLServer: Replication Agents** Stores the number of each type of agent that is running.

- **SQLServer: Replication Merge**   Provides data on merge rates. This object provides information on conflicts per second, uploads per second, and downloads per second.

The SQL Sever merge replication counters are not extremely helpful for determining performance problems. The best way to tune a merge replication system is to simply tune the SQL Server system as normal and pay special attention to the network. Look for normal performance bottlenecks and follow the guidelines given earlier in the chapter to determine if the distributor is overloaded.

Tuning the Merge Replication System

The main steps in tuning the merge replication system are to properly configure the system and monitor it as discussed previously, with a special emphasis on I/O and network performance. Once you have put the system into production you can monitor it via the Performance Monitor, but you will not find very useful merge data. Instead you must rely on other SQL Server counters and Windows NT counters in order to tune the system.

As mentioned earlier, you may want to modify the BCP and batch sizes if your system is doing a lot of updates. Increasing the BCP size will increase the performance of the original snapshot. Increasing the batch sizes will move more changes at a time, which may be more efficient. By moving more changes at a time you affect the system less frequently; however, each time you do, you perform more work, thus causing a larger effect on the system.

In addition to these changes, it is possible to change the polling interval, although the default polling interval usually works fine. Before tuning the polling interval, try changing the batch sizes instead. If you feel that you need merge replication to run more frequently or less frequently, then change the polling interval.

As with other replication types, you should monitor the network and increase its capacity if necessary. If your system appears to be performing well (that is, CPU and I/O usage are within their capacity limits) but the replication process seems to be taking too long, you may have a network problem. PerfMon does not have a counter that will show you network problems. A network monitor such as SMS (System Management Server) should be used. Look for network usage that is near the capacity of the network card. If you are near the capacity of your network, either purchase faster network cards or add a private network for the purposes of replication or backup and recovery, or both.

In addition to these tuning guidelines, remember that the publisher, distributor, and subscribers are SQL Server systems just like any other SQL Server system. Thus, you should follow the tuning guidelines given throughout this book.

Summary

SQL Server 7 offers three types of replication: snapshot, transactional, and merge. Tuning replication depends on what type of replication you are running, although there are some general tuning guidelines for the distributor because it is involved in all replication types. Only a few specific things need to be tuned for replication. Most of the tuning involves properly configuring the I/O subsystems of the publisher, distributor, and subscribers for replication, and then monitoring and reconfiguring those components as necessary. The next chapter explains how to configure and tune a system for high-performance backup and recovery.

Chapter 15
High-Performance
Backup and Recovery

Your company's most valuable asset may be the data in its databases. Therefore, one of the most important duties of the DBA is to protect that data by forming a backup and recovery strategy as well as a disaster recovery plan. Without such plans, you may lose data that may cost thousands or even millions of dollars.

As with any other activity that runs on the SQL Server system, backup and recovery comes at a cost. The backup process entails a certain amount of overhead on the system while it is running. It is therefore to your advantage to minimize this cost by improving the performance of backup operations. This chapter explains how to improve the speed of backup operations and how to set up the best backup and recovery solutions for your business. It also presents a variety of guidelines and tips for improving your backup and recovery strategy and for setting up a disaster recovery plan.

Backup and Recovery Concepts

Backup and restore are related topics that have to do with saving data from the database for later use and copying that data back to the system. Recovery has to do with the ability of the RDBMS to survive a system failure and replay transactions. Throughout this chapter the term *recovery* is used to describe restoring the database and then recovering transactions.

Backup and Restore

Database backup and restore operations are similar to the backup and restore operations that can be done with the OS. The backup operation involves copying data from the database to another location. This operation may be a full backup, in which the entire database is copied, or an incremental backup, in which only recent changes are copied. The transaction log is also backed up on a regular basis. The transaction log backup is used to restore transactions that have been done since the last full or incremental backup.

The restore operation involves copying the backup data to the database. This process should not be confused with recovery. These topics are separate and should be treated as such. The restore operation is essentially a reloading of the database from the backup files.

Recovery

Recovery is the ability of the database to replay (recover) transactions after a system failure. Because SQL Server does not write changes to the data files immediately to disk every time a change is made in the database, a system failure might leave the database in a corrupt state. To maintain the integrity of the database, SQL Server logs changes in the transaction log. Before a transaction can be committed, the change information must be written to the transaction log. In the event of a system failure, on restart SQL Server uses the transaction log to roll forward transactions that had been committed and roll back transactions that had not been committed at the time of the failure.

> **Caution** The transaction log is essential to the recovery of transactions in the event of a failure and is therefore essential to the integrity of the database. Because it is so important, the transaction log should always reside on a RAID 1 or RAID 10 (mirrored) volume.

When a transaction is rolled back by SQL Server, the transaction is nullified and all the data changed by this transaction is restored to its original values. This process is identical to concluding a transaction with the ROLLBACK command. When a transaction is rolled forward, the changes that it had made to the database are replayed in order to synchronize the data files with the current state of the database.

In the event of a system failure that requires the database to be restored using backup files, the transaction log and transaction log backups are used to recover the database to the point of failure. Thus, restore and recovery operations work together. In the event of a power failure or a spontaneous system reboot, only a recovery operation may be necessary.

Types of Backups

Several methods exist for performing backups. These methods differ by the type and amount of data being backed up. This section describes the different types of backups: the full backup, differential backup, and transaction log backup.

Full Backup

A full backup involves backing up the entire database. All the data files that are part of the database are backed up. In systems with multiple databases, all the databases should be backed up. Depending on how often the data is modified, these databases may be backed up on different schedules. With large databases this operation can be quite time-consuming. This chapter explains how to minimize this time by tuning the backup system. The backup time can also be reduced by performing differential backups or filegroup backups rather than full backups.

File or Filegroup Backups

File or filegroup backups involve backing up a single file or the files that make up a filegroup. This operation is much faster than backing up the entire database, but protects only the data that has been backed up. The entire backup is composed of individual file or filegroup backups from different times. In the event of a system failure that requires a restore, it may take much longer to restore the database from the collection of file or filegroup backups than from a full backup because you must restore all the transaction log backups that occurred after the last backup was performed on the file or filegroup that failed. If the entire database has to be restored and the file or filegroup backups are from different times, the transaction log backups must be applied from the time of the oldest individual backup component.

Differential Backup

Differential backups allow you to back up only the information that has changed since the last backup. Differential backups are faster and consume less disk space than full backups because they back up only part of the data. The downside is that differential backups are more difficult and time-consuming to restore than full backups. A differential backup requires the restoration of the last full backup and the last differential backup before failure.

Transaction Log Backup

As changes are made to the database, all information about them is logged in the transaction log. Because writes to the data files are not immediate, it is important to log these changes to a durable medium (that is, one that is not subject to power failures) such as a disk drive. If the changes were not logged to durable media and power were to be lost or the system were to fail, it would be impossible to recover unrecorded transactions. SQL Server therefore logs all changes to the transaction log. A transaction is not considered committed until the commit record has been written to the transaction log. Because the transaction log stores a large amount of data, it is necessary to periodically clear it out to make room for more log records. SQL Server clears the transaction log as part of the transaction log backup.

Factors Affecting Performance of Backup and Recovery

A number of factors affect backup and recovery performance. It is impossible to say which performance factor is most important, since any number of components can cause a performance bottleneck. This section explores the most common sources of backup and recovery bottlenecks, which include the I/O subsystem, the network, and SQL Server itself. First let's look at how these components work together to perform a backup.

The Backup Process

A typical backup operation for SQL Server consists of the following steps:

1. The data is read from the SQL Server database or file to be backed up. Because SQL Server recognizes that backup I/Os are sequential, these I/Os are combined into an I/O that is larger than the normal 8 KB page size. During backup and recovery operations, 64-KB I/Os are performed.

2. The data that has been read is either written to tape or disk or copied over the network to the network backup server. This backup thread will not read any more data until the copy has completed.

3. If a network backup server is being used, the data is copied to memory on the backup server and then the backup data is copied to disk. While this operation is taking place there is still no I/O activity on the SQL Server system because of the backup thread.

4. The control of the backup operation is returned to the backup process on the SQL Server system.

One problem with this process is that it is sequential. Parts of the system (either the SQL Server system or the backup server) are periodically idle while other components of the system are busy. By performing these operations in parallel, all components can be kept busy at the same time. We discuss this in more detail in the section "SQL Server" later in this chapter.

I/O Subsystem

The I/O subsystem can frequently be a cause of a backup and recovery bottleneck. The I/O bottleneck can occur either on the SQL Server system or on the backup medium itself. On the SQL Server system, I/Os for backups occur in the same manner as with any other disk operation. However, since the goal of the operation is to copy data from the database as quickly as possible, the I/O subsystem may often be overdriven. Because you are copying data from the database to a backup medium, this medium (disk or tape) may also be a bottleneck.

I/O on the SQL Server System

To configure your system for maximum backup performance, monitor it during backup operations as well as during normal day-to-day operations. When monitoring the I/O subsystem during a backup operation, look for the number of I/Os per second as well as the seconds per I/O. If disk latencies (seconds per I/O) exceed 25 ms, you may be experiencing an I/O bottleneck on the SQL Server system.

I/O on the Backup System

Your goal should be to minimize the time that a backup takes because running a backup creates overhead on the SQL Server system. While this additional overhead exists on the SQL Server system, the user community will experience degraded performance. The I/O capacity of the backup medium is often a bottleneck because the backup system may be underconfigured.

Backing Up to Tape

To determine if your backup performance is adversely affected by the performance of the tape device to which you are backing up, calculate the maximum throughput of the tape device and compare it with your backup times. If this comparison indicates that your backups are occurring at tape speed, then the tape device is a limiting factor.

For example, if you are using a tape drive that can write data at 1 GB per hour, and it takes 2 hours to back up 2 GB, then you are probably being limited by the speed of the tape device. Conversely, if you are backing up to a tape device that can write data at 1 GB per hour and it is taking 3 hours to back up 2 GB, then your problem probably lies elsewhere.

You can improve backup performance by taking any of the following actions:

- **Replace the tape device.** The tape device can be replaced with a faster device if your current device is too slow. The fastest tape devices claim backup performance of up to 150 GB per hour.

- **Add tape devices.** You can back up to multiple devices simultaneously, which increases the throughput of the backup by striping the data and by writing it in parallel.

- **Back up to disk as a first stage.** A typical method of increasing backup performance is to first back up all files to disk, either locally or over the network, and then copy those backup files to tape. This increases the performance of the crucial stage of the backup during which SQL Server is involved. This method is known as *staging* the backup, and the area on disk that is used as the intermediary area is known as the *staging area*.

As you can see, there are several methods of increasing performance of a backup to tape. These methods can be combined to provide for better backup performance, as discussed later in this chapter.

Backing Up to Disk

Backing up to disk is a common way of performing SQL Server backups. To optimize the performance of these backups, you should configure the I/O subsystem on the backup system to be able to handle large numbers of write I/Os. Since SQL Server will write to the backup system as fast as possible, you should make sure that the latter system is not a bottleneck.

To determine if the backup system is a bottleneck, use the Performance Monitor with the *diskperf* option. Look at the number of I/Os per second as well as the seconds per I/O. If disk latencies are greater than 20 ms, you are experiencing degraded performance. Increasing the performance of the I/O subsystem will increase backup performance. Remember that disk performance is degraded if the I/O rate exceeds 85 I/Os per second.

Because I/Os to the backup system are 100 percent writes, RAID 5 is inappropriate for backups because it has a high write overhead. RAID 10 is the recommended configuration (unless you are severely budget limited) because it offers a high degree of fault tolerance and incurs only one additional physical I/O for each write I/O.

Network

When performing SQL Server backups over the network, the network itself can be a bottleneck. It may surprise you to know that the network is often the cause of backup performance problems. Let's look at a few examples of how this can occur.

A typical 10BaseT network has a throughput of 10 megabits per second, which is approximately 1.25 MB per second. This network can back up approximately 4,500 MB per hour, or 4.4 GB per hour. It can take a significant amount of time to back up your database at this rate. In contrast, a 100BaseT network can achieve 44 GB per hour, and a Gigabit Ethernet network can back up 440 GB per hour. If you use a Gigabit Ethernet network and a fast I/O subsystem on the SQL Server system, you must ensure that the backup system can support the resulting I/O rates.

> **Note**   These performance ratings are theoretical maximums. Depending on the packet size, network traffic, and the individual components in your network, you may find that your actual throughput is less.

SQL Server

In addition to providing sufficient I/O and network capacity, you can also improve backup performance by providing sufficient SQL Server resources. You can do so through SQL Server configuration parameters and through the design of the database itself.

Backup Threads

When backups are run to more than one backup device, the backup operations will be done in parallel, thus improving the performance of the backup. Each backup operation requires a SQL Server thread in order to run. If the *max worker threads* parameter has not been set high enough or if the system is so busy that all the worker threads are in use, the backup operation must wait for another backup thread to finish before it can acquire a thread. Thus, it is important to make sure that the *max worker threads* parameter has a sufficiently high value. The default setting of 255 is usually sufficient to provide enough threads to achieve adequate parallelism on backups; if you have decreased this value for other tuning purposes, you may experience backup and recovery performance problems.

Multiple Backup Devices

When multiple backup devices are used, the backup operation will proceed in parallel, thus improving performance. By keeping enough backup threads active concurrently it is possible to keep the SQL Server system and the backup server active at the same time. In addition, RAID controllers thrive on concurrent I/Os. Since a disk array is made up of many disk drives, more concurrent I/Os mean that all the disk drives can be active at once, thus increasing performance.

Configuring the System for Maximum Backup and Recovery Performance

To achieve optimal performance on backup and recovery operations, it is necessary to properly configure the system so that there is sufficient I/O and network capacity to run the backup as quickly as possible. This section discusses methods for determining the capacity of the I/O subsystem and network and ways of configuring these devices in order to achieve better performance.

Analyzing Performance Needs of a Backup

It is always a good idea to start by analyzing the performance needs of your backup, then determine if you have hardware capable of meeting these needs. This analysis provides a goal to shoot for as well as to measure your success against. In addition, it provides valuable information that you can present to management if it is necessary to purchase additional hardware.

Determine the Goals

Determining a throughput goal is a fairly easy task. (In fact, this goal may already be defined in an SLA.) To determine the required throughput, simply determine the size of the backup set and divide by the allotted backup time window. This will tell you exactly what throughput you must achieve.

For example, if you have a database that is 250 GB and you are allotted a 4-hour time window for backups, the required throughput is 250 GB divided by 4 hours, or 62.5 GB per hour. This capacity may or may not be achievable with your current hardware configuration, as we will determine in the next section.

Calculate the Capacity

To calculate the throughput or capacity of the backup system, you must examine each component. The most likely outcome of this analysis is that you will find the throughput of the entire system to be limited by a single component. Charting the throughput of each link in the chain can determine which is the weakest link.

For example, consider a system that is backing up the large SQL Server system described earlier (a 250-GB database) to a backup system over a 100BaseT network. The database system is configured with 20 disk drives running RAID 10. The backup system has a disk subsystem configured with 7 disk drives running RAID 5. To analyze this system, you should look at the capacity of each of the components.

The system that is running SQL Server (the system that is being backed up) is configured with 20 disk drives running RAID 10. Using the rule of thumb of 85 I/Os per second per disk drive yields the following read capacity (remember that SQL Server backups use 64-KB I/Os):

*85 I/Os per second per disk * 20 disks * 64 KB per I/O = 108,800 KB/sec = 373.5 GB/hr*

As you have already seen in the section "Network," a 100BaseT network has a theoretical maximum of 44 GB/hr.

The backup system is configured as RAID 5, so each write causes four physical I/Os. Thus the capacity of the seven-disk RAID 5 disk subsystem is

*(85 I/Os per second per disk * 7 disks * 64 KB per I/O) / 4 I/Os per write = 9520 KB/sec = 32.6 GB/hr*

Write caching may help improve this performance. However, the RAID 5 write performance will be improved only slightly by adding the cache.

The I/O subsystem on the backup server and the network could both be limiting factors in this scenario, as you can clearly see from the values in the following table:

Component	Performance
I/O subsystem on the SQL Server system	373.5 GB/hr
100BaseT network	44 GB/hr (theoretical maximum)
I/O subsystem on the backup system	32.6 GB/hr

Note The figures in this example are simplifications of the actual performance of these components in order to illustrate the importance of each component. The actual performance depends on many different factors, such as block size, write caches, and controller performance. In other words, your mileage may vary.

Compare the Results

Once you have calculated the performance of the components that are available for performing the backup, you will have a good idea of how the system will behave. Comparing the values you obtain with your desired goals may also give you a clue as to how the system can be improved. In the example system, the required throughput of 62.5 GB/hr cannot be achieved because of the I/O limitation of 32.6 GB/hr on the backup system as well as the limitation of the network. Clearly a configuration change is necessary.

Configuring the Network

As you have seen, you must first determine your performance needs and then configure your system so that it is able to sustain the performance necessary to meet those needs. In the case of the network, several configuration options are available.

One way to achieve high performance is to use the fastest network hardware available. Hardware such as the Gigabit network performs well but can be quite expensive. If your budget allows for it, a high-performance network is an effective solution.

Another way to improve backup performance is to configure a dedicated network for backup and recovery operations. This alternative allows the entire bandwidth of the network hardware to be used for backups, thus speeding up performance. Ensuring that the overhead on the SQL Server system is not prolonged due to network problems is especially important for transaction log backups, as mentioned earlier.

If a dedicated network is not enough, you can improve backup performance by configuring multiple network cards in your system and creating multiple networks. These additional networks can be used specifically for backup and recovery. To configure multiple networks, create new subnets, each with its own IP subnet address. The backup system and the SQL Server system should each have an address on these new subnets. When configuring the backup devices, give them the IP address of the backup system. Assign each backup device an address on a different subnet, as shown in Figure 15-1.

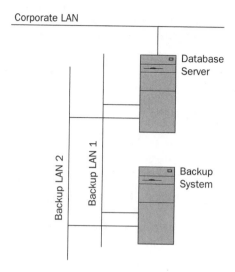

Figure 15-1 *Using multiple subnets for backup and recovery operations.*

You can configure the backup devices on the individual subnets within SQL Server Enterprise Manager. Select the database that you are going to back up, then select Backup Database from the Tools menu. Click the Add button to add a new backup device. Instead of providing a drive name, use the full UNC (Universal Naming Convention) name for the device path. In order to specify exactly which network device to use, specify the IP address as the server name, as shown in Figure 15-2.

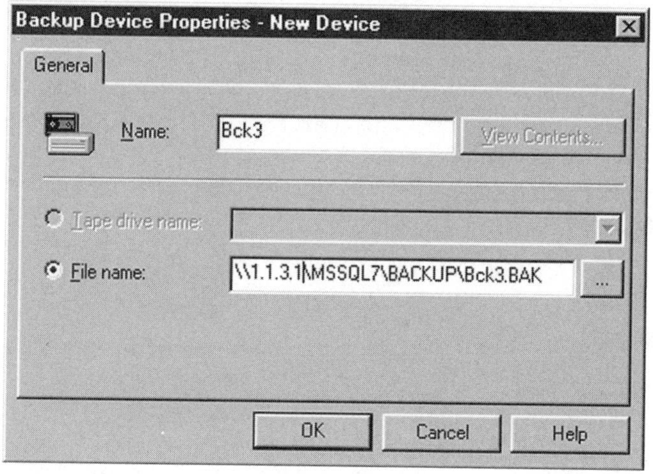

Figure 15-2 *Specifying the UNC name in the Backup Device Properties–New Device dialog box.*

If multiple network segments are needed, create multiple backup devices that each use a different segment. In this manner, the network bandwidth can be increased by adding more and more networks.

Configuring the I/O Subsystem

The configuration of the I/O subsystem on the SQL Server system is usually dictated by normal performance tuning activities. If your system operates under a heavy workload, you have probably already configured the I/O subsystem on your server. However, if your backup is experiencing a performance problem on the SQL Server system, you can monitor the I/O subsystem and add more disk drives if necessary.

Configuring the I/O subsystem on the backup server is a fairly straightforward activity. Once you know what performance is required, you can follow the guidelines given throughout this chapter to determine how many disk drives are needed and how they should be configured. Since the I/Os to the backup system's disk drive are 100 percent writes during the backup operation, you must consider the additional I/Os generated by RAID 5. Table 15-1 shows approximately how much throughput can be achieved when writing to disk subsystems using various RAID configurations.

Table 15-1 Throughput Comparisons for Different RAID Configurations (100% Writes)

Configuration	Throughput Capacity per Disk Drive
RAID 0 at 64 KB per I/O	18.7 GB/hr
RAID 1 or RAID 10 at 64 KB per I/O	9.3 GB/hr
RAID 5 at 64 KB per I/O	4.7 GB/hr

Although the figures in Table 15-1 are rough estimations of throughput, this information can help you calculate the number of disk drives necessary to achieve the desired backup performance. It is important to remember that if you exceed the recommended throughput as shown in the table, the I/O latency will increase, thus degrading I/O performance. Degraded I/O performance will degrade backup and recovery performance.

Backup Scenarios

This section suggests some methods for performing backup and recovery operations and discusses how they can be optimized. The examples in this section will give you ideas on how you can best configure your backup and recovery system for performance while customizing it based on your individual needs and budget.

Local Backups

Local backups are probably the most common type of configuration for small to medium installations. Here the backup device or devices are connected directly to the system where SQL Server is running, and the backup goes directly from SQL Server onto the tape drive or disk.

Advantages

Because the backup medium is local, there is no need to transfer data across the network, thus eliminating the network as a potential bottleneck. This can be a big advantage on systems that share a busy network. You also have the option to back up from SQL Server to disk and then copy the backup file to tape. This can reduce the time during which SQL Server performance is degraded. Local backups are the best choice for very large systems in order to avoid sending large amounts of data over a network.

Disadvantages

The major disadvantage of the local backup is that the backup files are local. If something were to happen to the system, such as a fire, the backup medium would be destroyed along with the database. In addition, if the server were disabled it would be necessary to recover the backup files before a new system could replace the problem system. Furthermore, for many systems a local backup is not feasible because of the number of SQL Server resources involved.

Configuration

If you are backing up directly to tape, you need to ensure that your tape system has the capacity to perform the desired backup in the desired time frame. This may involve purchasing faster tape hardware or striping the backup over several tape devices.

If you are backing up to disk, the disk drives should be configured in a RAID 10 array. RAID 5 cannot absorb all the required write I/Os without causing high latencies. This array should be separate from the transaction log and data arrays so that it does not interfere with their performance. Follow the procedures outlined earlier to configure sufficient I/O capacity.

Network Backups

Network backups are very common. They can range from a server supporting one or more SQL Server systems on a network with a shared disk or tape system up to a full-blown Enterprise backup server (which is the same thing on a larger scale). By using a network, resources that may be relatively unused for much of the time can be shared among several servers.

The most common scenario is a network backup server that stores the most recent full backups on disk, as well as storing the transaction log backups that have occurred since those full backups. Either on a regular schedule or triggered by an event, these backup files are then written to tape and archived in a safe storage facility. As needed, older backup files are removed from the disk subsystem after they have been archived to tape. In the event of a system failure, the latest full backup is on disk and can be easily and quickly restored, along with the latest transaction log backups.

Advantages

The main advantage of the network backup server is that the resources can be shared among multiple SQL Server systems. Instead of having several systems that back up to an array of two or three disk drives, you can combine the disks into a larger array. This larger array can perform the backup much faster because the I/O capacity is greater.

Disadvantages

The disadvantage of the network backup server is that the backup runs over the network, which can very easily become a performance bottleneck. More complex configuration and backup coordination may be needed to overcome this problem.

Configuration

You need to follow some tuning and configuration guidelines in order to effectively use a network backup server. These include the following:

- Configure the number of disk drives and the RAID level based on performance needs. Don't configure only for the amount of space needed, because this may leave you with an I/O bottleneck.

- Carefully schedule backups. If you are sharing the disk subsystem among several SQL Server systems, spread out the load. Alternate times so that only one system is backing up at a time.

- Regularly monitor the backup system and make sure that the network, the I/O subsystem, or both are not becoming bottlenecks. If a problem arises, you need to reconfigure.

- Keep at least two full backups online so that you can restore the older one if the new one is corrupted. If you delete the old backup before you do a new one and the system fails during the backup, you may be left with no alternative but to go offsite for your archived backup files.

- The files being restored will be loaded in bursts; thus, be sure to monitor all the peak times. This is when problems are most likely to show up.

Storage Area Networks

Other backup configurations include new hardware and software products such as the storage area network (SAN). A SAN allows components of the I/O subsystem, such as disk and tape arrays, to be shared among several servers. This can provide a high-performance solution that is fairly cost-effective because the shared resources need not be duplicated. These alternatives are new and will no doubt evolve and improve over time.

Backup Tips and Recommendations

In this section we provide a number of miscellaneous suggestions on how to make the backup and recovery process more efficient. These suggestions are categorized by the component to which they apply.

SQL Server System

The best way to tune the SQL Server system for backup is to simply tune the system in general. If you follow the guidelines and tips given throughout this book for configuring your system for excellent performance, you will find that backup and recovery are also well tuned. You can do a few additional things specifically for backup and recovery, as follows:

- **Configure multiple files.** SQL Server assigns backup threads to each file that is being backed up. A database with a single file will be allocated only one backup thread, whereas a database with multiple files will be allocated multiple threads during the backup process. Multiple threads allow for parallel operations, which increase performance.

- **Increase the size of network packets.** If backup performance is crucial, you can increase the size of network packets. Since backup and recovery use 64-KB pages, by increasing the network packet size you should see higher network performance. However, this is not generally recommended because it can degrade performance for other applications accessing SQL Server.

As you can see, there is not much that needs to be done on the SQL Server system besides normal tuning exercises.

Network

When performing network backups, you should be careful that the network itself does not become a bottleneck. The network is a fixed-bandwidth component that may or may not be busy when you want to perform your backup. Knowing what kind of network you have allows you to determine the maximum throughput, but you must keep in mind that other users and applications may be using some of that bandwidth. If possible, monitor the network and make changes as necessary. Some tips for increasing network performance include the following:

- **Use the fastest network available.** Doing so increases the bandwidth and may eliminate a bottleneck; however, this could be an expensive solution because the latest and fastest hardware is usually also the most expensive.

- **Use multiple networks.** Use several network segments for the backup operation. This allows you to increase the throughput to that of multiple network segments.

- **Use a dedicated network.** By dedicating a network to backups, not only will the backup performance be improved, but the user community will not experience performance slowdowns due to the network being used for other purposes.

Network components can easily cause a backup and recovery bottleneck. Carefully plan and implement the network with backup performance in mind.

Network Backup Server

The network backup server is a frequent source of backup and recovery bottlenecks. It is not uncommon for multiple backups to the server and a tape backup of the server to happen simultaneously. This can cause a tremendous load on the I/O subsystem. By properly configuring for these peak loads, you may be able to avoid this bottleneck. Some tips and guidelines to help in your configuration include the following:

- **Configure sufficient disk drives.** A disk drive can handle only so much I/O. You can overcome this limitation by adding multiple disk drives in a RAID array. Configure a sufficient number of disk drives to achieve the desired performance.

- **Use RAID 10.** A fault-tolerant RAID array is a must to protect your data. Because of the excessive overhead incurred by RAID 5 during write operations, RAID 5 is not a good candidate for this application.

- **Configure the Server service to maximize performance for file services.** This configuration will optimize the file system buffer cache for file service operations.

As with the other components, the network backup server should be carefully monitored. The I/O subsystem in particular should be carefully watched.

General Tips and Guidelines

Here are some tips that can be helpful in determining the best backup schedule for your system.

- **Plan full backups for off hours.** If your company does not run in a 24 × 7 environment, the off hours are the best time to do backups. This will both improve the performance of the backup and reduce the effect of the backup on the user community.

- **Schedule a full backup over several days.** If your database is very large and you cannot perform a full backup in the allotted time, split it up. You can do a file or filegroup backup on a piece of the database. Over a period of several days you can back up all the data in this manner.

- **Use differential backups.** If you cannot afford the time to do a full backup every night, you can do a differential backup during the week and a full backup over the weekend.

- **Use multiple backup devices.** Using multiple backup devices allows SQL Server to parallelize some of the backup operations. SQL Server creates a number of threads based on the number of data files and number of backup devices. Parallelization improves both backup and recovery performance.

- **Use multiple data files.** By using several data files rather than one large one, SQL Server will be able to parallelize the backup better and thus improve both backup and recovery performance.

- **Stage the backup.** The backup can be done as a disk backup initially, and then the disk backup files can be copied to tape. This method has the benefit of allowing faster backup performance as well as keeping the latest few backups available on disk, which improves the restore performance for those backup files.

- **Create a reasonable backup schedule.** One of the best ways to improve the performance on the system being backed up is to not do unnecessary backups. You must determine what the most effective backup schedule is based on your needs. Don't back up more than you need to, but don't sacrifice the security of your data for performance. Based on your needs, create a backup plan that is best for you.

- **Keep the most recent backups on disk.** In the event that a restore is necessary, a restore from a disk that is available on the network can be started immediately. A restore from tape may involve getting the tape from storage, loading the tape, and then restoring the backup from that tape.

As you can see, there are many different things you can do to improve backup and recovery performance. However, don't take chances with your backups: don't sacrifice the security of your data for performance.

Review of Component Capacities

Table 15-2 summarizes the various throughput capacities that have been given throughout this chapter. The disk I/O throughputs are based on the rule of thumb of 85 I/Os per second. Exceeding this I/O rate will cause latencies in excess of 20 ms, which can increase exponentially as the throughput is increased. These ratings are based on theoretical maximums that are usually unachievable in practice; your mileage may vary.

Table 15-2 Component Capacities

I/O Components (8 KB per I/O per Disk)	Capacity (100% Writes)
RAID 0	2.33 GB/hr
RAID 1 or RAID 10	1.16 GB/hr
RAID 5	0.58 GB/hr

I/O Components (64 KB per I/O)	Capacity (100% Writes)
1 disk drive, RAID 0	18.7 GB/hr
1 disk drive, RAID 1 or RAID 10	9.3 GB/hr
1 disk drive, RAID 5	4.7 GB/hr

Network Components	Capacity
10BaseT	4.4 GB/hr
100BaseT	44 GB/hr
Gigabit Ethernet	440 GB/hr

Summary

Backup and recovery are very important to the stability of your system. The data in your database may be one of the most valuable assets that your company has; its loss could be devastating to your business. It is therefore essential that this data be protected from permanent loss. This chapter presented a review of backup and recovery techniques and provided a number of guidelines and tips for improving those techniques.

Since the backup operation incurs a significant amount of overhead, tuning this operation is essential. By improving the performance of backup operations, you minimize the overall performance impact on the system. In this chapter you learned how to improve the speed of backup operations and how to configure your system for maximum efficiency. This information should help you to protect your data while minimizing the overhead on the system.

The next chapter begins Part IV, "Tuning SQL Statements." This part of the book discusses how to make SQL statements more efficient, as well as how to use hints and stored procedures to improve performance. The next chapter introduces SQL Server Query Analyzer and how you can use it to help tune SQL statements.

Part IV
Tuning SQL Statements

Chapter 16
Using SQL Server Query Analyzer

Microsoft SQL Server Query Analyzer is an important tool that provides information on the resources that a query consumes; this information aids in the performance analysis and tuning of your system. It is a graphical user interface for designing and testing SQL statements, batches, and scripts interactively. SQL Server Query Analyzer can be accessed from the Start menu or from the command line, or called directly from the Tools menu of SQL Server Enterprise Manager.

This chapter begins by exploring the different features of SQL Server Query Analyzer. It then looks at how to run queries and interpret the results, using sample SQL code to walk through the process. It also discusses how to use the Index Tuning Wizard and how to manage table statistics.

Features of SQL Server Query Analyzer

Microsoft SQL Server Query Analyzer offers the following features:

- **Free-form text editor**   The editor is used for entering and editing SQL statements. The free-form design gives you the flexibility to develop your own coding style. You can also modify and debug the SQL statements in the same window.

- **Color coding of SQL syntax**   Color coding improves the readability of complex statements. SQL Server Query Analyzer uses this color coding to indicate SQL keywords, such as SELECT and UPDATE, and to indicate strings in quotes. This latter feature assists you to debug SQL statements by highlighting unclosed quotation marks.

- **Customizable display mode**   Results can be presented in either a grid or a free-form text window.

- **Graphical diagram of the Showplan**   This diagram shows the logical steps that are built into the execution plan of a SQL statement. This feature allows you to better visualize the SQL statements and how they will execute. SQL Server Query Analyzer color-codes areas of your statements that need further attention. In addition, it provides a relative cost of the SQL query.

- **Index Tuning Wizard**   The wizard analyzes a SQL statement and the tables it references to determine if additional indexes will improve the performance of the query.

- **Context-sensitive T-SQL statement help**   Clicking on a T-SQL statement will bring up syntax and option information on the command.

Running SQL Server Query Analyzer

When you install SQL Server, either in client mode or server mode, you are given the option of installing SQL Server Query Analyzer. The default is to install it. It can run on either the database server or on any of your client machines.

Once installed, you can access SQL Server Query Analyzer by selecting Start, Programs, Microsoft SQL Server 7.0, and then Query Analyzer. You can also access it from the Enterprise Manager console on the Tools menu. A final method is to invoke it from a Windows NT command line by typing ISQLW and pressing Enter.

The Connection Process

After starting Query Analyzer, you are prompted to enter the SQL Server alias to which you wish to connect (see Figure 16-1). The available SQL Server aliases are constructed from those specified in the SQL Server Client Network Utility. You may type a SQL Server alias in the text box, select one from the drop-down list, or click on the ellipsis button (...) and select a SQL Server alias.

In the Connection Information area, specify either Windows NT or SQL Server authentication. If your database server is configured to accept Windows NT authentication, click the radio button for Use Windows NT Authentication. This instructs your system to log on to the database using the user ID and password with which you are currently logged on. If your system is configured for SQL Server authentication, click the radio button for Use SQL Server Authentication and enter your SQL Server login name and password in the appropriate text boxes. Click OK to log you on to your database system with the selected authentication.

The Query Window

Once the logon process has completed, you are presented with an empty window known as the *query window*. The query window is where you will primarily interact with SQL Server Query Analyzer. The icons in the query window assist you in analyzing your queries and stored procedures, as detailed here:

   New Query   The New Query icon allows you to start another connection to the current database server. It opens a new query window.

   Open Query File   This icon provides a dialog box that allows you to open an existing SQL batch or stored procedure and display it in the current query window.

   Save Query File   Clicking on the Save Query File icon allows you to save the query text in the query window to a specified file.

Figure 16-1 *The Connect to SQL Server dialog box.*

Clear Query Window   The Clear Query Window icon allows you to quickly delete all the text in the query window.

Check Syntax (Parse)   Clicking this icon directs Query Analyzer to parse your SQL statements and identify any syntax errors. This command will not execute the statements.

Execute Query   The Execute Query icon executes the SQL text in the query window.

Cancel Query   This icon allows you to cancel the currently executing query.

Execution Mode   The Execution Mode icon allows you to specify how the results of the query analysis are to be displayed. It has four options:

- Display the query results as text without the execution plan
- Display the query results as text with the execution plan
- Display the query results in a grid without the execution plan
- Display the query results in a grid with the execution plan

Estimated Execution Plan   Clicking on this icon displays the estimated execution plan(s) for the query text in the query window. It does not actually execute the query against the database.

Show/Hide Results   This icon allows you to either show or hide the lower pane of the query window. This pane contains the results of the query text.

In addition to the icons, the query window contains the DB field. This field is a drop-down list of all existing active databases on the database server to which you are connected. Selecting a database with this field is equivalent to the USE (*database name*) SQL statement.

Analyzing Queries

After you have connected to your database server, you can use the query window to enter the text of your SQL statements. You can either open an existing query file, enter new SQL statements, or extract the SQL statements embedded in your applications. Once the query text is displayed in the query window, you can execute all or part of the query text. To execute the entire batch of SQL statements, either click on the Execute Query icon, press F5, or press Ctrl-E. To execute portions of the query text, simply use the mouse to highlight the SQL statements you wish to execute and then either click on the Execute Query icon, press F5, or press Ctrl-E.

In either instance, the results are displayed in the lower pane of the query window. Depending on the option you chose for displaying the results, you will see any messages, any result sets, and any execution plans generated.

Execution Plans

One of the most important aspects of SQL Server Query Analyzer is its ability to display query execution plans. After you have opened your query text in the query window, select Show Execution Plan from the Query menu. The execution plan is then displayed in a graphical format in the results pane.

Logical and Physical Operators

The logical and physical operators in the execution plan describe how a query or update is executed. The *physical operators* describe the physical implementation algorithm used to process a statement, for example, scanning a clustered index. Each step in the execution of a query or update statement involves a physical operator. The *logical operators* describe the relational algebraic operation used to process a statement, for example, performing an aggregation. Not all steps required to process a query or update involve logical operations.

SQL Server Query Analyzer uses icons to represent the different aspects of query execution. The most common ones are listed here.

 Assert   The Assert logical and physical operator performs condition verification. It represents operations such as checking referential integrity constraints or performing any internal checks to ensure that a scalar subquery returns only one row. Each row is passed through the Assert operator, which evaluates the expression. If the expression evaluates to NULL, the Assert operator passes the row on. If it is a non-null value, the Assert operator raises an error condition.

Bookmark Lookup   The Bookmark Lookup logical and physical operator uses a bookmark (a row ID or clustering key) to look up the corresponding row in the table or clustered index. The operator includes an argument that contains the bookmark label used for the lookup, as well as the table name or the name of the clustered index in which the row was looked up. If the WITH PREFETCH clause appears in the argument, then the SQL Server query processor has determined that it is optimal to use asynchronous prefetching, or read-ahead buffering, when looking up bookmarks in the table or clustered index.

Clustered Index Delete   The Clustered Index Delete physical operator deletes rows from the clustered index specified in the Argument column. If a WHERE:() predicate is present in the Argument column, only those rows that satisfy the predicate are deleted.

Clustered Index Insert   The Clustered Index Insert physical operator inserts rows from the input into the clustered index specified in the Argument column. The Argument column also contains a SET:() predicate, which indicates the value to which each column is set.

Clustered Index Scan   The Clustered Index Scan logical and physical operator scans the clustered index specified in the Argument column. If an optional WHERE:() predicate is present, only those rows that satisfy the predicate are returned. If the Argument column contains an ORDERED clause, the query processor requests that the rows' output be returned in the order in which the clustered index has sorted them. If an ORDERED clause is not present, the storage engine will determine the optimal way to scan the index. This last method does not guarantee that the output will be sorted.

Clustered Index Seek   The Clustered Index Seek logical and physical operator performs row retrieval via the clustered index. The Argument column contains the name of the clustered index used by the operator, as well as the SEEK:() predicate. The SQL Server storage engine will select only those rows that satisfy the SEEK:() predicate. This operator can optionally include a WHERE:() predicate that further limits the scope of the seek. If the WHERE:() predicate is specified, the storage engine will not use the index.

If the Argument column contains an ORDERED clause, the query processor has determined that all the rows will be returned in the same order as the clustered index has sorted them. If an ORDERED clause is not present, the storage engine will determine the optimal way to scan the index. This method does not guarantee that the output will be sorted.

Clustered Index Update   The Clustered Index Update physical operator updates input rows in the clustered index specified in the Argument column. If a WHERE:() predicate is specified, only the rows that satisfy the predicate are updated. The SET:() predicate, if present, indicates the value to which each updated column is set. A DEFINE:() predicate indicates the list of values that this operator defines. These DEFINE:() values are referenced in the SET clause or elsewhere within the operator.

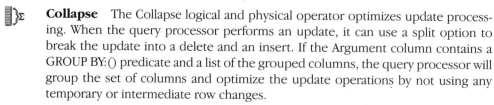

Collapse The Collapse logical and physical operator optimizes update processing. When the query processor performs an update, it can use a split option to break the update into a delete and an insert. If the Argument column contains a GROUP BY:() predicate and a list of the grouped columns, the query processor will group the set of columns and optimize the update operations by not using any temporary or intermediate row changes.

Compute Scalar The Compute Scalar logical and physical operator evaluates an expression to produce a computed scalar value, which can be returned to the user or referenced elsewhere in the query.

Concatenation The Concatenation logical and physical operator scans multiple inputs and returns each row scanned.

Constant Scan The Constant Scan logical and physical operator introduces a constant row into a query. It returns either zero or one row, which usually contains no columns. The Compute Scalar operator is often used to add columns to the row produced by a Constant Scan operator.

Deleted Scan The Deleted Scan logical and physical operator scans the deleted table within a trigger.

Filter The Filter logical and physical operator scans the input rows and returns only ones that satisfy the filter predicate. The filter predicate appears in the Argument column.

Hash Match The Hash Match physical operator builds a hash table by computing a hash value for each row from its build input. A HASH:() predicate specifies a list of columns to be used to create a hash value. This predicate appears in the Argument column. For each probe row (as applicable), this operator computes a hash value and scans the hash table for matches. If a residual predicate is present in the Argument column, that predicate must also be satisfied for rows to be considered a match. This operator's behavior will differ based on the actual logical operation that is being performed. The following list outlines the behaviors:

- If you are performing a join, the first input value is used to build the hash table, and the second input is used to probe the hash table. The output matches are dictated by the specified join type. If multiple joins use the same columns, the hashing operations are grouped for efficiency.

- For the Distinct or Aggregate operators, the input value is used to build the hash table. Duplicates are removed and aggregates are computed at this stage. After the hash table is built, it is scanned and all the rows are returned.

- If the Union operator is specified, the first input value is used to build the hash table, removing any duplicates as the table is built. The second input value, which must have no duplicates, is used to probe the hash table. All rows that have no matches are removed; the hash table is then scanned to return all the rows satisfying the Union operator.

Hash Match Root   The Hash Match Root physical operator coordinates all Hash Match Team, or grouped hash, operations directly below it. The Hash Match Root operator and all Hash Match Team operators directly below it will share a common hash function and partitioning strategy. This grouping is done for hash efficiency. The Hash Match Root operator always returns its output to an operator that is not a member of its team.

Index Delete   The Index Delete physical operator deletes input rows from the nonclustered index specified in the Argument column. If a WHERE:() predicate is present, then only those rows that satisfy this predicate are deleted.

Index Insert   The Index Insert physical operator inserts rows from its input into the nonclustered index specified in the Argument column. The Argument column also contains a SET:() predicate, which indicates the value to which each column is set.

Index Scan   The Index Scan logical and physical operator retrieves all rows from the nonclustered index specified in the Argument column. If an optional WHERE:() predicate appears in the Argument column, then only those rows that satisfy the predicate are returned. If the Argument column contains an ORDERED clause, it indicates that the query processor has determined that the rows returned will be in the order that the nonclustered index has sorted them. If the ORDERED clause is not present, then the storage engine will determine the most efficient way to search the index. This last condition does not guarantee that the rows returned will be sorted.

Index Seek   The Index Seek logical and physical operator indicates row retrieval via the nonclustered index. The Argument column contains the name of the non-clustered index used by the operator, as well as the SEEK:() predicate. The SQL Server storage engine will select only those rows that satisfy the SEEK:() predicate. This operator can optionally include a WHERE:() predicate that further limits the scope of the seek. If the WHERE:() predicate is specified, the storage engine will not use the index.

If the Argument column contains an ORDERED clause, the query processor has determined that all the rows will be returned in the same order as the nonclustered index has sorted them. If an ORDERED clause is not present, the storage engine will determine the optimal way to scan the index. This last condition does not guarantee that the output will be sorted.

Index Update   The Index Update physical operator updates rows from its input in the nonclustered index specified in the Argument column. If a WHERE:() predicate is specified, only the rows that satisfy the predicate are updated. The SET:() predicate, if present, indicates the value to which each updated column is set. A DEFINE:() predicate indicates the list of values that this operator defines. These DEFINE:() values are referenced in the SET clause or elsewhere within the operator.

Inserted Scan The Inserted Scan logical and physical operator scans the inserted table within a trigger.

 Merge Join The Merge Join physical operator performs the inner join, left outer join, left semi-join, left anti-semi-join, right outer join, right semi-join, right anti-semi-join, and union logical operations.

The Argument column contains the MERGE:() predicate if the operation is performing a one-to-many join. If the operation is a many-to-many join, then the Argument column contains a MANY-TO-MANY MERGE:() predicate. Within the predicates is a comma-separated list of the columns the query processor will use to perform the join. A merge join requires two inputs, both sorted on their respective columns. If required, an explicit sort will be inserted into the query plan by the query processor.

 Nested Loops The Nested Loops physical operator performs the inner join, left outer join, left semi-join, and left anti-semi-join logical operations. This operator first performs a search on the inner table for each row of the outer table. This is typically done using an index, if available. The query processor decides, based on anticipated query costs, whether to sort the outer input. This sort is done to improve locality of the searches on the index over the inner input. Any rows that satisfy the optional predicate in the Argument column are returned.

 Parallelism The Parallelism physical operator performs the distribute streams, gather streams, and repartition streams logical operations. The Argument column can contain a PARTITION COLUMNS:() predicate. This predicate will contain a comma-separated list of the columns being partitioned. The Argument column can also contain an ORDER BY:() predicate with a list of the columns for which the sort order is preserved during partitioning.

 Parameter Table Scan The Parameter Table Scan logical and physical operator scans a table that is acting as a parameter in the current query. Typically, this is used for INSERT queries within a stored procedure.

 Remote Delete The Remote Delete logical and physical operator deletes the input rows from a remote object.

 Remote Insert The Remote Insert logical and physical operator inserts the input rows into a remote object.

 Remote Query The Remote Query logical and physical operator submits a query to a remote source. The Argument column contains the text of the query that is sent to the remote server.

 Remote Scan The Remote Scan logical and physical operator scans a remote object. The Argument column contains the name of the remote object to be scanned.

 Remote Update The Remote Update logical and physical operator updates the input rows in a remote object.

Sequence The Sequence logical and physical operator drives wide update plans. The Sequence operator executes each input in sequence, from top to bottom. Each of the inputs is usually an update of a different object. Only those rows that come from its last or bottom input are returned.

Sort   The Sort logical and physical operator sorts all incoming rows. The Argument column contains a DISTINCT ORDER BY:() predicate if duplicates are removed by this operation, or an ORDER BY:() predicate with a comma-separated list of the columns being sorted. Each of the columns is prefixed with the value ASC if the columns are sorted in ascending order, or the value DESC if the columns are sorted in descending order.

 Stream Aggregate   The Stream Aggregate physical operator calculates one or more aggregate expressions returned by the query or referenced elsewhere within the query. It can optionally perform a group by a set of columns before the aggregate is calculated. If the Stream Aggregate operator is performing a group by columns operation, a GROUP BY:() predicate and the list of columns appear in the Argument column. If the Stream Aggregate operator computes any aggregate expressions, a list of them will appear in the Defined Values column of the output from the SHOWPLAN_ALL statement or the Argument column of the graphical execution plan.

 Table Delete   The Table Delete physical operator deletes rows from the table specified in the Argument column. If a WHERE:() predicate is included in the Argument column, only those rows that satisfy the predicate will be deleted.

 Table Insert   The Table Insert physical operator inserts rows from its input into the table specified in the Argument column. The Argument column also contains a SET:() predicate, which indicates the value to which each column is set.

 Table Scan   The Table Scan logical and physical operator retrieves all rows from the table specified in the Argument column. If a WHERE:() predicate appears in the Argument column, only those rows that satisfy the predicate are returned.

 Table Update   The Table Update physical operator updates input rows in the table specified in the Argument column. If a WHERE:() predicate is present, then only those rows that satisfy this predicate are updated. If a SET:() predicate is present, it indicates the value to which each updated column is set. If a DEFINE:() predicate is present, it lists the values that this operator defines. These values may be referenced in the SET clause or elsewhere within this operator and elsewhere within this query.

 Top   The Top logical and physical operator scans the input, returning only the first specified number or percentage of rows. The Argument column can optionally contain a list of the columns that are being checked for ties. In update plans, the Top operator is used to enforce row count limits.

Interpreting Graphical Execution Plans

The graphical execution plan that is displayed in SQL Server Query Analyzer is read from right to left and from top to bottom. Each query in the batch that is being analyzed is displayed, including the cost of each subquery as a percentage of the total cost of the query batch. Figure 16-2 shows a sample graphical representation of an execution plan.

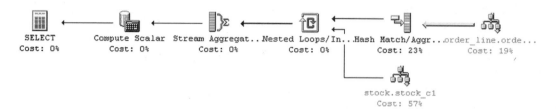

Figure 16-2 *An example of an execution plan displayed in SQL Server Query Analyzer.*

The execution plan diagrams use the following conventions:

- Each node in the tree structure is represented as an icon that specifies the logical and physical operator used to execute part of the query or statement.
- Each node is related to a parent node. All nodes with the same parent are drawn in the same column. An arrow connects each node to its parent.
- Recursive operations are indicated by an iteration symbol.
- Operators are shown as symbols related to a specific parent.
- When the query contains multiple statements, multiple query execution plans are drawn.
- The parts of the tree structures are determined by the type of statement to be executed.

SQL Server Query Analyzer breaks down a query into its components, each of which can be one of the five following types:

- **SQL statements and stored procedures** If SQL Server Query Analyzer determines that the statement is a stored procedure or T-SQL statement, it promotes it to the root of the graphical execution plan tree. A stored procedure can have multiple children that represent statements called by the stored procedure.
- **Data manipulation language statements** When the statement is determined to be a data manipulation language (DML) statement, such as SELECT, INSERT, DELETE, or UPDATE, the DML statement is made the root of a tree. A DML statement can have up to two children. The first child is the execution plan. The second child represents a trigger if used.
- **Conditionals** When SQL Server Query Analyzer identifies a statement as a conditional statement, such as IF..ELSE, it divides it into three children. The IF..ELSE statement is the root of the tree. The "if" clause becomes a subtree node. The "then" and "else" clauses are represented as statement blocks. SQL Server Query Analyzer processes WHILE and DO-UNTIL statements in the same manner.
- **Relational operators** Operations such as table scans, joins, and aggregations are represented as nodes on a tree.
- **Cursor declarations** When SQL Server Query Analyzer encounters a DECLARE CURSOR statement, it promotes it to the root of a graphical execution tree, with its related statement as a child or node.

Once you have displayed the graphical execution plan in SQL Server Query Analyzer, you can put your cursor over a node and view the context-sensitive information related to that part of the query statement (see Figure 16-4). The ToolTip box can include the following information:

- **Physical operation**   The physical operator used for the operation, such as Hash Join or Nested Loop.

- **Logical operation**   The logical operator that matches the physical operator. If the logical operator is different from the physical operator, it is listed after the physical operator and separated by a forward slash.

- **Estimated row count**   The number of rows output by the operator.

- **Estimated row size**   The estimated size of each row output.

- **Estimated I/O cost**   The estimated cost of all the I/O activity for the operation.

- **Estimated CPU cost**   The estimated cost for all CPU activity for the operation.

- **Estimated number of executes**   The number of times the operation was executed during the query.

- **Estimated cost**   The cost to the query optimizer in executing the operation. This includes the cost of this operation as a percentage of the total cost of the query.

- **Estimated subtree cost**   The total cost to the query optimizer in executing this operation and all operations preceding it in the same subtree.

- **Argument**   The predicates and parameters used by the query.

Example of Using Query Analyzer

Let's look at a sample query in Query Analyzer. The query we will analyze is based on one of the transactions in the Transaction Processing Council's TPC-C benchmark. The query is not too complex, but it does provide an excellent example of what to look for with SQL Server Query Analyzer. The SQL text of the query is as follows:

```
CREATE PROC TPCC_STOCKINFO    @W_ID       SMALLINT,
                              @D_ID       TINYINT,
                              @THRESHOLD  SMALLINT

AS

DECLARE  @O_ID_LOW    INT,
         @O_ID_HIGH   INT

SELECT   @O_ID_LOW    = (D_NEXT_O_ID - 50),
         @O_ID_HIGH   = (D_NEXT_O_ID - 1)
FROM     DISTRICT
WHERE    D_W_ID       = @W_ID AND
         D_ID         = @D_ID

SELECT   COUNT(DISTINCT(S_I_ID))
FROM     STOCK
WHERE    S_W_ID       = @W_ID AND
```

(continued)

(continued)

```
                S_QUANTITY    < @THRESHOLD AND
                S_I_ID        IN (SELECT DISTINCT(OL_I_ID)
                                  FROM    ORDER_LINE
                                  WHERE   OL_W_ID =   @W_ID AND
                                          OL_D_ID =   @D_ID AND
                                          OL_O_ID BETWEEN @O_ID_LOW
                                          AND @O_ID_HIGH)

SET        ROWCOUNT 20

SELECT     DISTINCT(S_I_ID),
           S_QUANTITY,
           S_YTD
FROM       STOCK
WHERE      S_W_ID        = @W_ID AND
           S_QUANTITY    > @THRESHOLD AND
           S_I_ID        IN (SELECT DISTINCT(OL_I_ID)
                             FROM    ORDER_LINE
                             WHERE   OL_W_ID =   @W_ID AND
                                     OL_D_ID =   @D_ID AND
                                     OL_O_ID BETWEEN @O_ID_LOW
                                     AND @O_ID_HIGH)

ORDER      BY S_YTD DESC,
           S_QUANTITY ASC,
           S_I_ID ASC

SET        ROWCOUNT 0
GO
```

Let's look at each piece of the query and its associated graphical execution plan. The first SELECT statement,

```
SELECT     @O_ID_LOW     = (D_NEXT_O_ID - 50),
           @O_ID_HIGH    = (D_NEXT_O_ID - 1)
FROM       DISTRICT
WHERE      D_W_ID        = @W_ID AND
           D_ID          = @D_ID
```

uses a warehouse identifier and a district identifier (which are passed in) to select the last 50 orders. The graphical execution plan generated by SQL Server Query Analyzer for this query is shown in Figure 16-3.

The first line of the text output gives you the relative weight of this query in the batch you presented to SQL Server Query Analyzer. In this example, with only one query active at a time, the query cost is 100 percent. The second line of the output displays the text of the query. The results pane displays the execution plan using an icon for each distinct part of the statement.

Query 1: Query cost (relative to the batch): 100.00%
Query text: select (d_next_o_id - 20),   (d_next_o_id - 1)   from district   where d_w_id = 1 and   d_id = 5

Figure 16-3 *Graphical representation of the execution plan for the first SELECT statement in the example query.*

By placing the cursor over one of the icons, such as the Clustered Index Seek icon, you can obtain detailed information about that portion of the statement, as shown in Figure 16-4. This display indicates that the physical and logical operations being performed are clustered index seeks. The Estimated Row Count is 1, and the Estimated Row Size is 11. The Estimated I/O Cost gives you an indication of the amount of I/O resources this portion of the query will use. The value in the example query, 0.00632, is acceptable. It takes into account that the columns used for the scan all have valid statistics and that there is a clustered index on the columns used. You should strive to keep I/O cost as low as possible. The appropriate use of index structures will help you achieve this goal.

The next statement is a little more complex. Figure 16-5 shows the execution plan that SQL Server Query Analyzer generates for the second part of our sample query batch. Several different icons are represented in this output. The query in question executes a clustered index seek operation, and then a hash match/aggregate operation. The result of the latter operation is then joined with the result of another clustered index seek. The Nested Loops/Inner Join icon represents this join. Following the join, an aggregate function is executed. Finally, the scalar computation is performed and the results are returned to the requestor.

Query 1: Query cost (relative to the batch): 100.00%
Query text: select (d_next_o_id - 20),   (d_next_o_id - 1)   from district   where d_w_id = 1 and   d_id = 5

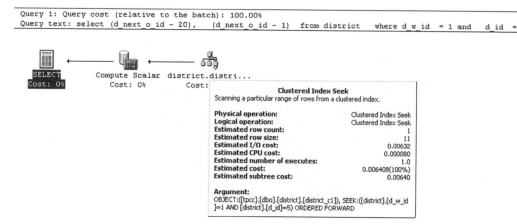

Figure 16-4 *Statement details.*

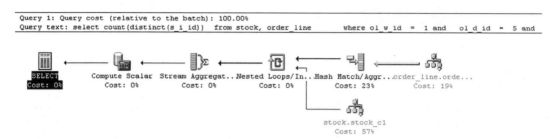

Figure 16-5 *Execution plan for example query.*

This query also illustrates another feature of Query Analyzer. The two clustered index seeks are color coded in red. When you move the mouse over the icon to display the operation details, a message appears that indicates that some statistics are missing for this table (see Figure 16-6). If you wish to create the missing statistics, right-click on the icon and select Create Missing Statistics from the context menu. SQL Server Query Analyzer then displays a window showing which column or columns in the table are missing statistics (see Figure 16-7).

In our example, SQL Server Query Analyzer suggests that we generate statistics for the *ol_i_id* column of the *order_line* table. Before clicking OK, you have the option to determine how much data is to be sampled. The default is to sample 25 percent of the rows in the table. This sampling allows the statistics creation to occur in a timely fashion. You may request that a different percentage of the rows be sampled, or have the statistics generated based on all rows. Be aware that creating statistics on all rows may require a great deal of time.

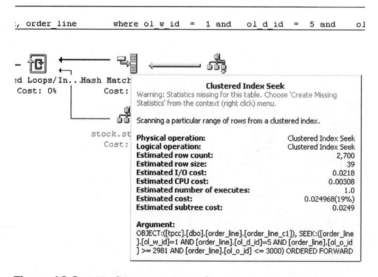

Figure 16-6 *A ToolTip message indicating missing statistics.*

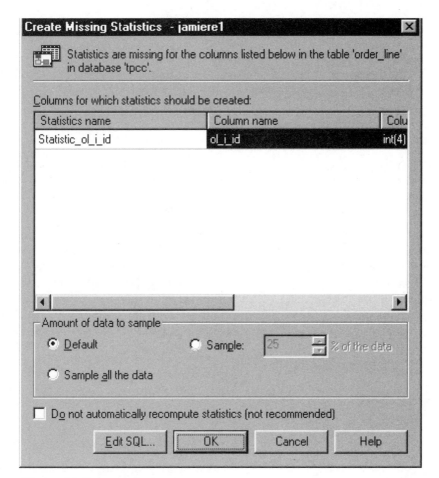

Figure 16-7 *Creating missing statistics.*

In addition, you can instruct SQL Server not to automatically recompute statistics. This option is not recommended for tables in which the data is dynamic. As you insert, delete, and update tables for which automatic recomputation of statistics has been disabled, the quality of the statistics will degrade. This will lead to decreased performance when seeking records in those tables. If you have tables that are static in nature, automatic recomputation of statistics is not necessary.

One other option you have in the Create Missing Statistics dialog box is to view and edit the actual T-SQL code that will be executed. After you have set your particular options, and when you are satisfied with the code, click OK to instruct SQL Server to generate the statistics. When the statistics have been computed, subsequent displays of the execution plan will no longer show up in red.

Earlier we looked at each piece of the batch of our queries separately. In each of those cases, the query cost was 100 percent. When we display all the statements of our batch together, we can get a feel for which areas of our batch are the most expensive in relation to other queries in this batch. Figure 16-8 shows the output for the entire query batch of our example. In this example, 4.73 percent of the time is spent on the first query in the batch, and 95.2 percent is used on the second query. Using the relative costs will allow you to properly focus your efforts on the most expensive parts of your query batch, thereby giving you the most return on your time investment.

Index Tuning Wizard

An integral part of SQL Server Query Analyzer is the Index Tuning Wizard. The Index Tuning Wizard allows you to select and create an optimal set of indexes and statistics for a Microsoft SQL Server database without requiring an expert understanding of the structure of the database, the workload, or the internals of SQL Server.

The Index Tuning Wizard requires a workload as its input. A workload can consist of a SQL script or a SQL Server Profiler trace saved to a file. A SQL Server Profiler trace is the recommended input for the Index Tuning Wizard. The more closely the input represents your actual environment, the more accurate the Index Tuning Wizard's recommendations will be. Furthermore, the longer the trace duration, the better the end analysis will be. Bear in mind, however, that using a long Profiler trace increases the amount of time the Index Tuning Wizard requires for its analysis. See Chapter 7 for more information on SQL Server Profiler.

Features of the Index Tuning Wizard

The Index Tuning Wizard offers the following features to assist you in your tuning efforts. It can

- Recommend the best mix of indexes for a database given a specific workload by using the query optimizer to analyze the queries in the workload. Bear in mind that the index mix recommended might not be optimal if the workload changes, even slightly, from that used in the Index Tuning Wizard.

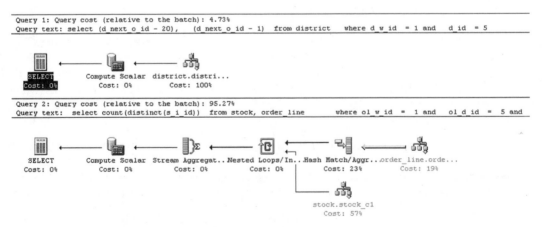

Figure 16-8 *Graphical representation of the execution plan for a complete SQL batch.*

- Analyze the effects of the proposed changes, including index usage, distribution of queries among tables, and performance of queries in the workload.

- Recommend ways to tune the database based on a small subset of queries used in your workload.

- Allow you to customize the recommendations by specifying advanced options such as disk space constraints.

After the Index Tuning Wizard completes its analysis, it presents several recommendations. A recommendation consists of SQL statements that can be executed to create new, more effective indexes and, if desired, to drop existing indexes that are ineffective. Once the Index Tuning Wizard has suggested a recommendation, it can either be implemented immediately, scheduled to be implemented later by creating a SQL Server job that executes a SQL script at a specified time, or saved to a SQL script so that it can be executed manually by the user at a later time, possibly on a different server.

Limitations of Index Tuning Wizard

The Index Tuning Wizard has some limitations that must be kept in mind. To begin with, the wizard does not recommend indexes on the following:

- Tables referenced by cross-database queries that do not exist in the currently selected database

- System tables

- Primary key constraints and unique indexes

Furthermore, the number of tunable queries allowed in the workload is limited to no more than 32,767. Any additional queries in the workload will not be considered. Queries with quoted identifiers are also not considered for tuning.

Because the Index Tuning Wizard gathers statistics by sampling the data, successive executions of the wizard on the same workload may result in variations in the indexes recommended as well as variations in the improvements that result from implementing these recommendations. You may also encounter a condition in which the Index Tuning Wizard will not make any suggestions. Normally, this indicates either that there was not enough data in the tables being sampled to come up with any meaningful recommendations or that the potential recommendations will not offer any significant performance improvements over the existing index structures.

If you encounter problems with excessive or unacceptable Index Tuning Wizard execution times, there are several things you can do to reduce the execution time:

- Clear the Perform Thorough Analysis option in the Select Server and Database dialog box. When you opt to perform a thorough analysis, you instruct the Index Tuning Wizard to go through an exhaustive analysis of all the queries in the input stream. This results in longer execution times.

- Restrict the Index Tuning Wizard to a subset of the tables in your database. When performing index analysis from Query Analyzer, the Index Tuning Wizard analyzes only the tables contained in the workload or query you opened. If you invoke the Index Tuning Wizard from Enterprise Manager, however, you can select a subset of your tables from the Tables object pane prior to starting the wizard.

- Reduce the overall size of the workload file.

If you select the Keep All Existing Indexes option, the Index Tuning Wizard will not recommend dropping any indexes. Only new indexes will be recommended, if appropriate. Clearing this option can result in a greater overall improvement in the performance of the workload. Additionally, the Index Tuning Wizard does not recommend dropping indexes on primary key constraints or unique indexes. However, it may drop or replace a clustered index that is not unique or currently created on a primary key constraint.

You can defer building the indexes recommended by the Index Tuning Wizard by saving the recommended SQL scripts using SQL Server Query Analyzer. You may then examine and edit the SQL statements. Once edited, the script can be run at a more convenient time.

Using the Index Tuning Wizard

Let's look at an example of using the Index Tuning Wizard. We will use the same SQL batch as earlier in this chapter (see p. 155). After you have loaded the workload by selecting Open from the File menu, you can access the Index Tuning Wizard by clicking Query in the menu and selecting Perform Index Analysis. You can also press Ctrl-I as a shortcut.

Now the system analyzes the queries and the existing index structures. Depending on the complexity of the workload and the tables involved, this process can take a while. When the Index Tuning Wizard finishes its analysis, a window is displayed that indicates the recommended index or indexes and the appropriate SQL statements for building them (see Figure 16-9). You can click on the Accept button to build the recommended index or indexes; alternatively, you can copy the SQL statements and execute them at a later time.

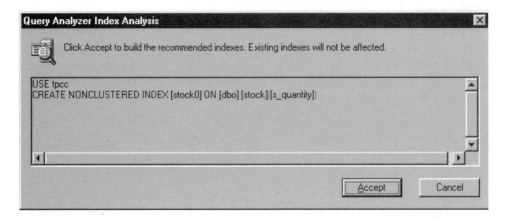

Figure 16-9 *Recommentations of the Index Tuning Wizard.*

Summary

In this chapter you learned about SQL Server Query Analyzer and the Index Tuning Wizard. You have seen how to use Query Analyzer to view the graphical execution plan and to view the details of each subcomponent of your queries. In addition, you have seen how to use the Index Tuning Wizard to enhance your query strategy. Now that you have been exposed to the tools available to optimize and tune your queries, let's look at the actual techniques you can use to get the most performance from your SQL statements.

Chapter 17
Tuning SQL Statements and Stored Procedures

An extremely important area of system performance involves the SQL statements used in your applications. In this chapter we explore techniques for effective application design, query design and tuning, and index design and tuning. Finally, we briefly look at *open database connectivity* (ODBC) techniques you can use to gain better performance in your applications that issue the same SQL queries many times.

Application Design

An efficient application design is critical to your system's performance. If you have purchased your application from a third party, it may be difficult or impossible to examine the actual database statements used. If you have implemented the techniques and tips from other chapters in this book and still find you have performance problems, it would be wise to contact the provider of your application for assistance.

If your application is of your own design, or home grown, then you have much more flexibility in tuning it and its associated queries. One way to think about your application is to view it and the client as a controlling entity. The application controls the flow of information and directs the SQL Server database's actions. Your application instructs SQL Server which queries to execute, when to execute them, and how to process the results. This in turn has a major effect on the type and duration of locks, the amount of I/O, and the processing (CPU) load on the server, and hence on whether performance is generally good or bad.

Thus, it is important to make correct decisions during the application design phase. A well-designed application allows SQL Server to support thousands of concurrent users. On the other hand, a poorly designed application prevents even the most powerful server platform from handling more than a few users.

Recommendations

Several areas can easily be analyzed, and corrected if necessary, to improve performance of your system and applications that run on it. You should always strive to eliminate excessive network traffic between the clients and the SQL Server system. The network round-trips are the conversational traffic sent between SQL Server and the clients for every batch and results set. Generally, you can exploit SQL Server stored procedures to minimize the round-trips. We examine stored procedures later in this chapter.

Another area to look at in your applications is the size of the result sets returned. You should attempt to minimize this size because retrieving needlessly large result sets for browsing on the client adds processor and network I/O load. It also can make the application less capable of remote use and can possibly limit multiuser scalability. It is advantageous to design the application to prompt the user for sufficient input so queries are submitted that generate modest result sets. You can use several techniques to control the size of the result set returned. For more information on properly sizing result sets, see "Efficient Retrieval of Data" later in this chapter.

You should not overuse wildcards, such as SELECT *, when building your queries. In addition, you should make certain input fields mandatory to ensure you have enough input data to construct a more efficient SQL statement. You should also consider using SQL statements such as TOP, PERCENT, and SET ROWCOUNT to limit the number of rows returned by the query. Finally, you can try to eliminate ad hoc queries from your client systems. Ad hoc queries typically are poorly constructed and will return far more rows than necessary. Eliminating ad hoc queries is a rather drastic step, but it is an option.

One area that is often overlooked is providing an application feature that allows a user to cancel a query and regain control of the processing. If a user or client makes a mistake, allowing them to cancel the query will eliminate needless processing on the system. A simple Cancel button can work wonders for system performance. When this feature is overlooked, it can lead to performance problems that are difficult to detect and resolve. Both ODBC and DB-Library connections provide an API for query cancellation. If you do allow cancellation of a query, you should make sure that the application issues either a commit or rollback to ensure data integrity, because canceling a query does not automatically commit or roll back the transaction.

Another easy technique you can use is to always implement a query or lock timeout. This measure prevents miscoded queries from running indefinitely, a common problem in environments that allow ad hoc queries. SQL Server and ODBC provide functions and statements to regulate the duration of query and lock timeouts.

Another common area of effective application design is the selection of application generation tools. Though we do not cover the selection of these tools, we do have a recommendation concerning their features. Some application generation tools do not allow you to control explicitly the SQL statements generated and sent to SQL Server. Tools that transparently generate SQL statements sound inviting, but they can and do cause performance problems. Tools such as these normally do not provide mechanisms for query cancellation, query timeout, or overall transactional control. You can often encounter problems due to locking and transactional blocking, which, as we have seen in other chapters, are critical to overall system performance.

You should minimize the use of database cursors in your applications when possible. Cursors are useful tools but are usually more expensive to use than regular, set-oriented SQL statements. In set-oriented SQL statements, the client application tells the server to update the set of records that meet specified criteria. SQL Server will figure out how to accomplish the update as a single unit of work. When updating through a cursor, the client application requires the server to maintain row locks or version information for every row in case the client asks to update the row after it has been fetched.

In addition, using a cursor implies that the server is maintaining client state information, such as the user's current rowset at the server. This state information is usually maintained in temporary storage. With a small number of users, this is usually not a problem. As the user population grows, however, maintaining this state becomes an expensive use of valuable server resources. A better strategy is for the client application to get in and out quickly, maintaining no client state at the server between calls.

If you find that you must use cursors, you should determine if the cursor query could be written more efficiently either by using a more efficient cursor type, such as fast for-ward–only, or by using a single query. We examine techniques for efficient cursor utilization later in this chapter.

You should avoid intermixing OLTP and decision support queries on the same system. Each type of workload has different requirements and functions that may compete if they are placed on a single system. We recommend having one or more systems for your OLTP workload, and having other systems that use offline data for your decision support queries. Decision support and OLTP systems are discussed in detail in Chapters 12 and 13.

Finally, you should attempt to keep the duration of transactions as short as possible to minimize blocking and improve concurrency. A long-running query can block other queries. A DELETE or UPDATE operation that affects many rows can acquire many locks that may even escalate to table locks. These locks can prohibit other transactions from executing. You should look for ways to optimize a long-running query by changing indexes, breaking a large, complex query into simpler queries, or running the query during off hours or on a separate computer. Execution of SQL statements in SQL stored procedures or in prepared execution statements can also improve application performance. Generally, long-running queries are decision support queries. Remember that you should try not to intermix your decision support and online transaction processing queries on the same database.

Critical-Path Transactions

Before analyzing your applications and queries, you should attempt to identify the transactions that are in your *critical path*. These are the transactions or database operations that could affect your system the most if they perform poorly or block other transactions. After you have identified the critical transactions or operations, you can easily focus on the areas that can provide the most return on your time investment.

One methodology you can use to analyze your critical transactions is to draw an execution matrix. Using a spreadsheet or graph paper, list the critical transactions or operations down the left side. Then for each transaction or operation, list the table and the type of access. Are you selecting, inserting, updating, or deleting rows? Also be sure to note if you are joining multiple tables in the transaction. Once you have your information plotted in the matrix, you can analyze it for concurrency or look for places where redundant data might be appropriate. If you find places where a transaction is doing a large join, for example, it might make sense to have redundant data in some tables to lessen the impact of the join. Figure 17-1 is an example of an execution matrix for two transactions. For each transaction, only those columns that are being accessed are displayed. This is done for readability in the example. For each column, the type of access is noted, as well as any joins that may be occurring.

Using Stored Procedures

Most SQL Server applications that are considered well designed are developed with stored procedures in mind. Stored procedures allow you to reuse queries on your system by simply specifying them by name and passing in the appropriate parameters.

A *stored procedure* is simply a group of SQL statements that are compiled into a single execution plan. SQL Server stored procedures can take input via input parameters and can return data in one of four ways: output parameters of either actual data or cursor variables, an integer return code, a result set for each SELECT statement, or a global cursor that can be referenced outside the context of the stored procedure.

Stored procedures allow you to achieve a consistent implementation of logic across all your applications. The SQL statements and logic needed to execute a commonly performed task can be designed, coded, and tested once and then reused. Each application that needs to perform the task can simply execute the stored procedure. In addition, if you code your business logic into stored procedures, you gain greater control in ensuring that your clients are using the most current versions of your business rules and procedures. The use of stored procedures allows you to isolate your normal application logic from the database layout. If you have a stored procedure that returns some values to your application, you can modify the database layout and stored procedure without changing the application. As long as you still return the expected number and type of values, the application code will not have to change.

Transaction # 1	District			Order-Line				Stock		
	d_id	d_w_id	d_next_o_id	ol_w_id	ol_d_id	ol_i_id	ol_o_id	s_w_id	s_i_id	s_quantity
Stock Information	= local var.	= local var.	Select	Join (s_w_id)	= local var.	Join (s_i_id)	= local var.	Join (ol_w_id)	Join (ol_w_id)	< local var.
									Return Count	

Transaction # 2	Customer					History			
	c_last	c_w_id	c_d_id	c_id	c_ytd_payment	h_c_id	h_d_id	h_w_id	h_date
Payment		= local var.	= local var.	= local var.	Update	Insert	Insert	Insert	Insert
					=val + local var.	= local var.	= local var.	= local var.	= local var.

Figure 17-1 *An execution matrix.*

Stored procedures also improve performance. Generally, an application performs a task as a series of SQL statements. The output of the first statement provides data for subsequent SQL statements, and a conditional expression determines which SQL statements will be executed. If you can combine these SQL statements and conditional logic into a stored procedure, they become part of a single execution plan on the server. This concept is illustrated in the following SQL code sample:

```
IF (@QuantityOrdered < (SELECT     QuantityOnHand
                        FROM       Inventory
                        WHERE      PartID = @PartOrdered))
     BEGIN
          <insert SQL Statements to do work if condition is true>
     END
ELSE
     BEGIN
          <insert SQL Statements to do work if condition is false>
     END
```

Even though there is a single execution plan now, you will still get some traffic between the client and the server. At the end of each SQL statement, SQL Server sends a response back to the client indicating the number of rows affected by the statement; these messages take up some network bandwidth. Once you are comfortable with the logic in your stored procedure, you can turn off these messages by issuing the SET NOCOUNT ON connection command. The results then do not have to be returned to the client to have the conditional logic applied; all the work is done on the server. This helps minimize the number of network round-trips required for execution.

Using stored procedures can also reduce network bandwidth because applications do not need to transmit all the SQL statements in the procedure. To execute the procedure, the application need only transmit either an EXECUTE or CALL statement containing the name of the procedure and the values of the parameters.

SQL Server 7, unlike previous versions of SQL Server, does not save a partially compiled plan for a stored procedure when the procedure is created. A stored procedure is compiled at execution time like any other SQL statement or batch. SQL Server retains execution plans for all SQL statements in the SQL Server procedure cache, not just execution plans for stored procedures. SQL Server uses an efficient algorithm for comparing any new SQL statements with the SQL statements used in existing cached execution plans. If it determines that the new SQL statement matches the SQL statement of an existing execution plan, it reuses the plan. This reuse reduces the relative performance benefit of precompiled stored procedures by extending execution plan reuse to all SQL statements.

You can create stored procedures by either coding SQL statements within a CREATE PROCEDURE wrapper or by using the Create Stored Procedure Wizard in SQL Server Enterprise Manager. The following code sample shows the creation of a stored procedure using the CREATE PROCEDURE SQL statement:

```
USE SALES
IF EXISTS (SELECT  NAME
            FROM    SYSOBJECTS
            WHERE   NAME = 'REGION_INFO' AND
                    TYPE = 'P')
   DROP PROCEDURE REGION_INFO
GO

USE SALES
GO

CREATE PROCEDURE REGION_INFO   @REG_NAME VARCHAR(40),
                               @BRAND VARCHAR(20)

AS
SELECT REGION_NAME,
       UNITS_SOLD,
       SALES_BY_MONTH,
       BRAND_NAME
FROM   REGION_DATA
WHERE  REGION_NAME = @REG_NAME AND
       BRAND_NAME  = @BRAND
GO
```

Let's look at this code in detail. The first thing we want to do is to find out if there is an existing stored procedure by this name in our database. Since we want to give our users the most current version, if we find an existing version we drop that version of the procedure. Next we issue a CREATE PROCEDURE command. This command names the procedure and, in this case, defines two parameters that will be passed to the stored procedure as input. We then use these input parameters in the subsequent SELECT statement. You can see that the stored procedure consists of regular SQL statements with an additional wrapper around them.

If you choose, you can use the Create Stored Procedure Wizard in SQL Server Enterprise Manager to build your stored procedure. To access the Create Stored Procedure Wizard, expand your list of databases in Enterprise Manager. Right-click on the desired database and select New and then Stored Procedure. The Create Stored Procedure Wizard window appears (see Figure 17-2). Enter your stored procedure text in the window. At any time, you can click on the Check Syntax button, which allows you to quickly make sure that you have entered the correct syntax in your stored procedure. In addition, you can choose to save the text as a template for the development of future stored procedures. This feature allows you to create a stored procedure style for your applications and queries and then easily maintain that style across other stored procedures you create.

Regardless of how you create your stored procedures, you will want to get data or result sets back from them. The following code illustrates three ways that stored procedures can return data to your application:

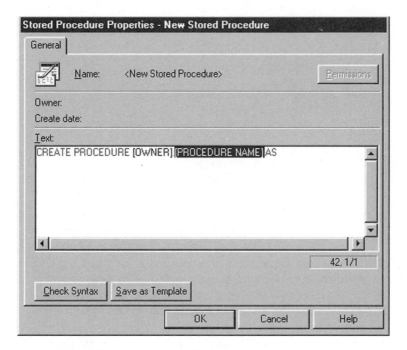

Figure 17-2 *The Create Stored Procedure Wizard.*

```
USE NORTHWIND
GO

IF EXISTS (SELECT NAME FROM SYSOBJECTS WHERE NAME = 'ORDERSUMMARY')
     DROP PROCEDURE ORDERSUMMARY
GO

CREATE PROCEDURE ORDERSUMMARY @EMPID INT

AS
DECLARE @MAXQUANTITY INT
IF (@EMPID >= 0)
     RETURN 1
ELSE
     BEGIN
        SELECT  ORD.EMPLOYEEID,
                SUMMSALES = SUM(ORDET.UNITPRICE * ORDET.QUANTITY)
        FROM    ORDERS AS ORD
        JOIN    [ORDER DETAILS] AS ORDET ON (ORD.ORDERID = ORDET.ORDERID)
        WHERE   ORD.EMPLOYEEID = @EMPID
        GROUP   BY ORD.EMPLOYEEID
```

(continued)

(continued)

```
        SELECT  @MAXQUANTITY = MAX(QUANTITY)
        FROM    [ORDER DETAILS]

        SELECT  @MAXQUANTITY AS 'MAX QUANTITY'
    END
GO
```

To run the stored procedure, use the following line of code:

```
EXEC @ORDERSUM = ORDERSUMMARY @MAXQUANTITY = @LARGESTORDER OUTPUT
```

This sample stored procedure first checks to see if the input parameter, @EmpID, is greater than zero. If it is not, we consider this an error condition and the stored procedure exits and returns 1 to the calling application. If the input parameter is greater than zero, the stored procedure issues a SELECT statement that returns a result set summarizing the sales activity from the Orders and Order Details table grouped by employee where the employee ID equals the input parameter. Next, the stored procedure issues another SELECT statement that fills an output parameter called @MaxQuantity. This value is not returned to the user at this time. Finally, the stored procedure performs another SELECT statement that returns the @MaxQuantity value back to the user

Caching Execution Plans

In addition to caching the execution plans of stored procedures, SQL Server 7 caches the execution plans of queries that are not stored procedures. If your users issue ad hoc queries, SQL Server 7 caches the execution plans. If a subsequent ad hoc query matches a cached plan, SQL Server 7 will reuse the plan.

SQL Server 7 also provides autoparameterization caching for simple queries. SQL Server guesses which constants in a SQL batch are parameters. Subsequent SQL batches that follow the same basic template can use the same execution plan as the original batch. As an example of autoparameterization, let's look at the two following queries:

```
SELECT BRAND, SW_UNITS, SW_SALES FROM REGION_SALES
    WHERE BRAND = 'MOUNTAIN DEW'
SELECT BRAND, SW_UNITS, SW_SALES FROM REGION_SALES
    WHERE BRAND = 'DR. ENUFF'
```

These two queries will use the same plan for execution. SQL Server will internally parameterize the *brand* condition. To avoid any possible performance degradation with autoparameterization, SQL Server will use the same execution plan only if the template is considered safe. The plan is safe if any change to the actual parameter will not change the execution plan.

Coding SQL Statements as Transactions

If you use SQL statements appropriately, you will reduce the amount of data transferred between server and client. Reducing the amount of data transferred will normally reduce the time it takes to accomplish a logical task or transaction. Transactions with long execution times are adequate for a single-user system, but they will inhibit proper scaling when your system encounters multiple users. As we have seen, to support transactional consistency, a database system must hold locks on shared resources from the time they are first acquired within the transaction until the transaction commits. If another user needs access to the same resources, the user must wait. As your individual transactions get longer, the queue of other users waiting for locks gets longer and system throughput decreases. Long transactions also increase the chances of a deadlock, which occurs when two or more users are each waiting on locks held by the other.

Some techniques you can use to reduce transaction duration in your applications are as follows:

- Commit your transactional changes as soon as possible within the requirements of the application. If your application includes large batch-oriented jobs, such as month-end summary processing, you should break the entire job into individual steps that can be committed without compromising your data consistency. If you can commit the changes as quickly as possible, you minimize the duration of locks that must be held.

- Take advantage of SQL Server statement batches. Statement batches are a means of sending multiple SQL statements from your clients to SQL Server at one time. These batches minimize the number of round-trips between the client and server, which shortens the time that locks must be held to complete a transaction. If you are forced to go back to the client after each piece of the overall transaction, you will increase the lock duration.

SQL Server provides an excellent tool for determining if you are exploiting the SQL batches and not delaying a commit: SQL Server Profiler, which can be used to monitor, filter, and capture all calls sent from client applications to SQL Server. It will often reveal unexpected application overhead due to unnecessary calls to the server. SQL Server Profiler can also reveal opportunities for gathering into batches statements that are currently being sent separately to the server. You can find more information on SQL Server Profiler in Chapter 7.

Efficient Retrieval of Data

The SQL language provides you with the ability to filter data at the server so you return only the minimum amount of data to the client. Using these facilities minimizes expensive network traffic between the server and client. You need to ensure that your WHERE clauses are restrictive enough to retrieve only the data that is actually required by the application. It is always more efficient to filter data at the server than to send it to the client and filter it in the application. This principle also applies to columns requested from the server. If an application issues a SELECT * FROM statement, the server is required to return all columns to the client even if the client application has not bound all the columns for use in the program. By selecting only the needed columns by name, you avoid unnecessary network traffic. As a result, your application is more robust in the event of table definition changes, because newly added columns are not returned to the client application.

SQL Server assumes that your application will fetch all the rows from a default result set immediately. Therefore, your application must use the client's resources to buffer any rows that are not used immediately but may be needed later. This requirement makes it especially important for you to specify your SQL statements properly so you are not forced to buffer any unneeded data.

On the surface, it would appear that requesting the default result set and having your application fetch rows as they are needed would be the most efficient means of getting your desired data. This is not normally the case. Unfetched rows from a default result can cause SQL Server to hold locks at the server, possibly preventing other users from updating the locked rows. This concurrency problem may not show up in small-scale testing, but it can appear later when the application is deployed and the user count increases.

Some applications cannot buffer all the data they request from the server. If an application queries a large table and allows the user to specify the selection criteria, it may return no rows or millions of rows. The user probably does not want to see millions of rows, so he or she will typically reexecute the query with narrower selection criteria. Thus, the application fetched and buffered millions of rows only to have them thrown away by the user, which wastes time and system resources.

Because there are many cases in which applications do need to select a large number of rows from large tables, SQL Server offers *server cursors*. These cursors allow an application to fetch a small subset or block of rows from an arbitrarily large result set. If the user wants to see other records from the same result set, a server cursor allows the application to fetch any other block of rows from the result set, including the next *n* rows, the previous *n* rows, or *n* rows starting at a certain row number in the result set. SQL Server fulfills each block fetch request only as needed and does not normally hold locks between these block fetches.

Server cursors also allow an application to do a positioned update or delete of a fetched row without having to figure out the source table and primary key of the row. If the row data changes between the time it is fetched and the time the update is requested, SQL Server detects the problem and prevents a lost update.

There is a downside to this cursor flexibility, however. If all the results from a given query will be used in your application, using a server cursor will always be more expensive than using the default result set. A default result set requires only one round-trip between client and server, whereas each call to fetch a block of rows from a server cursor results in a round-trip. Additionally, server cursors consume more resources on the server, and there are restrictions on the SELECT statements that can be used with some types of cursor.

For these reasons, you should use server cursors only when your application needs their features. If your particular task requests a single row by primary key, then by all means use a default result set. If another task requires an unpredictably large or updateable result set, use a server cursor and fetch rows in reasonably sized blocks. A good rule of thumb is to fetch a screen of rows at a time for user processing. You should also attempt to make use of fast forward–only cursors with the autofetch option enabled. These cursors can be used to retrieve small result sets with only one round-trip between the client and server, similar to a default result set.

Tuning SQL Queries

Most people with database system performance problems look at the system-level components: memory size, number and speed of processors, and so on. Tuning these components eliminates many performance problems, but may mask some underlying problems that can be alleviated by tuning the actual SQL queries your applications or users are issuing. The SQL queries can be contained in an application, generated by a third-party application development tool, or issued from an ISQL command prompt or SQL Server Query Analyzer.

As you start to look at tuning queries, it is helpful to understand how the SQL Server query optimizer parses and determines the execution plan for a query. The first thing the query optimizer does is to parse each clause of the query and determine if the clause can be used to limit the amount of data that must be scanned for the query. Such a clause can be used as a search argument in an index. After the query is parsed for any search arguments, the query optimizer determines if an index exists for the search argument and decides the usefulness of the index. Next the optimizer derives a query execution plan. Finally, the query optimizer estimates the cost of executing the plan to find the rows that satisfy the search argument.

The query optimizer determines the usefulness of an index based on the answers to the following questions:

- Is the first column of the index used in the search argument?
- Does the search argument specify an upper bound, lower bound, or both to limit the scope of the search?
- Does the index contain every column referenced in the query?

If the query optimizer finds an index that contains all the columns referenced in the query, referred to as a *covering index,* it uses it. This is normally the fastest data access. Because all the required information to satisfy the query is held in the index, the system does not have to access the actual data pages. This provides a large savings in physical I/O for this query.

Once the query optimizer determines that it has a useful index, it evaluates the index by using the index's statistics. SQL Server generates the index statistics automatically unless you disable the *auto update statistics* option. As the database ages, you may encounter a condition in which the statistics are out of date. When SQL Server detects this condition, it will automatically update the statistics unless you have explicitly disabled the automatic statistics update feature. You can force an update by issuing the UPDATE STATISTICS command. The index statistics contain an even sampling of values associated with the index key. The query optimizer accesses the statistics from the *sysindexes* system table in SQL Server. In addition to the statistics information, the *sysindexes* table includes the number of pages in the table or index.

The last piece of information that the query optimizer uses is the *density*, or uniqueness, of the index. The more selective an index is, the more useful it is. A unique index leads to greater density because each index item points to exactly one data item.

Once the query optimizer has gathered its data, it costs the access method for the data. It is possible that even though an index has been deemed useful, its relative cost will be higher than other indexes. The query optimizer evaluates the index to estimate the number of potential cache hits based on the density and step values in the index statistics. Once this value is determined, the query optimizer estimates how many rows qualify based on the search argument discussed earlier in this chapter. The query optimizer will analyze multiple indexes, if they exist, as well as performing a simple table scan. It will finally decide on the access method that results in the smallest number of logical reads. Table 17-1 shows the different access methods and their estimated costs.

Table 17-1 Data Access Methods and Their Estimated Costs

SQL Server Access Method	Estimated Cost in Logical I/Os
Table scan	The total number of data pages in the table.
Clustered index	The number of levels in the index plus the number of data pages to scan. (Data Pages to Scan = Number of Qualifying Rows / Rows per Data Page)
Nonclustered index on a heap	The number of levels in the index plus the number of leaf pages plus the number of qualifying rows.
Nonclustered index on a table with a clustered index	The number of levels in the index plus the number of leaf pages plus the number of qualifying rows times the cost of searching for a clustered index key.
Covering nonclustered index	The number of levels in the index plus the number of leaf index pages. Because this is a covering index, the actual data pages need not be accessed.

In addition to using SQL Server Query Analyzer and SQL Server Profiler, you can also check query performance by using the SET statement. With the SET statement, you can enable the SHOWPLAN, STATISTICS IO, STATISTICS TIME, and STATISTICS PROFILE options. Each of these options is described here.

- **SHOWPLAN** Displays the method chosen by the SQL Server query optimizer to retrieve data
- **STATISTICS IO** Reports information about the number of scans, logical reads, and physical reads for each table referenced in the statement
- **STATISTICS TIME** Displays the amount of time (in milliseconds) required to parse, compile, and execute a query
- **STATISTICS PROFILE** Displays a result set after each executed query that represents a profile of the execution of the query

Remember, you can also use the graphical execution plan option in SQL Server Query Analyzer to view a graphical representation of how SQL Server retrieves data. Chapter 16 discusses SQL Server Query Analyzer in detail.

The information gathered by these options allows you to determine how the SQL Server query optimizer is executing a query and which indexes are being used. With this information, you can determine if performance improvements can be made by rewriting the query, changing the indexes on the tables, or perhaps modifying the database design when possible.

As mentioned previously, SQL Server creates statistics regarding the distribution of values in a column automatically on indexed columns. You can also create statistics on nonindexed columns either manually, by using SQL Server Query Analyzer or the CREATE STATISTICS statement, or automatically, by setting the *auto create statistics* database option to TRUE. The query optimizer will also use statistics on the nonindexed columns to determine the optimal strategy for evaluating a query. Maintaining additional statistics on nonindexed columns involved in join operations can improve query performance. See Chapter 16 for more information about using SQL Server Query Analyzer to create statistics.

Some queries are inherently resource intensive due to fundamental database and index issues. For example, highly nonunique WHERE clauses and queries returning large result sets can be resource intensive. These queries are not inefficient, because the query optimizer will implement the queries in the most efficient fashion possible; however, they are resource intensive, and the set-oriented nature of SQL can make them appear inefficient. No degree of query optimizer intelligence can eliminate the inherent resource cost of these constructs. Although SQL Server will use the optimal available access plan, it is limited by what is fundamentally possible.

General Recommendations

The query tuning information provided in this chapter can be put to good use by following the guidelines given here.

- Add more memory to the server. If the system runs many complex queries, this can improve general query performance. See Chapter 2 for more information about memory management in SQL Server.

- Run SQL Server on a computer with more than one processor. Multiple processors allow SQL Server to make use of parallel queries. Chapter 4 discusses this in more detail.

- Consider rewriting the query if it uses cursors. Look into using a more efficient type of cursor.

- If your application uses looping, consider putting the loops inside the query. Often an application contains a loop that includes a parameterized query, which is executed many times and requires a network round-trip between the computer running the application and SQL Server. Instead, create a single, more complex query using a temporary table. Only one network round-trip is necessary, and the query optimizer can better optimize the single query.

- Do not use multiple aliases for a single table in the same query to simulate index intersection. SQL Server automatically considers index intersection and can make use of multiple indexes on the same table in the same query.

- Make use of query hints only if necessary. Queries using hints executed against earlier versions of SQL Server should be tested without the hints specified. The hints can prevent the query optimizer from choosing a better execution plan. For more information, see Chapter 19.

- Make use of the *query governor cost limit* configuration option. This option can be used to prevent long-running queries from executing, thus preventing system resources from being consumed. By default, the *query governor cost limit* configuration option allows all queries to execute, no matter how long they take. However, the option can be set to a maximum number of seconds that all queries for all connections, or just the queries for a specific connection, are allowed to execute. Because the *query governor cost limit* option is based on estimated query cost, rather than actual elapsed time, it does not have any runtime overhead. It also stops long-running queries before they start, rather than running them until some predefined limit is hit.

Queries Using Joins

If you require joins or merge functions in your queries, there are additional techniques for analyzing and enhancing your queries. SQL Server performs sort, intersect, union, and difference operations using in-memory sorting and hash joins. For query plans that use these operations, SQL Server supports vertical table partitioning, sometimes called *columnar storage*. SQL Server supports nested loop joins, merge joins, and hash joins.

When one join input is quite small (10 rows or less) and the other join input is fairly large and indexed on its join columns, the index nested loops operation is the fastest join operation because it requires the least I/O and the fewest comparisons. If the two join inputs are not small but are sorted on their join column, then a merge join is the fastest join operation. If both join inputs are large and the two inputs are of similar sizes, the merge join with prior sorting and the hash join offer similar performance. However, hash join operations are often much faster if the two input sizes differ significantly from each other.

Hash joins can process large, unsorted, nonindexed inputs efficiently. They are useful for processing intermediate results in complex queries for the following reasons:

- Intermediate results are not indexed, unless explicitly saved to disk and then indexed, and often are not produced suitably sorted for the next operation in the query plan.

- The query optimizer only estimates intermediate result sizes. Because estimates can be an order of magnitude wrong in complex queries, algorithms to process intermediate results not only must be efficient but also must degrade gracefully if an intermediate result turns out to be much larger than anticipated.

Hash joins reduce the need to denormalize the database. Denormalization is typically used to achieve better performance by reducing join operations, in spite of the dangers of redundancy, such as inconsistent updates. Hash joins allow vertical partitioning, which represents groups of columns from a single table in separate files or indexes.

Index Tuning Recommendations

An integral part of application and query tuning is having an effective index strategy. Selection and creation of the correct indexes on your data can make or break a system's performance. In this section we look at some recommendations for effective indexing. Chapter 18 covers indexes in depth.

One very attractive aspect of indexes is that they can be dropped, added, and changed without affecting the database schema or application design. Efficient index design is a critical component of good system performance. Since you can readily create or modify indexes, you should not hesitate to experiment with different indexes. One excellent aid in this experimentation is the SQL Server Index Tuning Wizard (see Chapter 16). This tool can be used to analyze your queries and suggest which indexes should be created.

In a majority of cases, the SQL Server query optimizer will reliably choose the most effective index. As we discussed earlier in this chapter, the query optimizer analyzes many different areas of the index to determine its potential effectiveness. Your overall design strategy should be to provide a good selection of indexes to the query optimizer and trust it to make the right decision. Having a good selection will reduce analysis time and result in good performance over a wide variety of situations.

You cannot always equate the use of an index with good performance, however. If using an index always produced the best performance, the query optimizer's job would be simple. In reality, an incorrect choice of indexed retrieval can result in less than optimal performance. Therefore, the query optimizer's task is to select indexed retrieval only when it will improve performance and to avoid indexed retrieval when it will negatively affect performance.

One potential negative impact of indexes is the overhead required to maintain their effectiveness. As you update or insert data, SQL Server updates the indexes to keep them valid and useful. If you are writing queries that update rows, you should strive to update as many rows as possible in a single statement rather than use multiple queries to update the same rows. When you use only one statement, the optimized index maintenance that SQL Server provides can be exploited.

Other index recommendations are as follows:

- Use the Index Tuning Wizard to analyze your queries and make index recommendations. We cannot stress this recommendation enough.

- Use integer keys for clustered indexes. Also, clustered indexes benefit from being created on unique, non-null, or IDENTITY columns.

- Create nonclustered indexes on all columns frequently used in queries. This can maximize the use of covered queries.

- The time taken to physically create an index is largely dependent on the disk subsystem. Important factors to consider are the following:
  - The RAID level used to store the database and transaction log files. As you saw in Chapter 3, the different RAID levels may require more system resources, as well as time, to perform the reads and writes.
  - The number of disks in the disk array. If you can spread the reads and writes across more physical disks, you will decrease the amount of data a single disk must process and decrease the index creation time.
  - The size of each data row and the number of rows per page. This determines the number of data pages that must be read from disk to create the index.
  - The columns in the index and the data types used. This determines the number of index pages that have to be written to disk.
  - Examine data distribution in indexed columns. Frequently, a long-running query is caused by indexing a column with few unique values or by performing a join on such a column.

Prepared Execution

The ODBC API defines *prepared execution* as a way to reduce the compiling overhead associated with repeatedly executing a SQL statement. The application builds a character string containing a SQL statement and then executes it in two stages. First, it calls SQLPrepare once to have the statement compiled into an execution plan by the database engine. Next, it calls SQLExecute for each execution of the prepared execution plan. This method saves the compiling overhead on each execution. Prepared execution is commonly used by applications to repeatedly execute the same, parameterized SQL statements.

For most databases, prepared execution is faster than direct execution for statements executed more than three or four times primarily because the statement is compiled only once, whereas statements executed directly are compiled each time they are executed. Prepared execution can also reduce network traffic because the driver can send an execution plan identifier and the parameter values, rather than an entire SQL statement, to the data source each time the statement is executed.

SQL Server 7 reduces the performance difference between direct and prepared execution through improved algorithms for detecting and reusing execution plans from SQLExecDirect. This makes some of the performance benefits of prepared execution available to statements executed directly.

SQL Server 7 also provides native support for prepared execution. An execution plan is built on SQLPrepare and later executed when SQLExecute is called. Since SQL Server 7 does not need to build temporary stored procedures on SQLPrepare, there is no extra overhead on the system tables in *tempdb*.

If you call either SQLDescribeCol or SQLDescribeParam before calling SQLExecute, you will generate an extra round-trip to the server. On SQLDescribeCol, the driver removes the WHERE clause from the query and sends it to the server with SET FMTONLY ON to get the description of the columns in the first result set returned by the query. On SQLDescribeParam, the driver calls the server to get a description of the expressions or columns referenced by any parameter markers in the query. This method also has some restrictions, such as not being able to resolve parameters in subqueries.

Excessive use of SQLPrepare with the SQL Server ODBC driver degrades performance, especially when connected to earlier versions of SQL Server. You should not use prepared execution for statements that are executed a single time. Prepared execution is slower than direct execution for a single execution of a statement because it requires an extra network round-trip from the client to the server. On earlier versions of SQL Server it also generates a temporary stored procedure.

In SQL Server 7, prepared statements cannot be used to create temporary objects; this is also true in earlier versions of SQL Server if the option to generate stored procedures is active. With this option turned on, the prepared statement is built into a temporary stored procedure that is executed when SQLExecute is called. Any temporary object created during the execution of a stored procedure is automatically dropped when the procedure finishes.

Some early ODBC applications used SQLPrepare any time SQLBindParameter was used. SQLBindParameter does not require the use of SQLPrepare; it can be used with SQLExecDirect. For example, use SQLExecDirect with SQLBindParameter to retrieve the return code or output parameters from a stored procedure that is executed only once. Do not use SQLPrepare with SQLBindParameter unless the same statement will be executed multiple times.

Summary

In this chapter, we discussed techniques for ensuring that your applications and queries do not inhibit your system's performance. We looked at overall application design considerations, query design, and query tuning. In addition, we explored how to use indexes and how the SQL Server query optimizer selects the appropriate index to use for your query. Finally, we briefly looked at how you can use specific ODBC API calls to enhance performance in applications in which you issue the same SQL statements multiple times. Now that you have your SQL statements optimized, we need to look, in detail, at the indexes in your database. The next chapter explores indexes and how to use and tune them.

Chapter 18
Using and Tuning Indexes

The use of indexes on your SQL Server tables is critical to the performance of data operations. But you must understand how to use indexes in order to benefit from them. In this chapter, we discuss index fundamentals as well as the different types of indexes and when you should use them. We also give general guidelines to follow when building your indexes, show you how to analyze and tune indexes for better query performance, and discuss how to form your queries so they will use the indexes you create.

Index Fundamentals

An *index* is an auxiliary data structure used to assist SQL Server in accessing data. Indexes are created on tables. One table may have more than one index that refers to its data. Depending on the type of index, the index data may be stored either with the table data or separate from it. Regardless of the type of index, the basic concept of how it works is the same. A database index is like an index in a book or the guide words in a dictionary: by looking up the term in the index or by using the guide words, you can quickly find where the data is located without searching every page.

Without an index, all retrieval of data must be done through table scans, in which all the data in a table must be read and compared against the data that you are requesting. You should avoid table scans because of the high amount of I/O that this operation generates (unless you want to select a large percentage of rows from the table). If the table is large, it could take a lot of time and system resources to perform a table scan. By using an appropriate index, the number of I/Os needed to find data rows can be greatly reduced. This speeds up the access to the data as well as frees up system resources for other operations.

The structure of an index is typically a *B-tree*. The B-tree structure begins with a *root node;* this root node is the start of the index. The root node contains index rows (rows of index data) that contain ranges of index key values and pointers to the next index nodes, known as *branch nodes*. Branch nodes in turn contain index rows with further refined ranges of values that point to other branch nodes. Each level of branch nodes is known as an *index level*.

The nodes in the lowest level of the index tree are called the *leaf nodes*. The leaf nodes contain the index key data plus either information indicating where the referenced data resides or the data itself, depending on whether the index is nonclustered or clustered. (These different index types are explained later in this chapter.) The number of index levels that must be traversed to reach a leaf node determines the number of I/Os necessary to find the desired row of data. Figure 18-1 illustrates all the terms discussed thus far. Each node does not necessarily contain only two pointers as shown in Figure 18-1. Actually, each index row in a node contains a pointer to another node, as shown in the general index structure of Figure 18-2.

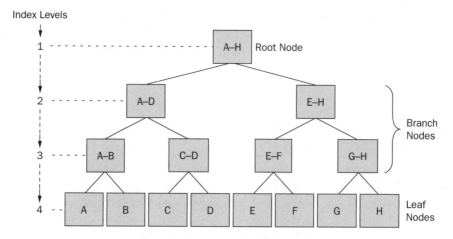

Figure 18-1 *A sample index.*

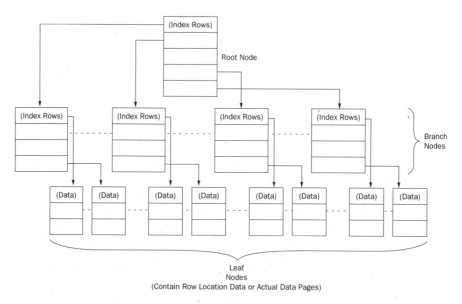

Figure 18-2 *An index structure.*

Indexes are helpful not only with SELECT statements, but with UPDATE and DELETE statements as well because SQL Server must find a row before it can update or delete it. For the remainder of this chapter, when we speak of finding data or performing queries we are referring to any of these three types of operations.

Index Keys

Index keys are the columns for which an index is created. To access a row of data via the index, you must include an index key value or values within the WHERE clause of the SQL statement. You may create an index on one or more index key columns.

An index with only one index key is called a *simple index*. For example, a simple index may be created on the customer ID column of a customer table. This index will be used for queries that search for a particular customer ID. Note that the customer ID must be included in the WHERE clause of the SQL statement in order for the index to be used.

An index with more than one key column is called a *composite index*. A composite index may be created on the last-name column and first-name column of the customer table. This index will be used for queries that search for a particular customer by last name only, by first name only, or by last name and first name. For more information on index keys, see the section "Choosing the Index Key Columns" later in this chapter.

Types of Indexes

SQL Server supports two major types of indexes: clustered and nonclustered. For either of these two types of indexes, you can specify whether the index should be a unique index. (A unique index is sometimes considered a third type of index, but it is actually a characteristic of either a clustered or nonclustered index.) Another kind of index, called the *full-text index*, is more like a catalog. The full-text index has characteristics different from those of clustered and nonclustered indexes and thus stands in a category of its own. The following sections explain the characteristics of each type of index and discuss when each type is useful.

Clustered Index

A *clustered index* is an index that indicates the order in which table data should be physically stored. The table data is sorted and stored according to the key column or columns specified for the clustered index. This type of index is analogous to a dictionary, which stores information in alphabetical order and provides guide words to help locate the information quickly; the data is found on the same page as its guide words. The clustered index is similar in that it includes the index pages as well as the actual data pages, which make up the lowest level (the leaf node) of the clustered index, as shown in Figure 18-3. Each row in the root node will point to a branch node, whose rows may point to other branch nodes (only one set of branch nodes is shown in Figure 18-3). The last set of branch nodes will finally point to the leaf nodes. When you get to the lowest level of the index (to the leaf nodes), you thus have reached the actual data page as well. Since the data is physically stored in a specific order, you can only create one clustered index per table.

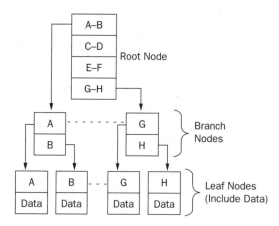

Figure 18-3 *The structure of a clustered index.*

Clustered indexes are very efficient when created on columns that will be searched for a certain range of values. For example, you may want to frequently retrieve all rows from a customer table that contain last names beginning with the letters *A* through *C*. By using a clustered index on the last-name column, the data will be physically stored in order of the last name. When the query is performed, the row with the first selected value is found (the first occurrence of a last name that starts with *A*); the subsequent rows are guaranteed to be physically adjacent. Therefore the rows will be retrieved quickly until the last row containing a last name that starts with *C* is reached.

Another case in which clustered indexes are particularly efficient is when you frequently need to sort the data that is retrieved. If you create a clustered index on the column or columns that you would need to sort by, then the rows will be physically stored in that order (and thus presorted), eliminating the overhead of sorting the data after it is retrieved.

Clustered indexes are also efficient when you frequently perform queries to find a row that contains a specific value for a column that contains all unique values, such as a customer ID column (assuming each customer has a unique customer ID). Creating a clustered index on that column provides the fastest path to retrieve a row in this case. You may want to make this clustered index unique, which means that no duplicates of that column will be allowed to be inserted into the table. SQL Server will provide an error message if you attempt to insert a duplicate value into the index key column or columns.

Because you can only have one clustered index per table, you must look at what search conditions your queries will be using (such as searching for a range of values or for a particular customer), how frequently they will be performed, and how much data is involved with each query (that is, the size of the table to be queried). You want to create the clustered index so that it will be most beneficial for your situation. For instance, if you create the clustered index to service a particular query that is run only once each night, you may be causing performance to suffer for other queries that run more often during the day by not building the clustered index to satisfy the more frequently run queries. On the other hand, the nightly query may take too much time to complete if the clustered index is not built to speed that query.

> **Note**   When you create a primary key constraint on a column, SQL Server automatically creates a unique clustered index for that constraint if one does not already exist and if you do not explicitly specify that the index should be a unique nonclustered index.

Nonclustered Index

Unlike the clustered index, a *nonclustered index* does not contain the actual table data in its leaf nodes (Figure 18-4). Instead, the index itself is completely separate from the data, similar to a book with an index in the back—the index indicates which page to go to, but the data is not with the index itself. The leaf nodes of the nonclustered index contain index rows that hold index data and information that determines the exact location of a row.

The location information can be one of two types, depending on whether there is a clustered index on the table. If there is a clustered index, then for each row the key value of the clustered index is stored in the leaf node of the nonclustered index as the row locator. This value is then used to directly locate the data, which, as you recall, resides in the leaf node of the clustered index. If the clustered index is not a unique index, SQL Server automatically assigns an internal value to any duplicate index key values to make them unique for use with nonclustered indexes. The internal values are not visible to users.

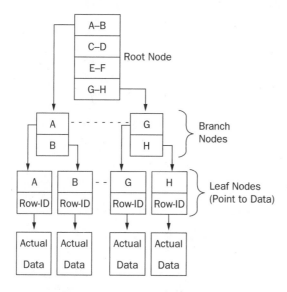

Figure 18-4 *The structure of a nonclustered index.*

If there is no clustered index on the table, then each leaf node contains a row ID as the row locator, instead of a key value of the clustered index. The row ID is a pointer made up of the file ID, page number, and row number in the page. This pointer indicates exactly where the row is found, so that once the row ID is reached, only one more I/O is required to read the row of data. Figure 18-4 illustrates the structure of a nonclustered index.

SQL Server allows a maximum of 249 nonclustered indexes on a table. Remember that the more indexes you have, the more overhead is incurred when performing inserts, updates, and deletes because the index pages must be maintained to include those modifications as well. Thus you do not want to create unnecessary indexes.

Unique Index

A *unique index* is either a clustered or a nonclustered index that is created specifically to be unique. Values inserted into the key value column or columns must be unique; duplicates of the key values are not allowed. For composite keys, that means that the combination of the values must be unique. For example, if you have a unique index created on the last-name and first-name columns of a customer table, no duplicate last-name and first-name pairs may be inserted; you may insert two or more rows with the same last name, but they must have unique first names to go with them and vice versa. A case in which you would want the unique index to be on only one column is when you want a single column to be unique in itself, such as a column containing social security numbers. You can create a unique index on that column to ensure that there are no duplicate social security numbers in the table.

You remember that you can also use another method to enforce uniqueness of data for certain columns: you can create a UNIQUE constraint. When you create a UNIQUE constraint, SQL Server automatically creates a unique nonclustered index to enforce the constraint. Once you have a unique index on a table, SQL Server will prevent duplicates from being entered into the table and will give you an error message stating that a duplicate row insert was attempted.

Full-Text Index

The *full-text index* is more complicated than the previously discussed indexes. The full-text index is actually like a catalog. Instead of simply searching in an ordered B-tree fashion, the full-text index allows you to search by groups of keywords. The full-text index is part of the Microsoft Search Service. It is used extensively in Web site search engines and other text-based operations.

Unlike B-tree indexes, the full-text index is stored external to the database, but is maintained by the database. This is done so that the index can maintain its own structure. The following restrictions are placed on creating and maintaining full-text indexes:

- Full-text indexes can be created only on columns of type char and varchar.
- Only one full-text index is allowed per table.
- A full-text index is not automatically updated, unlike B-tree indexes.
- A full-text index is created, managed, and dropped using stored procedures or the Full-Text Indexing Wizard.

The full-text index has a wealth of features that cannot be found in normal B-tree indexes. Because this index is designed to be a text search engine, it supports more than normal text search capabilities. With the full-text index you can perform the following types of operations:

- Searching for words or phrases
- Searching for single words or groups of words
- Searching for words that are similar to each other

Note   To use full-text indexing, you must have installed the Full-Text Search Service with SQL Server Standard or Enterprise Edition. To select the option, you must choose the custom install.

See SQL Server Books Online for more information on the full-text index. We will focus on tuning clustered and nonclustered indexes for the rest of this chapter.

Tuning Indexes

An efficient index is one that helps you to find data with fewer I/Os and less system resource usage than a table scan. Since an index involves traversing the B-tree to find an individual value, it is not efficient to use an index when retrieving large amounts of data. A rule of thumb is that for queries that access more than 20 percent of the rows in a table, it is better to do a table scan than to use an index.

Upon the execution of a query, the SQL Server query optimizer evaluates the costs of the possible methods of finding the data and chooses the method that is most efficient to use as the query execution plan. SQL Server will determine whether to use an index, and which of the available indexes to use. (If it is more efficient to use no index to satisfy the query, SQL Server will do so.) In earlier versions of SQL Server, only one index could be used in a query execution plan. With SQL Server 7, index intersection or index union may be performed in order to make use of more than one index to satisfy a query. SQL Server may also join two indexes defined on the same table to satisfy a query.

Basically, creating an appropriate and efficient index is the first step in tuning the index. You must make several decisions when creating indexes, including the following:

- Which column or columns to include in the index
- Whether to add a PRIMARY KEY constraint or UNIQUE constraint to the table, which will allow SQL Server to automatically create an index for you (you may have already done this at table creation)
- Whether the index should be clustered or nonclustered
- Whether the index should be unique or nonunique
- Whether to use a fill factor and, if so, what percentage to choose (for more information, see the section "Fill Factor" later in this chapter)

To help in making these decisions, you must look at your SQL statements to determine which tables and columns are being accessed and how they are being accessed. We discuss this in more detail in later subsections. But first, let's go over some general guidelines for creating indexes:

- Determine if most of the queries are SELECT statements, or if there are significant numbers of INSERT, UPDATE, or DELETE statements. As the number of indexes on a table increases, so does the amount of overhead required to maintain those indexes for INSERT, UPDATE, and DELETE statements. For queries with a lot of these statements, therefore, be conservative with the number of indexes you create on the modified tables. If your queries are mostly SELECT statements, then having more indexes may allow better performance by providing SQL Server more indexes to choose from for its query execution plans. Usually you will have to find a balance between these two cases.

- You should attempt to build your indexes to aid specific queries—do not just generalize or guess about what columns to use as the index keys. After creating an index, you should check the execution plan for the query or queries for which it was built and verify that the index is being chosen by SQL Server as you expected. We explain how to do this in the section "Using SQL Server Query Analyzer" later in this chapter.

- Indexing very small tables may hurt performance because it may be more efficient for SQL Server to perform a simple table scan. The query optimizer should detect this fact; however, it is not perfect, so be aware of the possibility that SQL Server may try to use an index where one is available.

- Avoid having too many index keys in the index, because the greater the amount of data in the index, the more data will have to be updated when modifications are made to the table, thus causing more overhead. An index with one to a few key columns is called a *narrow index;* an index with many key columns is called a *wide index*. A narrow index will take up less space than a wide index and is preferable when possible.

- Avoid choosing columns with large data types as index keys. For example, a column of type integer is a good choice for an index key, whereas a column of type varchar is not a good choice because the varchar data may require a lot of space and therefore more overhead for maintenance.

Now let's look at some guidelines concerning what type of data search clauses in queries will most benefit from indexes:

- **Searches that match a specific value**   These queries will retrieve only a few rows that match a specific equality. For example: `WHERE customer_ID = 19`.

- **Searches that match a range of values**   These queries will also retrieve a small number of rows. For example: `WHERE customer_ID BETWEEN 19 AND 22` or `WHERE customer_ID >= 19 AND customer_ID <= 22`.

- **Searches that are used in a join**   Columns that are used as join keys often are good candidates for indexes. For example: `FROM customer_table as cust, customer_detail_table as cust_det WHERE cust.customer_ID = cust_det.customer_ID`.

- **Searches that retrieve data in a specific order**   If you wish the resulting data set to be sorted, you can use a clustered index on the column or columns by which you wish to sort. Because the data is already sorted within the index itself, no sorting is required when the results are returned. An example is assuming a clustered index on customer_ID: `WHERE customer_ID < 100 ORDER BY customer_ID`.

Creating and verifying index usage is a continual process as your queries grow and change. In the next sections we discuss in more detail how to choose the index key columns for an index, how to use a fill factor, and how to use SQL Server Query Analyzer to determine the execution plan chosen for a query by SQL Server.

Choosing the Index Key Columns

An index is most beneficial when searching for only a few rows. Therefore, an index should be designed with good selectivity. The *selectivity* of an index is based on the number of rows per index key value. An index with poor selectivity is one that has multiple rows per key value, such as an index key on a gender column that holds one of two values: "M" for male and "F" for female. An index with good selectivity has one or a few values per index key, such as an index on a customer ID column. A unique index has the best selectivity.

Information about the selectivity of an index is stored within the index distribution statistics. An index with good selectivity is more likely to be used by the query optimizer than an index with poor selectivity. You can view the selectivity of an index by using the command DBCC SHOW_STATISTICS (*table_name*, *index_name*). The lower the density returned in the output, the higher the selectivity. Index statistics are updated automatically by default, but can be manually updated with the command UPDATE STATISTICS *table_name*. For more information about these two commands and their syntax, search for them by name in SQL Server Books Online.

The selectivity of an index can be enhanced by using a composite index. Several columns with poor selectivity can be joined together in a composite index to form one index that has good selectivity. Although a unique index provides the best selectivity, be sure to choose an index type that fits your data model. For instance, you should not create a unique index on a customer last-name column if duplicate last names are allowed in your table.

For a clustered index with a composite key, the order in which the key columns are listed in the CREATE INDEX statement is also important. When creating such an index, the data is sorted first by the first key, then by the second key, and so on, according to the order in which the columns were specified when you created the index. For example, if you create a clustered index for a customer table on the customer last-name column and then on the customer first-name column, the data will first be sorted by last name; if there are any rows with the same last name, those rows will also be sorted by first name. If there are 100 entries with the last name of Smith, for example, the Smith duplicates will be sorted in order of the first names after the data is sorted by last name. Therefore, a query using this index will be more efficient either if both last name and first name are included in the WHERE clause or if the last name only is in the WHERE clause. A less efficient query would search for first name only, because all last names will have to be checked for the matching first name. In all three cases, the clustered index will be used to satisfy the queries, and each will be performed more efficiently than if there were no index on the table.

In contrast, the order in which the columns actually appear in the WHERE clause does not matter. (This is true for both clustered and nonclustered indexes.) For example, the following two queries will use the index just described in the same manner (that is, they will have the same execution plan):

```
SELECT CUSTOMER_ID FROM CUSTOMER WHERE LAST_NAME="SMITH" AND FIRST_NAME="PENELOPE"

SELECT CUSTOMER_ID FROM CUSTOMER WHERE FIRST_NAME="PENELOPE" AND LAST_NAME="SMITH"
```

Another important concept when choosing your index keys is to try to cover a query. *Covering* a query means that each of the columns in the SELECT list is included as an index key within the same index, so that the data retrieved resides in the index keys themselves, and the actual data pages will not have to be read at all. The covered query needs to read data only from the index and can bypass the table data pages. For example, if a query selects only columns *A* and *B,* and a composite index on that same table has columns *A* and *B* as the index keys, then the query is covered. Even if the index is created on columns *A, B,* and *C,* the query is still covered.

Fill Factor

As inserts, updates, and deletes are performed on a table that has indexes, the indexes must be updated to reflect the changes in the table. The index rows are stored in order based on the index keys. Therefore, particularly for inserts and updates, new index rows must be added in the appropriate location to maintain order in the index. As index pages fill up, space for additional index rows must be created. SQL Server accomplishes this by moving approximately half of the rows in the index page to a new page. This operation is known as a *page split*. Page splits result in increased system overhead because of the CPU usage and additional I/Os they incur. One way to avoid page splits is by tuning the fill factor of the index pages. The *fill factor* specifies the percentage of the page to fill when creating the index. This allows you to leave room in the index pages for additional index rows.

You can specify the fill factor on an index by using the FILLFACTOR option with the CREATE INDEX command or, if using Enterprise Manager, by opening the database diagram, right-clicking on the table you want, and selecting Properties from the menu. Click the Indexes/Keys tab, select the index from the drop-down list, and enter the percentage you want in the Fill Factor section. The value of the fill factor varies from 0 to 100, indicating the percentage of the index page that should be filled upon index creation. If the fill factor is not specified, the system default (the value set for the SQL Server configuration option *fillfactor*) will be used. This value is set to 0 when SQL Server is installed.

Note The fill factor parameter only specifies how the index is originally created. It has no effect once the index has been built.

When 0 is specified for the fill factor, the leaf pages are packed to 100 percent, but the branch nodes have some space left free. This is the SQL Server installation default, and it usually works well. A value of 100 for the fill factor specifies that all index pages are completely filled when the index is created. This is optimal for tables that never have new data inserted into them (that is, read-only tables). Both the leaf pages and upper-level pages are completely packed; thus, any insert will cause a page split. The benefit of packing the index pages is that the index requires less storage space.

Using a low value for the fill factor will allow a great deal of space for inserts, but will require a lot of extra space in which to store the index. Unless you will be doing constant inserts into the database, a low value for the fill factor is usually not recommended. If you are experiencing a great deal of page splits, try decreasing the value for the fill factor by a small percentage, then recreate the index and see if the problem is solved.

The number of page splits per second that your system is experiencing is displayed in the SQL Server statistic Page Splits/sec. This value can be found in the Performance Monitor under the SQLServer: Access Methods object. If this value is high, you may need to rebuild the index with a lower fill factor.

Using SQL Server Query Analyzer

SQL Server Query Analyzer has many functions, but we focus here on three particular functions that help with index tuning. First, we show how Query Analyzer can be used to perform index analysis on a query; SQL Server will recommend a possible index to help with the execution of the specified query. Next, we show how Query Analyzer can be used to display the estimated execution plan that SQL Server will use to execute a query, without actually executing the query. Finally, we show how to display the actual execution plan that SQL Server used to perform a query.

For the examples of index analysis, we use our own sample database *salesdb*. (We don't use the installed sample databases because they have so little data that SQL Server will not make any index recommendations.) You should be able to follow along and do similar testing with your own databases.

We use SQL Server Query Analyzer to help us determine what indexes would be helpful for some queries to the *customer* table of our *salesdb* database. This table currently has no indexes and contains 300,000 rows of data. First we open Query Analyzer and select *salesdb* as the database in the DB drop-down menu. Then we type in our query, which searches for all rows with a last name of "Smith," as shown in Figure 18-5. Next we select Perform Index Analysis from the Query menu. After waiting for a few seconds, SQL Server responds with its recommendation, as shown in Figure 18-6.

In this case, SQL Server recommends a nonclustered index, named *customer0*, on the *customer* table, with c_last as the index key. We can choose to either accept the recommended index and let SQL Server create it or to cancel the analysis. We choose to cancel this window so we can perform index analysis on another query. You probably should perform index analysis on more than one query before deciding which indexes to create. There may be another query, for example, that searches for the customer by last name and first name, in which case the recommended index would be a nonclustered composite index on both the c_last and c_first columns. This one index would cover both of the queries discussed here.

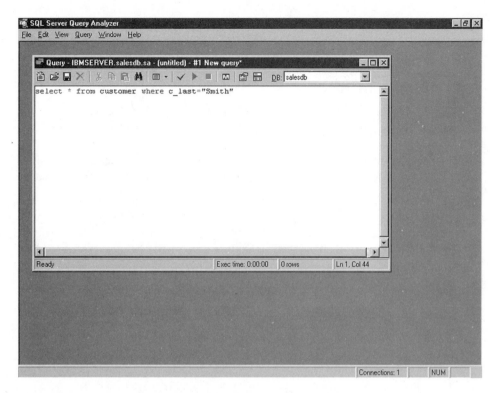

Figure 18-5 *SQL Server Query Analyzer.*

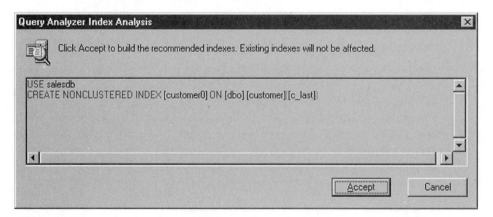

Figure 18-6 *Index recommendations after index analysis.*

Let's look at another example of index analysis using a query that searches for a range of the *c_id* (customer ID) column. The query and the results of running Perform Index Analysis are shown in Figure 18-7. SQL Server did not suggest an index for this query because of one of the three reasons listed in the output. Note that SQL Server Query Analyzer will not recommend a clustered index when tuning a single query. Therefore, because this query searches for a range of values (which is a good candidate for a clustered index), we can assume that the reason SQL Server did not make a recommendation is that it would have recommended that the index be a clustered one. It is difficult to determine by just looking at this one query if the clustered index should really be built on the *c_id* column. You will have to decide which column or columns should be part of a clustered index by using your knowledge of the characteristics of your table and your query. Let's assume that most queries performed on our *customer* table search for rows by customer last name, not by customer ID. In that case it would be more beneficial to create the clustered index on the last-name column than on the ID column.

Note   SQL Server Query Analyzer will not recommend a clustered index when tuning a single query with the Perform Index Analysis option.

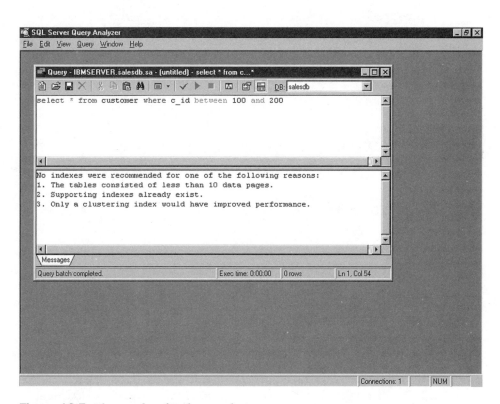

Figure 18-7 *The results of index analysis.*

Before we create any indexes on our *customer* table, let's look at the same query on customer ID as before, but this time let's choose the option Display Estimated Execution Plan from the Query menu. This option displays the estimated execution plan without executing the query. This is helpful when you suspect that the query may take a long time to complete and you do not want to execute it, but you want to find out what execution plan SQL Server would choose if it did execute the query. The results for our query are shown in Figure 18-8.

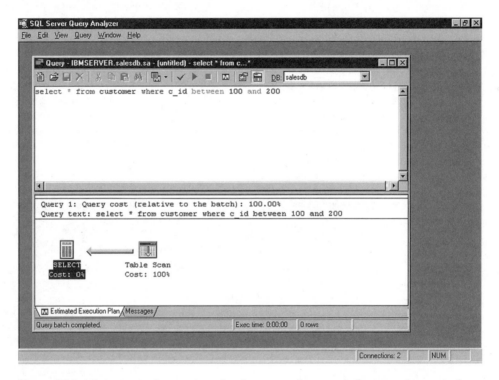

Figure 18-8 *The estimated execution plan for a sample query before creating an index.*

To understand the output, you read from right to left (following the gray arrow) and from bottom to top (had there been more levels of information). As you see in Figure 18-8, SQL Server would perform a table scan to complete our query. A table scan is not desirable since it requires reading every row in the table, so we create a clustered index on the *c_id* column using the following command:

```
CREATE CLUSTERED INDEX cust_indx_1 on customer (c_id)
GO
```

Now we display the estimated query plan again, and we obtain the results shown in Figure 18-9. This time, SQL Server chose to use the index we just created in its execution plan. If you move the mouse over the icon and the name of the index in the displayed results, you will see a window pop up with statistics about the index operation, as shown in Figure 18-10. Move the

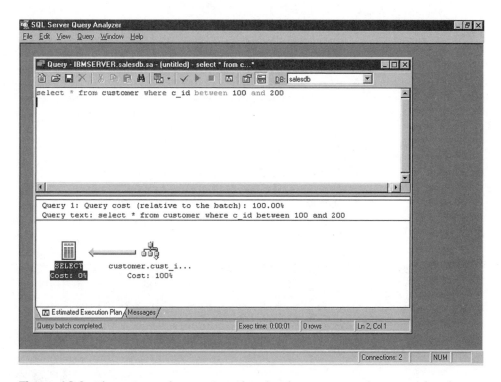

Figure 18-9 *The estimated execution plan for the same sample query after the index has been created.*

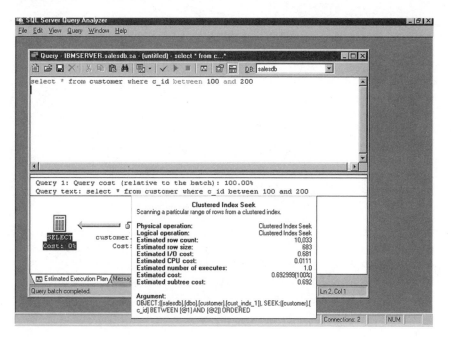

Figure 18-10 *Details of the clustered index seek.*

mouse to point at the arrow between the SELECT and index icons, or above the SELECT icon, and you will see more statistics windows pop up. See Chapter 16 and SQL Server Books Online for details on what the icons signify and what the statistics mean.

Now let's actually run this query and see if the estimated execution plan is the same as the execution plan SQL Server really uses. First, we change the query to select only *c_last* instead of *, so that less data is returned. Next select Show Execution Plan from the Query menu, so that the icon to the left is highlighted in light gray (this indicates that it is enabled). Then we click on the green arrow to run the query.

Once the query has been completed, the query results are displayed in the Results tab, and the execution plan that was used is displayed in the Execution Plan tab. We click on the Execution Plan tab and see the results shown in Figure 18-11. If we hold the mouse over the index icon again, we see the query execution statistics for that index seek operation, as shown in Figure 18-12.

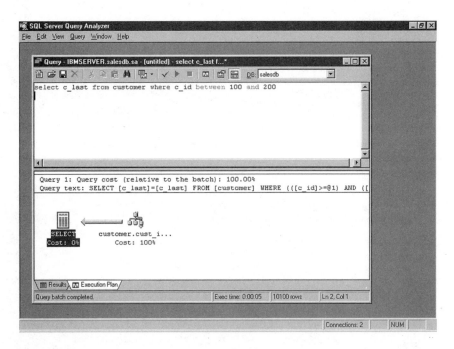

Figure 18-11 *The actual execution plan.*

If we compare this set of statistics for the index operation with the set from Figure 18-10 (the estimated execution plan), we can see that the row count is greater and the row size is less. However, the actual cost of the index operation is the same in both cases (0.692), so the estimate was fairly accurate.

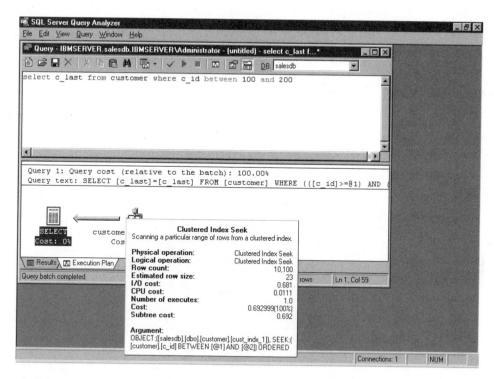

Figure 18-12 *Query execution statistics.*

Now that you have seen how to use SQL Server Query Analyzer, you should be able to display the execution plans for your queries to help you determine whether your indexes are being used or not, and if the right index is being used.

Summary

This chapter focused on tuning SQL Server indexes. You first learned the fundamentals of indexes—the different index types and their structures. Then, as part of tuning, you learned that it is important to properly create your indexes and to test them for specific queries. Choosing the columns for the index keys should be based on the columns used in the search conditions of the queries for which you are creating the index. You should build indexes that are useful for your queries. We showed you how to use SQL Server Query Analyzer to determine the execution plan for a query and to recommend possible indexes for a query. Remember, index usage should be evaluated often to determine if indexes are being used properly, especially if new queries are added to your application or new indexes are created. In the next chapter you will learn how to use hints to direct certain behaviors of SQL Server.

Chapter 19
Using Hints in SQL Server

SQL Server 7 allows you to include hints that instruct the SQL Server query processor how to handle your query. You can override the normal processing to meet your specific needs. This chapter discusses the different isolation levels and what they mean. It also explains how to apply hints to your query statements to take advantage of these isolation levels.

Isolation Levels

Before you can start exploring the hints available in SQL Server, you must understand the isolation levels available. When you use locking as a concurrency control mechanism, you have solved the concurrency problems. The locking strategy, either at the table, page, or row level, allows all transactions to run in complete isolation from one another, although there can be more than one transaction running in SQL Server at any one time.

The basic concept underlying isolation is *serializability*, a property of the database system such that the database state achieved after running a set of concurrent transactions must be equivalent to the database state that would be achieved if the set of transactions were executed serially in some order. This property ensures that all the data stored and retrieved from the database is correct and consistent. Without serializability, we could receive different answers to our concurrent queries depending on the order in which they were run. That would be unacceptable.

We can think of serializability by using the analogy of several writers working on different chapters of the same book. Any author can submit chapters to the overall project at any time. However, after a chapter has been edited, an author cannot make any changes to the chapter without the editor's approval. This way the editor can guarantee the accuracy of the overall project at any point in time, regardless of when new unedited chapters arrive.

Although serializability achieves the goal of maintaining data integrity, it does so at the expense of performance. To get around the performance problem and still maintain data integrity, database developers determined that some queries do not require full isolation in order to be acceptable. This led to the establishment of isolation levels. You can think of an isolation level as the threshold below which a transaction will not accept inconsistent data. When you run at a low isolation level, you gain higher concurrency but at the expense of data correctness. Conversely, when you run at a higher isolation level you ensure data correctness, but your overall transaction concurrency will be negatively affected. It is important to look at your transactions and determine the appropriate isolation levels required.

SQL-92 defines four isolation levels, all of which are supported by SQL Server:

- **Read Uncommitted**   This is the lowest level of isolation, which ensures that transactions are isolated just enough so that they do not read corrupt data.
- **Read Committed**   This is SQL Server's default isolation level, which ensures that transactions are isolated enough so that they read only committed data.
- **Repeatable Read**   This isolation level ensures that if a transaction reads the same item twice without updating it in the interim, the read returns the same value.
- **Serializable**   This is the highest level of isolation, in which transactions are completely isolated from one another.

Now that we know what the four isolation levels are, let's look at the four concurrency problems that they help alleviate. If we did not have locking and isolation, the following problems could occur:

- **The lost update problem (dirty write)**   The lost update problem arises when two or more transactions select the same row and then update the row based on the value originally selected. Because each transaction is unaware of other transactions, the last update overwrites the updates made by the other transactions. Therefore, data is lost.

    Returning to our book-authoring example, suppose we have two editors who each make an electronic copy of the same document. Each editor changes his or her copy independently and then saves the changed copy, thereby overwriting the original document. The editor who saves his or her changed copy last overwrites changes made by the first editor. The first editor's work has been lost without anyone knowing it, causing problems later on. It would be better if the second editor could not make changes until the first editor had finished.

- **The uncommitted dependency problem (dirty read)**   This condition occurs when a transaction modifies a data element and a second transaction reads the data before the first transaction commits the changes. If the first transaction performs a rollback of the change, then the second transaction will have used a value that was never committed and therefore may be incorrect.

    Using our book example, suppose an editor is making changes to an electronic document. During the changes, a second editor takes a copy of the document that includes all the changes made so far and distributes it to the intended audience. The first editor then decides the changes made so far are wrong and removes the edits and saves the document. The distributed document contains edits that are no longer valid and should be treated as if they never existed. It would be better if no one could read the changed document until the first editor determined that the changes were final.

- **The inconsistent analysis problem (nonrepeatable read)**   This condition arises when a transaction reads a data element, and then a second transaction comes along and modifies or deletes the data element and performs a commit. If the first transaction were to reread the data element, it may receive a modified value or discover that the data element has been deleted.

For example, an editor reads the same document twice, but between each reading, the author rewrites the document. When the editor reads the document for the second time, it has completely changed. The original read was not repeatable, leading to confusion. It would be better if the editor could read the document only after the author had completely finished writing it.

- **The phantom problem (phantom read)**   The phantom read problem manifests itself when a transaction reads a set of values that satisfy some search criteria. A second transaction then generates additional data that also satisfy the search criteria of the first transaction. If the first transaction were to repeat its initial read with the same search criteria, it would obtain a different set of values.

Once again, we can return to our book example to illustrate this problem. An editor reads and edits a document submitted by an author, but when the edits are being incorporated into the master copy of the document by the production department, they find that new, unedited material has been added to the document by the author. The document contains material that previously did not exist, leading to confusion and problems. It would be better if no one could add new material to the document until the editor and production department finished working with the original document.

Session-Level Isolation

Occasionally, your application may require either more or less strict isolation than the default SQL Server Read Committed isolation level. If the entire SQL batch requires the same isolation level, you can override the SQL Server default setting for this session. You set the isolation level for a session by issuing the SET TRANSACTION ISOLATION LEVEL statement.

When you specify the isolation level, the locking behavior for all SELECT statements in the SQL Server session operates at that isolation level and remains in effect until the session terminates or until you specifically set the isolation level to another value. For example, if you wish to set the transaction isolation level to Serializable, ensuring that no phantom rows can be inserted by concurrent transactions into a *SALES* table, you would execute the following SQL statements:

```
SET TRANSACTION ISOLATION LEVEL SERIALIZABLE
GO
BEGIN TRANSACTION
SELECT monthly_mountaindew_sw FROM SALES
GO
```

You can also query SQL Server to determine what transaction isolation level is in effect by using the DBCC USEROPTIONS statement. The following SQL batch and its output illustrates this:

```
SET TRANSACTION ISOLATION LEVEL REPEATABLE READ
GO
DBCC USEROPTIONS
GOs
```

The following output is produced:

```
Set Option          Value
Textsize            4096
Language            us_English
Dateformat          mdy
Datefirst           7
isolation level     repeatable read
```

SQL Hints

SQL Server provides several options and hints that you can set to affect the results and performance of your SQL statements. These options can affect SQL Server at the index or table level. To determine which option or hint takes precedence, SQL Server follows a hierarchical sequence. As we explore the different hints and options available, you should keep in mind the following sequence.

If the option or hint is available at more than one level, then SQL Server determines the level on which the option or hint will be applied. The base level consists of server options, which are set via the *sp_configure* command. Any database option, specified via the *sp_dboption* command, overrides a server option. The database option can be overridden by a SET command. Finally, a hint at the statement level will override a SET option. This hierarchy allows you to determine which behavior of the server you want to be the default. You can then easily override that setting for special queries or SQL statements.

The most flexible method for providing hints is at the SQL statement level. Hints at this level override any option or hint set at any other level. SQL Server allows you to specify three different types of transactional hints: join hints, table hints, or query hints. We explore each of these in detail.

> **Caution**   The SQL Server query optimizer usually selects the best execution plan for a query. Incorrect or inappropriate join hints can have a negative impact on the performance of the system. For that reason, join hints, query hints, and table hints should be used only as a last resort by experienced database administrators.

Join Hints

SQL Server 7 provides a mechanism for modifying the default behavior during a table join operation through the use of join hints. For example, you can force SQL Server to use a hash join by specifying the following join hint:

```
SELECT    region_id,
          region_name,
          sales_ytd
FROM      sales INNER HASH JOIN regions
          ON sales.region_id = regions.region_id
```

You can specify whether the SQL Server query optimizer should use a loop, hash, merge, or remote method for the join.

The *loop join,* also called *nested iteration,* uses one join input as the outer input table and one as the inner input table. The outer loop consumes the outer input table row by row. The inner loop, executed for each outer row, searches for matching rows in the inner input table. In the simplest case, the search scans the entire inner input table or index. A loop join is particularly effective if the outer input is quite small and the inner input is preindexed and quite large. In many small transactions, such as those affecting only a small set of rows, loop joins are far superior to both merge joins and hash joins. In large queries, however, loop joins are often not the optimal choice.

The hash join method has two inputs: the build input and the probe input. The query optimizer assigns these roles so that the smaller of the two inputs is the build input. Hash joins are used for many types of set-matching operations, such as inner joins; left, right, and full outer joins; left and right semi-joins; intersections; unions; and differences.

A hash join can be used only if there is at least one equality (WHERE) clause in the join predicate. However, because joins are typically used to reassemble relationships (expressed with an equality predicate between a primary key and a foreign key), most joins have at least one equality clause. The set of columns in the equality predicate is called the *hash key,* because these are the columns that contribute to the hash function. Additional predicates are possible and are evaluated as residual predicates separate from the comparison of hash values. The hash key can be an expression, as long as it can be computed exclusively from columns in a single row. In grouping operations, the columns that appear in the GROUP BY clause are used as the hash key. In set operations such as intersection, as well as in the removal of duplicates, the hash key consists of all columns.

The merge join requires both inputs to be sorted on the merge columns, which are defined by the WHERE clauses of the join predicate. The query optimizer typically scans an index, if one exists on the proper set of columns, or places a Sort operator below the merge join. Since each input is sorted, the Merge Join operator will get a row from each input and compare them. For example, for inner join operations, the rows are returned if they are equal. If they are not equal, whichever row has the lower value is discarded and another row is obtained from the same input as the discarded row. This process repeats until all rows have been processed.

The merge join operation may be either a regular or a many-to-many operation. A many-to-many merge join uses a temporary table to store rows. If there are duplicate values from each input, one of the inputs will have to rewind to the start of the duplicates as each duplicate from the other input is processed.

The merge join itself is very fast, but it can be an expensive choice if sort operations are required. However, if the data volume is large and the desired data can be obtained pre-sorted from existing B-tree indexes, a merge join is often the fastest available join algorithm.

The remote join method should be specified only when you are explicitly performing a join between remote tables. Specifying a remote join when the tables are both local will result in the SQL Server query optimizer ignoring the join hint.

Table Hints

One of the more common places for passing hints to SQL Server is at the table level. These hints are specified in the SELECT, INSERT, UPDATE, and DELETE statements and allow you to override the locking scheme that SQL Server would use on the selected table.

Locking Hints

SQL Server provides a range of table-level locking hints. These locking hints instruct SQL Server how to lock and access the table or tables used in a query statement. Remember that these table-level locking hints override any systemwide or transactional isolation levels. These hints will modify the system behavior so you can exploit the system performance.

Generally, the SQL Server query optimizer automatically makes the correct table-locking determination. You should use these locking hints only when absolutely necessary. Specifying an incorrect or inappropriate table-locking hint can negatively affect the overall performance of your system.

The table-locking hints are specified in all data manipulation statements. For example, the following SQL statement will access the table using a table-locking hint of HOLDLOCK:

```
SELECT    monthly_mountaindew_sw
FROM      sales (HOLDLOCK)
GO
```

The table-locking hints that SQL Server allows are summarized in Table 19-1.

Table 19-1 Table-Level Locking Hints

Locking Hint	Description
HOLDLOCK	This hint instructs SQL Server to hold a shared lock until the transaction is completed instead of releasing the lock as soon as the required table, row, or data page is no longer required. HOLDLOCK is equivalent to SERIALIZABLE.
	HOLDLOCK can negatively affect concurrency of your system. Any other concurrent transaction will not be able to access the locked table.
NOLOCK	The NOLOCK hint instructs SQL Server not to issue shared locks and not to honor exclusive locks. When this option is in effect, it is possible to read an uncommitted transaction or a set of pages that are rolled back in the middle of a read. Dirty reads are possible.
	This table-locking hint applies only to the SELECT statement.
PAGLOCK	This hint instructs SQL Server to use a page lock rather than a single table lock, which would normally be used.
READCOMMITTED	When you specify READCOMMITTED, SQL Server will perform a scan with the same locking semantics as a transaction running at the Read Committed isolation level. By default, SQL Server operates at this isolation level.

READPAST	This table-locking hint instructs SQL Server to skip any locked rows it encounters. This option causes a transaction to skip over rows locked by other transactions that would ordinarily appear in the result set, rather than to block while waiting for the other transactions to release their locks on these rows.
	The READPAST lock hint applies only to transactions operating at Read Committed isolation and will read only past row-level locks. It applies only to the SELECT statement.
READUNCOMMITTED	The READUNCOMMITTED table-locking hint is equivalent to the NOLOCK hint.
REPEATABLEREAD	This table-locking hint instructs SQL Server to perform a scan with the same locking semantics as a transaction running at the Repeatable Read isolation level.
ROWLOCK	The ROWLOCK table-locking hint tells SQL Server to use row-level locks rather than the coarser-grained page-level and table-level locks.
SERIALIZABLE	Specifying the SERIALIZABLE hint instructs SQL Server to perform a scan with the same locking semantics as a transaction running at the Serializable isolation level. This hint is equivalent to HOLDLOCK.
TABLOCK	The TABLOCK table-locking hint instructs SQL Server to use a table lock rather than using finer-grained row-level or page-level locks. SQL Server will hold this lock until the end of the statement.
	If you also specify HOLDLOCK, the table lock is held until the end of the transaction.
TABLOCKX	The TABLOCKX table-locking hint tells SQL Server to use an exclusive lock on a table. This lock prevents other transactions from reading or updating the table and is held until the end of the statement or transaction.
UPDLOCK	The UPDLOCK instructs SQL Server to use update locks instead of shared locks while reading a table. It also instructs SQL Server to hold the locks until the end of the statement or transaction.
	UPDLOCK has the advantage of allowing you to read data (without blocking other readers) and update it later with the assurance that the data has not changed since you last read it.

In addition to the table-locking hints, SQL Server provides other table hints, which are summarized in Table 19-2.

Table 19-2 Table Hints

Table Hint	Description
FASTFIRSTROW	The FASTFIRSTROW hint instructs the SQL Server query processor to optimize the query for retrieval of one row.
INDEX =	When you specify the INDEX = table hint, you instruct SQL Server to use the specified index or indexes for a table. This will override the normal SQL Server index selection process.

Query Hints

In addition to the table hints, you may specify query hints. These hints instruct SQL Server to modify its default processing of a query. You specify the query hints by using the OPTION clause of SELECT, UPDATE, or DELETE SQL statements. The INSERT SQL statement does not allow query hints. The following SQL sample illustrates the use of query hints.

```
SELECT    region_id,
          region_name,
          sales_ytd
FROM      sales INNER HASH JOIN regions
          ON sales.region_id = regions.region_id
          GROUP BY region_id
          OPTION (ORDER GROUP, ROBUST PLAN)
```

When using query hints, you should keep several things in mind. You can specify a query hint only once. You may specify multiple query hints, but only one of each type. If you have multiple queries in your statement, you must use the OPTION clause on the outermost query. The query hint will then affect all operators in your statement. If you happen to specify one or more query hints that cause the SQL Server query optimizer to generate an invalid execution plan, SQL Server will recompile the query and ignore your query hints. For debug purposes, SQL Server will issue a SQL Server Profiler event. The query hints available in SQL Server are summarized in Table 19-3.

Table 19-3 Query Hints

Query Hint	Use with Clause	Description
HASH	GROUP	Instructs SQL Server to use hashing when performing the aggregations specified in the GROUP BY clause of the query.
ORDER	GROUP	Instructs SQL Server to use ordering when performing the aggregations specified in the GROUP BY clause of the query.
CONCAT	UNION	Instructs SQL Server to use concatenation when computing a UNION set. If more than one UNION hint is specified, the optimizer selects the least expensive strategy from those hints specified.
HASH	UNION	Instructs SQL Server to use hashing when computing a UNION set. If more than one UNION hint is specified, the optimizer selects the least expensive strategy from those hints specified.
MERGE	UNION	Instructs SQL Server to use merging when computing a UNION set. If more than one UNION hint is specified, the optimizer selects the least expensive strategy from those hints specified.
FORCE ORDER	FROM	Instructs SQL Server to process the tables in exactly the same order specified in the FROM clause.
ROBUST PLAN	N/A	Instructs SQL Server to use the query plan that will work for the maximum potential row size. This could force SQL Server to use a plan that may degrade performance. This option is useful when you have large VARCHAR columns. These columns may cause an overflow condition on SQL Server's internal rows that will produce an error. The ROBUST PLAN will eliminate any potential plans in which this condition could occur.

Though query hints can be useful and possibly can enhance the overall system performance, you should use them with caution and only if necessary. If you are migrating queries using hints that you executed against earlier versions of SQL Server, you should test the queries without using the hints because incorrect or inappropriate hints can prevent the SQL Server query optimizer from choosing a better execution plan.

Bulk Copy Hints

In addition to the join, table, and query hints, SQL Server 7 provides several hints for use for bulk copying data into your tables. These hints allow you to customize how the *bcp* utility loads your tables so that you can optimize the efficiency of the bulk copy process. You can combine two or more of the following hints to achieve the desired behavior:

- **ORDER (*column* [ASC | DESC], ...)**   This hint notifies SQL Server of the sort order of data within specified columns in the input data file. The bulk copy performance is improved if the data being loaded is sorted according to the clustered index on the table. If the data file is sorted in a different order or there is no clustered index on the table, the ORDER hint is ignored. The names of the columns supplied must be valid columns in the destination table. By default, the *bcp* utility assumes the data file is unordered.

- **ROWS_PER_BATCH = *bb***   This hint allows you to specify the number of rows of data per batch (as *bb*). This option is generally used when the *[en]b* (batch size) parameter is not specified. If you do not specify ROWS_PER_BATCH or batch size, the entire data file is sent to the server as a single transaction. SQL Server will optimize the bulk load according to the value *bb*. By default, ROWS_PER_BATCH is not used, and the bulk copy is done as one transaction.

- **KILOBYTES_PER_BATCH = *cc***   This hint specifies the approximate number of kilobytes of data per batch (as *cc*). By default, KILOBYTES_PER_BATCH is not used.

- **TABLOCK**   The TABLOCK hint instructs SQL Server to acquire a table-level lock for the duration of the bulk copy operation. This hint significantly improves performance because holding a lock only for the duration of the bulk copy operation reduces lock contention on the table. When you specify the TABLOCK hint, a table can be loaded from multiple clients concurrently if the table has no indexes. By default, locking behavior is determined by the table option specified in the *table lock on bulk load* database option.

- **CHECK_CONSTRAINTS**   The CHECK_CONSTRAINTS hint instructs SQL Server to honor any constraints on the destination table. All constraints are checked during the bulk copy operation. Checking the constraints will negatively affect bulk copy performance because each row copied must be verified against any existing table constraints. By default, constraints are ignored.

You specify hints on the *bcp* command line via the *-h* option. For example, the following command will bulk copy the SWSales.txt file into the *SALES* table in the *SOFTDRINKS* database using the TABLOCK and ROWS_PER_BATCH hints:

```
bcp 'SOFTDRINKS..SALES' in SWSales.txt -c -w -Usa -P
    -h"TABLOCK,ROWS_PER_BATCH=200"
```

Summary

This chapter explored the various hints that are available in SQL Server 7. The hints range from those specified for joins and queries to those available for bulk copying data. Specifying hints is a very powerful and flexible method for modifying the default behavior of SQL Server. This power and flexibility should be used with caution, however, because specifying the wrong hints may cause SQL Server to use inefficient execution plans or may affect the concurrency of the system.

Part V
Appendixes and Glossary

Appendix A
SQL Server
Configuration Parameters

You can adjust the behavior of SQL Server through the settings you assign configuration parameters. This appendix lists the configuration parameters available with SQL Server version 7 and reviews how to set them. Keep in mind that the list of parameters may change as newer versions of SQL Server become available.

Note A complete description of these parameters can be found in the SQL Server Books Online.

- *affinity mask* A bitmask variable that defines the number of CPUs on which SQL Server is allowed to run. The default value of 0 lets the Windows NT scheduler determine which CPUs to use. Since the variable is a bitmask, the binary representation of the value determines the number of CPUs. The binary values are as follows:

```
0=0000
1=0001
2=0010
3=0011
4=0100
. . .
```

For example, when using a four-processor system, you can set the *affinity mask* parameter to 15 (1111) to allow SQL Server to run on all CPUs.

If SQL Server is the only application running on the system, you should consider setting the bitmask to allow SQL Server to run on all CPUs. If you are running on a system that is experiencing a high number of interrupts, you may prefer to bind the interrupts to one CPU and exclude SQL Server from running on that CPU.

In addition to specifying which CPUs SQL Server should run on, *affinity mask* also specifies that processor affinity should be used. Processor affinity specifies that a thread of execution that has run on a specific CPU should run on that CPU the next time it runs. The granularity of affinity is a SQL batch; thus, the entire batch will run on the same CPU.

- ***allow updates*** Allows users with sufficient privileges to update system tables directly. When *allow updates* is set to 0 (the default), the system tables can be updated only via the system stored procedures. We recommend keeping the default configuration.

- ***cost threshold for parallelism*** Specifies a cost to be used in determining whether parallelism should be used for queries. If the cost of the query in serial mode exceeds the value of *cost threshold for parallelism,* the query will be parallelized. The default value is 5.

- ***cursor threshold*** Specifies the minimum number of rows in the cursor set that will cause the cursor keysets to be created asynchronously. If the number of rows is less than the value of *cursor threshold,* the keysets will be created synchronously. The default value of –1 specifies that all cursor keysets will be created synchronously.

- ***default language*** Specifies the identification number of the default language used by SQL Server. The default of 0 is English.

- ***default sortorder id*** Specifies the ID of the sort order (ascending or descending) used by SQL Server. The parameter value is set when SQL Server is installed with the custom option. The *default sortorder id* parameter cannot be changed without rebuilding the entire database, since indexes are built with that sort order.

- ***extended memory size*** Specifies extended memory above 4 GB. This parameter is usable only on systems on which the hardware and software supports the PSE-36 memory extensions. Please check with your hardware vendor to determine if this parameter can be used with your system.

- ***fillfactor*** Specifies how densely SQL Server packs index pages when it creates them. A value of 1 specifies that pages are mostly empty; a value of 100 specifies that SQL Server completely packs index pages. The default value of 0 specifies that leaf pages are fully packed but upper-level pages have some space left in them.

- ***index create memory*** Specifies the amount of memory to be used for sorts that take place during index creation. The default value of 0 allows SQL Server to determine this value dynamically.

- ***language in cache*** Specifies the maximum number of languages that can be held in cache. This parameter is designed to save memory by limiting the cached languages. The default value is 3.

- ***language neutral full-text*** Specifies whether the language-neutral word breaker is used for full-text processing. The default value is 0 (FALSE), which uses the Unicode character set for the word breaker.

- ***lightweight pooling*** Specifies whether SQL Server uses Windows NT fiber mode scheduling to reduce context switching. Context switching incurs a lot of system overhead and is reduced by allowing SQL Server to do its own scheduling. The default value is 0, which specifies that fiber mode scheduling is not used. Systems with large numbers of concurrent jobs, such as a busy OLTP system, may benefit from setting lightweight pooling to 1 (TRUE).

- ***locks*** Specifies the maximum number of locks. The default value of 0 allows SQL Server to dynamically allocate and deallocate locks. You can monitor the number of locks in the system with the Windows NT Performance Monitor; if this tool reveals many allocations and deallocations, you may want to statically allocate locks. The default value of 0 is the recommended setting.

- ***max async IO*** Specifies the maximum number of outstanding I/O requests that SQL Server can have against each data file in the system. The default value is 32. This parameter is one of the most important that you can set in the system. When setting this value, keep in mind how many disk drives each file is made up of. A data file that is configured on a disk array with 20 to 30 disk drives will do better with a higher value for *max async IO*. A single disk drive that has multiple data files configured on it may require a lower value. Try the default and increase the value if it appears that you are having an I/O bottleneck. The *max async IO* parameter should be increased on I/O controllers with large numbers of disk drives. Remember that this is a per-file parameter; multiple data files on the same disk will allow this number of I/Os per file, not per disk drive.

- ***max degree of parallelism*** Specifies the maximum number of threads that can be allocated for use in a parallel execution. The default value of 0 specifies that the number of CPUs in the system is used. A value of 1 disables parallel execution. Because parallelism can help in I/O-bound queries, you may find that you can achieve better performance with a larger value for the *max degree of parallelism* parameter. The maximum value is 32.

- ***max server memory*** Specifies the maximum amount of memory that can be dynamically allocated by SQL Server. This parameter works in conjunction with *min server memory* to determine how much memory is used. If you want to reserve additional space for other processes, you can use this parameter. The default value of 0 specifies that SQL Server automatically allocates memory. Usually the default value works well.

- ***max text repl size*** Specifies the maximum number of bytes of text and image data that can be added to a replicated column in a single SQL statement.

- ***max worker threads*** Specifies the maximum number of Windows NT threads that SQL Server allows in its pool of worker threads. This parameter can be adjusted in order to allow more threads for processing within SQL Server. Too many threads may overload a Windows NT system; too few threads may cause a thread bottleneck. When *lightweight pooling* is enabled, you may not see the *max worker threads* value listed in the Performance Monitor because each thread will have multiple fibers associated with it.

- ***media retention*** Specifies the number of days that a backup medium is retained. SQL Server will not overwrite a backup medium until this time has been exceeded.

- ***min memory per query*** Specifies the minimum amount of memory that will be allocated for a query. The default value is 1024. This parameter can help performance with large sorts and hashing operations by allocating the memory when the query begins.

- **min server memory**   Specifies the minimum amount of memory that can be dynamically allocated by SQL Server. It is used in conjunction with *max server memory* to manually set the minimum and maximum amount of memory that SQL Server can use. The default value of 0 specifies that SQL Server automatically allocates memory. The default is usually sufficient for most systems. Exceptions to this are discussed throughout the book.

- **nested triggers**   Specifies whether a trigger can initiate another trigger. The default value of 1 signifies yes.

- **network packet size**   Specifies the size of incoming and outgoing data packets for SQL Server. The default value of 4096 specifies a packet size of 4 KB. If many of your result sets are large, you may want to increase this value.

- **open objects**   Specifies the maximum number of objects that can be opened at one time in the SQL Server database. The default number of open objects is 500.

- **priority boost**   When enabled (set to 1), specifies that SQL Server runs at a higher Windows NT scheduling priority than it normally would. The default value of 0 disables priority boost. This parameter can improve SQL Server performance but can keep other processes from getting sufficient CPU time. If SQL Server is the only program running on the Windows NT system, you may enable this setting. This parameter can cause erratic results if you are not careful; change it at your own risk.

- **query governor cost limit**   Specifies the maximum time (in seconds) that a query can run. Before a query is executed, the optimizer will estimate the amount of time that the query will run. Therefore, when set, this option prohibits long queries from running.

- **query wait**   When there is insufficient memory for a query to run, SQL Server will queue the query until the resources become available. By default (a setting of –1), the wait time is 25 times the estimated cost of the query. By setting the *query wait* parameter, you can specify the timeout value in seconds.

- **recovery interval**   Sets how often checkpoints occur by specifying the maximum amount of time that SQL Server can take to recover in the event of a system failure. The default value of 0 lets SQL Server determine the recovery interval automatically.

- **remote access**   Specifies whether remote logins from other SQL Server systems are allowed. The default value of 1 allows remote logins.

- **remote login timeout**   Specifies how long a remote login waits before timing out. The default value is 5 seconds.

- **remote proc trans**   By setting the *remote proc trans* parameter to 1, remote transactions with Distributed Transaction Coordinator (DTC) support ACID properties of the transactions.

- **remote query timeout**   Specifies how many seconds must elapse before a remote query times out. The default value of 0 specifies that queries do not time out.

- **resource timeout**   Specifies the number of seconds to wait for a resource before timing out. The default value is 10.

- **scan for startup procs**   Specifies whether to automatically scan for scheduled jobs at startup. The default value of 0 specifies not to scan for jobs.

- **set working set size**   When the *set working set size* parameter is enabled (set to 1), it specifies that SQL Server memory does not get paged out, even when SQL Server is idle. If the system becomes idle, and then suddenly becomes active, having the memory not paged out will avoid having to page it in If you are allowing SQL Server to allocate memory dynamically, do not enable *set working set size*. This parameter can be very important for performance and works in conjunction with *min server memory* and *max server memory*.

- **show advanced options**   When this parameter is enabled (set to 1), *sp_configure* will display the advanced parameters.

- **spin counter**   Specifies the maximum number of times that SQL Server spins waiting for a resource to become available. On a multiprocessor computer the default value is 10000. If the resource is not freed by that time, the thread will go to sleep, which is an expensive operation. In I/O-limited systems, you may experience a performance benefit by increasing this parameter. This change should be made with caution.

- **time slice**   Specifies how long (in milliseconds) a thread can run without voluntarily relinquishing itself. The default value of 100 is a good starting point. Decreasing this value can cause additional overhead. Increasing the parameter value can cause slower response times because threads may hold the CPU longer.

- **two digit year cutoff**   Specifies the behavior of the SQL Server 7 Y2K fix.

- **unicode comparison style**   Specifies the method of sorting with Unicode character sets. This parameter can be used to specify options such as case sensitivity. Changing this option requires a rebuild of the master database.

- **unicode locale id**   Specifies the Unicode location code.

- **user connections**   Specifies the maximum number of users that can be connected to SQL Server. By default SQL Server will dynamically adjust the number of allowed user connections, but this dynamic operation causes additional overhead. This parameter allows you to statically set the number of allowed user connections. The default setting is recommended under most conditions.

- **user options**   Used to specify global defaults for all users.

Setting Parameters

Configuration parameters are set in one of two ways: by using the system stored procedure *sp_configure* or by selecting properties on a database from SQL Server Enterprise Manager.

Changing Parameters with *sp_configure*

The *sp_configure* stored procedure is invoked with the following syntax:

```
Sp_configure 'parameter_name', value
```

For example, the *max worker threads* configuration parameter can be set to 200 with the following command:

```
Sp_configure 'max worker threads', 200
Go
```

Some of the configuration parameters are advanced parameters; in order to change such parameters using *sp_configure,* the *show advanced options* parameter must first be set to 1. (If you are using Enterprise Manager to set advanced parameters, you do not need to worry about enabling this parameter.)

Some parameters take effect immediately; others require a SQL Server restart. Table A-1 specifies which configuration parameters require restarts as well as which are advanced options.

Table A-1 Characteristics of Configuration Parameters

Parameter	Advanced Option	Restart Required
affinity mask	Yes	Yes
allow updates	No	No
cost threshold for parallelism	Yes	No
cursor threshold	Yes	No
default language	No	No
default sortorder id	Yes	Yes
extended memory size	Yes	Yes
fillfactor	Yes	Yes
index create memory	Yes	No
language in cache	No	Yes
language neutral full-text	Yes	No
lightweight pooling	Yes	Yes
locks	Yes	Yes
max async IO	Yes	Yes
max degree of parallelism	Yes	No
max server memory	Yes	No
max text repl size	No	No
max worker threads	Yes	Yes
media retention	Yes	Yes
min memory per query	Yes	No
min server memory	Yes	No

(continued)

Table A-1 *(continued)*

Parameter	Advanced Option	Restart Required
nested triggers	No	No
network packet size	Yes	No
open objects	Yes	Yes
priority boost	Yes	Yes
query governor cost limit	Yes	No
query wait	Yes	No
recovery interval	Yes	No
remote access	No	Yes
remote login timeout	No	No
remote proc trans	No	No
remote query timeout	No	No
resource timeout	Yes	No
scan for startup procs	Yes	Yes
set working set size	Yes	Yes
show advanced options	No	No
spin counter	Yes	No
time slice	Yes	Yes
two digit year cutoff	No	No
unicode comparison style	Yes	Yes
unicode locale id	Yes	Yes
user connections	Yes	Yes
user options	No	No

Changing Parameters with Enterprise Manager

You can modify many of the configuration parameters through Enterprise Manager. You set these parameters by right-clicking on the server icon in Enterprise Manger and selecting Properties.

General Tab

The initial tab of the SQL Server Properties dialog box is the General tab (see Figure A-1). The General tab does not have any configuration parameter options associated with it. However, you can select some autostart options here. You also have the ability to change some startup parameters, which are accessed by clicking the Startup Parameters button.

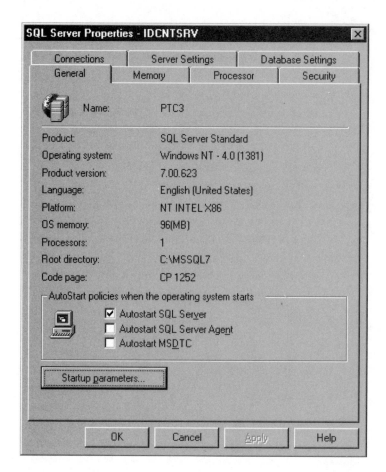

Figure A-1 *The General tab of the SQL Server Properties dialog box.*

Memory Tab

The Memory tab (Figure A-2) allows you to choose whether memory is dynamically allocated or statically chosen. You can set the amounts by moving slider bars. You can also set the minimum query memory used by SQL Server in this tab.

The parameters you can set in the Memory tab are as follows:

- *min server memory*
- *max server memory*
- *min memory per query*

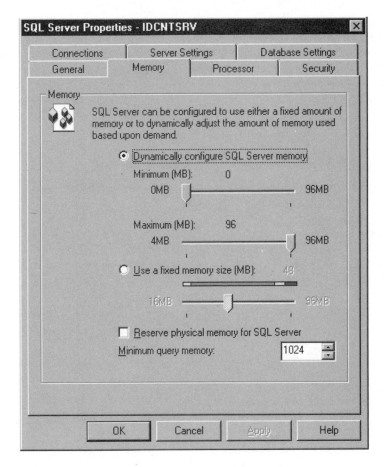

Figure A-2 *The Memory tab of the SQL Server Properties dialog box.*

Processor Tab

The Processor tab (Figure A-3) gives you the option of selecting CPUs that are available for SQL Server use. You can also set the maximum number of worker threads. Other check boxes allow you to boost SQL Server's scheduling priority and to use Windows NT fibers. Finally, you can specify how SQL Server parallelizes queries.

The parameters you can set in the Processor tab are as follows:

- *affinity mask*
- *max worker threads*
- *priority boost*
- *lightweight pooling*
- *max degree of parallelism*
- *cost threshold for parallelism*

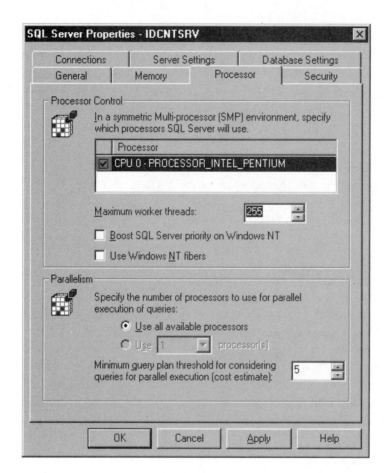

Figure A-3 *The Processor tab of the SQL Server Properties dialog box.*

Security Tab

The Security tab (Figure A-4) does not deal with tuning parameters. Instead you can specify the authentication method, the audit level, and the Windows NT accounts in which to start up and run SQL Server.

Connections Tab

The Connections tab (Figure A-5) provides a number of settings related to the user connections. Here you can set the maximum number of users and specify the level of constraint checking. You can also configure remote connection settings, such as allowing RPC connections, setting the query timeout, and enforcing distributed transactions.

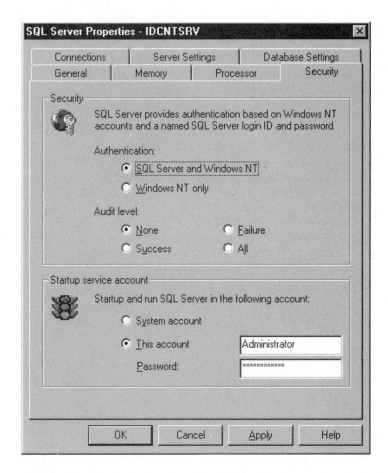

Figure A-4 *The Security tab of the SQL Server Properties dialog box.*

The parameters you can set in the Connections tab are as follows:

- *user connections*
- *user options*
- *remote access*
- *remote query timeout*
- *remote proc trans*

Server Settings Tab

The Server Settings tab (Figure A-6) deals with general server parameters. Here you can set the default language for the user, as well as set options to allow catalog modification and to allow triggers to fire other triggers. You can also enable the query governor and specify its cost limit. This tab also allows you to configure the SQL mail profile and year 2000 support.

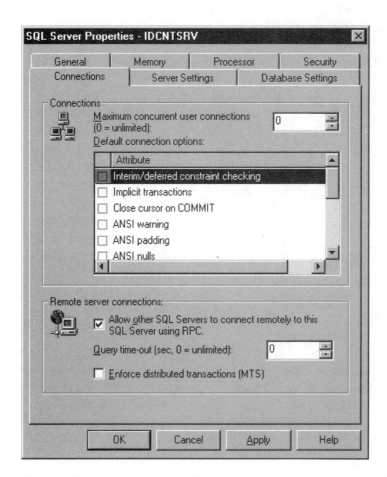

Figure A-5 *The Connections tab of the SQL Server Properties dialog box.*

The parameters you can set in the Server Settings tab are as follows:

- *default language*
- *allow updates*
- *nested triggers*
- *query governor cost limit*
- *two digit year cutoff*

Database Settings Tab

The Database Settings tab (Figure A-7) gives you the option of setting the database fill factor as well as backup parameters and the recovery interval.

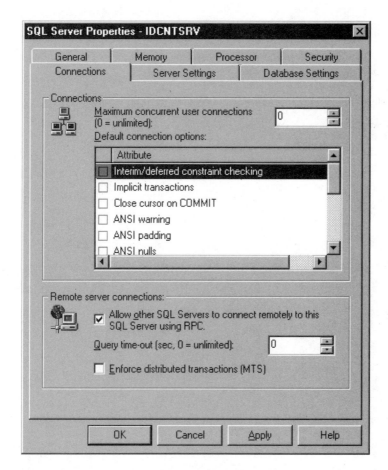

Figure A-6 *The Server Settings tab of the SQL Server Properties dialog box.*

The parameters you can set in the Database Settings tab are as follows:

- *fillfactor*
- *media retention*
- *recovery interval*

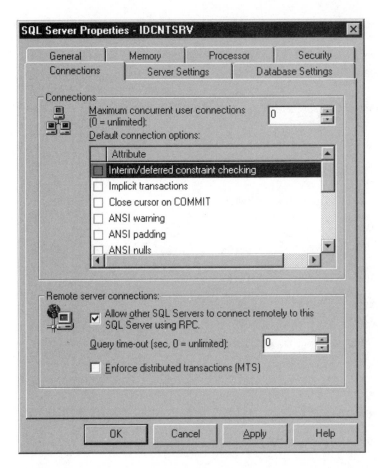

Figure A-7 *The Database Settings tab of the SQL Server Properties dialog box.*

Appendix B
SQL Server Monitoring

SQL Server provides a number of counters that can be read by the Windows NT Performance Monitor. This appendix presents a reference to those objects and counters that SQL Server installs.

SQLServer: Access Methods

The performance counters under the SQLServer: Access Methods object represent different object access methods and properties. The counters include the following:

- **Extent Deallocations/sec** The number of extents released per second by SQL Server.
- **Extents Allocated/sec** The number of extents allocated per second by SQL Server.
- **Forwarded Records/sec** The number of records retrieved through forward record pointers.
- **FreeSpace Page Fetches/sec** The number of pages returned per second by free space scans.
- **FreeSpace Scans/sec** The number of scans done per second to find free space for record insertion.
- **Full Scans/sec** The number of full table or index scans per second. If this counter shows a value greater than 1 or 2, you should analyze your queries to see if table scans are really necessary and whether the SQL queries can be optimized.

SQLServer: Backup Device

The single counter for the SQLServer: Backup Device object reports the performance of backup devices. Each instance has its own counter.

- **Device Throughput Bytes/sec** The number of bytes per second being transferred to a backup device during a backup operation. This counter is useful both for monitoring the throughput as well as the balance of I/Os through the various backup devices.

SQLServer: Buffer Manager

This object contains a number of counters related to the SQL Server buffer cache and how it is operating. The counters are as follows:

- **Cache Size (pages)** The number of pages that currently make up the SQL Server cache. Since the SQL Server buffer cache is dynamic, this is your indication of how big it is. You can monitor this counter and look for the constantly changing size. If the counter shows large swings during the day, you may want to fix the cache size by using the min server memory and max server memory parameters.

- **Checkpoint Writes/sec** The number of pages per second flushed for a checkpoint operation. If this counter shows a large value constantly, you may be experiencing too frequent checkpoints. How often you should checkpoint is based on your specific needs. Frequent checkpoints guarantee faster recovery time; less frequent checkpoints offer higher performance.

- **Committed Pages** The number of buffer pages committed.

- **ExtendedMem Cache Hit Ratio** The percentage of page requests that were satisfied from the extended memory cache. (The extended memory cache will not be implemented until SQL Server 7.5.)

- **ExtendedMem Cache Migrations/sec** The number of pages per second migrated into the extended memory cache. (The extended memory cache will not be implemented until SQL Server 7.5.)

- **ExtendedMem Cache Requests/sec** The number of pages per second requested from the extended memory cache. (The extended memory cache will not be implemented until SQL Server 7.5.)

- **Free Buffers** The number of free (nonused, but allocated) buffers available in the buffer cache. Don't worry if this value seems low. Remember that SQL Server dynamically creates more buffers as necessary.

- **Lazy Writer Buffers/sec** The number of buffers per second examined by the lazywriter.

- **Lazy Writes/sec** The number of buffers per second written by the lazywriter.

- **Page Reads/sec** The number of physical database page reads issued per second.

- **Page Requests/sec** The number of buffer page requests per second.

- **Page Writes/sec** The number of physical database page writes issued.

- **Readahead Pages/sec** The number of pages per second that are read in anticipation by SQL Server. These pages have not been requested by a user yet, but SQL Server is guessing that they soon will be, based on previous requests.

- **Reserved Page Count** The number of reserved pages in the buffer cache.

- **Stolen Page Count** The number of pages that have been stolen from the buffer cache to satisfy another memory request.

SQLServer: Cache Manager

This object is used to maintain overall cache manager statistics. Each of the counters is available for the following instances: ad hoc SQL plans, miscellaneous normalized trees, prepared SQL plans, procedure plans, replication procedure plans, and trigger plans. The counters are as follows:

- **Cache Hit Ratio** The ratio between cache hits and misses. This is a very good counter for seeing how effective the SQL Server cache is for your system. If this number is low, you may want to add more memory.
- **Cache Object Counts** The number of cache objects in the cache.
- **Cache Pages** The number of 8-KB pages used by cache objects.
- **Cache Use Counts/sec** The number of times each type of cache object has been used.

SQLServer: Databases

The SQLServer: Databases object contains a set of counters for each database in the system. The instances represent the database that you can monitor and include master, model, msdb, and tempdb as well as Northwind, pubs, and all your user-created databases. The counters are as follows:

- **Active Transactions** The number of currently active transactions in the database.
- **Backup/Restore Throughput/sec** The throughput of active backup and restore operations.
- **Bulk Copy Rows/sec** The number of rows per second currently being copied via a bulk copy operation.
- **Bulk Copy Throughput/sec** The number of kilobytes per second currently being copied via a bulk copy operation.
- **Data File(s) Size (KB)** The total size of all the data files in the database.
- **DBCC Logical Scan Bytes/sec** The logical read scan rate for DBCC commands.
- **Log Bytes Per Flush** The number of bytes in the log buffer when it is flushed.
- **Log Cache Hit Ratio** The percentage of log reads that were satisfied from the log cache.
- **Log Cache Reads/sec** The number of log cache reads per second.
- **Log File(s) Size (KB)** The size of the log file or files, in kilobytes.
- **Log Flush Wait Time** The total wait time for log flushes, in milliseconds.
- **Log Flush Waits/sec** The number of log flush waits per second.
- **Log Flushes/sec** The number of log flushes per second.
- **Log Growths** The number of log growths; that is, how many times the log has extended itself.

- **Log Shrinks** The number of log shrinks; that is, how many times the log has shrunk itself.
- **Log Truncations** The number of times the log has been truncated for this database.
- **Percent Log Used** The current percentage of the log that is being used.
- **Repl. Pending Xacts** The number of pending replication transactions in this database.
- **Repl. Trans. Rate** The number of replication transactions per second.
- **Shrink Data Movement Bytes/sec** The rate at which data is being moved by an autoshrink operation.
- **Transactions/sec** The number of transactions per second for this database. This counter gives you a good idea of the activity going on in your system. The higher the value, the more activity is occurring.

SQLServer: General Statistics

This object represents some general user connection information about SQL Server, including the following:

- **Logins/sec** The number of logins per second
- **Logouts/sec** The number of logouts per second
- **User Connections** The number of users currently connected

SQLServer: Latches

This object is used to show SQL Server latch statistics, including the following:

- **Average Latch Wait Time (ms)** The average time, in milliseconds, that a SQL Server thread has to wait on a latch. If this number is high, you could be experiencing severe contention problems.
- **Latch Waits/sec** The number of waits per second on latches. If this number is high, you are experiencing a high amount of contention for resources.
- **Total Latch Wait Time (ms)** The total amount of time, in milliseconds, that latch requests had to wait in the last second.

SQLServer: Locks

This object contains a number of counters that keep track of lock activity. Separate instances of these counters keep track of the following SQL Server lock types: database locks, extent locks, key locks, page locks, RID (row locks), and table locks.

These counters give you a good idea of the types and frequencies of locks that are being used in the system. The counters are as follows:

- **Average Wait Time (ms)** The average time, in milliseconds, that a thread waits for this type of lock.
- **Lock Requests/sec** The number of requests for this type of lock per second.

- **Lock Timeouts/sec** The number of times per second that a lock could not be obtained by spinning. The number of times that a thread spins before timing out and sleeping is governed by the SQL Server configuration parameter *spin counter*.

- **Lock Wait Time (ms)** The total wait time for locks, in milliseconds, for the last second.

- **Lock Waits/sec** The number of times a lock request caused a thread to wait in the last second.

- **Number of Deadlocks/sec** The number of lock requests that resulted in a dead-lock.

SQLServer: Memory Manager

This object contains information about SQL Server memory other than the buffer cache. The counters are as follows:

- **Connection Memory (KB)** The amount of memory, in kilobytes, that is used for maintaining connections.

- **Granted Workspace Memory (KB)** The amount of memory, in kilobytes, that has been granted to processes for sorting and index creation operations.

- **Lock Blocks** The current number of lock blocks in use on the server.

- **Lock Blocks Allocated** The total number of allocated lock blocks.

- **Lock Memory (KB)** The amount of memory, in kilobytes, that is allocated to locks.

- **Lock Owner Blocks** The number of lock owner blocks that are currently in use on the server.

- **Lock Owner Blocks Allocated** The number of lock owner blocks that have been allocated on the server.

- **Maximum Workspace Memory (KB)** The total amount of memory that has been allocated to executing processes. This memory may be used for hashing, sorting, and index creation operations.

- **Memory Grants Outstanding** The current number of processes that have acquired a workspace memory grant.

- **Memory Grants Pending** The current number of processes waiting for a work-space memory grant.

- **Optimizer Memory (KB)** The amount of memory, in kilobytes, that the server is using for query optimization.

- **SQL Cache Memory (KB)** The total amount of memory that the server is using for the dynamic SQL cache.

- **Target Server Memory (KB)** The total amount of dynamic memory, in kilobytes, that the server may potentially consume.

- **Total Server Memory (KB)** The total amount of dynamic memory, in kilobytes, that the server is currently consuming. Because SQL Server dynamically allocates and deallocates memory based on what is available in the system, this counter is your view of what is currently being used. If there are large swings over the course of a day or when special events occur, you may want to fix the amount of memory that SQL Server is using by setting the *min server memory* and *max server memory* parameters.

SQLServer: Replication Agents

This object displays information on the number of running replication agents. The following counter is available:

- **Running** The number of running replication agents

SQLServer: Replication Dist.

This object is used to view information about distributors and subscribers. The following counters are available:

- **Dist: Delivered Cmds/sec** The number of commands per second delivered to the subscriber
- **Dist: Delivered Trans/sec** The number of transactions per second delivered to the subscriber
- **Dist: Delivery Latency** The amount of time between when transactions are delivered to the distributor and when they are applied to the subscriber

SQLServer: Replication Logreader

This object is used to view information about distributors and publishers. The following counters are available:

- **Logreader: Delivered Cmds/sec** The number of commands per second delivered to the distributor
- **Logreader: Delivered Trans/sec** The number of transactions per second delivered to the distributor
- **Logreader: Delivery Latency** The amount of time between when transactions are applied to the distributor and when they are delivered to the distributor

SQLServer: Replication Merge

This object pertains to the replication merge process and has the following counters:

- **Conflicts/sec** The number of conflicts per second occurring during the merge process
- **Downloaded Changes/sec** The number of rows per second merged from the publisher to the subscriber
- **Uploaded Changes/sec** The number of rows per second merged from the subscriber to the publisher

SQLServer: Replication Snapshot

This object pertains to the snapshot replication process and has the following counters:

- **Snapshot: Delivered Cmds/sec** The number of commands per second delivered to the distributor
- **Snapshot: Delivered Trans/sec** The number of transactions per second delivered to the distributor

SQLServer: SQL Statistics

This object is very interesting in that it offers useful statistics on SQL statements that have been run. The counters are as follows:

- **Auto-Param Attempts/sec** The number of autoparameterization attempts per second
- **Batch Requests/sec** The number of SQL batch requests per second that have been received by the server
- **Failed Auto-Params/sec** The number of autoparameterization attempts that have failed per second
- **Safe Auto-Params/sec** The number of safe autoparameterizations per second
- **SQL Compilations/sec** The number of times per second that SQL compilations have occurred
- **SQL Re-Compilations/sec** The number of times per second that SQL recompilations have occurred

SQLServer: User Settable

The SQLServer: User Settable object represents a set of user counters that you can define. Each counter can be set from within any SQL statement by calling the appropriate system stored procedure *sp_user counter1* through *sp_user counter10* followed by an integer value to which you want to set the counter. You can read these counters through the Performance Monitor by viewing the following counter:

- **Query** Represents the user-settable value. This counter has 10 instances associated with it: User counter 1 through User counter 10. The value displayed is the value that your program or SQL statement has set.

Glossary

A

Active Server Page (ASP) A Web page that creates HTML pages dynamically on the server. ASPs are commonly used to access SQL Server from the World Wide Web.

ad hoc A term used to describe a spontaneous query. Typically an ad hoc query is not optimized and is typed into SQL Server Query Analyzer, ISQL, or OSQL, rather than used through an application. The Latin words mean "this is."

agent A program that runs independently within Windows NT to perform a service. Agents usually have a particular task, such as scheduling operations or performing replication tasks. The equivalent in the UNIX world is a daemon.

aggregate function Function that performs an operation on a set of values and returns a single value. The SQL Server aggregate functions are AVG, COUNT, DISTINCT, GROUP BY, HAVING, MAX, MIN, STDEV, STDEVP, SUM, VAR, and VARP.

API *See* application program interface.

AppleTalk The Apple networking protocol.

application The code that interfaces with the end user. The application in turn communicates with the RDBMS.

application program interface (API) The standard and documented interface that programs are coded to. By coding to an API one can create programs that use external functions, such as SQL Server access.

article A table or subset of data that is selected to be replicated.

ASP *See* Active Server Page.

Asynchronous Transfer Mode (ATM) A network hardware protocol.

B

backup A duplicate copy of the contents of a SQL Server database to be used in the event of a system failure. The backup can be copied back into the database in order to return the database to the state in which it was when the backup was performed.

bandwidth The throughput capacity of a device or system. This term is typically associated with a network device or computer bus.

batch processing system A system distinguished by scheduled loading and processing of data in groups. These long-running jobs are done offline with little or no user intervention.

BCP *See* bulk copy program.

bit The smallest unit of data. A bit is either on (1) or off (0).

block *See* page.

bottleneck A performance-limiting component. The term comes from an analogy to a bottle containing liquid: the narrowing of the neck slows the flow of liquid.

branch node An intermediate node in an index. Branch nodes are between the root node and the leaf nodes.

buffer cache *See* cache.

bulk copy A generic term relating to the act of copying large amounts of data to or from a SQL Server database. Typically a bulk copy will use the BULK INSERT T-SQL statement.

bulk copy program (BCP) A program provided with Microsoft SQL Server that is used for loading data from text files into the database.

BULK INSERT A way of copying large amounts of data from a data file into a SQL Server table from within SQL Server. Whereas BCP is an external program, BULK INSERT is a T-SQL command.

bulk load The act of loading the database using bulk insert operations. This can be accomplished either by using the BULK INSERT T-SQL statement or by using the *bcp* utility.

byte A sequence of eight binary bits. A byte is the basic unit of data used in computers. It is made up of bits (ones and zeros) that represent numbers, characters, and so forth.

C

cache Random access memory (RAM) used to hold frequently accessed data in order to improve performance. SQL Server contains its own cache made up of Windows NT memory used to hold commonly accessed pages. This is referred to as the SQL Server buffer cache or page cache. CPU chips contain their own on-board caches, and some I/O controllers also contain caches.

capacity planning The activity of planning for the increased utilization of the system and, by doing so, anticipating capacity that must be added. This task is performed in order to maintain the level of service expected by the user community while the load on the system is increasing.

capacity planning measurement A collection of performance statistics (counters) used to determine the resource consumption of a workload in order to plan for additional hardware resources. This type of measurement is of a longer duration than a performance measurement (usually hours or even a day).

Cartesian product The product of a join that does not have a WHERE clause. The size of the resulting data set is the number of rows in the first table multiplied by the number of rows in the second table. A Cartesian product is usually an unintentionally desired result of a query.

Central Processing Unit (CPU) The brains of the computer; that is, the chip that processes data.

checkpoint An operation that is performed to synchronize the data files with the current state of transactions. This is done in order to reduce the necessary recovery time needed in the event of a system failure. The checkpoint process traverses the list of dirty pages and flushes them to disk.

client/server model A programming model in which the user interface portion of the program resides in an executable on a desktop PC and accesses data in a database on a server. The application logic is divided between the client (PC) and the server.

cluster *See* clustered index, Microsoft Cluster Server.

clustered index A combination of index and table. The index is stored as a B-tree, and the data is stored in the leaf nodes of the index.

collision A collision occurs when two controllers are attempting to use the network at the same time. Each controller detects the collision and waits a usually random amount of time before trying again. In a heavily utilized network, collisions can cause a performance bottleneck. This term is usually associated with an Ethernet network.

column A collection of corresponding fields in all rows of data in a table. Each column has a data type associated with it. All the columns in a row make up a database record.

COMMIT The SQL statement that finalizes a SQL transaction. Until the COMMIT statement has been issued the transaction can be undone by issuing the ROLLBACK statement.

Component Object Model (COM) A set of APIs and tools developed by Microsoft. These applications run under the control of Microsoft Transaction Server (MTS) on the server system and under the control of DCOM (Distributed COM) on client systems. COM clients are developed using platforms such as Visual Basic and Visual C++. Applications can also be made up of newer technologies such as ASPs (Active Server Pages) and Internet Server Application Programming Interface (ISAPI).

composite index An index that is created on a combination of two or more columns.

configuration parameter A variable that allows you to change the behavior of SQL Server. These parameters are used to tune the SQL Server engine. Configuration parameters affect things such as SQL Server memory allocation, thread counts, and number of user connections.

constraint A restriction placed on a table to guarantee referential integrity.

CPU *See* central processing unit.

cube A multidimensional representation of both detail and summary data. Cubes are typically used in online analytical processing.

D

database A repository of data. This can be anything from a small list of names to a record of the entire population of the world.

database administrator (DBA) The person or persons responsible for maintaining the database. The DBA's role can vary depending on your company's needs.

database consistency checker (DBCC) A utility for finding and correcting problems in the consistency of the database.

database management system (DBMS) The programs, files, processes, and memory that make up the database. SQL Server is a relational DBMS (RDBMS).

database role A collection of permissions that represents the permissions granted to a set of users. Rather than assigning individual permissions to individual users, a role can be created and assigned to the users.

data definition language (DDL) SQL statements that are used in the definition or declaration of database objects. A DDL includes statements such as CREATE DATABASE and DROP DATABASE.

data file The physical operating system file that is used to hold the data associated with a filegroup and, in turn, the database. Under SQL Server this can be an NTFS file or a Windows NT raw device.

data integrity *See* integrity.

data manipulation language (DML) SQL statements that are used to insert, update, delete, or retrieve data from the database.

data mart A decision support system created from company online transaction processing (OLTP) data. A data mart differs from a data warehouse in that the former is typically used by one business segment, such as Accounts Receivable or Accounts Payable.

Data Transformation Services (DTS) The Microsoft SQL Server facility for transforming data between systems.

data warehouse A decision support system created from company online transaction processing (OLTP) data. A data warehouse is usually a very large system, which can reach terabytes.

DBA *See* database administrator.

DBCC *See* database consistency checker.

DBLIB Abbreviation of DB-Library; a SQL Server connectivity protocol.

DBMS *See* database management system.

DDL *See* data definition language.

decision support system A database system that is used to aid in business decisions based on data in the database. These decisions can be based on sales trends, product sales, and so forth.

differential backup A mode of backup that saves only the data that has changed since the previous backup. This mode can back up the database faster than a full backup, but usually takes longer to restore the database.

dirty page A page in the SQL Server cache that has been modified but has not been written to disk.

disk In this book, the term identifies a fixed disk drive. A fixed disk drive is a magnetic medium that is used to store data. A disk is persistent storage: data remains on the disk even after power is removed.

Distributed Transaction Coordinator (DTC) The Microsoft SQL Server facility that coordinates transactions between systems by performing two-phase commits.

distributor The intermediary component in SQL Server replication. A distributor takes replication data from a publisher and presents it to a subscriber.

DML *See* data manipulation languge.

domain A Windows NT network group. Systems in a domain share the same user list and passwords.

DSS *See* decision support system.

DTC *See* Distributed Transaction Coordinator.

DTS *See* Data Transformation Services.

E

encryption Encoding data or stored procedures with password protection for security reasons.

enterprise A term for a system that services the entire company.

Enterprise Manager The main utility used to administer the SQL Server RDBMS.

equijoin A join that uses an equality operator in the WHERE clause of the SQL statement performing the join.

Ethernet A popular network hardware protocol.

execution plan The method that the parsed SQL Server statement uses to perform operations on the database.

F

fault tolerance The ability of a subsystem to continue functioning after a component has failed. This is accomplished via the use of redundant components. Fault tolerance is typically associated with the I/O subsystem and RAID controllers, but other subsystems such as power supplies can also be fault tolerant.

fiber or **fiber optics** A network hardware protocol.

fiber channel A new I/O protocol that operates using either copper wire or fiber optic connection hardware.

field *See* column.

filegroup A group of files that is used as a repository for SQL Server objects. A filegroup can be made up of one or more data files. When SQL Server objects are created they can be assigned to a specific filegroup.

filegroup backup A new form of backup introduced in SQL Server version 7 in which a filegroup is backed up and restored, rather than the entire database. This method allows for the entire database backup to be spread over several days.

foreign key A field in a table that is also a primary key in another table.

foreign key constraint A requirement that a foreign key be a valid primary key in the database. This type of constraint is typically used to verify that referenced data is available.

full backup A backup that saves all data in a database.

full table scan A select operation in which all rows in the table are read in order to find the desired data. A full table scan is not usually desired because of the heavy I/O overhead involved.

G

gigabyte (GB) 230 bytes, 1,024 megabytes, or 1,073,741,824 bytes.

graphical user interface (GUI) An interface that is graphical in nature in order to simplify the use of the application. A GUI can be used to show data in a format that is easier for the human mind to comprehend.

GROUP BY A SQL clause used to divide a table into groups of data. These groups can consist of column names or results in computed columns.

GUI *See* graphical user interface.

H

HBA *See* host bus adapter.

hint An addition to SQL statements to allow you to give the query optimizer information on how you would like the execution plan to be constructed.

host bus adapter (HBA) A computer adapter used to communicate with an I/O bus.

hub A passive network device that is used to connect the network cards from multiple systems. A hub is an electrical device that has no application logic; thus, it is very fast.

I

index An auxiliary data structure used to speed access to data within the database.

index scan An operation that occurs when a group of index entries have to be read in order to find the desired data. Such a scan is used when a composite index is accessed and not all the columns that make up the index are supplied in the WHERE clause.

input/output (I/O) The movement of data from one computer component to another. The term can be used to describe the disk subsystem or other data transfer components.

integrity A property of a database that ensures the quality of the database by allowing only valid (within the business model) data in the database.

I/O *See* input/output.

I/O capacity The amount of work that can be supported by the I/O subsystem. The I/O capacity is constrained by either the number of I/Os (if random seeks are the limiting factor) or throughput (if seeks are sequential).

IPX/SPX A network protocol used in Novell networks.

ISQL An application supplied by Microsoft that allows access into the SQL Server RDBMS. ISQL uses the DBLIB protocol; OSQL uses the ODBC protocol.

J

JBOD An acronym for "just a bunch of disks." A non-RAID disk configuration.

join An operation that allows you to retrieve data from two or more tables by taking advantage of the relationship between the tables.

K

key The column or set of columns that is used to define the access point into an index. If a composite index is made up of two columns, those two columns make up the index key.

kilobyte (KB) 210 bytes, or 1,024 bytes.

L

latency The time a process spends waiting for an operation to be completed. The term is typically used to describe the time a thread waits for an I/O to finish.

lazywriter The thread that takes dirty blocks from the SQL Server cache and writes them to disk. It is called the lazywriter because it is a background process that operates on its own schedule and priority.

leaf node The lowest node in an index. The leaf node contains either a pointer to the row data or the data itself (in the case of a clustered index).

level 1 (L1) cache Memory built in to a CPU chip that is used for holding data and instructions to speed access from the CPU. Usually 16 KB or 32 KB.

level 2 (L2) cache Memory that is either built into or external to a CPU chip and that is used in addition to the level 1 cache as an overflow.

lock An object that is used to allow only one thread to access a resource at a time. Locking can be very important, especially in a symmetric multiprocessor system, because many threads may be trying to access resources simultaneously.

log *See* transaction log.

logical disk drive A virtual disk drive that appears to the operating system as a physical disk drive, but in reality is made up of two or more disk drives in a RAID system.

log writer The SQL Server thread that is responsible for reading the log buffer and writing the contents out to the transaction log.

M

measurement configuration The set of performance counters that is selected for the system to monitor.

medium (plural: **media**) An object to which data is written. Both physical disk drives and tapes are media.

megabyte (MB) 220 bytes, 1,024 kilobytes, or 1,048,576 bytes.

memory A term used to describe random access memory (RAM) that is allocated and used by the operating system and SQL Server. The term *memory* in this book refers to main memory. The main use of SQL Server memory is as a database cache. Memory is not durable; its contents are lost upon loss of power.

merge replication A replication method that is similar to transactional replication in that it keeps track of the changes made to articles. However, instead of propagating transactions that have made changes, merge replication will periodically transmit all changes that have been made to the database.

Microsoft Cluster Server (MSCS) An add-on to SQL Server that allows another SQL Server system to operate in standby mode for the primary server. In the event of a failure with the primary server, the secondary server would take over.

Microsoft Transaction Server (MTS) A framework for developing three-tiered distributed applications.

mirroring Creating a duplicate of a component, thus providing a redundant copy that can be used in the event that the original fails. The term is usually associated with I/O subsystems. Both RAID 1 and RAID 10 use mirroring.

N

Named Pipes A secure net-library that supports several underlying network protocols, such as IPX/SPX, NetBUEI, and TCP/IP. Named Pipes is required for SQL Server Windows NT installations.

network packet Data and control information that is transferred across the network as a unit. A SQL Server request may fit into one network packet, or multiple network packets may be required.

NWLINK The SQL Server network library that supports Novell's IPX/SPX network protocol.

O

ODBC *See* Open Database Connectivity.

OLAP *See* online analytical processing.

OLAP Services An add-on component to Microsoft SQL Server 7 designed to assist you with online analytical processing (OLAP); you can use it to access data in your data warehouses and data marts.

OLTP *See* online transaction processing.

online analytical processing (OLAP) The manipulation of data for analytical purposes. OLAP is usually associated with data marts or data warehouses.

online transaction processing (OLTP) Database processing characterized by many users accessing different data while waiting for that processing to be completed. These users are online and active; thus, response time is critical for OLTP systems.

Open Database Connectivity (ODBC) A Microsoft-designed database connectivity API that can be used to communicate from applications to a multitude of different RDBMSs.

optimizer *See* SQL Server query optimizer.

ORDER BY A clause that specifies the sort order of columns returned in a SELECT statement.

OSQL An application supplied by Microsoft that allows access into the SQL Server RDBMS. OSQL uses the ODBC protocol; ISQL uses the DBLIB protocol.

outer join An operation that returns all rows from at least one of the tables or views mentioned in the FROM clause, as long as those rows meet any WHERE or HAVING search conditions.

P

packet *See* network packet.

page The fundamental unit of data storage in SQL Server. This is the smallest unit of data that will be written to or read from disk or memory. The page size for SQL Server 7 is 8 KB; it was 2 KB for SQL Server 6.5.

page lock *See* lock.

paging Should Windows NT and SQL Server use more memory than is physically available, some of this data is temporarily copied to disk. This is known as paging. When paging occurs, the performance of the system is severely degraded. Also known as *swapping*.

parity Extra data (or pseudodata) that is used to validate or correct the base data. Typically, parity refers to a bit that is used to force the underlying data bits to be either even or odd. By checking the data in order to determine if the data is even or odd, the system can validate that it is correct. RAID 5 uses parity to protect its data.

parse A process performed by SQL Server to break down a SQL statement into its fundamental components before passing it to the query optimizer.

partitioning Dividing a table or database into separate components in order to create smaller and more easily managed data sets.

peak utilization period The time the machine is most stressed during a measurement or a working day.

performance counter A unit of collection that reflects resource usage.

performance measurement A collection of performance statistics (called performance counters) used to tune a computer system. This type of measurement is of short duration (usually seconds, minutes, or sometime hours) in order to capture anomalies in the system performance and correct them.

Performance Monitor (PerfMon) A utility that ships with the Windows NT and Windows 2000 operating system that allows you to look at various performance counters within the operating system and SQL Server.

physical memory The chips that are used for memory within the system.

predictive analysis The use of mathematics in order to predict the outcome of a specific change to the system. Predictive analysis can be used to predict the effect of adding users to the system.

primary key A column or combination of columns whose values uniquely identify each row in the table. This column (or columns) is used to enforce the entity integrity of the table.

procedure cache The part of SQL Server memory used for caching stored procedures and parsed SQL statements. The procedure cache is used to improve SQL Server performance.

processor Another term for central processing unit (CPU); the brains of the computer. A standard computer system consists of one or more CPUs, main memory, and disk storage.

Profiler *See* SQL Server Profiler.

publication A group of articles that is replicated from a publisher.

publisher The SQL Server system that is replicating its data to other systems. The receiver of the replication is called a subscriber.

pull subscription A form of replication in which the replication is initiated by the subscriber.

push subscription A form of replication in which the replication is initiated by the publisher or distributor.

Q

query A SQL SELECT statement that is used to retrieve data from the database. When this book refers to a *query,* we are talking about a read-only operation.

Query Analyzer *See* SQL Server Query Analyzer.

query optimizer *See* SQL Server query optimizer.

queue The list of processes, or threads, that are awaiting processing.

queueing The act of waiting in line for processing. Queueing occurs throughout SQL Server, the operating system, and in the hardware itself.

R

RAID (redundant array of inexpensive disks) A disk array that is used to form one large logical disk drive by partitioning or distributing the data across many physical disk drives. RAID controllers can be configured in different ways, each of which has different fault-tolerance and performance characteristics.

RAID level The RAID configuration being used.

RAID 0 The RAID level that provides for data striping and no fault tolerance. This is the most economical and fastest RAID level, but it provides no tolerance for disk failures.

RAID 1 Commonly known as mirroring. RAID 1 volumes consist of two disk drives that are exact copies of each other.

RAID 5 Known as distributed parity RAID. This RAID level creates a parity for each stripe. It is economical and provides fault tolerance.

RAID 10 The RAID level that combines both disk mirroring and disk striping. RAID 10 is sometimes referred to as RAID 0+1 or RAID 1/0.

random access memory (RAM) Nonpersistent storage that is used for data

processing. RAM is faster than disk, but all data is lost upon the removal of power.

raw device A method of accessing a disk drive through a raw interface, that is, by bypassing the OS file system.

RDBMS *See* relational database management system.

record A single row in the database.

recovery An operation in which SQL Server is restarted after a system failure; the transaction log is used to roll forward all committed transactions and roll back all noncommitted transactions in order to bring the database to the state in which it was at the point of failure.

recovery interval The amount of time it takes for SQL Server to recover in the event of a system failure.

referential integrity *See* integrity.

relational database management system (RDBMS) A database system that stores data according to a relational data model; that it, the hierarchy of the data is made up of relations between objects. SQL Server is one example of an RDBMS.

replication An add-on to SQL Server that allows you to automatically create copies of SQL Server objects or subsets of objects to other systems. Replication comes in three forms: snapshot, transactional, and merge.

response time The length of time between when the user submits the request for data (executes the transaction) and when that data is returned to the user. Often the response time is used to judge the performance of the system.

restore To copy a SQL Server backup back into the SQL Server database. This operation takes the database back to the state in which it was when the backup was created.

role *See* database role.

ROLLBACK The SQL Server statement to undo a transaction. Prior to committing a transaction, you can issue a ROLLBACK statement that will undo all the activity performed by that transaction.

root node The top node in an index.

rotational latency The time it takes for the disk drive to rotate to where the requested data resides.

router A network devices that passes data from one subnet to another based on the network addresses.

row A single record in the database. A row or record of data represents one entry in the database. This entry is a set of different pieces of data known as columns or fields.

row lock *See* lock.

S

SAN *See* storage area network.

schema A collection of objects associated with a database. Schema objects consist of tables, indexes, views, and so on.

SCSI *See* Small Computer System Interface.

seek time The time it takes for the disk heads to move from the current track to the track where the desired data resides.

selectivity The ability of an index to identify objects. An index with very few unique values is said to have poor selectivity. A unique index has excellent selectivity.

self join A join of a table with itself.

service level agreement (SLA) A contract between the provider of computer or database services and the user of those services. This agreement specifies the minimal level of service that is guaranteed and usually is in the form of maximum response times for certain transactions.

sizing The task of determining the proper amount of hardware (CPU, memory, disks) for a computer system. The system needs to be sized before it is designed and built. After it has been in production, capacity planning is used to plan for future growth.

SLA *See* service level agreement.

Small Computer System Interface (SCSI) An I/O interface that is very popular in today's computer systems. SCSI disks are disks that use the SCSI interface.

SMP *See* symmetric multiprocessor (SMP) system.

SMS *See* System Management Server.

snapshot replication A form of replication in which the entire publication is periodically copied from the publisher to the subscriber.

snowflake schema A schema in which dimension tables are joined with other dimension tables before being joined to the fact table. Several layers of dimension tables can be involved before joining to the fact table. The schema thus looks like a snowflake.

SPID *See* system process ID.

split seek A feature of RAID 1 and RAID 10 whereby both disks in a mirror can simultaneously seek for data.

SQL *See* structured query language

SQL Server Microsoft's RDBMS product.

SQL Server Agent Formerly known as the SQLExecutive in SQL Server 6.5. Its primary function is scheduling tasks and handling alerts. The SQL Server Agent scheduler is used for execution of other agents, such as the replication agents.

SQL Server Profiler A SQL Server utility that is used to monitor server performance and activity. SQL Server Profiler is a very nice tool for tracking events within SQL Server.

SQL Server Query Analyzer A tool that allows you to type in SQL statements and view the results in another pane; it also allows you to debug SQL statements by displaying the execution plan. SQL Server Query Analyzer has replaced ISQL-W (ISQL Windows Version) as the preferred tool for ad hoc SQL Server access.

SQL Server query optimizer An internal component of SQL Server that analyzes SQL Server and object statistics to determine the optimal execution plan. Users do not access the query optimizer; instead, the parser passes parsed SQL statements to the query optimizer.

staging table A temporary table in which to insert data so that it can then be extracted or transformed and copied into permanent tables. Using staging tables is a common way of transforming data within a database.

star schema A single fact table surrounded by dimension tables. The dimension tables are used to form the basis of the analysis of the data in the fact table. Each of the dimension tables is joined to a column in the fact table. If you imagine a fact table surrounded by dimension tables you can see how it resembles a star. A star schema is very common for data warehouses.

steady state The average utilization factor of a machine for either a measurement or a working day.

storage area network (SAN) An I/O subsystem in which multiple computer systems can share the same RAID subsystem.

stored procedure One or more T-SQL statements compiled into a single execution plan.

This compiled plan is stored in the SQL Server database.

striping Spreading data among two or more disk drives in equal chunks. With RAID controllers, data is distributed among all the drives in the logical volume in equal pieces.

structured query language (SQL) A common language used with relational databases. Standards for SQL are defined by both the American National Standards Institute (ANSI) and the International Standards Organization (ISO). Most modern DBMS products support the Entry Level of SQL-92, the latest SQL standard (published in 1992).

subscriber The recipient of SQL Server replication data.

swapping *See* paging.

switch A network device in which the path from one connector to another is electronically connected based on network addresses. This differs from a hub, in which all connectors see all traffic, and from a router, in which packets are modified.

symmetric multiprocessor (SMP) system A system with multiple CPUs that each share the same memory and that function equivalently. Each CPU in an SMP system typically has cache memory, but no main memory associated with it.

system administrator The person or persons responsible for maintaining the hardware and operating system. The system administrator's role can vary depending on how a company is organized.

System Management Server (SMS) Microsoft's enterprise management platform.

system process ID (SPID) A unique integer (smallint) assigned to each user connection when the connection is made. The assignment is not permanent.

T

table lock *See* lock.

table scan An operation in which all rows in the table are read before the desired data is found. A table scan is not usually a desirable way to perform a query.

TCP/IP *See* Transmission Control Protocol/Internet Protocol.

terabyte (TB) 240 bytes, 1,024 gigabytes, or 1,099,511,627,776 bytes.

thread A feature of Windows NT and Windows 2000 operating system that allows application logic to be separated into several concurrent execution paths. All threads are part of the same process and share the same memory.

throughput The data capacity of a data conduit such as a network or CPU bus. The term is used to describe how much data can pass through that bus or network hardware in a particular time.

Token Ring A popular network hardware protocol developed by IBM.

transaction A set of SQL statements that ends with either a COMMIT or ROLLBACK statement. The term *transaction* is usually used for those statements that modify data, and the term *query* is usually used for SELECT (read-only) statements.

transactional replication A form of replication that operates by duplicating on the subscriber each transaction that has run on the publisher.

transaction log A file in the database that is used to record all modifications to the database. Information on the transaction that performed each modification is also kept in the transaction log. The transaction log stores enough information to undo the transaction (in case of a rollback) or to redo the transaction (in case of a roll forward).

Transact-SQL (T-SQL) The procedural SQL language that is used by SQL Server. Transact-SQL is a superset of SQL.

Transmission Control Protocol/Internet Protocol (TCP/IP) A popular network protocol.

trigger A special type of stored procedure that fires or runs automatically whenever a predefined event occurs. This event can be an UPDATE, INSERT, or DELETE statement executed on a table.

truncate To remove all rows from an object without deleting the object itself. A table can be truncated with the TRUNCATE TABLE command. The transaction log can also be truncated.

two-phase commit A protocol used to coordinate a transaction between two independent systems by guaranteeing an all-or-nothing approach to the commit. The two-phase commit splits the commit operation into two parts. The first part is the prepare phase; the second part is the commit phase. These phases are initiated by a COMMIT command from the application.

U

UNION A SQL statement used to combine the results of two or more queries into a single result set consisting of all the rows that are returned from all the queries in the UNION statement.

unique A value with no duplicate values. SQL Server can be used to enforce uniqueness by either creating a constraint or a unique index.

Universal Naming Convention (UNC) name A full Windows NT name of a resource on the network. The UNC name conforms to the syntax of \\servername\sharename. Here *servername* is the name of the network server, and *sharename* is the name of the shared resource. The UNC name can and usually does include the directory path under the name; for example, \\servername\share-name\directoryname\filename.

UPDATE The SQL statement used to modify a record in the database.

V

view An auxiliary data structure that is used to create a virtual table. This virtual table is defined by a SQL statement that makes the table appear as either a subset or superset of the underlying objects.

Vines The Banyan network protocol.

virtual memory Memory created through the use of paging and swapping, which allows the operating system to access more memory than is actually present in the system. Only a portion of the virtual memory is actually in physical memory at any one time.

W

WHERE A clause in a SQL statement used to define the conditions for the data that you desire. It is used to refine search criteria to access specific data.

wizard A user-friendly tool provided by Microsoft in order to ease the jobs of administering the system and performing configuration tasks.

working set The amount of memory that is currently being used by a process.

Index

Steve Adrien DeLuca   Program Manager responsible for developing performance tools at Microsoft Corporation since 1998, Mr. DeLuca is currently developing performance and capacity planning solutions for Microsoft's Enterprise Server Division. Prior to working at Microsoft, Mr. DeLuca worked as an architect engineer at Oracle Corporation, where he co-invented and developed the Oracle System Sizer. In addition to his work at Microsoft and Oracle, Mr. DeLuca has performed the function of performance engineer specializing in sizing and capacity planning for such organizations as DEC, Tandem, Apple, and the U.S. Air Force. Mr. DeLuca has been participating in performance benchmarks, developing performance tools, and lecturing about them around the world since 1980.

Marcilina Garcia   Mrs. Garcia is a senior consultant of Performance Tuning Corporation (www.perftuning.com), a consulting company specializing in database performance, administration, and backup/recovery solutions. Prior to Performance Tuning Corp., Mrs. Garcia worked at Compaq Computer Corporation in Houston, Texas, as a database performance engineer. As a consultant, she has worked for many companies in the areas of database performance benchmarks, SQL Server performance and database design, and system configuration and tuning. Previously, she has written several whitepapers and a magazine article. This is her second book.

Jamie Reding   A performance engineer with the SQL Server team at Microsoft Corporation, Mr. Reding is responsible for developing and maintaining the Transaction Processing Council (TPC) benchmark kits and analyzing SQL Server system performance. Prior to Microsoft, Mr. Reding worked at the Compaq Computer Corporation in the capacity of database performance engineer. Mr. Reding has been participating in performance benchmarks and systems analysis since 1984. In addition to his work at Microsoft and Compaq, Mr. Reding spent 11 years with the IBM Corporation.

Edward Whalen   Mr. Whalen is president of Performance Tuning Corporation (www.perftuning.com), a consulting company specializing in database performance, administration, and backup/recovery solutions. Prior to Performance Tuning Corp., Mr. Whalen worked at Compaq Computer Corporation in the capacity of OS developer, and then as database performance engineer. He has extensive experience in database system design and tuning for optimal performance. His career has consisted of hardware, OS, and database development projects for many different companies. Mr. Whalen has published with Marcilina Garcia a previous book on SQL Server entitled *Microsoft SQL Server 7.0 Administrator's Companion,* as well as two books on the Oracle RDBMS, *Oracle Performance Tuning and Optimization* and *Teach Yourself Oracle8 in 21 Days.* In addition, he has worked on numerous benchmarks and performance tuning projects with Microsoft and Oracle. Mr. Whalen is recognized as a leader in database performance tuning and optimization.

Powerhouse resources to minimize costs while maximizing performance

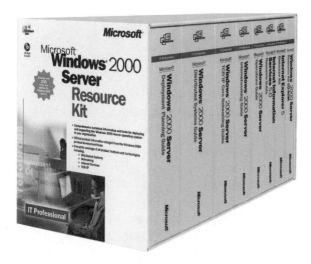

Deploy and support your enterprise business systems using the expertise and tools of those who know the technology best—the Microsoft product groups. Each RESOURCE KIT packs precise technical reference, installation and rollout tactics, planning guides, upgrade strategies, and essential utilities on CD-ROM. They're everything you need to help maximize system performance as you reduce ownership and support costs!

Microsoft® Windows® 2000 Server Resource Kit
ISBN   1-57231-805-8
U.S.A. $299.99
U.K.   £189.99 [V.A.T. included]
Canada $460.99

Microsoft Windows 2000 Professional Resource Kit
ISBN   1-57231-808-2
U.S.A. $69.99
U.K.   £45.99 [V.A.T. included]
Canada $107.99

COMING SOON

Microsoft BackOffice® 4.5 Resource Kit
ISBN   0-7356-0583-1
U.S.A. $249.99
U.K.   £161.99 [V.A.T. included]
Canada $374.99

Microsoft Internet Explorer 5 Resource Kit
ISBN   0-7356-0587-4
U.S.A. $59.99
U.K.   £38.99 [V.A.T. included]
Canada $89.99

Microsoft Office 2000 Resource Kit
ISBN   0-7356-0555-6
U.S.A. $59.99
U.K.   £38.99 [V.A.T. included]
Canada $89.99

Microsoft Windows NT® Server 4.0 Resource Kit
ISBN   1-57231-344-7
U.S.A. $149.95
U.K.   £96.99 [V.A.T. included]
Canada $199.95

Microsoft Windows NT Workstation 4.0 Resource Kit
ISBN   1-57231-343-9
U.S.A. $69.95
U.K.   £45.99 [V.A.T. included]
Canada $94.95

Microsoft Press® products are available worldwide wherever quality computer books are sold. For more information, contact your book or computer retailer, software reseller, or local Microsoft Sales Office, or visit our Web site at mspress.microsoft.com. To locate your nearest source for Microsoft Press products, or to order directly, call 1-800-MSPRESS in the U.S. (in Canada, call 1-800-268-2222).

Prices and availability dates are subject to change.

mspress.microsoft.com

Gain work-ready expertise as you prepare for the Microsoft Certified Professional (MCP) exam.

For information about Microsoft Press® products, visit our Web site at **mspress.microsoft.com**

NO POSTAGE NECESSARY IF MAILED IN THE UNITED STATES

BUSINESS REPLY MAIL
FIRST-CLASS MAIL   PERMIT NO. 108   REDMOND WA

POSTAGE WILL BE PAID BY ADDRESSEE

MICROSOFT PRESS
PO BOX 97017
REDMOND, WA 98073-9830